THE IMPERIAL FACTOR IN SOUTH AFRICA

THE IMPERIAL FACTOR IN SOUTH AFRICA

A Study in Politics and Economics

C. W. De KIEWIET

NEW YORK

RUSSELL & RUSSELL · INC

1966

FIRST PUBLISHED IN 1937
REISSUED, 1966, BY RUSSELL & RUSSELL, INC.
BY ARRANGEMENT WITH FRANK CASS & CO. LTD., LONDON
L.C. CATALOG CARD NO: 66-11637

Printed in Great Britain

To

A. G. H.

A NOBLE LIFE

CONTENTS

PREFACE

THIS BOOK HAS DEPENDED to a large extent on the original papers in the Public Record Office, including the Carnarvon and Granville Papers which are deposited there. Because of the destruction of a large proportion of the original official correspondence much material can be found only in the Confidential Prints in the Colonial Office. The permission to consult these, generously given, was most valuable, although for obvious reasons it has not been possible to refer to them.

The purpose of this book is to reach some explanation of British policy which will take into account the realities of South African history. In no part of the Empire has there been more "history". Yet in no part of the Empire have those realities been more persistently obscured or ignored. The last generation before the Boer War was already unhappily skilled in the game of make-believe, and versed in the pretence that a dangerous native problem was miraculously unrelated to the fortunes of the white population. These years of South African history were chosen because in no other period can the racial, social and economic issues be so clearly and conveniently studied. Because this is a study of these issues and not a detailed history the attempt has been made to dispense with the detailed references of a monographic work. Footnotes like friends should not be made to bear too much responsibility for a writer's judgments.

This book owes much to many people. Without the generous attitude of the administration of the State University of Iowa and especially of Dr W. T. Root, head of the Department of History, I could not have found the leisure to write it. To Dr H. G. Plum and others who read the manuscript I owe thanks for advice of real value. Advice, protection and punctuation I needed greatly, and I received them all from my wife. Mr Bernard Holm, M.A., helped me tirelessly with the labour of editing.

C. W. DE KIEWIET

February 1937

CHAPTER I

INTRODUCTION

MOST of these pages speak of South Africa in the 'seventies and 'eighties of the last century; and yet they are also about to-day. The problems here are curiously of our own time, unsolved some of them and grown so large that they are now the problems of a whole continent. It is the special temptation of the historian, as Goldsmith said of Samuel Johnson, to make his little fishes talk like whales. Yet in what other region of the Empire has the past thrust itself so relentlessly upon the future, or woven its stuff more closely into the history of the Empire? The evolution of South Africa as a great self-governing society sustained by industries of importance to the whole world, its contributions to the annals of war, statesmanship and finance, of names that are household words far beyond its own borders—these are already enough to make its chapter in the book of imperial history a full one. But none of these can explain why its story stands unmatched and apart. Not even the shades of violence and wrong thrown across an entire century can warrant such a claim. The history of South Africa is important, not because of the colour of its wars, nor the tragedy of its disasters, but because it cannot be ignored. It cannot be ignored because in a modern world beset by problems of race, and in an Empire that has made its subject peoples a special charge, South Africa, past and present, holds a uniquely instructive place. To the black man, not to the white man, does South African history owe its special significance.

It is not easy to read the materials of that history with detachment and fairness. The oppositeness of colour rules the facts dogmatically, elevating what is white and depressing what is black; or marshalling each against the other, as civilization against barbarism, and progress against stagnation. Actually the most distinctive feature of the history of whites and natives is not race or colour, but a close economic association. In spite of their wars South Africa's frontiers were much less lines of separation than areas of absorption and fusion. They were the gateways through which the natives entered European society. At no time was any one of the European communities even remotely successful in segregating the natives. Each war served only to drive them more deeply and inextricably into the ranks of their conquerors. Each war helped but to prove the indestructible character of native life, ready to change its form in order to preserve its being, to surrender independence for subjection in order to continue to live. In the face of European colonization the natives neither decreased nor retreated. Each blow that fell upon them drove them, not outwards into estrangement, but inwards into greater intimacy. The borders that should have excluded them, the wars that should have decimated their manhood, the alcohol and diseases that should have stricken their life in loin and womb, finally did none of these. Their minds learned new habits of life in crowded locations and slums; their blood diluted the poisons that entered it; and their bodies were yielding to the ways of diamond fields and railway construction camps. The pressure of white colonization pumped them into every artery and limb of South Africa's social body, until they could not be drained from it safely. The greatest social and economic fact in the history of the century is not gold nor diamond mining, nor even agriculture, but the universal dependence upon black labour.

Out of the heaving and thrusting of the nineteenth century there has emerged no romantic tradition comparable with the literature of adventure in which the North American Redskins were the heroes. The explanation is at least partly to be found in the different social and economic position of the descendants of Pontiac, Sitting Bull, or Osceola in the forgotten and inoffensive Indian reservations of modern America, and the descendants of Hintza, Chaka, and Sekukuni in the packed and controversial reserves, in the compounds of industrial towns and in European kitchens. In the inglorious change from an enemy to a servile proletariat there is little room for romance. South African schoolboys play at Cowboys and Indians, not at Boers and Zulus; for Zulus, Basuto and Bechuana are too manifestly an unheroic and desperate social problem.

The pioneer exploits of the Great Trek and its battle-scarred aftermath have created the impression that South African society was competitive. Actually its striving was to maintain itself unchanged. There was within it little room for the development of liberal ideas about the status of a servile population. The process of European colonization was not a process that enlightened the natives, or emancipated them or enriched them. The swiftly expanding, land-hungry Europeans turned the bulk of the native population into a proletariat, governed by laws that bound rather than unloosed, that restricted their liberties rather than widened their opportunities. Economically their life, even of those that managed to cling to the land, became a fretful going to and fro between the white man's world and their own, each alike in that neither provided them with adequate sustenance or privilege. Political rightlessness and economic inferiority, narrow opportunities and restricted rewards seemed the pillars on which white society strove to keep itself aloft.

A disastrous war between Great Britain and the Dutch Republics, and the understandable self-pity of much local historiography, have focused attention too exclusively upon the political vicissitudes of the two white races. The political disharmony of English and Dutch was really never a true measure of their relationship; for they were at all times more sincerely bound together by common interests than they were separated by their misunderstandings. In native matters it is impossible not to be impressed by the bundling of their interests and the knotting of their roots. Uniting them was always a sense of closely related purposes that was very similar to the relationship of political parties held together in the same constitution. Passions scorched men's hearts, and there were deep resentments that died hard. Nevertheless, the history of the two white races, when it is calmly reviewed, was till the end of the century singularly free of those unyielding animosities that know no reconciliation, and those cold treacheries that know no forgiveness. Right through the worst confusion of the period runs a path, trodden by both, that led finally to a natural and logical constitutional co-operation. It is for these pages to tell of the tangling of the strands by which the European population was being woven into a life that was more English than Dutch, and more South African than either. But for that tangling the two races would have spent less time on the road to that relationship with one another that the eighteenth century saw grow between English and Scotch. In spite of the frequent comparison of South Africa with Ireland, the Dutch stood more surely in the place of the Scotch, amenable to the same institutions as the English, excellently fitted for a common political experience, with a coincidence and mutual toleration that made the growth of an exclusively racial patriotism not a natural but an unnatural phenomenon.

Upon British policy has fallen much of the blame that the century was so crossed with adversity. Great Britain, in this view, was the violator of republican independence and the enemy of colonial liberties. The following pages will not seek to obscure the shortcomings of British policy. They were many and grievous. Only a mind incurably unfair would seek to resolve British policy of the ambiguities and purge it of the contradictions that were, after all, natural to it. In South Africa, of all places in the British Empire, it is essential to appreciate the amazing accumulation of difficulties with which both imperial and colonial statesmen had to contend. In 1874, for example, when Lord Carnarvon became Colonial Secretary, it was not simply sixty years of erratic British rule, but two centuries of European activity that had gone to form a terrain so seamed with political divisions, so broken with social and economic inequalities, that movement in any direction could not be made without stumbling and slipping. Above all it was true that the desperate sickness of the relations between black and white had reached a point where it was ready to discharge its suppuration upon the land in an incredible series of wars on every frontier. In the assumption, therefore, that such acts as the annexation of the Transvaal were shaped by sinister motives and a secret malignity that worked behind the scenes, there is a serious misapprehension of the nature and aims of British policy. In the atmosphere of South African history the dominant notes are not the unmoral notes of intrigue, craft and violence which can be so plausibly associated with the names of Carnarvon and his successors. Violence there was, and intrigue, yet the real bitterness of the century is in the failure of high motives and worthy ends.

The charge of ignorance can be directed against British policy as little as the charge of a fundamental *mala fides*. Its blunders were hasty blunders, pinchpenny blunders, soldiers' blunders, before they were ignorant blunders. True it is that Downing Street cannot be absolved from the guilt of making far too little use of the knowledge and skill of the men on the spot. Yet no one who has dwelt in intimacy with the officials of the Colonial Office can listen with respect to the frequent accusation that Downing Street applied a doctrinaire inexperience to practical situations upon which local experience alone could speak competently. Few hours are better spent than those devoted to the minute papers of the Colonial Office. The handwriting upon them is good and bad. It varies from Fairfield's graceful hand to the tiny illegibility of Hicks Beach or Leonard Courtney. The minutes themselves are lengthy memoranda or hasty scraps. Sometimes they are naughtily illustrated by caricatures of a bad-tempered Governor or a British soldier hiding from a Basuto warrior. But in them the historian will always find enlightenment, most frequently a skilful handling of facts, and a flexible understanding of involved questions. Above all he will clearly find that the real traditions of the Colonial Office were those of a fairmindedness and a devotion to duty that was larger than insular patriotism or imperial greed.

It does not, therefore, betray a lack of understanding of the peculiar problems of South African history to insist that every student of colonial problems must at some time or other in his investigations take his stand firmly in London so that he may look outwards upon Canada, Australia, New Zealand or South Africa, and for a while see them as joined to each other by a vast network of influences that make the history of any part unbalanced unless it is written as both local and imperial history. Such a detachment, resolutely maintained, also discloses the true contours of each colony's history. It shows that although South Africa entered the same orbit as the other colonies in its constitutional movement, it was thrust forth again by its unique native problems. Through these problems it was made to stand apart from the other colonies, and made the object of a special imperial concern. The virtues of self-government and the need of a closer political co-operation between the European communities were as real in South Africa as elsewhere. Yet an enlightened judgment cannot deny that the relationship between Europeans and natives raised problems far more pressing than those of republican independence or colonial self-determination.

It is but justice to Carnarvon to recognize that he saw in the confusion and danger of native matters an obligation to which the Mother Country could not be indifferent. It is an ignorant and false tradition that Great Britain undertook nothing that did not serve some profitable and material end. Not all the penetration into the shadier and more obscure processes of imperial action can seriously disturb the conviction that there was in England a genuine feeling of concern over the native tribes. True, it was a feeling far weaker than the earlier militant zeal that had sacrificed life and treasure in the pursuit of its object. Already shocked by the Indian Mutiny, Great Britain shared with the United States the disillusionment that followed the Civil War. It was, however, more than humanitarian feeling that brought Downing Street back to South Africa after it had made such a deliberate gesture of withdrawal by the grant of self-government to the Cape Colony in 1872. The Empire had belied the pessimism of sixty years by refusing to fall apart, however amiably. The colonies themselves showed few signs of desiring that separation that had been periodically prophesied for them. For an imperial process that positively was not one of devolution nor of dissolution there was need of new values and new principles. Clumsily and tactlessly but enthusiastically Carnarvon sought to apply them. It is undoubted that immediately after the passage of the British North America Act a new attitude towards the Empire began to develop and slowly to gain in strength. The imperial process began to appear as one of evolution and integration. There appeared an optimism that conceived of the Empire as an organism evolving from the lower to the higher, from the inchoate to the orderly, and therefore susceptible to organization and consolidation. An important ingredient in Carnarvon's mind was an idealism that left little room for uncertainty in matters where his convictions were set. His idealism had one trait proper to the age in which he lived—a belief in the moral power of rationalism. The unsettlement of South Africa was irrational and therefore progressively amenable to order. Its statesmen could be persuaded to see their true course, if it were only fully and authoritatively explained to them. It was this quality of mind that gave Carnarvon a somewhat overweening confidence in himself and his ideas. The same quality of mind explains the political tactlessness that tried to give public instruction to colonial politicians. It will not be easy to discover how far his energetic intervention in South Africa was warranted, yet it is well to remember that it was he who first set his face against the neglect and pessimism that had been a leading cause of the country's worst difficulties.

The problem of Great Britain's presence in South Africa was whether she could successfully maintain that certain interests were imperial. Defence and the integrity of the coastline, none would deny, were such interests. Was confederation such an interest? Above all, were native matters an imperial "reason of state"? An affirmative answer meant that the British Government was bound to continue to be an active force in the subcontinent. When Carnarvon rendered this affirmative answer it followed that the entire political development of South Africa was itself an imperial "reason of state"; for only by intimate participation in the building of a new political order could the Home Government hope to find some more ample place for the native population. Therein lay what excuse there was for a forward hand in South African politics. The failure of Carnarvon's policy was thus not primarily the failure of confederation. Union of some sort, even if its road lay through fire and blood, was destined for South Africa. The failure of Carnarvon's policy was that it did not win for the natives a higher and better place in the future of the land they lived in.

The responsibility for that failure rests with no man, with no party, with no principle. That it rests with the Home Government rather than with the colonial communities is probably true. Failure was the punishment of a policy that was never master of

B

itself, being such a patchwork of expedients and compromises, that its firmness was temporary, its promises illusory and its means deficient. It was a policy that strained under the burden of its own past, a phoenix-like policy that arose and died, and arose again from the ashes of its previous failures, questing vainly for a consummation that seemed always to elude it. In the person of its chief agent, Lord Carnarvon, it made the mistake of haste, arrogance and over-confidence, forgetting, in what was perhaps its capital blunder, that colonists of the nineteenth century, no less than of the eighteenth century, were jealous of their privileges and quick to resent peremptoriness from over the sea. "...perché sempre, ancora che uno sia fortissimo in sugli eserciti, ha bisogno del favore dei provinciali ad entrare in una provincia."

Once British policy had shot its bolt it had few reserves of strength. However much Disraeli and Carnarvon were responsible for encouraging a closer identification of national with imperial interests, by conceiving of the Empire as a measure of British strength rather than as a source of weakness, it is easy to over-estimate their success. British public opinion remained remarkably diffident. It knew more about the emancipated slaves of America than it knew of the causes and effects of Kafir wars. The continued lack of Parliamentary interest in colonial questions was such that Lord Stanley's plea in 1834 that "the House would bear with him, though he was aware how difficult it was to command attention on such a subject..." could still be made forty years later.

Notwithstanding Disraeli's Crystal Palace speech it remained as imperative as ever before that all extensions of colonial territory be made a charge on colonial revenues, and that other forms of colonial enterprise be self-supporting. The "Empire Builders" who made the Colonial Office so nervous were even more feared by the Treasury, always by its nature more inclined to pocket an injury or forgo an uncertain risk. Not even the heightened sense of responsibility for the colonies and for the subject races in particular availed anything in unloosening the purse strings of the Treasury. It is without doubt that the Gladstonian budget was, till the appointment of Chamberlain, a controlling influence in British colonial policy.

The story of British humanitarianism is compromised at every point by the insufficient financial support which its advocates received. Even Carnarvon's humanitarianism, as the following pages will show, was a faith alloyed by Treasury qualms, and perverted by a belief that vigorous policies could be reconciled with cheapness and made to pay their own way. British humanitarianism was stronger in sentiment than in guiding principles, easily aroused, whether in Jamaica, Bulgaria or the Transvaal, but nervous and uncertain before demands for sustained efforts towards reform.

Carnarvon's ambitions were greater than his power to achieve them. His own position in the Cabinet was a lowly one, nor did the Colonial Office rank as yet amongst the most important departments of state. He was able, it is true, to force Disraeli to agree to the annexation of the Fiji Islands; and he exercised an unusual freedom in colonial policy. It was nevertheless a freedom that was easily lost. The Colonial Office was not one of the departments of great expenditure. Since its place in the budget was comparatively small, sudden requests of large sums for colonial purposes were unusual and provoked severe scrutiny both in Parliament and the Treasury. There can be no question that the development of the Empire in the nineteenth century was frequently determined less by the positive initiative of the Colonial Office than by insistence upon economy, by limitations upon appropriations or by the refusal on occasion to guarantee loans. It is hardly an exaggeration to say that the Treasury and the exigencies of the British budget have made as much colonial history as the Colonial Office itself. The answer to the criticism, therefore, that Great Britain poured vast sums into South Africa is that it was money which she neither wished nor intended to spend. The British Government made it almost a rule of conduct to pay only for disasters.

In colonial policy there is always the head, the heart and the hand. Yet if the hand be not open, it is vain to ask attention to the dictates of the head or the promptings of the heart. It is hardly surprising that men like Molteno insisted that true responsibility could only rest with those that executed measures and paid for them. The policy of confederation tried to attain its goal cheaply, and at a time when South Africa as a whole was spending more money and needing more money than at any time in its history. The Cape and Natal placed burdens upon themselves until their resources strained in order to modernize their transport and hasten their economic development. Yet of all moments this was the moment when the British Government urged them to undertake still greater responsibilities. It was but natural that Molteno should shake his hard head at such a bargain for the Cape Colony. What South Africa needed was more credit. The country as a whole suffered from dear land, dear labour and dear capital. Unnaturally dear land produced the disturbing pressure upon native areas; wasteful and therefore dear labour caused the outcry for measures to compel a readier flow of labourers; timid and therefore dear capital excited tariff rivalries between the European communities, and caused the denial of adequate funds for native improvement. The easing of financial strain would almost certainly have disposed all the communities more favourably towards political co-operation. Not Shepstone and twenty-five policemen, but credit and financial advice were needed to save the Transvaal in 1877. When the money came it was unhappily given into wasteful and ignorant hands. A colony that had been annexed because it was bankrupt was permitted to sink into a still more inexcusable bankruptcy, and finally abandoned in a spirit too ungenerous to go long unpunished.

This is a tale that will be told again. Another telling will seek to know more about men like Shepstone, and more of the internal history of the Republics. It will notice that between 1873 and 1886 Great Britain passed through a great financial and commercial crisis; that the part is never greater than the whole; that Treasury economies are the life-blood of a sound financial system. It will show how an apparently disjointed, halting and undefined policy can yet have elasticity and continuity. It will disclose a tenacity and obstinate power of resistance against error, a power of compromise and vigorous recovery that has enabled imperial statesmanship to travel far beyond the vision of its original framers. It will explain more lucidly the paradox how Great Britain, in the very act of scuttle, could annex a million and more square miles, and create in Basutoland, Bechuanaland, and Zululand, native reserves that constitute possibly the most important contribution to native policy in the nineteenth century.

CHAPTER II

A HOUSE DIVIDED

WHEN SIR HENRY BARKLY was sent in 1871 to consummate Cape self-government, Lord Kimberley had seen in the responsibility of the Mother Colony a force powerful enough to absorb the unannexed territories on its borders, and attractive enough to draw Natal and the Republics into its orbit as a confederated group. But it would be a development in which the Home Government was to take no initiative and assume no responsibility. "Not a soldier or a shilling." With Cape self-government, Kimberley had hoped that the British Government would be able to withdraw decently as a principal from South African affairs. His hopes were immediately belied. Responsible government brought with it prosperity and confidence for the Cape, but no relief for the British Government. The Cape did indeed take over Basutoland. It refused, however, to annex the diamond fields, despite a vague pledge made in 1871. In the opinion of Molteno, later to become the first Prime Minister, the annexation would compromise self-government. To make matters worse Barkly had clumsily introduced his annexation bill in the beginning of the session of 1872 at the very moment when Molteno was making his final bid for self-government. It was intolerable to Molteno that a bill to which his Dutch supporters in the West objected should be introduced at a moment when he needed their support. Moreover, the mob of republicans, colonials and foreigners at the diggings would certainly endanger the success of the new Government with their conflicting cries for Brand, the President of the Free State, the Union Jack and a free diggers' republic. At best, hating Cape Town, they would throw in their lot with the Separatist party in the East. The worst offending of Barkly's bill in Molteno's sight was that the Easterners tried to exploit it in their struggle for separation from the West. Those who in the previous session had been loudest in their cries for annexation, veered suddenly round to oppose the bill, in the hope that the British Government would withhold its consent and eventually attach the diamond fields to a separate Eastern colony.[1]

Henceforth, until the spectre of separation was laid, Molteno's face was set against annexation. The diamond fields were British territory; their trade and transport were practically a Cape monopoly. It would be folly for the Cape to quarrel with the Free State over their possession, or to attempt to pit its inexperience against the discordant elements at the diggings. More than that, the problems of the diamond fields involved every major problem of South African life. As long as Brand obstinately refused to recognize the British annexation, as long as the Transvaal insisted on its title to the territory to the east of the diamond fields, there could be neither understanding nor confederation with the Republics.

Worst of all, Griqualand had suddenly revealed, to a South Africa that was as yet too unenlightened to be properly startled, a new native difficulty of the utmost seriousness. The effects of the native wars of the past two generations and of the unrelieved pressure of the European population upon the native lands had hitherto been obscured by the congestion in the native areas and the squatting on European farms. Now the stream of natives from every part of South Africa that came to the diamond fields seeking employment and guns was at once evidence of the disruption of tribal life and economy, and the cause of still more rapid social change. Though the individual labourers still returned whence they had come, South Africa had now to face a new and serious complication of its native problems—namely the dependence of a growing proportion of the native population upon European employment for existence, and the creation of a detribalized and landless urban proletariat. What had hitherto been a rural and even a frontier problem now was fast becoming an urban problem as well. It was a new social disease that was destined to become chronic. Into the new urban and industrial communities the native policy of the frontier farmers intruded itself. In a South Africa that the British Government hoped would soon be a self-governing federation, able in its strength

[1] G.D. 6/32, Barkly to Carnarvon, 25 May 1874.

and security to develop a calm and liberal native policy, it was actually the attitude of the frontier that was everywhere to the fore. In very truth the Great Trek was coming out of exile and avenging itself. The old Cape liberalism was losing ground on all sides. The story of the failure of Lord Carnarvon's South African policy will be seen to be a story not so much of imperial blundering, as of the essential incompatibility between a point of view that, while favouring colonial self-government, cherished some regard for native interests, and a colonial point of view that called for the reduction of native power and looked upon even the very hesitant and timid humanitarianism of the British Government as ignorant, wrongheaded and dangerous interference.

The knowledge that is requisite to a true and full understanding of South African history does not lie in the creeds of party and race and colour; it lies ever in the understanding of the process that taking two independent racial groups—not the Dutch and the English, but the black and the white—produced during the course of a century a single society in which the main line of division was not one of race and culture, but of possession and authority.

And everywhere with diamonds, renewed prosperity, railways and plans for railways, the demand for reliable native labour became more insistent. Reliable labour, as diggers, farmers and transport riders defined it, meant essentially detribalized labour, restricted in its freedom of movement, dependent upon "wages and keep" rather than upon the produce of its own agriculture. In the Cape the prosperity of the 'seventies was disturbed by bitter complaints that still greater prosperity was retarded by the scarcity of labour. The shortage of railway and domestic labourers was acute. There was noticeable an ominous resentment against the policy that permitted natives to settle in locations instead of keeping them as labourers. The feeling grew that the natives should be compelled by special laws to come out from the native locations. The familiar sentiment that natives not in European service were necessarily living in idleness was already common. More than ordinary pressure was brought upon the Cape Parliament in 1874 for the enactment of stricter labour laws. Envious glances were even cast at Natal's coolies. Fingers pointed to the Republics as places where men really knew how to deal with their natives. It is clearly not out of place to note that the universally increased demand for native labour came in a decade that experienced the most widespread native disturbance and the most serious wars South Africa had known.

Diamonds introduced other striking changes. Without any navigable rivers and with but a primitive system of communication by land, South Africa had hitherto lived in the eighteenth century. The discovery of diamonds provided, directly and indirectly, the capital and the incentive to modernize transport. Diamonds brought the nineteenth century and the Industrial Revolution to South Africa. The telegraph and the progress of transportation from the ox waggon to the more regular and speedy post cart and ultimately to the railway meant a progress from isolation and localism to coherence and interdependence; for a complex and efficient system of transportation presupposes an advanced political development. The interior began to be drawn out of its remoteness to participate in a more general and active life. The men of diversified occupations and aims that moved more numerously into the interior, the commodities that flowed more briskly and in greater variety, announced a revolution. From its effects the Republics could not possibly escape. Even less could British policy. The policy of the Sand River and Bloemfontein conventions that had tried to outlaw the Republics and their problems by making them independent, that had even looked regretfully upon the Cape Colony as the price Great Britain had to pay for its naval bases at Cape Town and Simon's Bay, was imperatively altered. It is only the narrowest interpretation of South African history that can seek to explain the eventful years leading to the Boer War by dwelling exclusively upon the sins of Downing Street and British Secretaries of State.

Kimberley in 1873 was a town of canvas, mud and iron that glittered from afar in an arid plain set with stunted and valleyless hills that one traveller called four hundred miles of vacuity. In the town and in the diggings around were gathered together with the diggers the dregs and parasites of the subcontinent, hastened thither to batten upon digger and native alike. The result was drunkenness, thievery and gunrunning, with which the ragged and inefficient police force was powerless to cope. The Cape laws which Lieutenant-Governor Southey's untried administration sought to maintain had been framed primarily to apply to Hottentot peasants and farm labourers. Applied to the slums of tents and huts on the diamond fields, they were incapable of checking crime and abuse. The civil service, made up to some extent of aged or incompetent civil servants with whom the Cape Government found it economical or convenient to endow Southey, soon became demoralized and remained demoralized until the Cape finally annexed the territory in 1880. A large proportion of the civil servants lived in chronic indebtedness, hypothecating their salaries to moneylenders at rates as high as 10 per cent. per month. Some officials had to do extra clerking after hours to earn enough for even the necessities of life. As late as 1877 many were still living in tents because they could not afford even the makeshift houses the diamond fields provided. Rents and the most essential commodities, let alone the Havana cigars and Monopole champagne of lucky diggers and profiteers, were exorbitantly high. The transport of building material, machinery and provisions from the Cape Colony cost thirty to fifty shillings per hundredweight. Transport was still dependent upon grass. When the dryness of the inland winter hardened the roads there was likely to be insufficient grass for the draught animals; when rain fell the roads were heavy and often impassable. In the latter part of 1873 the drought in the eastern districts of the Cape was so severe that transport was almost at a standstill and costs impossibly high. Then in February 1874 unpredecented rains flooded the diamond fields, so saturating the ground that mines collapsed and filled with 15 feet of water. That South African native wars frequently broke out in periods of drought when transport was difficult is incidentally one explanation of the length of these wars and their high cost to the British Government.

Lieutenant-Governor Southey's position in Griqualand West was from the beginning almost impossible. Of farming in the new territory there was practically none. The revenue came from an essentially unreliable commodity, in which violent fluctuations occurred soon after the British annexation. The sudden and steep increase in the world's supply of diamonds depressed prices.

The world-wide financial crisis that began with the crash on the Vienna Bourse in 1873, the imminent Egyptian bankruptcy, and finally the Russo-Turkish War which dislocated an important market, combined with collapsing and flooded claims to make the returns from diamonds uncertain in the extreme. The glamour of the first eager years when each digger felt that he was treading hard on the heels of fortune, and when the "niggers" were kept firmly in their place, was fading. Instead taxation, profiteering, illicit diamond buying, wasteful mining, and native labourers who stole, drank and decamped, brought steadily closer the day when organized capital would consolidate the claims and reduce the independent digger to the status of overseer and employee. The introduction of high finance would be yet another step towards achieving the incredible social complexity of twentieth-century South African life.

Richard Southey was an autocrat in the midst of a heterogeneous and restless population, an imperialist in the face of the Republics, a humanitarian amongst men clamouring for class legislation. Popularity he never had. He was doubly unwelcome because, coming from the liberal Western Province of the Cape, he resisted the demands for severer Master and Servant Laws, although he had neither the money nor the police to make his native policy more than a record of endless bickerings with the diggers on labour agreements, vagrancy and thievery. He was indeed as great an offender as the diggers themselves in fomenting social disorder. Canteen licences were to be had for the asking. A committee sitting in 1874 found that there was one canteen for every forty people, and in addition there were numbers outside the camps, most of them a cloak for illicit diamond buying, where white loafers bought drink for the natives. The committee recommended as an important reform that canteens should not be allowed to open before five o'clock in the morning! Conditions elsewhere in South Africa, it must be admitted, were hardly better. Denied a market abroad for their wine, the Cape growers unlearned the skill that had formerly produced at least one excellent wine, and made bad brandy for the natives. The best efforts of magistrates and missionaries on the Eastern Frontier and in Basutoland could not prevent the sale of "Cape smoke" in such quantities that it was a matter for wonder amongst observers that the widespread befuddlement amongst the natives did not decimate the population. Even the Free State, strict enough with its own population, permitted farmers and storekeepers on the Basuto border to sell Cape brandy and worse Hamburg "fire water" to the Basuto.

The most serious abuse on the diamond fields was the traffic in guns and ammunition. It was an abuse that Southey deliberately aided and abetted. The diamond fields needed native labourers and the virtual free trade that was permitted at the diggings was excellent bait. Guns brought labourers; guns stimulated trade with the interior tribes and attracted that trade to Griqualand West. To stop the traffic would merely destroy a lucrative British trade and surrender it to other and more unscrupulous merchants. In Southey's sight the maintenance of the traffic was actually a patriotic duty. In his dislike of the Republics he even found it possible to reconcile the trade with the advancement of civilization amongst the natives and with the maintenance of the highest principles of justice. During the last nine months of 1873 over 18,000 guns were introduced into Griqualand West. In the same period nearly 10,000 permits of sale were issued.

Nothing betrays more signally than this traffic the disunion and local selfishness of the South African communities, not merely in the vital matter of native policy, but in everything that concerned their general interests. The three British colonies, struggling with each other for trade and revenue, were determined to keep whatever advantages they each had. Every gun that was imported meant revenue, twenty shillings in the Cape, ten shillings in Natal, and twelve shillings and sixpence in Griqualand West. In the Cape the law did demand a bond from the exporter. But fearful of losing its interior trade and diminishing its revenue, the Government made no attempt to ascertain to whom the guns were sold, so that the provision became a farce. The Natal law requiring all guns to be registered was only occasionally applied before 1874. When Natal requested the Cape to assimilate its laws to those of Natal, the Cape Government retorted by suggesting that Natal might double her import dues, and unhelpfully passed the request on to Griqualand. And Southey declared in turn that in a colony like Natal that oppressed its native subjects, it might be as well for the natives to be armed.

The traffic in guns was highly objectionable to the Republics. That the superior attraction of the diamond fields should drain the farms of their labour was serious enough. But most offensive to the Republics was the sight of their own natives and those on their borders becoming daily richer in arms. Protests to Barkly were unavailing. The High Commissioner even seemed to welcome their embarrassment and made no effort to curb the unreasonable discourtesy which Southey displayed towards the Free State and its President. Even more, the Free State was denied the right to control at least that part of the traffic that passed through its territory. Individual farmers tried to prevent Zulus and Basuto from reaching the diamond fields. Some few natives returning from the diamond fields with guns in their hands were shot at sight, till they adopted the device of traversing the country in armed bands. A clash with irate burgher patrols was inevitable. Southey and Barkly indignantly reported to Downing Street that the Republic was molesting British subjects. Violent though the actions of the Free State were, they at least betokened a sense of responsibility in which the British authorities were lacking. The time was not yet come when the Cape would sacrifice treasure and life in undoing the very evil which its own selfish indifference had provoked.

Brand knew that he was fighting for more than the right of the Free State to control the natives upon its own soil. Behind his quotations from Vattel that Barkly found so disconcerting, behind his efforts to win recognition of his Government by foreign powers, and his unsuccessful attempts at direct correspondence with the British Foreign Office, behind his insistence on foreign arbitration on the issue of the diamond fields, lay his determination that as long as the Free State was independent, it should have the full status of a foreign power. The tendency of British policy was otherwise. Barkly and Southey maintained that republican independence was strongly qualified by British paramountcy in the subcontinent. Both regarded the return of the Republics under the British flag as the aim of British policy in South Africa. Barkly himself lost no opportunity of commenting on the dangers of republican independence. "The position of these petty republics is most anomalous", he privately complained to Carnarvon. "President Brand of the Free State is still a member of the Cape Bar, and might be recommended to me for Chief Justice. His father is the Speaker of the Cape Assembly, his wife is an Englishwoman, and his eldest son is now studying at the Middle Temple, and yet he can declare war on me tomorrow."[1]

Although the Colonial Office frequently was able to discern the exaggeration and unfairness of some of the attacks on the Free State, it could not but allow its attitude to be influenced by the representations of the men on the spot. "These Boers must be taught to respect British subjects", testily exclaimed Knatch-bull-Hugessen, when Barkly informed him of the clashes between the burghers and Basuto in the Free State. "Every day shows in stronger light the mistake that was made in abandoning the Orange River Territory. These people are worse neighbours than the Kafirs."[2] It was an unjust criticism. In the face of the rank and often malicious vocabulary of Southey's correspondence, Brand habitually observed a decorous and correct attitude. Unyielding in its defence of what it considered its rights, bitterly though it resented the annexations of Basutoland and the diamond fields, the Free State Government had loyally respected the new boundary lines. When it comes to the question of the inability of subsequent British policy to win the support of the Free State, the resentment caused by the tone of the letters from Cape Town and Kimberley, so offensive as to be sometimes uncouth, must be borne in mind.

The controversy over the diamond fields had long since reached deadlock. Brand still insisted vainly on foreign arbitration. His determination seemed to grow stronger as the correspondence with Barkly grew vaster. As new evidence was uncovered and old motives were more fully explained, it became clear to impartial minds that the British Government would have difficulty in winning its case before such a tribunal as Brand proposed.

[1] G.D. 6/32, Barkly to Carnarvon, 6 April 1874.
[2] C.O. 48/465, D. 40, Barkly to Kimberley, 4 April 1873.

Rapidly becoming more serious than the quarrel with the Free State was the refusal of the Transvaal to abide by the Keate Award.[1] The weakness of the Award was that it had provided no means to secure the land to the natives. Once the Cape had refused to annex the diamond fields, there was no authority capable of resisting Transvaal encroachment. The farmers originally within the line stayed where they were. The further expansion of their fellows was easy and natural. Although the Award had declared the magistracy of Bloemhof to be outside the Transvaal, the republican Government showed its contempt by moving its magistracy to Christiana, thirty-five miles deeper still into the disputed territory. The British Government practically encouraged the encroachment of the Dutch farmers. Twice the perpetual Augustan edict *de coercendo intra fines imperio* of British Secretaries of State had been flouted. Twice the British Government had found itself saddled with the government of unwanted territories. Especially incensed at the Cape refusal to take over the diamond fields the Secretary of State now roundly declared that the British Government would make no effort to defend the Keate Award by force. Small wonder that the new Transvaal President, Thomas François Burgers, who knew the contents of British Parliamentary Papers as well as the High Commissioner himself, ignored the protests of the Lieutenant-Governor.

In the Transvaal frontier districts the Government followed whither the individual farmers led. Its proclamations and treaties and annexations were merely an imprimatur which it set upon the arbitrary actions of the burghers themselves. On the western frontier of the Transvaal the impetus to expansion came from the land-hungry farmers. Except for the establishment of British authority over Griqualand West only occasional scuffling would have marked the process by which the Dutch farmers were steadily turning the native population into labourers and rightless squatters or forcing them into the drier and less desirable areas.

Land in the disputed area, even in spite of Southey's objections, was being alienated to the Europeans rapidly enough. It

[1] In October 1871 Lieutenant-Governor Keate awarded the land between the Harts and Vaal Rivers to the independent tribes, denying the Transvaal claim.

was the familiar story of every South African frontier. Grazing privileges obtained from the natives became permanent ownership of the land itself; intimidation and force were resorted to freely; water courses were diverted, or natives were prevented from watering their cattle, and forced to move away. Although the territory was itself vast enough, having an area of over 30,000 square miles, the pressure of a relative handful of farmers was enough to have the severest effects on the original population. Farms of 3000 morgen were expanded by the simple process of "jumping" land on either side, so that farms of 8000 morgen (rather more than 16,000 acres) were not uncommon. Much more serious than the mere acreage of European farms was the loss to the natives of the all-important frontage to the rivers, of the springs and watercourses. The distribution of European settlement provided in effect a fairly reliable map of the country's water supply.

The Boer expansion had at least the merit of a certain economic pressure, and the majority of the farmers really occupied their farms with their families and cattle. Not so the land speculators that accompanied them. Declaring themselves for the Transvaal or for Southey and British intervention as they saw fit, they descended upon the helpless chiefs. The struggle between rival groups of land sharks, aided by missionaries and traders, was accompanied by a fishwives' chorus of abuse, threats and scurrility. Confused by bullying and fair promises the natives soon began to sign away their own land or that of their neighbours. The unwillingness of the British Government to assume any further obligations beyond the limits of Griqualand West gave the Transvaal and its supporters the advantage. Although Mankoroane, the most important of the chiefs, was won for the "British" side, the Transvaal made such progress that by March 1874 it issued a proclamation annexing the whole of the Baralong territory.

Richard Southey fought Boer westward expansion with all the means he had. He was the most ardent imperialist in South Africa before Rhodes. South Africa, he declared, was vast and rich in mineral wealth. A wise policy of British annexation would open up territory able to absorb thousands of Englishmen now a burden on the British taxpayer. Griqualand West and the disputed territory were the gateway into the interior. Transvaal settlement and annexation threatened to close that road to British trade. On the other hand the expansion of Griqualand West would give it a monopoly of trade and access to native labour that would free it of its dependence upon Basuto and Zulu labourers. There would then be an end to the social unsettlement and financial instability of its administration. Above all British intervention would secure the natives against Transvaal encroachment upon their lands. However wholehearted Southey's dislike of the Republics, however compromising his association with land speculators, however great his desire to press the natives into service on the mines, he was genuine in his belief that British intervention would relieve the natives from the severe pressure upon their lands. But then even the land sharks and cutpurses of Empire that sought to batten upon the chiefs were also convinced that because they opposed the Transvaal their crimes were headed by an absolving imperial virtue.

By protests to the Transvaal, complaints to Downing Street, and open encouragement of well-disposed chiefs, Southey sought to curb and embarrass the Transvaal. No occasion was neglected of discrediting it and inciting the British Government either to annex the disputed territory or to establish over the tribes some form of protectorate. Not content with reporting the high-handed actions of farmers and republican officials, he even raked up stories of Transvaal blackbirding, more than fifteen years old and of the most doubtful authenticity. Full well, as an old Cape official, did he know that those in England who abominated blackbirding in the Pacific and who were sorely perplexed at the continued activity of the African slave traders, would look with a more than usually troubled conscience on the disturbed South African scene.

At Cape Town the High Commissioner was in full accord with Southey that the Republics should be compelled to accept British leadership in their native affairs. "It must be borne in mind", Barkly wrote to Carnarvon, "that the key to South African politics is the question of the treatment of the natives."[1] Pro-

---

[1] G.D. 6/32, Barkly to Carnarvon, 25 July 1874.

C

tests and counter-proclamations were useless as long as the British Government published Blue Books announcing to all the world and President Burgers that it would not spend a shilling to uphold the Keate Award. If the British Government would only speak firmly the weak Republics would desist. Their military resources "in an aggressive point of view" were negligible. In the Zoutpansberg, on the Zulu border and on the road to Delagoa Bay, where dwelt Sekukuni, the Transvaal lived in daily dread of native outbreaks. In an emergency President Burgers might conceivably raise a force of a thousand men, tolerably well armed. Yet even these could only hold the field for a short while. "This at least is clear from past experience," Barkly informed Carnarvon, "that neither the Boers who form the bulk of the population, nor the more restless and ambitious British Subjects who are their Rulers, have the slightest desire to come into collision with Great Britain, and she has only plainly and firmly to indicate her will, in order to secure submission to it."[1] Was it not true that the Boers had withdrawn before a determined British attitude in Basutoland and Griqualand West? If a "decided tone" were adopted, the prey would be dropped again. Thus Barkly taught the Colonial Office a contempt for the strength and fighting qualities of the Republics that was not without influence on its final decision to annex the Transvaal, and was to be punished disastrously on Majuba Hill.

Barkly was not the first High Commissioner who had taken it upon himself to exceed instructions from Downing Street. Convinced that the Transvaal could be browbeaten, he held such violent language towards Burgers that Carnarvon in England took fright. In the belief that Barkly was intending to back up his words with military force, he wrote a peremptory letter forbidding any movement of troops in the direction of the Transvaal western border. Burgers knew himself to be secure behind this veto and the controversy degenerated into a lengthy and acrimonious correspondence in which both complained with justice of the discourtesy of the other. Burgers was a redoubtable opponent. His handling of Barkly's didactic and admonitory letters was a fine example of ingenious invective and subtle argu-

[1] G.D. 6/32, Barkly to Carnarvon, 25 May 1874.

ment. He knew well how to refute Augustine by Augustine. Not even his desperate and almost fatal illness when, already ill of the dropsy, he was prostrated by an internal haemorrhage in March 1874, served to chasten the defiance of his Government.

Rebuffed by Burgers and aware that he could expect no support from the Cape, where Molteno's fear of alienating the Dutch vote made him a virtual supporter of the Republics, Barkly nevertheless refused to accept defeat. If the victims of Transvaal aggression could not be annexed, then it might be possible to annex the aggressor. Burgers was unpopular in the Transvaal. He supported the western borderers, it is true, but the farmers frowned upon his opposition to their demands for more stringent native pass laws, and disliked the ambitious innovations of the Hollanders whom he had introduced into the civil service. The merchant fraternity, with headquarters in the Cape or Natal, favoured more amicable relations with the British colonies. The goldminers at Lydenburg and the prospectors drifting about in search of the gold that everybody seemed convinced would be found, were a valuable focus of British influence. Both in the colonies and Republics federation was discussed widely and with growing favour, even though Brand was still irreducibly opposed to any understanding with the British Government or its colonies until the Free State claims to the diamond fields were settled. If Burgers died—his Kimberley doctors were convinced that he could not live—an opportunity for bringing the Transvaal under British influence might easily present itself.

Successors to the presidency were already being freely discussed. The foremost was the Attorney General Buchanan, who was however an advanced republican. But there was also favourable mention of Green, who in the course of a chequered career had been a British commissariat officer, British Resident in the Orange River Sovereignty, Civil Commissioner in the Cape, and member of the Griqualand West Legislature. If a candidate favourable to British influence could be found, reflected Barkly, "all would be safe".[1] If it were true, as Southey confidently reported after a personal reconnaissance into the Transvaal, that

[1] *Ibid.* Barkly to Carnarvon, 24 June 1874.

two-thirds of the population were well disposed to the British
Government, the Transvaal might even welcome the British
flag.

In hopeful preparation Barkly took "sure and secret" means
to feel the pulse of the Transvaal population as to British rule.[1]
He clearly recognized all the valuable results that might flow
from the acquisition of the Transvaal, notably the easier adjustment of the Griqualand and Natal frontier disputes and the control of Zululand that would be held between two British territories. Above all the Orange Free State would be isolated, and
probably forced to come to terms. Without such pressure the
Free State would remain intractable. While it had been engaged
beyond its strength in fighting the Basuto, and greenbacks were
worth eight shillings in the pound, the idea of federation with the
Cape had been popular. But now that the Cape Government
kept the Basuto in order, now that trade and transport were
thriving, and the greenbacks had risen to par, any movement
that threatened republican independence was frankly unpopular.
Brand's position and popularity were beyond challenge. Neither
British threats nor promises would move him, as long as the
Griqualand West dispute remained unsettled. "Nothing that the
British Government could do for him would improve" his
position, Barkly explained to the Secretary of State. His emolu-
ments were twice those of the Lieutenant-Governor of Natal,
so that he had personally nothing to gain by the change to British
rule. But if the Transvaal "would come under our flag again the
Orange Free State must, hemmed in as it would be on all sides,
sooner or later follow".[2] And once the Republics were under the
British flag, the Cape would be released from the neutrality in
which Molteno's fear of offending his Dutch electorate held it.
As early therefore as the middle of 1874 the road to South
African co-operation and federation seemed to lead first of all
to the establishment of British influence in the Transvaal by
peaceful and legal or otherwise by violent means.

The return of the Republics under the British flag—Barkly
seemed to echo the thought of Carnarvon in England. The
British Government had first tried to turn its back upon the

[1] G.D. 6/32, Barkly to Carnarvon, 25 July 1874.   *Ibid.*

Republics. It had then imperiously halted their expansion by forceful intervention. There remained the policy of compromise and reconciliation. Had the Cape consented to annex the diamond fields, Carnarvon might have agreed to the use of suasion against the Transvaal. Molteno, however, made it completely clear that the Cape Government would not assume either Griqualand West or the Keate Award. Thus Carnarvon was forced to try to win the Republic for his policy. "Improved relations if possible with the Dutch States" must be the aim of British policy.[1]

Amongst the carefully tended prejudices of South African history is the tradition that Carnarvon was, of all British Secretaries of State before Chamberlain, the most aggressive and the least respectful of republican independence. Yet in its first years at least, his South African policy was one of reconciliation. In spite of the aggressive impatience of Southey and Barkly at the "petty republics", he recognized, and indeed never failed to recognize, that the consent of the Republics rather than their coercion would most surely achieve the federation that he made the leading object of his policy. It must be remembered that the positive and energetic intervention of the British Government in South African affairs during his regime did not seek to add new territories to the Empire, but sought virtually the opposite—the opportunity for the Mother Country to withdraw decently from a land in which co-operation and a common understanding between the various communities should have replaced the confusion of separate and conflicting ambitions.

Southey's proposal that the disputed area on the Transvaal western border be added to Griqualand West, Carnarvon rejected out of hand. The British Government had been jockeyed into accepting the diamond fields, although it considered the Cape morally bound to take them over. Certainly it must refuse to be the catspaw for further annexations of territory. Moreover, there could be no confidence in the continued prosperity of the diggings. The experience of Australia and California pointed to the early exhaustion of even the most valuable mineral deposits. Already every mail brought news of discouragement, loss of population, and the growing financial instability of the Griqua-

[1] G.D. 6/32, Carnarvon to Barkly, 22 Aug. 1874.

land West Government. The addition of new territory could only mean that at no distant date a swollen and insolvent colony would collapse upon the hands of the British Government.

If only the Transvaal could quietly and unobtrusively absorb the territory, it might be possible for the British Government to close its eyes. "Her Majesty's Government", wrote Carnarvon to Barkly, "are not prepared...to interfere to prevent the peaceful and unconstrained union of such tribes with the Transvaal Republic." "I fail to see", he added privately, "that the Imperial Government are bound to support through thick and thin an award in which they are very indirectly interested, should one or both of the parties on whose behalf it was pronounced retire from it; it may be very unfortunate and very dishonourable of the Free State [*sic*], but it is obviously no light matter to commit the home government to the risks of a doubtful and highly unsatisfactory collision with the Republic." Perhaps, he suggested somewhat helplessly, the High Commissioner could impose an embargo on guns for the Transvaal, or arm the native enemies of the Transvaal, or place higher duties on all goods intended for Transvaal consumption. Would it be possible to swamp the Dutch in South Africa by an influx of British immigrants?[1]

The position of the Colonial Secretary was most embarrassing. "These South African questions", he complained, "are a terrible labyrinth of which it is very hard to find the clue."[2] The entries in his memorandum book clearly indicate his indecision. Conflicting scraps of sentences frequently occur: "repress aggression by aggression"; "no wish to annex"; "wish to arrive at understanding"; "if Cape will not support us must leave Griqualand to itself"; "if the Rep[ublic] only exercise suasion are not justified in opposing it". The British Government could not but fear the grave consequences of republican expansion which Barkly and Southey so darkly described. Yet it shrank from violent action. Where would these piecemeal and unco-ordinated annexations end? Natal, if Lieutenant-Governor Pine was to be believed, had within the past year come perilously close to a disastrous native uprising, and Theophilus Shepstone was urging

[1] G.D. 6/32, Carnarvon to Barkly, 24 April 1874.
[2] C.O. 48/469, D. 82, Barkly to Carnarvon, 25 Aug. 1874, Minutes.

the British Government to relieve Natal of its dangerous excess of natives by annexing yet more disputed territory, claimed already by Zulus and the Transvaal. And inevitably the Home Government would be asked to sanction the annexation of the native areas beyond the Cape Eastern Frontier, and the indeterminate length of coastline and hinterland beyond the Cape northern boundary.

It became clear that the British Government must free itself of embarrassment and indecision, and seek more resolutely to resolve the complexities by which it was faced. There was nothing to be expected from the benevolent neutrality Kimberley had suggested. Every complaint against the Republics from Barkly and Southey, every spasm of irritation and fear in Natal, every bottle and gun that found its way into Basutoland pointed to the need of a vigorous intervention in South Africa. If British policy in this period be judged less by its setbacks and errors than by the conditions that called it forth, the criticism that Downing Street thrust itself upon a land that was quietly if slowly solving its own problems, must lose its force. The conditions that called forth Carnarvon's intervention were frontier quarrels, an intransigent localism, the certainty of native wars, and above all a fatal lack of leadership either in the British colonies or the Republics. Brand had sunk into a deep moral obstinacy that did him personal credit, but did not help the cause of co-operation. Molteno, afraid of offending the Dutch vote, and concerned with orthodox ambitions for the Cape, would speak only vaguely of an uncertain future when the Cape would absorb the rest of South Africa. There remained, therefore, the sovereign power—the British Government.

Confederation came to appear as a political necessity to be urgently pursued, so urgently pursued that the British Government felt compelled to advance it by every means in its power. The possession of the Transvaal, the Colonial Office had been informed, would bring the Free State under the British flag. The common allegiance of all the South African communities would indeed be a long stride towards confederation. The following pages will show how Carnarvon's failure to persuade South Africa to accept confederation brought him back finally to what he himself considered the *ultima ratio*—the extinction of the Transvaal's independence.

But before he would have recourse to compulsion Carnarvon decided to explore the gentler and more persuasive paths that might lead to this end. Froude had said of the Boers that they had been much and unfairly maligned. The Boers knew that ultimately they must come under the British flag. Given fair play and generous treatment they would come readily.[1] Anyway the British colonies were in their way as great obstacles to confederation as the Republics. In Carnarvon's eyes there was little to choose between Brand in the Free State and Molteno in the Cape, between provocative Transvaal borderers and the dangers of a weak native policy in Natal. Indeed it was in Natal that there occurred the crisis which brought the Secretary of State to show his hand.

[1] G.D. 6/49, pp. 126–9.

CHAPTER III

QUASI CROWN COLONIES

THE HISTORY of the colony of Natal, more than that of any other colony, is the history of native policy. Yet for a whole generation that policy had been concealed beneath the mantle of Theophilus Shepstone, Secretary for Native Affairs. Until 1873 there had occurred no serious crisis, nor had there been a single important innovation that might serve to draw attention to the manner in which a great native population was faring in the midst of the European colonists. The illusion has accordingly been created that the period of Shepstone's rule was a kind of golden age of peace and native contentment. Actually the same ubiquitous problems of land and labour were developing in Natal as well, although without the alarums of the Cape Eastern Frontier, and the hurly-burly of the Transvaal western border. The Natal colonist demanded a plentiful supply of reliable labour, courts of law that carried out the Masters and Servants Laws in a proper and summary manner, a minimum of expenditure for purely native purposes and security against uprisings. Not unlike the farmers of the Republics he believed that the natives held too much land, which was an encouragement to idleness, that they held it in too large areas, which made them a military menace. The need of native policy in his view was a reduction in the amount of land held by the natives and a system of taxation calculated to force them more freely into the labour market.

In the absence of reliable figures it is impossible to discuss accurately the numbers and distribution of the Natal native population. But it is certain that the colony was already menaced by serious overcrowding. This was not due to a positive shortage of land, but to the land hunger of the farmers and the operations of the selfsame land speculators that had descended upon Griqualand West. Large areas of valuable land near the towns and close to the principal roads had fallen into their hands, and were held for speculative purposes. It was a notorious fact that settlers from England and the Cape were unable to pay the exorbitant prices asked for company land. As the lands still held by the Crown were for the most part difficult of access or disadvantageously located, immigration was almost at a standstill. Because company land was rented to native squatters, who had never been assigned reserves or had been squeezed out of them, the colonists received the impression that the natives had an abundance of land. Superficially they were not incorrect. The natives of Natal were certainly far better off than the population of British Kaffraria, for example. But too much of it was land that the natives occupied on sufferance, to which they had no legal claim whatever. To those like Shepstone, who looked into the future, it was obvious that the coming of railways and the inevitable growth of the European population would reveal the inadequate provisions made for native land.

Theophilus Shepstone was looked upon by his contemporaries as a great native administrator, and his fame is undimmed to this day. He was the first of South Africa's native administrators to be a practical sociologist. He had not merely an unusual knowledge of native law and custom, but a sympathetic understanding that was rewarded by the respect of the tribes. That Natal lived in security for over twenty years is the amplest tribute to his prestige and authority. Modern criticism must insist upon judging men like Shepstone not simply by their understanding of the native mind, but by what they did to meet the problems that the contact between whites and blacks inevitably produced. Of his own work he said towards the end of his career that he had spent his life making bricks without straw. It was true that he was at all times starved of money and men. Yet of him it may be said that although he did superlatively well with the means he had, he failed to transcend the limitations thrust upon him. It was one thing to be versed in native matters and keep an unenterprising peace; it was another to affront boldly and constructively the confusion that was Natal's native policy. Shepstone's contributions to creative native policy are surprisingly unimportant. Though he had a peculiar reticence that makes it difficult to dwell with him in intimacy, it is easy to recognize that he was essentially at one with the colonists. It is significant that he was never unpopular with them. It is an important explanation of his impressive reputation that he did not in the days of his greatest power seriously oppose the European demand for labour and land. He was even eager that the country should be more numerously settled by white colonists. True, he saw clearly the dangers of a situation that permitted masses of natives to squat upon European-owned land without any security for the future. He foresaw better than any of his contemporaries a future in which an increased native population would be deprived of the temporary relief that squatting afforded them. He knew full well that land was the most imperative need of the natives. Yet in solution he put forward fanciful and vain proposals which have a claim to attention only because uncritical minds still periodically suggest them.

Shepstone's native policy went far to meet popular demands. He affirmed like any colonist that the mass of natives in the colony were a hindrance to European expansion. He agreed that the Europeans could not grow in wealth unless they could draw more fully upon the reservoirs of labour in their midst. He agreed that as long as the Tugela River was all that divided Natal from the great independent Zulu tribe the peace and prosperity of the colonists were in jeopardy. Zulu impis fording the Tugela, a sympathetic rebellion amongst the Natal natives themselves, a mass of Zulus stampeded into Natal by Transvaal commandoes —these were favourite terrors in Natal. Such terrors greatly strengthened the conviction which ever more strongly came to obsess the mind of white South Africa, that if the power of the tribes be not broken, there must inevitably come an awful day when a vast uprising would pour its destruction from the Zoutpansberg Mountains to Grahamstown, and in the favourite language of frontier scaremongers "drive the white man into the sea". And what would be the fate of a colony outnumbered by its own subjects and surrounded on all sides by Zulus, Pondos and Basuto? Although Shepstone was by no means the tool and mouthpiece of public opinion, these mingled hopes and fears find a clear reflection in his activity.

In spite of the mystery with which his admirers have sought to enshroud his policy, the ambitions of his mature years are not obscure. They were quite simply to forestall a clash of races in Natal by thrusting part of its native population over the Tugela, where it would serve the additional purpose of checking Dutch pressure upon Zululand. Zululand would be opened up to Natal influence and, what is even more to the point, to Natal settlement. Lacking as he did a land policy which sought to achieve within the limits of Natal a wiser and richer mode of association between the races, despairing of ever finding popular support for such a policy, he accepted, possibly against his own better judgment, the *refoulement* of its natives as the inevitable accompaniment of Natal's growth. "Natal," he wrote to Carnarvon, "with her overwhelming and ever-increasing native population finds herself hemmed in on all sides by Governments anxious to acquire and retain extensions of Territory. The Population per square mile far exceeds that borne by any Territory of equal extent in South Africa. The occupation by natives of farms and Crown lands unoccupied by whites as yet prevents much inconvenient pressure, but should any sudden and considerable accession of white population take place,—a matter beyond the control of any Government,—it is impossible to foresee what solution will be found to so serious and dangerous a problem. A safety valve in the shape of adjoining Territory has always been looked to as the only source of relief...."

The safety valve Shepstone desired for Natal was nearly a thousand square miles of Zulu land and a strip of what he termed "disputed territory" lying between the Transvaal and the Zulus. To this land the Transvaal had an apparently legal claim; for its pressure upon the Zulu border, as upon its western border, had resulted in one of the "treaties" that gave the European farmers the "right" to settle over the heads of the natives, reducing them to squatters and servants or expelling them to find what room they might in the diminishing areas of native settlement. Natal's policy as it was directed by Shepstone sought to prevent the further encroachment of the Republic upon native land. But at root Natal merely aimed at substituting its own encroachment for that of the Dutch farmers. That ultimately the "safety valve" would be "occupied by Europeans", Shepstone frankly confessed, "cannot be doubted; but if the land can be acquired, and put to the purpose I have suggested, the present tension in Natal will be relieved, and time be gained to admit of the introduction of a larger proportion of white colonists". But it would be a mistake, he further revealingly admitted, "to suppose that the relief afforded by this measure would be but temporary, or that the difficulty it is proposed to abate could ever again reach its present dimensions, because the outlet being to the North, the abatement permits of permanent extension towards a climate unsuited to Europeans but not so to natives".[1] Shepstone, in other words, seems to have been the creator of that useful but imaginary vacuum somewhere to the miasmatic north that has so often since his day threatened to solve all South Africa's native ills.

Such language sheds a very clear light upon some of the strongest motives that ruled native affairs in Natal, and goes far to explain the atmosphere in which Natal plunged so readily into the disastrous Zulu War. Such language, strongly supported by Lieutenant-Governor Pine, shows how impossible it is to uphold the belief of the Colonial Office that Natal was a buffer against the territorial greed and oppressiveness of the Transvaal. Indeed the rivalry between the Transvaal and Natal for control of Zululand is one illustration the more of how the subdivision of the land into independent governments bred disharmony and made of the natives and their land a prize for selfish competition.

In earlier years the ignorance in the Colonial Office of South African geography and local conditions had been occasionally almost staggering. But now there was no longer the attitude of a former day when officials did little more than initial despatches that dealt with native customs and conditions—*Graecum est non legitur*. Colonial newspapers now were carefully examined and filed; officials were conversant with local idiomatic expressions probably a decade or more before some of them passed violently into the English language; and they had stopped imposing a German spelling upon Dutch place-names. Certainly the body of information in the Colonial Office on native subjects was large enough to permit a critical and informed approach to the affairs of South Africa.

[1] G.D. 6/23, Shepstone to Carnarvon, 30 Nov. 1874.

The contumacy of a petty Natal chief was the occasion that determined the Colonial Office to invade the mysterious reaches of native policy. In 1849 the tribe of Langalibalele, dubbed "Longbelly" by Wolseley's stiff tongue, was settled in the county of Weenen to act as a buffer against the marauding fragments that the native wars and the Great Trek had driven into the Drakensberg Mountains. *But Jeshurun waxed fat and kicked.* Left in peace for many years, Langalibalele gained some reputation as a witch doctor and earned the hatred of the missionaries among whom he found not a single defender in his hour of trial. When diamonds were discovered some of his men joined the stream to the fields and returned with guns. Though the law of the land forbade the possession of firearms by natives without the express sanction of the Lieutenant-Governor,[1] its operation was inconsistent, desultory and confusing. It was not the only law affecting the natives that was applied in an unequal and arbitrary fashion. Magistrates returned or retained guns brought for registration as they saw fit, so that inevitably the law was evaded and ignored. Such was the weakness of native administration that it could not carry out any unpopular law lest its commands be disobeyed by a population too numerous to coerce.

The temptation to terrorize was powerful in a colony where there was a great disproportion between whites and blacks. Therefore, when Langalibalele laid violent hands upon some Government native messengers sent to bid him to the capital, the Natal Government felt that through its very weakness it was forced to inflict the most complete punishment upon his tribe. In Natal, as throughout all the land, it was held that indecision in the face of the natives was dangerous folly. The opinion that natives, though easily contented with their lot, submit to no control save that of force, and accept no bond save that of expediency, is of the essence of much South African native policy. In a community that remembered the violence of the Cape and Free State borders, the conviction that an armed force was the only possible answer to native unrest was necessarily strong. Langalibalele's disobedience was but a single footprint, yet to a nervous Natal its meaning was fearfully clear. "There was no alternative left",

[1] Law 5 of 1859.

Shepstone later submitted, "between attempting to coerce, and listlessly and criminally allowing the reins of government to be dragged in the dust." And so the cry was raised, and with kennels ayelp, the colonists and loyal blacks of Natal set off in pursuit of the terrified and fleeing tribe. Of fighting there was practically none, although *The Times* laconically announced "another little war". Langalibalele was captured in Basutoland and brought to Natal for trial.

A specially constituted tribunal headed by the Lieutenant-Governor himself tried the chief. Two of its members had lost relatives in the skirmish. At the time of the trial news of the Ashanti War arrived in Natal. The Ashanti War, roundly declared Pine, who knew West Africa, had all risen out of the absence of a summary form of native justice. There would be no Ashanti War in Natal. The "smouldering fire" of native unrest must be stamped out. Langalibalele was sentenced to lifelong confinement on Robben Island.

There is small need to discuss the irregularities and the arbitrariness of the trial. What merits attention was the proclamation issued before the trial utterly dispersing the Amahlubi and Putili tribes and confiscating their land and cattle. The dispossession of the tribes was essentially an intemperate and vindictive manifestation of the desire of the colonists to destroy what they conceived to be the too great economic independence of the natives, to limit their lands, and finally to remove the "restraints" that kept them from freely entering the labour market. That almost the entire religious body of Natal applauded Pine's conduct was due partly to their abhorrence of the "rain maker" chief—it was God Almighty in his righteous judgment who had come down upon them—but more especially to the fact that the Gospel was making insufficient headway against tribal organization and custom. The detribalized natives could be more easily Christianized than tribes bound together by their own laws and sustained by some measure still of economic independence.

In the ranks of the clergy Langalibalele found one defender— Bishop Colenso, whose controversial work in biblical criticism had made his name a household word in England. The Pentateuch was played out, his enemies declared, and Langalibalele gave him a new sensation. The weight of his name and the energy of his onslaught upon Lieutenant-Governor Pine, forced the trial into the focus of British Parliamentary and public attention. The Colonial Office was shocked by the manner in which the trial had been conducted. Carnarvon felt that the British Government could not escape the duty of using all its influence to secure the release of Langalibalele from Robben Island, and to restore their property to the dispersed tribes. The action of the Colonial Office was, however, by no means guided by Colenso. Carnarvon was anxious not to affront colonial opinion too seriously, and ultimately prevailed upon the stormy bishop to drop his threats of an appeal to the Privy Council, not to "make triumph" in Natal and to become reconciled with Shepstone.

The real problem that faced the Secretary of State was not merely whether the chief should be released and the tribal lands restored, nor even the admittedly serious need of passing under review Natal's native administration. At the very beginning of his period of office Carnarvon was unexpectedly forced to answer questions that lay at the heart of his whole South African policy. What were the limits of imperial power? What authority did the Home Government possess in the internal problems of the subcontinent? By what means could it exercise its authority? Only ten years earlier a cry would have been raised in Parliament and the press that England could not withdraw its feet too promptly from the slough of colonial dominion. Now almost abruptly and still a year before the purchase of the Suez Canal shares, the slough of dominion had become an imperial responsibility not to be lightly abandoned, and even the right of colonists to govern their own affairs was a subject of debate. In other words, the simple question of justice or injustice towards a petty native chief was much less important than the assertion of the policy that in a conflict between white and black the Imperial Government had a responsibility that made interference a duty.

It was deeply unfortunate however that the new Secretary of State was compelled thus early to make a forceful declaration of policy on so explosive a question. Try as he would to be tactful he could not avoid serious offence to colonial feeling. The Graaff

Reinet *Herald*, conservative in its judgment and English in its leanings, uttered the warning that it would probably go far to sever the connection of the Colony with the British Empire if the chief were liberated.[1] Another newspaper ended a fierce article by grimly warning the Imperial Government "that next year will be the centenary of American Independence."[2] On all sides men held up their hands in horror at such cynical and dangerous meddling. As if it were not obvious to every man who "knew" the native character that the release of Langalibalele would provoke an unrest amongst all the tribes from Zululand to the Eastern Frontier![3] From Weenen County in upper Natal came a memorial suggesting that the best guarantee against future difficulties with the Imperial Government would be an independence "far greater than we now possess". It was inevitable that a demand for constitutional changes should be the outcome of the crisis. It was equally inevitable that the Home Government should envisage the opposite possibility— the limitation instead of the expansion of Natal's constitutional liberties.

The attitude of the Secretary of State to self-government in Natal was influenced by the physical and political weakness which the crisis had disclosed. To a greater extent still it was influenced by the discovery that self-government could be a serious hindrance to an authority that, claiming to be the paramount power in South Africa, was determined to effect an early and direct change in the political structure of the country as a whole. By Act III of 1874 the Parliament of the Cape Colony had given its consent to the imprisonment of Langalibalele on Robben Island. Carnarvon's insistence that the chief be removed to the mainland brought about a collision with the Cape Government. Barkly also warned the Secretary of State that in forcing his will upon the Cape Parliament he would undermine his influence in the Republics. Molteno made a dark allusion to the Anti-Convict Agitation. But since he was not prepared to engage in open conflict with the Home Government or to provoke an imperial disallowance of the Act, he sullenly complied with Carnarvon's

[1] 26 Dec. 1874.   [2] G.D. 6/32, Barkly to Carnarvon, 5 Feb. 1875.
[3] *Ibid.* Barkly to Carnarvon, 25 Jan. 1875.

D

wishes.[1] But he had not long to wait for his revenge. The Act that imprisoned Langalibalele on Robben Island was repealed just when the ship bearing Carnarvon's famous despatch on South African confederation was approaching Table Bay. That the despatch was received with an ill humour was not very strange.

For Natal there could be no self-government. Instead there were to be a new Governor and a new Government. A policy that aimed at self-determination for the entire subcontinent was thus unhappily inaugurated by a quarrel with the Cape and arbitrariness in Natal. Pine had come to Natal because he was old and worn, and wished to round off his career in a restful place. Now he was recalled and in spite of a rumour that he was to be the next President of the Transvaal Republic, left Natal an ill and embittered old man to join the diminished heads of so many South African governors. The despatch recalling him significantly crossed in mid ocean a bill "To Amend the Constitution", passed by the Natal Legislature. It was a forlorn request. Instead of self-government Natal was to have Jamaican government. Even Molteno agreed that "it would be madness to give Natal Responsible Government".[2] In Natal the Imperial Government would no longer plough with an ox and an ass together. The constitution had to go.

The appointment of Sir Garnet Wolseley to succeed Sir Benjamin Pine as Lieutenant-Governor of Natal was intended to secure Natal for Carnarvon's South African policy.[3] Griqualand West was already a Crown Colony; it was Wolseley's chief task to reduce Natal to the same standing. Natal was in a sense the *corpus vile* upon which Carnarvon experimented before he approached the larger problems of the federation which he believed was close at hand.

Natal's constitutional privileges had been granted under the Royal Charter of 1856, and the Natal Legislature had exercised them for close on twenty years. How could they be abrogated? The problem is deserving of attention. What power did Her

[1] G.D. 6/32, Barkly to Carnarvon, 4 June 1875.
[2] G.D. 6/49, p. 113.
[3] G.D. 6/38, Carnarvon to Wolseley, 15 July 1875.

Majesty's Government have over Colonial governments? What were the limits of imperial authority? Could the Colonial Office turn the exceptional experience of Jamaica into an accepted precedent, and so open a permanent imperial re-entry into colonial institutions? Not since Sir James Stephen had Downing-Street spoken with such firmness. Carnarvon and his associates were convinced that there should be greater room, particularly in South Africa, for the exercise of imperial authority. "This should be a warning", wrote Lowther, the Parliamentary Under-secretary, "against the Imperial Government granting these Constitutions at all except in very exceptional cases and under safeguards which seem to have been omitted."[1]

Would it be possible to abrogate the Natal Constitution by simple Letters Patent? It was a very important and revealing question for the Colonial Office to put to the Law Officers. The Queen could give constitutions; but could her ministers advise her to take them away? The Law Officers were of the opinion that the Queen had the power to issue an amending charter. But their views were given falteringly and timidly. Vaguely defined as were the powers of any single constitution within the Empire, they felt, and the Colonial Office agreed instinctively, that once legislative institutions had been granted to any community it would be highly unconstitutional to repudiate them by arbitrary process. And what was unconstitutional could be decided not by law nor even by precedent, but rather by that feeling for appropriate and acceptable conduct which has always been the inspiration of imperial constitutional development. If the constitution of Natal were to be changed, it should be changed either by the Colonial Legislature itself or by the Imperial Parliament. That meant inevitably that any amendments would have to be accepted by the Natal colonists; for the nineteenth century still had to see the Cabinet that brought a difficult colonial issue into the focus of Parliamentary attention without the very greatest reluctance.

No one can follow the incidents of Wolseley's Natal campaign without fascination. He handled his mission like a campaign. Soldier-like he was prepared to use whatever tactics promised

[1] C.O. 179/119, L.O. to C.O., 14 Jan. 1875, Minutes.

success. The strategic advantage was his; for over the head of Natal hung the threat of coercive imperial legislation. Though it was natural that the cry of secession should be raised, Natal knew that as long as Zulu impis mourned their unbaptized assagais, as long as its railways were unbuilt, British regiments and British credit were more valuable than constitutional privileges.

While he was still on the high seas Wolseley, with an immediate insight into Natal's needs, wrote back to Carnarvon urging that more troops be sent to Natal, and that the Imperial Government guarantee a loan of a million pounds for railway construction. Armed with such a guarantee he could more easily coax the Natal Legislature to take the cash and let the constitution go. No change of constitution no guarantee.[1] Carnarvon shook his head. Troops Wolseley could probably have. That could be arranged between departments. But for an imperial guarantee the Secretary of State would have to approach Parliament. He was already committed to the necessity of asking Parliament for a small guarantee for Fiji. "Two guarantees for Colonial objects in one session would be a severe test of the patience of Parliament."[2] British colonial policy, even when it aimed at the federation of an entire subcontinent, had still to be sparing.

Wolseley turned to other means. Knowing that wine and good food never did a government any harm, he sweetened the bitter draught with sherry and a brilliant manner. Where his old and enfeebled predecessor had scarcely ever been north of Maritzburg, he visited the inland districts, and suggested that his successor be more of a country squire, glad to hunt or chat with sheep-farmers. To his critics he adopted a frank and pleasant conduct. The waverers he awed with his utter confidence in the success of his mission. His whirlwind activity touched the society of Durban and Maritzburg at every point. Politically and socially the two towns had never been so entertained, so flattered and so browbeaten. Accustomed to lustreless Governors they could not deny their admiration to a man who worked tirelessly yet could meet all men and entertain them splendidly.

[1] G.D. 6/38, Wolseley to Carnarvon, 27 Feb. 1875, at sea.
[2] Ibid. Carnarvon to Wolseley, 2 March 1875.

"He frightens these small folk with his amazing energy and decision", chuckled Broome, his Colonial Secretary and press agent. After a meal with Wolseley, the overpowered mayor of Maritzburg gasped that he felt as though he had been put "through a cullender".[1]

Wolseley scored a more practical success by capturing the principal executive offices. The Colonial Treasurer and the Immigration Officer conveniently departed on furlough, and their offices were filled by Colonel Colley and Major Butler, both members of Wolseley's military staff. The new broom was ready to sweep clean, and the capital beheld the unwonted spectacle of punctuality, zeal and hard work in the public offices. Three of the newspapers were persuaded into "something like reason". With the editor of the *Durban Mercury*, Broome took a "great deal of trouble...writing him articles and many private letters". The Maritzburg *Times* became the Government organ. Members of Wolseley's staff furnished it with four articles every week. The editor of the Maritzburg *Witness*, Ridley, though dying, alone stood savagely at bay. He would have nothing to do with the policy of a "howling humanitarian fanatic" like Carnarvon or Wolseley.[2]

To an original distrust of colonial self-government Wolseley added a particular disbelief in the fitness of Natal for self-government. "I am as sensible as anyone can be", he declared, "of how unfitted these people are for framing laws that should in any way whatever affect the interests of the Kingdom...."[3] In the departments of Government his aides found confusion and mismanagement. Accounts of all sorts were muddled; numerous irregularities had been tolerated. Revenues had been under-estimated, estimates inadequately prepared, and eked out by long strings of supplementary items. There were even ugly rumours that railway contracts had brought corruption into high Government places. Though he flattered men in public Wolseley was privately of the opinion that the colony did not contain enough men of "sense and ability" to fill the offices of Government under a responsible regime. Such men of ability as there

---

[1] G.D. 6/38, Broome to Carnarvon, 26 April 1875.   [2] *Ibid.*
[3] *Ibid.* Wolseley to Carnarvon, 29 May 1875.

were amongst the "noisy clique" of Responsibles, were self-seeking, or failures in every walk of life who had taken to politics as a last resort.[1] There he spoke with a soldier's disdain for politicians. In reality he was afraid that these whom he affected to despise would cause the failure of his mission. His private state of mind stood in the greatest possible contrast with his public statements. He made every move with uncertainty. The amending bill was rushed through its readings lest its opponents find time to swing public sentiment against him. When it was passed few were more relieved and surprised than he himself. Even with the full support of Shepstone and the suborned news-papers, he was afraid till the last that it would be necessary after all to have recourse to the Imperial Parliament.

To secure the passage of his bill he had been forced to compromise with his opponents. He had hoped to obtain a thorough-going Crown Colony government by reducing the number of elective members. Instead he had to be content with raising the number of nominated members to equality with the elective members. The equality meant that only a popular administration could work well with the legislature, and that an unpopular administration would either have to endure deadlock or exploit the factious temper of the elective members.

Yet it is true that Natal as a whole was not antagonistic to the changes he had wrought. His success, qualified though it was, was due, not to his sherry, nor to the promises of Indian labour he made to the coast members, but to the unwillingness of the Natal colonists to resist a measure which had the support of the Home Government. A change in the direction of responsible government would have been greatly more welcome, but if the new Government would watch the Zulus, build the railways, and keep the executive offices clean of the inefficiency and sloth of previous administrations, loyal Natal was willing to give the new system a fair trial.

The amendment was on its way to Downing Street. Wolseley's successor, Sir Henry Bulwer, had not yet arrived. But he did not abate his activity. Except for a cloud in Burma that might or might not spell another "little war", the imperial horizon was

[1] G.D. 6/38, Wolseley to Carnarvon, 29 May 1875.

clear. Till November it was the "off season" for campaigning in Burma.[1] Beseeching that he be kept in mind he turned to Natal's natives. Now that the offending constitution was out of the way it was Carnarvon's wish that the new administration should introduce reforms into the system of native finance and management. But when the Lieutenant-Governor turned to carry out the Secretary of State's will, he found himself confronted by Shepstone. True, reforms were needed. Those that Wolseley introduced were excellent. That reforms had not been carried out before was because Natal could not hope to carry out even existing laws. Without a complete change in her military position reforms could only succeed in irritating the native population. Shepstone pointed beyond the borders of Natal. There lay the rub. How could reforms be safely carried out with uncontrolled Zulu impis under a despotic and cruel ruler chafing beyond the Tugela, and with an independent Republic exploiting their unrest, covetous of both their lands and a road to the sea? Was not Burgers about to tour the capitals of Europe in search of funds for a railway that would imperil the success of Natal's own railways and make out of Delagoa Bay an outlet for the commerce of the interior? The crying problem of Natal, Wolseley discovered, was not an internal social problem but an external military problem. The unreal humanitarianism of British statesmen in the past had fouled the paths of Natal's natural development. His words to Carnarvon were blunt. "England with her humanitarian notions of governing barbarians is really responsible for the dangers now existing within Natal."[2] Had the British Government not forced its high philanthropic sentiments upon the colonists they could have followed the superior example of the Dutch and purged their land of two-thirds of its native inhabitants. The third that remained would have been properly and wholly subordinated to European influence. Pine and his irregular cavalry, he plainly hinted, had not erred when they sought to crush Langalibalele. As it was, the interference of the British Government had left the natives in a frame of mind so dangerous that if Natal were to be spared a "fearful catastrophe" strong measures could not be delayed. Natal had to be the

[1] G.D. 6/38, Wolseley to Carnarvon, 12 June 1875.   [2] *Ibid.*

undisputed mistress in her own house. To accomplish that she must be freed from the explosive menace of external dangers, or Great Britain had better for its own reputation cease to hold the colony altogether. Like Frere later, Wolseley came to reform and remained converted.

Encouraged by such sympathy Shepstone abandoned the lesser project of annexing the disputed territory for the more ambitious annexation of all Zululand. From missionary interests in Zululand, baffled in their work of Christianization by the hostility of Cetywayo, came a persuasive language. "I think the present a most opportune time for making the attempt to obtain the land you covet", wrote Robertson,[1] his chief informant in Zululand. The Testament advanced more smoothly where soldiers had gone before. Robertson did not shrink at the prospect of spilling pagan and unbaptized blood. "Had you found it consistent with honour and humanity to let the late war fever take its course I believe you would have had the whole country at your disposal by now", he told Shepstone.[2] All Zululand would be a better "safety valve" for Natal's excess population than a mere strip. A thousand men, learned Wolseley, would suffice to bring the Zulus under the British flag.[3] A thousand men, relayed Wolseley to Carnarvon, would give the Empire Zululand and all the coastline to the Portuguese possessions. Gone would be the threat of a Zulu war and disasters within Natal. The borders of British Zululand would be as undisturbed as those of British Basutoland. There could be no Transvaal railway built to the coast. Great Britain would control the hub and rim of the South African wheel, and republican spokes must needs spin at her behest. Dependent upon British railways and British ports the Republics could not but agree to confederation.

That Zululand would ultimately be annexed was as certain as it was desirable. It is almost certain that Cetywayo's despotic

[1] G.D. 6/38, Robertson to Shepstone, 25 June 1875.
[2] *Ibid.* Robertson to Shepstone, 18 June 1875. Shepstone was afraid lest his attitude and activities be publicly known. His letters were secretly sent and received. The letters he wrote were at his urgent request "reduced to ashes". Cp. R. Robertson to Shepstone, 18 June 1875.
[3] *Ibid.* Wolseley to Carnarvon, 8 July 1875.

rule could have been easily overthrown in 1875. The disaster at Isandhlwana in 1879 with its mournful Inkermann roll of British dead does indeed give the historian pause. Yet Isandhlwana was an illogical disaster, as unnecessary as it was bloody. It happened. That is almost all that can be said about it. In 1875 conditions in Zululand were clearly favourable to annexation. There were factions amongst the chiefs. Cattle disease had swept off great numbers of beasts. Shepstone's name, though it did not stand as high amongst the Zulus as he believed, was still powerful and a rallying point for those that loved not Cetywayo.

In a political sense Shepstone and Wolseley advocated nothing that was new. Natal's native difficulties, like any other South African difficulty such as currency, communications, or gunrunning, transcended the mere borders of any single community. For nearly two years this truism had been the burden of Carnarvon's despatches. The novelty lay in the insistence upon prompt and forcible action. Wolseley's response to what he saw was imperious and abrupt, and seemed to have little place for the more persuasive and diplomatic path that Carnarvon had hitherto trodden. With Wolseley, as Gilbert and Sullivan were quick to see, the British army achieves a new type, more brilliant and thrusting, with a dash of romantic bravura, less restrained by the cautiousness of their fathers, more active and more venturesome, certainly happier in the new found energy of the late Victorian Empire. Wolseley, it is not irrelevant to remark, was of the generation that succeeded Cardwell's abolition in 1871 of the purchase of army commissions. This reform sharpened the desire of ambitious army officers to see active service, and make their achievements speak in their behalf. In later years Wolseley himself advised young and enterprising officers to take every opportunity of getting themselves killed in action. It has been said more than once that military exploits in French Northern Africa have been encouraged by military men eager for promotion and distinction. In South Africa the ardour of army officers to enhance their reputation, and the renown and strength of their Sovereign, is not unrelated to the more vigorous departures of British policy.

Mark the puffing words of Major Butler, one of Wolseley's

military staff. "Our possessions are vast in South Africa, but they are yet small compared to the limits of their possible future, and it will be found that here as elsewhere throughout the world, that policy which retains in an unrelaxing grasp every foot of British territory, be it but a waste of wilderness, is alone the policy which suits our safety and our honour.... South Africa must follow that irrevocable rule which gives Empire alone to British race and tongue."[1] Sir Henry Barkly himself told the story of "War Horse" Cunynghame, commanding officer of the Cape regiments, who at the time of the war scare on the Eastern Frontier in 1876, not merely revealed the plans of the Government, but in the face of all efforts to allay a dangerous panic, made a Trafalgar speech, asking the head of each military department whether he was ready, and ending with an enquiry of the Chief Medical Officer on the number of tourniquets he had in store! "I feel bound to say", commented Sir Henry, "that if another Kafir War has been avoided it has not been due to prudence on the part of the Military Authorities."[2]

While it would be gravely unjust to the reputation of so distinguished a soldier as Wolseley to accuse him of deliberately imperilling the peace of a British colony, it is certain that he brought to Carnarvon's attention more emphatically than before the possibility of achieving his ends in South Africa by direct and forceful means. It was he more than any other who implanted in Carnarvon's mind the thought that a more summary conduct would relieve the deadlock that his negotiations with the Cape and the Republics finally reached. Whatever blunders the Secretary of State committed, his policy in its inception was an effort to reach an agreement with the Cape and the Republics through the regular channels of political discussion. If his effort were to fail, either through his own fault or the fault of South African statesmen, the temptation to follow Wolseley's advice would be strong. The temptation was made stronger by events in Griqualand West. Hard upon the heels of the crisis in Natal came the threat of the collapse of the Government of Griqualand West, of race riots and rebellion at the diamond fields. These happenings

[1] C.O. 179/118, Conf., Wolseley to Carnarvon, 27 Aug. 1875.
[2] G.D. 6/32, Barkly to Carnarvon, 6 Feb. 1877.

seemed to challenge the British Government to grapple firmly and promptly with its problems in South Africa.

At the close of 1874 the diamond fields were on the verge of collapse. The European population had dropped to almost 6000. It was a population that had to face the difficulties of falling diamond prices, the high cost of living, increased taxation, collapsing and unworkable claims, and the inroads of speculators and mining companies. The Government was fast breaking down. Its responsibilities grew in magnitude as its revenues declined. Import dues, the most certain and obvious source of revenue, were absorbed by the Cape. A very conservative estimate placed upon the dues collected by the Cape on goods destined for the diamond fields was £56,000 for 1875, but as dues collected on guns alone in 1875 were reliably given as £20,000,[1] it is certain that the Cape must have collected very considerably more. In addition the Cape Government levied a tax of £15,000 on cheques and bank notes in circulation at the diamond fields. Land, instead of being a source of revenue, was a heavy charge. Land-jobbers under an assumed authority from the native chiefs had unscrupulously disposed of their dubious land claims to others, so that almost every acre in the territory was in dispute. When Southey naturally refused to recognize these claims, the speculators and their dupes joined in the attempt to embarrass the Government and secure Southey's recall. Indeed, every element of the population felt it had reason to oppose the Government. The proprietors of the diamond-bearing ground protested their rights to raise rents *à merci*; capitalists and company promoters with money from London approached members of the Government with bribes and schemed to buy out the claim holders and work the mines themselves; the diggers with their backs against the wall abused the administration for not pumping out the water that flooded their claims and for not keeping the natives in their proper and servile place. These discontents were exploited by a ring of speculators and agitators, the most notorious of whom was Aylward, an incredible personage, assassin, Fenian, correspondent for the *Daily Telegraph*, a Government spy in Dublin Castle, racy raconteur and newspaper editor, a partisan of many

[1] G.D. 6/36, Lanyon to Carnarvon, 1 Jan. 1876.

causes, though a martyr to none, a man of undoubtedly superior education who claimed that an early attempt to train him as a Roman Catholic priest had sent him wrong.

The rumour was spread that the Lieutenant-Governor's own hands were not clean of land speculation, and the rumour, though it was false, was widely believed, for Southey was a hotbed of intrigue in himself. While he opposed the speculators within Griqualand West he supported their brethren across the borders in their claims against the Republic. It was alleged that his underpaid civil servants embezzled public funds and betrayed the contents of cipher messages to their former colleagues at the Cape. The Colonial Secretary, John Blades Currey, was the evil genius of the diamond fields. Once a police magistrate at Cape Town and an intimate of Barkly, he was now Southey's closest associate. He cynically used his influence in favour of a land-jobbing friend. His insolent and browbeating manner toward those who came to his office, together with Southey's own austere and unapproachable mood, made the administration completely unpopular. It was in such bad odour that if a drain were not cleaned out or if there were a fall of earth in the mine the blame was placed upon the administration. If a digger woke up with a headache, it was declared he would toss in his bed and curse John Blades Currey. Men were too alike in their interests and their manner of living to take kindly to the officiousness and the pretensions of an administration that, with a shack for a Government House, and living for the most part in tents and mud huts, had not even the trappings of authority, let alone the income to provide the wines and charades that Wodehouse had found it well to offer his opponents. Worst of all, the Government could not even show a united front. The personal animosities and the bickerings of the Executive Council ended by making it ridiculous in the sight of all men.

The Home Government might have been inclined to look upon the confusion in Griqualand West as the inevitable condition of mining communities, had it not been for Southey's extreme financial embarrassment. In 1874 and 1875 the Colony drifted steadily closer to bankruptcy. Mulcted by the Cape, with falling diamond prices and a dwindling population, Southey was at his wit's end for revenue. The expenditure soared above the estimates; and indebtedness to the all too accommodating Cape banks mounted apace. Ever more expenditure was forced upon Southey. The land disputes called for expensive surveys; the mining camps needed a police force, which if it was inefficient was still costly. Taxation that had amounted to £3 a head in 1872 rose to £10 in 1875. The natural financial difficulties were made worse by an almost incredible incompetence. Estimates were prepared three months after the beginning of the financial year and arrived in England too late to be useful. Vouchers were prepared months after payments had actually been made. The accounts for 1873 were "cooked" and entered upon the books only in 1875.[1] It is a story in itself to observe from the minutes in the Colonial Office how Carnarvon's eagerness to effect confederation and bring about the annexation of the fields to the Cape grew with the gathering crisis at the fields.

In spite of his ambition Carnarvon was as nervous as his most cautious predecessors of incurring expense on behalf of the colonies. It is indeed a mark of the mid-Victorian Empire that it did not seek to colonize the wilderness. It was an imperialism that was mainly interested in colonies and enterprises that could pay their own way. Carnarvon's plan for South Africa was a broad and dignified ambition as he explained it to Parliament, but it is only just to Molteno and those who opposed the British Government to see the obverse side of the medal, to realize that confederation was pursued also as a means of more surely relieving the Mother Country of the expense and responsibilities that a divided South Africa threatened to unload upon her. Granted that co-ordination was the country's greatest need, Carnarvon's policy was mainly acceptable to the British Government and Parliament because it would, in the phrase of sixteenth-century Spanish viceroys, spare Her Majesty's purse and relieve her conscience.

All through the beginning of 1875 the tempest kept rising at Kimberley. At one time Carnarvon had agreed that Southey was

---

[1] G.D. 6/23, Crossman to Ommanney, 8 Jan. 1876. Currey was again the principal culprit. "I am in the middle of the accounts. I never saw anything so disgraceful." Crossman to Ommanney, 26 Nov. 1875.

the best man in South Africa. Now he wondered whether he should not be replaced. It would be idle to blame Southey's personality or the shortcomings of his subordinates for the collapse of his administration. Even as the diamond fields were South Africa's first industrial community, so for the first time was South Africa confronted by the naked problem of capital and labour. In the development of South Africa the problem of the diamond fields was now not whether they belonged to the Free State or even whether they should be annexed to the Cape. What Southey saw and what Carnarvon certainly did not see was that there was being decided at Kimberley the question how mining enterprise, with which the whole economic and social future of South Africa was destined to be bound up, was to be organized and controlled. Could South Africa at the outset of its industrial history discipline the resourceful and powerful interests that came to draw profit from her unusual wealth? In 1875 the question was not merely rhetorical. An interim Government, itself seized in the toils of the banks, and unsupported by the Home Government, could not hope to force terms upon the men, British and foreign, Gentile and Jew, who could buy up-to-date machinery and hire the best skill of British and American mining science. Richard Southey, imperialist, opponent of colonial self-government, and enemy of republican independence, ruined himself politically in defending the digger, the small independent worker against companies and organized wealth. A man born to follow Rhodes had he been younger; yet he set himself resolutely in the path of the "free" play of those sovereign economic forces that gave Cobden's England its wealth and its power. To the company promoters he let it be known "that the immense wealth yet to be obtained from our diamond mines should be carefully guarded, in order that the people of South Africa may derive the profits accruing from them, rather than that such profit should go out of the country to foreign companies". He secured the passage of three ordinances which declared that the Government of Griqualand West was not content with the narrow function of keeping down the burden of taxation and protecting men in their divine right to property; nor was it just a municipality that kept roads in order and put drunken and absconding native servants in gaol. Ordinance 5 of 1874 called in question the right of the proprietors to mineral rights and cleared the ground for a test case that would permit the Government to scotch the claim of the proprietors to be free of its control. Ordinance 9 of 1874 took the additional step of conferring upon the Government powers to regulate the stand rents imposed upon the diggers and shopkeepers, and to prevent the proprietors from destroying the small worker with crushing rentals. A third ordinance, No. 10 of 1875, known as the Mining Ordinance, disqualified any individual or company from holding more than ten claims. But the British Government had the power to disallow the legislation of Crown Colonies, not to speak of "quasi Crown Colonies". Ordinance 5 and Ordinance 9 were both disallowed, even though Barkly, with his Australian experience, spoke disparagingly of the "capitalists" and ventured to suggest that the diggers were waging the fight of labour against capital. Carnarvon's Tory economics was deeply shocked. Labour against capital forsooth! The diggers were nothing but the disturbers of the peace and the enemies of property rights. Her Majesty's Government would not hamper the beneficent free play of classical economic laws.

The disallowance of the two ordinances doomed both digger and Government.[1] It was the digger who suffered most from rising taxation and diminishing returns. The Cape banks and the more designing "capitalists" had been most insidiously liberal in advancing credit with 12 per cent. as the lowest rate on good security. There had ensued in 1872 and 1873 the same reckless overtrading and speculation that had been Natal's downfall in 1868. The Government itself, lured into ambitious spending, plunged into such poverty and indebtedness that it dared not displease the banks by restricting their dangerous activities. When credit collapsed, the embarrassment of the small men was the opportunity of the strong. Against them Southey was equally powerless. The Home Government had bound him hand and foot and delivered him into their hands. The provisions of Ordinance 10 that no company could hold more than ten claims

---

[1] G.D. 6/32, Barkly to Carnarvon, 15 July 1875, for a bitter comment by Barkly on conditions in Griqualand West.

could not be applied. The very diggers themselves, because they were diggers and not yet hired workmen, resented it and bought titles under fictitious names. The registrar of the du Toit's pan mine had in good or bad faith neglected to keep a claims register during three years of office. Abandoned claims were disposed of without legal notice. Blank licences were issued without number or signature, and claims continued to accumulate quietly in a few patient and designing hands.[1] The proprietors of the farm Vooruitzigt which contained the richest soil, welcomed the disallowance of the restrictive ordinances by raising the claim rents to £50 a year. Not Southey but the proprietors won a test case permitting them to eject the diggers who did not pay this exorbitant amount. The fires of discontent at last broke out. Aylward and his agitators, some of them almost certainly the agents of the proprietors and company promoters, fanned the flames. A babel arose in which men cursed the Government and the owners alike, called for the Free State, self-government, confederation, less taxation, new mining regulations, more land and less pampering of the natives. Men were united only in their detestation of Southey's Government. Bitterest were the diggers themselves. In Southey's attempt to regulate mining they could see only a bungling officiousness. To his defence of their interests they were blinded by their horror of his native policy. They clamoured against the ineffectiveness of the Vagrancy Laws and the difficulty of securing convictions against natives in the courts.[2] Their discontent was aroused not so much by drunkenness or thieving as by the sight of "unemployed hordes" that through their "idleness" raised the cost of labour. A violent outburst in the *Diamond Field*[3] measured to the full their abomination of the place that Southey was disposed to accord the native in their society. "Ruin, financial ruin for the whites, moral ruin for the natives, these are the results of the attempt to elevate in one day the servant to an equality as regards the right to hold property with his master.... Class legislation, restrictive

[1] G.D. 6/36. See F. W. Stow to Capt. C. C. Edwards, Private Secretary to Her Majesty's Special Commissioner, 9 Jan. 1876.

[2] *Ibid.* Lanyon to Ommanney, 15 Jan. 1876. "One of my greatest troubles here has been contending against this leaning towards legislation against the natives."   [3] 28 Nov. 1874.

laws and the holding in check of the native races, till by education they are fit to be our equals, is the only policy that finds
favour here.... With a government determined to protect white
interests from danger at the hands of unlettered vicious savages,
but yet giving opportunities to the savage to work out their social
elevation by holy ennobling honest labour, and the slow but
steady progress of education, there is and must be a glorious future
before us." To those who wish to understand the factors that
determined the development of South Africa's native problems
the extract is as illuminating as was the request of a leading
digger that he be excused from a jury because "he hated the
nigger" so much that he could not find it in his power to acquit
him of anything.

The diggers established a committee grimly called a Committee of Public Safety. Aylward ran up the Jolly Roger and
men began to arm and drill. Southey, perceiving some fantastic
relationship between the Committee and the Reign of Terror,
called for volunteers and refused to parley with the "revolu-
tionaries". To Cape Town went urgent appeals for military aid.
Currey, police magistrate that he was, recklessly announced that
a little bloodshed would put the diggers in their places. His
remark lost the administration what support it had had. Barely
180 volunteers presented themselves, whereupon the Government took the insanely injudicious step of beginning to arm
natives. Fortunately better counsels prevailed in time to stop
what might have become South Africa's first urban race riots.
When the police arrested a digger for selling guns the mob of
armed men marched to the court house and took up firing forma-
tion. Overawed the Government released its prisoner, although
it saved its face by accepting in lieu of a fine a cheque which it
promised not to cash. It was the end.

The military arrived in May and fraternally drank beer with a
populace suddenly become meek, not because it was afraid of the
troops but because in spite of Aylward there was no disloyalty
against the Crown. The Government was destroyed, but so also
were ultimately the diggers. In making Southey's recall inevitable they had played into the hands of the proprietors and
the company promoters.

E

Southey, Carnarvon decided, had to go. "The whole thing", grumbled Herbert, "has been a huge mistake."[1] The ultimate dismissal of Southey and the reorganization of the Government removed what small possibility there had been of developing the mining industry in the interests of the independent workers and buyers. And yet, though there were men besides Southey and Barkly who recognized the social implications of the struggle, it is more than doubtful whether Southey could have succeeded. The expenses of administration as they increased came to rest ever more heavily on an irrational, disorganized, and wasteful industry, which was incapable of bearing the taxation imposed upon it. An inexperienced and incompetent Government that was harassed by emphatic orders from Downing Street to practise economy and yet more economy, that was baulked in its attempts to legislate, could not hope successfully to embark upon a radical industrial experiment. The view of Francis Oats, the Provincial Engineer, was bound to prevail. "Without arguing upon the good policy or otherwise of the existing Mining Ordinance, which restricts the quantity of ground that may be held in any of the mines by an individual or company, still on the question of the economic working of the mines, I do not hesitate to say that the fostering of a large number of individual holdings is most adverse to economy of working." The public meetings and drillings of the populace had led to no real organization. Their leaders were adventurers who decamped when the troops appeared. Their riots merely hastened the arrival of companies by adding to the administration's already heavy load of debt the sum spent on the military detachments. Undoubted as were their grievances, they had to be sacrificed in the interests of the economy that was the leading principle in the British Government's South African policy.

Southey's successor was Captain Owen Lanyon. His appointment, like that of his brother officer Wolseley in Natal, has its special significance. Since the departure of General Cathcart in 1854 South Africa had been governed by civilians, by an order of men to whose work throughout the Empire decent justice has still to be done. The secret of a whole vital generation of imperial

[1] C.O. 48/475, D. 95, Barkly to Carnarvon, 15 Aug. 1875, Minutes.

government and development lies hidden in their often modest lives; in the long absences from England that practically made colonists of some of them; in the personal charm and resourcefulness that softened the asperities of colonial political life, and guided their legislatures and ministries to develop their liberties in ways that were compatible with the imperial bond; even in the occasional disobedience or arbitrariness that brought upon their heads the anger of Downing Street or the colonists, so that their sacrifice might appease angry tempers, and give colonial and imperial Governments a chance to reconsider their positions. They were men who in general did not seek to assume greater powers, but rather to yield to the growing demands of the colonies; who, because nobody knew what their powers and responsibilities really were, could absorb the shock of what might otherwise have been dangerous impacts. In the annals of colonial government the numbers are not small of men who sacrificed high intrinsic qualities for the humdrum mediocrity of arduous service.

But with Wolseley and Lanyon, and later Colley and even Frere, there returned to South Africa the Indian and military tradition of government. Although they were men of superior parts they necessarily adopted in the matters of their Governments a more imperative attitude that came both from habits of obedience to instructions and from a professional predilection for clear ends and positive achievement. Though encompassed by the sounds and scenes of an unfamiliar land, they set deliberately about the Empire's work, which was in their soldiers' eyes, to increase the Queen's power, her territories, and her renown. They were, therefore, the ready instruments of Carnarvon's eager and impatient policy. They came to South Africa and reconnoitred it, were interested in its roads and in the military strength of the Republics and native tribes. They looked upon the embarrassments and procrastinations of colonial legislatures with impatience, and preferred to cut the Gordian knot with a stroke. They most certainly influenced the course of events between 1874 and 1880 in a manner that was aggressive and peremptory.

Another military officer, Colonel Crossman, was sent to the diamond fields at the end of 1875 to examine into its financial position and to recommend the strictest economies. His reports[1] are interesting documents in the history of the mining industry; for their principal recommendations were almost entirely carried out. Griqualand West, Crossman stated in effect, had no business to be a colony. It was a mining camp and its administration should be little more than a municipality. The "province" and its debt should be taken over by the Cape Colony. It would be better still if an arrangement could be made by which the Orange Free State once again became the "Sovereignty" and, under the British flag, attached the fields to itself. The control over the mines and the mining areas should be surrendered to an organization created by the mining interests themselves. A capable Civil Commissioner could, at a cost not exceeding £12,000 a year, maintain sufficient mining inspectors to look after the safety of life, with police and magistrates to keep the peace and protect property. Ordinance 10 should be rescinded. Thus was the way made clear to company control and operation.

The determination to cut down the expenses and responsibilities of Government made company mining inevitable. In the field of free competition organized capital alone could hope to work the mines economically and profitably, check illicit diamond buying, and regulate the supply of diamonds according to the demands of the world market.

Not the least interesting outcome of the sweeping changes introduced was the death blow administered to Southey's native policy. There was an end now to the grogshops and the black prostitutes that had made a Kimberley Saturday night a scene to marvel at. Gone too were the native gun shops that encouraged stealing and the "swell niggers" who were the "go-betweens" of the illicit diamond dealers. But equally was there an end to the rights of natives as Southey had conceived them. They could no longer be permitted to hold claims or wash the débris. In the interests of efficiency and economy natives on the diamond fields could henceforth only have one status—that of labourer. It is perhaps idle to wonder what might have been the possibilities of Southey's liberal interpretation of the native's place in South Africa's first industrial community. It is sufficient to say that it

[1] C.O. 107/3, Crossman to Carnarvon, 5 Feb. 1876 and 1 May 1876.

was at the diamond fields that the gate to all but low paid and unskilled labour was slammed against the native in industry.

The breakdown of Southey's administration still left unsettled the vital question of responsibility for the territory. What time Griqualand West had been drifting into chaos Carnarvon had been engaged in the most important negotiations of his policy in an attempt to persuade the Cape Colony not merely to take over Griqualand West, but to assume the leading role in effecting an early South African confederation in which the local difficulties of Natal and the diamond fields and the Republics would become the concern of a central Government.

CHAPTER IV

A BUNDLE OF STICKS

THE FIRST PRIME MINISTER of the Cape Colony, John Charles Molteno, immediately became, after Brand, the most important political figure in South Africa. Born the year before Waterloo he was already past the prime of life. Thick-set and full-bearded, he looked very like the Western Dutch farmers who were amongst his strongest supporters. After almost forty years in South Africa he had become a man not unlike some of the Dutch leaders themselves, shrewd, conservative and except when a notoriously violent temper broke down his restraint, reticent and uncommunicative. Although he was an indifferent speaker and put pen to paper with such unwillingness that Wolseley later accused him of being "wholly uneducated", he owed his political ascendancy to the same practical sense that had made him a prosperous merchant and a large land-holder. His followers admired his solidity and the political realism that distinguished sharply, too sharply perhaps for real statesmanship, between what was certain and what was speculative, between immediate profit and uncertain return. It was almost with a merchant's eye for their possible financial and commercial effects that he judged Carnarvon's schemes.

His ambitions for the Cape were of an orthodox nature—railways, an untroubled Eastern Frontier, the success of responsible institutions. To wider and more ambitious designs, to the design for example of an early confederation of the South African communities, his vision, like the weak sight he kept sheltered behind blue glasses, did not so readily extend. There was reason enough. The credit of the Cape was good; that of the republics and especially the Transvaal was bad. Confederation was like multiplying his difficulties by three or four, adding the call of at least three other mouths for a share of the Cape's revenues. If there were still periodic alarums and panics on the Eastern border, the Cape had never felt so secure in the face of the natives; while Natal's white population still lived precariously in the shadow of Zulu power, and friction with the natives in the Transvaal was chronic. Controlling the most important ports, the Cape already dominated the bulk of the interior trade. The banks of Griqualand West and the Republics were Cape banks, and it was the Cape that built most of the waggons that were still the only means of transport. It monopolized the wine and spirit trade. To Molteno's practical mind confederation therefore promised little and threatened much. If it came before self-government had been fairly tried, it would drain the Cape of the revenues it needed for its own railways, harbours and police, involve it in the native troubles of the Republics and Natal, and draw upon it the ill will that the Republics now bore the British Government.

Rumour had it that in former days he had been involved in a dubious land operation. In his political life he did not always show an austere regard for consistency. He was prone, perhaps because his resentments were strong, to place false interpretations upon the acts and motives of his opponents. Perhaps also because it is of the nature of young and untried governments to lay the stronger stress on their rights and privileges, he was sometimes guilty of political tactlessness, and lacked the dexterity of experienced politicians who avoid open breaches and leave the way clear to compromise by dwelling rather upon points of agreement than difference. But Barkly, whose experience of young colonial parliaments was great, understood him. After five years he had even come to regard him with feelings of friendship. He found him "more easily led than driven; somewhat impatient of contradiction; and apt from overcaution to become suspicious", yet, so he informed Carnarvon, "you will find him straightforward and reasonable enough, and honourable in all his dealings".[1] There were not wanting those both in South Africa and England who grew impatient of Molteno's plodding and called him pigheaded rather than shrewd, narrow rather than sensible. The neutral stand he felt compelled to take towards the problems of the rest of South Africa limited the area of his political effectiveness. But to his dour and unhurried mind

[1] G.D. 6/32, Barkly to Carnarvon, 24 Dec. 1875.

Carnarvon and the agents of his policy—Froude, Wolseley, Lanyon, Frere—were men in a hurry, impatient and doctrinaire. Thorough colonist that he was, he felt that he understood better than a distant Colonial Secretary or the brilliant but transitory representatives of the Queen, the dangers of rapidly transforming the South African scene.

He had won the fight for Cape self-government: his first duty was therefore towards the new institutions, lest the talk of separate provinces under federation cause the Easterners to revive again their demand for separation from the West. After 1872 the Eastern and Western parties had soon begun to lose the coherence which their attitude towards responsible government had given them. Grahamstown and Port Elizabeth still quarrelled with Cape Town, nor had the Easterners altogether abandoned their hopes for separation. But more and more were constitutional differences displaced by the competition between East and West for a share of Government expenditure, railway building and interior trade. Molteno, who always declared that he was a Westerner only by accident, divided the Cape into seven electoral districts that ignored the geographical distinction between East and West. In the new Parliament also voting often ignored party loyalties. Neither Molteno nor his principal opponent Paterson could depend upon any steady following. Members were very apt to be guided by regional, racial or personal motives, so that it was never safe to predict the course of political events, especially where in such a small Parliament the vote of a single member was equivalent to a dozen votes in the British Parliament. It was a situation that inevitably forced the Government to depend in an unusual degree upon Parliament, and made it unwilling to take any important step without the assurance of parliamentary support. If it be remembered that the most stable group amongst Molteno's supporters were inclined to take their cue from the Republics, it can readily be understood how difficult even the most willing Ministry would have found it to give Carnarvon unequivocal support. Molteno's policy therefore was to sponsor measures that were popular or unavoidable, such as the creation of new magistracies, educational reform and railway construction. Provided it was not asked to subsidize the rest of South Africa the Cape had money and credit enough for its own projects. The success of self-government and the development of prosperity seemed, therefore, to require a certain isolation from the rest of South Africa. If the Cape could guard itself against a distraction of its interests and a dissipation of its resources, its immediate future was bright.

Revenue was expanding with expenditure. In the first years of the new administration prosperity and contentment were general. Besides prosperity there were other auspicious circumstances that explain the local success which the new institutions almost immediately had. They were fortunate in attracting more men of property and position, and fewer of the mere political adventurers that at times marked Australian and Canadian political development. Owing to the comparative poverty of the country, truly large fortunes and powerful vested interests were absent. An unusual social complexity enhanced the importance of political action. The presence of a numerous native population made property qualifications especially important. Consequently public life and those professions connected with or actually leading to public office proved attractive to many of the most capable men of the country. Lord Carnarvon might betray a patrician scorn for colonial talent when he referred to a certain judge as "good for a South African". The Cape parties might be lacking in tradition and be ruled by the family cliques that were so characteristic of the older Western districts. Yet it cannot be denied that such men as the young de Villiers whom Molteno appointed as his Chief Justice, the little hunchback Saul Solomon who held the political balance between East and West, and John X. Merriman were able men. It was a most healthy portent for the future political life of South Africa that the modest financial rewards did not deter men of capacity from seeking public office. Early Cape self-government bequeathed a high order of political conduct to the future.

The emphasis upon property placed a premium upon the more conservative elements and obstructed the emergence of liberal ideas on such important matters as the economic and political status of the natives. Cape institutions showed little of the tendency so marked even in the early Australian legislatures to undertake what were for the times radical social and political reforms. The conservative Eastern and Dutch vote gave the sentiments of the frontiersmen and the voortrekkers a strength that Molteno could not possibly afford to ignore.

The attention paid by students of the nineteenth-century Empire to purely constitutional developments and problems has tended to obscure the effect of social and economic questions on imperial relations. The quarrel between the Cape and Home Governments that so profoundly influenced the course of South African history, no doubt took place mainly in those ill-defined constitutional borderlands upon which Molteno's aggressive defence of the privileges of self-government and Carnarvon's strong sense of imperial responsibility both encroached. But it was the acute question of Natal's native policy that really precipitated the conflict. No Colonial Secretary had ever spoken as sharply as Carnarvon on native policy. It was with surprise that Cape opinion had listened to him taking Natal to task for its native policy and the conduct of the Langalibalele affair. With displeasure it had seen the Cape Government itself forced to repeal the statute legalizing the imprisonment of the Natal chief on Robben Island. Public opinion resented the dismissal of Lieutenant-Governor Pine. Disturbed by what it considered a dangerous interference on the part of the Home Government with the mysteries of native management, it was inclined to look upon the Secretary of State's subsequent proposals and actions with suspicion. It is difficult to exaggerate the effect which Carnarvon's pronouncements upon South African native problems had upon the manner in which his confederation proposals were received by the Cape administration.

Behind Molteno's resistance to Carnarvon's proposals lurked a profound unwillingness to face those native problems that confederation would reveal for the first time in their full girth and universal urgency. As long as the subdivision of South Africa continued it remained possible to maintain the illusion of separate problems for which responsibility was equally separate and local. Moreover, because liberal opinion was unorganized and because there was wanting the great body of ordered information on laws, customs, population and needs that are ever the essential basis for calm and constructive legislative and social action, the feeling was widespread that the natives were mainly a military problem, and that in the event of confederation the principal responsibility of the Cape would be to help in "breaking" the power of the Zulus and the other powerful tribes of the interior. The continued subdivision of South Africa was a compulsion that kept England responsible for Natal and Griqualand West, and prevented the departure of British regiments from South Africa. The subdivision of South Africa and the protective presence of British troops, in other words, were a guarantee that the Cape could stay at home and not be called forth to adventure abroad. This truth is part of the explanation of Molteno's attitude to confederation.

In 1872 a Commission had reported that there was little feeling in the country for closer federal union.[1] Nearly three years later the same Commission could not conscientiously have questioned the urgent need for at the very least some common understanding between Governments that were steering their courses "each to a sev'ral coast". It was impossible to observe the folly of gun-running, the corrupting liquor traffic, the ugly tempers on the Transvaal-Zulu border, the threats of bankruptcy in the Transvaal, of civil disturbance in Griqualand West, and the unregulated competition for the unannexed native territories without the very gravest concern. To a Secretary of State fresh to office a survey of the Empire at large caused South Africa to stand out in vivid relief. In New Zealand Maori and Pakeha lived together peaceably at last, and an energetic decade was devoted to building roads and railways, to breaking up the selfish accumulations of land speculators, and encouraging immigration. In Australia the excitement of gold was over, nor was the time quite yet when French and German activity in the Pacific would provoke a cry for British action. Arbitration and negotiation had eased the tension between Canada and its great neighbour, so that the new confederation could turn its mind to building its railways, exploiting its resources and opening up its vast hinterland. Even the Cape was building railways and borrowing its money easily at 4½ per cent. But the Cape was not South Africa.

[1] de Kiewiet, *British Colonial Policy*, p. 298.

It was inevitable that Carnarvon should consider seriously the possibilities of an early South African confederation. Within the last decade one great war had been fought to preserve a federal union, and another had been fought to achieve it. Italy had become a power through unification. In the British Empire, Canada and the Leeward Islands had become federations. Even the British expansion in India was in one sense a federative process. The Empire, far from breaking loose from the Mother Country, seemed to be moving towards consolidation and greater strength. And to Carnarvon, concerned with the organization of an imperial system of defence, the consolidation of a land that lay behind two such vitally strategic points as Cape Town and Simonstown was a necessary step to a well-buttressed Empire. It is well to remember that Carnarvon always had in mind the imperial and strategic value of a federated South Africa, and it is specially significant that the earliest document contained in Carnarvon's Memoranda on South African Affairs is a discussion between Froude and Herbert in which a consideration of the value of Simonstown led directly to Herbert's conclusion that in South Africa "strength is therefore to be sought in federation".

South African federation was then not merely a matter of local interest. It was influenced by the mounting conviction of the last Victorian generation that an Empire which refused to fall apart should be given greater coherence and strength. This conviction was encouraged by the attitude of the colonies themselves. They began to appreciate as never before that in the face of the industrial, national, and finally imperial rivalries of the new world powers, the Mother Country was their shield and buckler. Great was the uneasiness of the British colonies in the face of a possible foreign attack after 1871. Just as in South Africa the moral and physical advantage of British regiments was keenly felt, so in the Empire at large did an appreciation of the value of the British fleet serve to strengthen the attachment to the Mother Country. It does not lessen the genuine sentimental attachment to Mother Country and Crown to recognize that it was British naval prestige that enabled the colonies to devote their limited resources, upon which the necessity of an entire self-defence would have made drastic inroads, almost wholly to the needs of settlement and economic development. Hence not merely the strength of the imperial bond but in some measure at least the development of colonial society along characteristic democratic and unmilitary lines was partly due to the security that the British fleet afforded.

In South Africa there was in the native question room for conflicts of principle between local opinion and the Home Government severe enough to strain loyalty to Great Britain. It is only by recognizing the unusual physical dependence of South Africa on England, both internally and externally, that one ceases to wonder why the bitter controversies of the 'seventies did not raise more explicitly the demand for separation.

Confederation came increasingly to appear as the answer to various urgent needs. It was a step towards a better ordering of both imperial and local defences. It gave the colonists self-government and relieved the Mother Country of onerous internal responsibilities. "The ultimate effect of Lord Carnarvon's South African policy", the Cabinet was informed in a special memorandum in January 1876, "would be to relieve the British Exchequer not only from the ordinary (and serious) charge for the Natal and Cape garrisons, but also from a contingent liability of vast proportions of which there is no way of divesting ourselves, while the civilized states are yet isolated one from another." As in the days of Richard Cobden when he recommended self-government as the proper "cure" for South Africa's native ills,[1] so now there was in and out of Parliament much sympathy for the view that confederation and local responsibility were the only means of relieving the "less well to do people of the United Kingdom" of the burden of native wars. It was no less a person than Lord Cadogan, Carnarvon's Parliamentary Under-secretary, who informed Parliament that "confederation will involve, we hope, self defence, which will remove the liability under which we labour of spending our blood and our money upon these wretched Kafir quarrels in South Africa".[2]

Amongst those in England who supported Carnarvon's confederation policy there were some few who welcomed it solely

[1] de Kiewiet, *op. cit.* p. 44. [2] Hansard, vol. 244, col. 1669.

as a means of lightening England's burdens and who were therefore indifferent to the political future of confederation. But now more than at any earlier period of the century the strongest groups of opinion held that separation and independence were not the inevitable and desirable outcome of the development of responsible institutions. Rather did they believe that England could never wholly abrogate her colonial responsibilities, that under responsible government there was still room, and necessary room, for the exercise of the imperial power. Most strongly was this attitude held toward colonies with subject native populations. Within the Colonial Office and later in parliamentary discussions the position of the South African native population under a self-governing confederation caused the greatest uneasiness. Men like Earl Grey who believed that "no tyranny was so grievous as that of an Assembly which represented, not the whole of the population, but only a minority",[1] were even inclined to question the wisdom of self-government at all in South Africa. Even Herbert felt compelled to admit that responsible government was a system that was unsuited for any colony in which natives formed the majority of the population. "I think we must expect", he remarked, "that a strong South African Federation will be disposed to legislate unfairly and oppressively on Native Affairs. We shall almost certainly come into collision with it on these subjects."[2]

The attitude that the welfare of the natives was a grave imperial responsibility might seem in all logic to demand that the Mother Country abandon none of her powers over either colonists or natives. Actually such a procedure was unthinkable. Colonial policy could not escape the discipline of time and circumstance. There might be reason to regret that Great Britain had ever recognized the independence of the Republics; it was possible to question the opportuneness of the grant of self-government to the Cape. But in 1874 the Republics were independent and the Cape was self-governing. Any political reform that the British Government undertook in South Africa that did not deliberately aim at ultimate self-government could only court frustration and failure.

[1] Hansard, vol. 233, col. 1662.　　　[2] G.D. 6/49, p. 17.

It was a most trying dilemma that faced Carnarvon. How could he reconcile the safety of British strategic interests with the need for economy, the need for economy with humanitarian motives, and humanitarian motives with the accepted right of the Europeans to self-government? He might have done what Kimberley had planned to do—withdraw British regiments and leave the Cape to guide South Africa to political unity in its own good time. Yet could South Africa wait? When a colony like Natal blanched with fear at the recalcitrance of a petty tribe; when bankruptcy and civil disturbance threatened in Griqualand and the Transvaal; when the Republics loved neither their neighbours nor one another, a Secretary of State might well feel that action was urgent and that the initiative lay with the paramount power.

Early confederation seemed to Carnarvon and his colleagues the only means of meeting the crisis. "The advantages of Federation", he informed the Cabinet, "are very obvious. European immigration and capital flow slowly into countries under small and isolated Governments whose financial solvency is questionable, and where there is no adequate security for property and no confidence in prudent legislation. Federation would greatly improve and cheapen the administration of affairs in almost every branch and greatly lessen the probability of a demand for aid in the shape of Imperial money or troops. But the most immediately urgent reason for general union is the formidable character of the native question, and the importance of a uniform, wise and strong policy in dealing with it....The policy of establishing through Confederation a great South African dominion is indeed recommended by other considerations connected with the advance of civilization in Africa and the general interests of the Empire; but it is in respect of its influence on the solution of the native question that Confederation has become a matter of immediate concern to Parliament and the United Kingdom."

Such confederation could not be achieved by the South African communities alone, and certainly not without adequate guarantees for the welfare of the native races. Since Carnarvon did not intend the British Government to relinquish its supervision over the natives even when confederation was achieved,[1] he felt that the British Government had to take an active and forward part in all steps leading to a reform of South African political life. Only thus is it possible to understand what to the colonists seemed a doctrinaire interference with their own affairs. The British Government did not intend to make its withdrawal an act of scuttle.

On first assuming office Carnarvon had held a tentative and even hesitant language on confederation. During 1874 he showed none of the headlong eagerness to apply a ready-made Canadian experience to South Africa that has been attributed to him. "Some form of federation" seemed desirable enough. What that form should be and when it might be achieved could only be determined by the trend of events. Federation might even, he was ready to admit, prove impracticable. But by the end of the year his doubts had left him. Events in every colony and Republic conspired at once to proclaim the folly of delay. Froude, given the task of reading the current materials on South Africa in the Colonial Office—a task he performed with thoroughness—announced that federation was imperative. He suspected that the Republics had been treated with less than justice, went out to South Africa on Carnarvon's request to investigate, and in the course of a flying tour that gave him too little time to sit at the feet of Barkly and Southey, but enough to write some half dozen sensible reports, still further convinced the Secretary of State that the British Government could not escape the obligation of intervention. The British Government alone was in a position to make amends to the Free State. The British Government alone could break the deadlock and bring the obstinate South African heads together in conclave. Even Shepstone, who had passed Froude in mid-ocean, admitted that a federal government, although certain to be quarrelsome on native matters, was preferable to the prevailing state of affairs.[2]

---

[1] G.D. 6/49. "Probably the safest course will be for this country to retain in its own hands—if possible—all native policy, requiring the Governor General, in his Imperial capacity, to assent to no law, and empowering him to veto if necessary any executive action, affecting natives whether within or without British territory." Statement by Herbert.

[2] G.D. 6/49, p. 29.

At the very time then that Barkly and Southey were abusing the Republics and their presidents, the Colonial Office itself was reaching the conclusion that British policy could not make progress without republican good will. Carnarvon seemed almost to regret that the diamond fields had ever been annexed. As long as Griqualand West hung unstably and uncertainly as a "quasi crown colony" between the Cape and the British Government it remained an affront to the Free State and the Transvaal. Better that it be restored to the Free State than remain for ever a bone of contention. "I should be very glad if Griqualand were assigned [by a 'strong Arbitration Court'] to the Orange State, and Bechuana [land] to the Trans Vaal."[1]

By the beginning of 1875 there was no longer any hesitation in Carnarvon's mind. The anti-republican policy of Barkly and Southey was openly disavowed. The abrupt recall of Lieutenant-Governor Pine, the release of Langalibalele from Robben Island, the appointment in April of Sir Garnet Wolseley for the declared purpose of reducing Natal to the status of a "quasi crown colony" like Griqualand West, were ominous portents of a new imperial policy that would not hesitate to be heavy handed. But the Cape Constitution? It could not be abrogated. Nor could the Colony be forced into confederation against its will. And yet it was the very citadel through which lay the main road to confederation. As it could not be reduced like Natal by direct assault, Carnarvon decided to undermine it.

For forty years the British Government had floundered in a morass of annexations and abandonments, threats and evasions. Now suddenly it showed a disposition to confront all its difficulties at once, and at a moment that no optimism could call propitious. The paramount power was going to win back the republics and introduce a more enlightened native policy. These, perhaps its two strongest ambitions, were the most fiercely incompatible. The importance of Carnarvon's schemes in the entire history of South Africa becomes startlingly clear when it is realized that never again was the British Government in a position to face the problem of European and native with the same power and the same chance of even moderate success; for when at the end of the

---

[1] C.O. 48/471, D. 140, Barkly to Carnarvon, 3 Dec. 1874, Minutes.

F

Great Boer War, South Africa lay helpless at her feet, Great Britain could only think how she might most speedily raise the stricken Republics and reconcile them to herself. In such an aim there was no longer any real room for a courageous native policy. The historian, free of the trammels of patriotism and race, must regret the suffering and bitterness that the ultimate failure of Carnarvon's schemes wrought, but even then he cannot escape the serious duty of pointing out that the great virtue of what Carnarvon planned to do was his desire to create an order in which there was room and hope not merely for Dutch and English, but also for the native majority of the population.

That Carnarvon blundered needs little comment. It was a powerful source of error that he could more readily envisage an Empire developing under the direction of Downing Street than by local initiative. His blunders have come to seem greater as the status of colonial self-government has grown to an equality with the British Government itself. But it may be some palliation of his mistakes to recall that, recklessly maybe, he took upon his shoulders the accumulated errors of forty years, and that his confederation was intended for South Africa and not a part, for all races and not the Europeans alone. South African history, if it is not to be merely a branch of patriotism, must recognize these facts. British policy in this eventful decade had the merit of a drama in which the contradictions of localism and imperialism clashed together. The outcome vindicated the prestige of self-government, but unhappily left the native population even more thoroughly than before at the mercy of communities whose disunion and sense of weakness encouraged a narrow and coercive rule.

On 4 May 1875 Carnarvon launched his famous despatch on South African confederation. It was framed, in the words of Carnarvon's official biographer, "on most considerate and non-dictatorial lines ".[1] It recommended that a conference of delegates from the colonies and republics should meet "to deliberate and report, but not to take any action on the subjects which might come before it ". And if "the all-important ques-

[1] Hardinge, *Life of Carnarvon*, vol. II, p. 184.

tion of a possible union of South Africa in some form of confederation should arise, Her Majesty's Government will readily give their earnest and favourable attention to any suggestions that may be made". The Secretary of State had no established opinion on the form of confederation. Once the principle were adopted there was no reason why each province should not have a form of government in accordance with its own traditions and desires. Let it be understood, he emphatically concluded, that "the action of all parties, whether the British Colonies or the Dutch states, must be spontaneous and uncontrolled". Nothing could sound more considerate and less dictatorial. Yet these inoffensive words acted like a "bombshell" to Molteno and the Cape Parliament.

They acted like a bombshell because they proclaimed that the Home Government had decided to exercise an active influence as the paramount power in the land. For all its moderate language the despatch was nothing if not a manifesto to the whole of South Africa. Three times, once in an official despatch, once in a private letter, and lastly in a cablegram sent to catch the mail steamer at Madeira, Barkly was ordered to give the most immediate and widest publicity to its contents. In private letters to Barkly the tentative note of the despatch gave way to a revealing peremptoriness. "The real and essential consideration is to make the conference succeed; first because I believe that the present happens to be an unusually favourable opportunity: secondly *because success is necessary.*"

The obstacles to that success in Carnarvon's judgment were Barkly himself and Molteno. Barkly he especially distrusted. He was "clever and probably the instigator and inspirer of Molteno". He was "'cold-blooded' and entirely and at heart opposed to all my policy". These were the reasons he gave himself privately for his distrust of the governor.[1] He quite accurately realized that in a policy that aimed to reconcile the Republics Barkly could have no responsible place. They detested him too cordially. Had the language of the public despatch not been so tentative, Barkly might have been recalled. But popular sentiment might be aroused; Southey's recall was imminent and

[1] G.D. 6/49, p. 156.

Pine's recall had created stir enough. There were more ways than one to curb an unwilling Governor. In courteous but unmistakable words Carnarvon hinted to Barkly that he would "readily understand" it if the presidency of the conference were given to Sir Arthur Cunynghame. And both as a gesture to the republics and as a further restraint upon Barkly, Froude, *son éminence grise* of the Colonial Office, was sent after the despatch with authority to read all correspondence and to represent the Imperial Government on the conference. At Molteno and the Cape Ministry an equally shrewd blow was directed by the suggestion that Paterson, the leader of the Easterners in the Cape Parliament, be made one of the delegates. The intention to undermine and weaken the place of Molteno on the conference was clear. The suggestion was an open appeal to the Easterners to support the Secretary of State's policy, and was virtually a promise that in the event of confederation they would have separation from the Western Province. A Memorandum subsequently presented to the Cabinet fully explained Carnarvon's purpose. "The mention of a distinct representation of the Eastern and Western Provinces of the Cape has profoundly affected the Eastern (district)...of the Colony. These parts have long resented the supremacy of Cape Town in Colonial politics. The great remoteness of Cape Town...gives its professional politicians an undue share of political influence. The East is virtually disfranchised, from its inability to find Representatives who have the leisure to represent it. The East regards the proposal as affording a hope of separation under a larger federal union; but the politicians of Cape Town, and especially the present Ministry, little relish a scheme which would deprive them of their present command of Parliament.

"The Confederation Cabinet would not be the present Cape Cabinet, and Mr Molteno might perhaps not be the Premier of South Africa. In any case Cape Town must forego its supremacy, and be outweighted in a federal Parliament by four or five rival Provinces."[1] Thus while the constitution of the Cape could not be abrogated the attempt could be made to weaken it, and by an appeal to popular sentiment to discredit it.

[1] Jan. 1876.

The despatch angered Molteno, even though, by the curious power that colonial communities have always had of guessing at the contents of important despatches before they are received, he was not unprepared. Appreciating the threat to his Ministry he acted with swiftness and resolution. Swiftness was essential if the Secretary of State's intention was to be frustrated. Instructions or no, Barkly was not to publish the despatch. If he did the Ministry would resign.[1] Barkly's obedience to the Prime Minister's will illustrated the truth of Sir Henry Taylor's maxim that "the hand which executes a measure should belong to the head which propounds it, otherwise the hand, if an unassenting one, will carry an advantage over the head".[2] Barkly agreed with Molteno all the more readily because he had no sympathy with a despatch that addressed the Republics as if they were already loyal British colonies. Contrary to Carnarvon's most emphatic instructions the despatch was kept secret for five days. When it was finally laid before the House it was accompanied by a hostile minute that the interests of the Cape would not be promoted by pressing forward such a conference as the Secretary of State proposed. A resolution was immediately rushed through the House without giving members more than two days in which to consider their opinion. Only three weeks later were copies of the despatch uselessly sent to the Orange Free State and the Transvaal. Molteno had stolen Carnarvon's thunder. One of the ministers called the despatch "balderdash", and a member hailed the resolution as a "slap in the face to Lord Carnarvon". Within a week of its arrival and a week before Froude could arrive the design of the despatch had been frustrated, and the Cape Parliament had been committed to Molteno's support.

Molteno had adroitly turned the first step in Carnarvon's confederation policy into a blunder. How big or serious really was the blunder? There was universal agreement that confederation was desirable and ultimately necessary. But there was hardly any agreement on the method of achieving it or the ends it would serve. Natal wished for confederation because it was too weak

[1] G.D. 6/32, Barkly to Carnarvon, 15 June 1875.
[2] Sir Henry Taylor, *The Statesman*, p. 64, reprinted Cambridge, 1927, ed. H. J. Laski.

to protect itself and confederation alone would endow it with self-government. British Kaffraria under Sprigg would have none of confederation if it involved separation between East and West. The die-hard separatists in the East looked to confederation to divorce them from the West. Then they could starve the Kaffrarian port of East London and monopolize the customs collected at their own port of Port Elizabeth on all goods destined for the diamond fields, the Free State and the interior. The Western Province was jealous for the supremacy and commercial ascendancy of Cape Town and favoured the creation of a single state by the gradual absorption of the Republics and territories. In the Free State there was undoubted sympathy for confederation. With the exception of Visser, chairman of the Volksraad, who was a "patriot" and bitterly opposed to British influence, several of the prominent members of the republican administration were not ill-disposed to the main lines of British policy. Such men as Hohne, the government secretary, Venter, the Landdrost of Bloemfontein, married in Australia to an Irish wife, Kleinveldt, the educated son-in-law of Pellissier, the French missionary, and Frazer, Secretary to the Raad, were not committed against the new policy. But none in the last resort would act without Brand. His prestige was such that the Volksraad would certainly go wherever he led. It was not without reason therefore that Carnarvon wished his despatch to appeal directly to the Republics; for in the Transvaal as well it was by no means certain that a liberal form of union would be rejected out of hand. It is significant that the radical suggestion of making Brand the first Governor General of the new confederation was sympathetically received in Downing Street.

James Anthony Froude, sent to be Carnarvon's ears and eyes and mouth, landed at Cape Town a fortnight after the despatch had been received. He stepped from the boat into controversy. Barkly was his most cold-blooded and frigid self. In swift revenge Froude pointedly refused his hospitality at Government House, and insisted on attending as his first public engagement a dinner given by Molteno's opponents. As was only proper the Governor, the Speaker, and the President of the Council refused to attend. At the dinner Froude declared war on the Ministry by defending Carnarvon's despatch, and entirely estranged Barkly by hinting that the annexation of the diamond fields had been mismanaged. He did what Carnarvon's despatch had been intended to do—appeal to those elements in the colonies and Republics that might be persuaded to support the policy of confederation. In spite of his own subsequent denials he acted and spoke like the fully empowered agent of the Secretary of State, even rebuking Barkly for his submissiveness to his ministers, and calling upon him to display more energy in advancing the views of his superiors. Barkly, in his turn, did not conceal that he resented Froude's mission, and thus forced him still more into a position which gave his every word a sinister meaning, and made every action appear like an open attack on the Ministry. And yet there is much to be said for the actions of both men.

Their conflict arose out of the ill-defined constitutional responsibilities of the Governor of the Cape. In all the colonies of the Empire the position of the Governor was still anomalous. By 1875 his uncertain position between a responsible ministry and the Home Government had not yet been defined by an accepted body of precedent, just as indeed there was not yet a workable understanding on the extent of the imperial power in internal affairs. It was actually not until the Imperial Conference of 1926 that a Governor General definitely ceased to be a representative of the British Government supervising imperial interests in the colonies. It was the Statute of Westminster that unequivocally defined him as the personal representative of the Crown which itself was "the symbol of the free association of the members of the British Commonwealth".

The position of a Governor of the Cape in 1875 was additionally complicated because he was also Her Majesty's High Commissioner with duties that extended beyond the borders of the Cape, and therefore strictly beyond the control of a responsible ministry. Under representative institutions the two functions had been compatible. Sir Philip Wodehouse had been responsible to the Secretary of State in both capacities. Under self-government, however, the two functions were no longer compatible. Neither the constitution of 1872 nor subsequent instructions had attempted to regulate the High Commissionership. In principle, therefore, Barkly was wholly responsible to the Secretary of State in all matters that lay outside the borders of the Cape. In practice it was impossible to maintain any clear distinction between Barkly's two functions, more especially where the tribes beyond the Cape Eastern Frontier were concerned. At the time of the unrest in 1872 and 1873 the Cape Ministry were at first doubtful whether they could properly give the High Commissioner advice on native matters. When Charles Brownlee, the Secretary for Native Affairs, went to inspect the affected region in 1873, his mission was attacked as the unauthorized assumption on the part of the Ministry of a responsibility properly attaching to the Imperial Government. The Kaffrarian Sprigg moved for the production of any new commission issued by the Queen since the introduction of responsible government. Barkly, however, refused to admit that there could be any radical distinction drawn between his two offices, claiming that the Cape Ministry had the right to give him advice both as Governor and High Commissioner.[1] His decision was in entire accord with the policy of Lord Kimberley; for Kimberley had enjoined upon him the necessity of co-operation in all matters with the Cape responsible ministry, so as to stress in the clearest manner the wide responsibility the Home Government desired the new Government to possess. It was an important part of Kimberley's policy that whatever took place beyond the Cape borders should be acceptable to and indeed guided by the parent colony. A policy, however, that sought to limit the powers of the Cape Government by claiming for the Imperial Government the duty of leadership and guidance was bound to resist the constitutional relationship that was growing up between the High Commissionership and the Cape Ministry, and bound to remind Barkly sharply that his first obligation was to the Imperial Government and not to Molteno.

Although Barkly was on the side of the future development of colonial constitutional practice, his attempt to abandon the special position which the High Commissionership gave him was as yet impracticable and ill-advised. With the exception of the Eastern Frontier, the wide range of transfrontier affairs lay wholly out-

---

[1] C.O. 48/478, D. 33, Barkly to Carnarvon, 27 March 1876.

side Cape jurisdiction. Without the consent of the Home Government the Cape Government could annex no territory nor take any important step affecting other states. Relations with the other colonies and Republics were altogether an imperial concern entrusted to the High Commissioner.

Carnarvon recognized that his policy had received a serious reverse, but his determination hardened. It was not his place nor had he the slightest wish, he stiffly informed Barkly, to take any part in the internal affairs of the Colony. But it was the right and the duty of the Home Government to advise on matters that related to South Africa as a whole. To Barkly was administered a stinging rebuke. "I will not deny that it has been with disappointment and regret that I have become aware of the little support which I have had at your hands." A Governor was the representative of the Queen and the Imperial Government, and owed the Secretary of State his wholehearted support. A colonial minister, he said, mixing magnanimity with a little scorn, might well fail to appreciate the intentions of the Home Government. At the hasty interpretations and impetuous language of a colonial cabinet an Imperial Secretary of State need not take umbrage. But when a Governor withheld his assistance "at the very pinch of the most crucial question", and a question which was moreover "entirely without the limits of Responsible Government", the service of the Crown could no longer be promoted by a "continuance of our relations". Barkly was to co-operate with his superior or resign.[1]

Barkly refused to do either. The imperial policy carried out by Froude was an agitation that threatened to range East against West, Dutch against English and "possibly Kafirs against both".[2] He had not failed in his duty, he bluntly retorted. He certainly would not resign. Twenty-five years of service during which close upon a score of Secretaries of State had come and gone had surely taught him what were the duties of a constitutional Governor.[3] By his own lights Barkly had done his duty well, better certainly than Carnarvon knew. He had done his best to

[1] G.D. 6/32, Carnarvon to Barkly, 4 Aug. 1875.
[2] *Ibid.* Barkly to Carnarvon, 25 June 1875.
[3] *Ibid.* Barkly to Carnarvon, 18 Nov. 1875.

appease Molteno's irritation at the despatch of 4 May, and had even tried to heal the breach between the Ministry and the Secretary of State by endeavouring to slip a passage favourable to the Conference into the Address closing the session. But as long as Froude was in the land undermining the Government Molteno would know nothing of compromise, and the conciliatory passage was omitted.

Froude marched from success to success. Bulwer called his campaign against Molteno a triumphant progress. In the Eastern Province he spoke in a high imperial strain, and pointedly praised the Mayor of Port Elizabeth upon the loyalty of the town to the British Empire. To the Free State he let it appear that what wrongs had been done would be righted. The tide of popular sentiment began to flow so strongly against the Ministry that Barkly told Molteno that it was his duty to bow to the widespread approval that Carnarvon's policy was receiving, by calling a special session of Parliament to reconsider its decision.[1] Molteno was himself inclined to rue his impetuousness and was probably not opposed to an honourable retreat. If only Froude and his attacks did not force him into ever deeper obstinacy. This agitation from abroad, as Merriman termed it, was a menace to constitutional government and the solidarity of the colony. Froude's actions, Molteno informed the Governor, "must have the effect of rendering any giving way in the direction of the proposed Conference utterly impossible—even should circumstances appear favourable".[2] He refused to admit that circumstances were favourable, and he would lift no finger to make them so. From the Cabinet, therefore, came a Memorandum that was nothing but a boycott of the Home Government's ideas and suggestions. The Secretary of State had suggested the need for co-operation in native matters, the Memorandum deliberately misunderstood his meaning, and held that a uniform native policy was undesirable. Froude had reported that the Cape and Natal were in immediate contact with two million natives, increasing "like the Irish", and with whom a collision was very probable. The Memorandum pooh-poohed the possibility of a general native

[1] G.D. 6/32, Barkly to Carnarvon, 18 Sept. 1875.
[2] *Ibid.* Barkly to Carnarvon, 3 Oct. 1875.

rising. Native wars or no the Cape Government refused to consider a federation in which it would have to defend the whole subcontinent against its native enemies. The Memorandum refused to accept the principle of even a deliberative conference for fear the Cape should be placed before an awkward decision if the rest of the conference recommended policies objectionable to it.[1] The Governor had the greatest difficulty in dissuading the Ministry from injecting its wrath against Froude into the opening Address for the special session of Parliament.[2] Baulked in this Molteno raised more strenuously the cry of the constitution in danger, and plunged forward to charge the Imperial Government with having encouraged an unconstitutional agitation for the purpose of forcing its views upon the Colonial Government. Now even Barkly's patience came to an end. Rather than permit a Minister of the Crown to submit such a resolution to Parliament he threatened to precipitate a constitutional crisis. Sullenly Molteno retorted that he did not care whether he submitted the resolution as a Minister of the Crown or not. Other colonial ministers had held strong and direct language to a Secretary of State before now.[3] But Molteno knew and Barkly knew that Froude had done his work well and that the Ministry was dangerously close to defeat. The resolution was tempered and became a mild complaint that an agitation had been created "in the name of the Imperial Government". Even then it was defeated in the Assembly. The Legislative Council voted in favour of the conference.

There could no longer be any constitutional objection to a dissolution and an appeal to the electorate. Yet abandoned by Carnarvon, estranged from Molteno, at loggerheads with Froude, the Governor held his hand. His hesitation was less a reflection upon his boldness and initiative than proof that he was not prepared even now to strike a decisive blow in favour of confederation. It was fortunate for Molteno that before he had been completely abandoned by Parliament Carnarvon announced that he had given up the project of a local conference in favour of a

[1] C.O. 48/476, D. 129, Barkly to Carnarvon, 20 Oct. 1875.
[2] G.D. 6/32, Barkly to Carnarvon, 10 Nov. 1875.
[3] *Ibid.* Barkly to Carnarvon, 16 Nov. 1875.

meeting in London. With relief the Ministry swallowed its words.

What had really happened? The answer is that Carnarvon had come to the conclusion that he must not yield but proceed more vigorously yet. Confederation had to make swifter headway. Its course could not be silted up by the resistance of a Colonial Ministry. The hesitations and objections of the Cape meant that the Secretary of State must open up new channels and exploit new possibilities.

Molteno, on the other hand, had been discovering the perils of a protracted quarrel with the Home Government, and was fast reaching a more tractable frame of mind. The Cape had need of the Home Government. Without the goodwill of Downing Street it could not extend its boundaries to the north and the east. If the British Government could not forcibly thrust the diamond fields upon the Cape as it had thrust British Kaffraria upon it in Wodehouse's day, even less could the Cape annex territories without imperial sanction. It came to pass that at the very time the Cape was doggedly resisting confederation, it began to sense the need to expand in other directions, beyond the Kei and the Orange Rivers. It had been obvious since Grey had settled the Griqua chief Adam Kok in East Griqualand in 1861 that the Cape would ultimately have to annex and rule all the territory from the Kei to the Natal boundary. The disgruntlement of the natives within the Eastern Frontier was serious enough. Beyond it old lackland Kreli had come within an ace of precipitating a general outburst in 1872, and was still treading dangerously on the toes of the luckier Tembus and Fingos. Deeper in the Transkeian territories the Griquas had lived uneasily for years under the menace of Nehemiah Moshesh's Basuto, whom the Free State pressure on Basutoland had squirted into Kafirland. In the direction of Port St Johns reaving and quarrelling kept the Pondos and Xesibes in a snarling of dogs. Already the appointment of some half a dozen magistrates to different tribes had paved the way to annexation. The British Government was in principle more than eager that the Cape should assume responsibility for the Transkeian territories. This eagerness came not merely from military and financial motives, strong though they were, but also from a nervous conviction that too much of the African coastline lay invitingly open to foreign covetousness. The award to Portugal of the whole of Delagoa Bay by the French President in July 1875 was a shock to men like Wolseley, who immediately declared that England "ought by some means or other to obtain entire possession" of what was "the key to the whole position".[1] The award unsettled British commercial and anti-slavery sentiment. Anti-slavery sentiment, it cannot be forgotten, lies at the root of all British thought on African questions in this period, even though it was not slow to see, as Livingstone himself saw, the positive commercial advantages of an extensive British control of the African coast. It is a refreshing corrective to "local" South African history to see how after 1874 South Africa is drawn on to the international stage. The discovery that the South African coastline was part of the African coastline, that its ports were valuable links in the organization of an Empire whose monopolies were no longer unchallenged, destroyed for ever the illusion that South African affairs were remote and local. The status of the Republics and the management of the natives were drawn out of isolation to influence and be influenced by the rivalry of contending imperialisms, which caused England ultimately to establish herself in Cyprus and Egypt, to send regiments to Afghanistan, to quarrel with France and Germany in Africa, the Pacific, and the China Seas. Thus when, in addition to desiring Tembuland, the Cape raised its eyes to the coastline north of the Orange River, its desire aroused immediate interest in England.

Events in the Congo basin, and the reports of foreign activities (intrigues they were still called) on the African coast alarmed both Barkly and the Home Government in England. "It is imperatively necessary", wrote Herbert, "to declare the whole coast up to the Portuguese boundary[2] to be British....And I think the consent of the Cabinet should at once be obtained to this proclamation of British territory. It cannot be avoided, nor postponed without danger. I should think it very desirable at the same time...to notify that Her Majesty's Government claim all

[1] G.D. 6/38, Wolseley to Carnarvon, 27 Aug. 1875.
[2] Said by the Foreign Office at this time to be Cape Frio, 18° S.

the coast South of the Portuguese boundaries on the west and east side."[1] Carnarvon agreed to bring the matter to the attention of the Cabinet, but actually his mind was turning away from Molteno and the Cape Colony and was pre-occupied with advancing his confederation schemes by direct negotiations with the Free State and a conference in London. When the question of the territory to the north of the Cape is again mentioned it will be to explain how it became not British territory but a German colony.

The entries in Carnarvon's private memoranda on South African affairs at this time show a moral enthusiasm for his policy that led him to look upon those who stood in his way as perverse and ignorant. "Solidarity has always been (the) foremost element in every conception of ideal life", he reflected. Was it not Seneca who had said that the "Gods divided man into men that he might be more helpful to himself"?[2] These were not the thoughts of a man ambitious for narrow personal ends, who therefore was given the strength and energy of vanity and selfishness. They were rather the thoughts of a man who considered himself to be entitled to a special authority and competence given him by his patrician status and the office he held in the Imperial Parliament. In his handling of colonial matters there is frequently discernible an annoyance at the hardihood of colonial ministers who presumed to speak with as convinced a voice as a Minister of Her Majesty's Cabinet. Unfortunately he did not possess those qualities of mind that might fuse the desire to serve the Empire with the authority of high position and elevate them to true statesmanship. He placed too much reliance upon the prestige of his office and the high aims of his policy to take proper account of colonial susceptibilities and convictions which, even if they were colonial, were none the less real, and so he drifted slowly out of an initial effort to co-operate and compromise into an increasing peremptoriness and a mounting assurance that opposition to him was disloyalty to the Empire itself. In his notes and comments there is clearly noticeable a progressive inclination to abandon negotiations and take the im-

[1] C.O. 48/476, D. 167, Barkly to Carnarvon, 5 Dec. 1875, Minutes.
[2] G.D. 6/49, p. 167.

perious path that led to the dismissal of a Governor and the summoning of presidents and colonial statesmen to his own ante-rooms. "The best plenipotentiary", he assured himself, "is the Secretary of State for the Colonies and the best place of meeting Downing Street."[1]

The London Conference of 1876, to which were invited Shepstone, Brand and Molteno, was a final attempt to salvage some common accord from the wreckage and controversy of 1875. There was no man on the spot whose prestige and personality could attract the discordant views of men and Governments into common consultation. Barkly was the last person under whose guidance either Republic could ever agree to co-operate. The appointment of another Governor, although ultimately inevitable, was at the moment impolitic, if only because Barkly's recall would have plunged Molteno into deeper recalcitrance.

But Carnarvon's attention was no more upon Molteno. It was directed towards the Orange Free State and its President. Was it after all impossible to win republican support? A direct discussion conducted by the Secretary of State himself might calm the resentment that the provocative language of Barkly and the quarrelsome tone of Southey had aroused. Were the Republics after all so seriously in the wrong, or so intractable? Froude had written favourably even of their native policy. Burgers, sitting in one of Carnarvon's own chairs, had spoken feelingly of his desire to see the composition of all quarrels and the achievement of unity. If the Free State could be won for confederation how could the Cape longer stand aloof? It was almost fortunate that the Free State had grievances, so that the Secretary of State might generously remove them. That those grievances were great Carnarvon could not deny. It was clear now that Barkly's annexation of the diamond fields had ridden roughshod over a Free State case so strong that four years of acrimony and debate had failed to weaken it. Froude was so impressed with the injustice done that he counselled withdrawal from Griqualand West and the payment to the Free State of a share of Natal's customs dues.[2] Colonel Crossman, who had penetrated deeply into the affairs

[1] C.O. 48/476, D. 157, Barkly to Carnarvon, 19 Nov. 1875, Minutes.
[2] G.D. 6/49, p. 130.

of the diamond fields, reported that of the disputed Ramah-Vetberg lines the one claimed by the Free State was alone acceptable. The British Government could hardly hope to emerge successfully from any arbitration.[1]

Carnarvon decided to sweep aside the accumulation of years of contention and approach Brand directly. Both parties had long since exhausted all the possibilities of fresh argument and invective, so that the controversy was feeding upon itself in mere rewording and repetition. It was not in Carnarvon's mind, however, to make simple restitution to the Free State. Restitution could only be made if it were also an instrument for forwarding confederation. To light a fire beneath the obstinacy of Brand, he announced that the British Government was no longer prepared to submit the issue to any tribunal however constituted. Brand was not so easily intimidated.

In March 1876 Judge Stockenstrom delivered his famous judgment in the Land Court of Griqualand West. The judgment amply corroborated the claims of the Free State. Although not unimpeachable on legal grounds it had meaning chiefly because it was really a political pronouncement, not unlike those judgments of the United States Supreme Court that are often guided by public opinion or political exigency rather than by the law and its letter.

Strengthened and justified, Brand now came to London. But he did not come cap in hand. He came not to negotiate or to bargain. He came simply to ask justice for the Free State. In the face of such an attitude the Colonial Office was deeply embarrassed. It was impossible to coerce a man who spoke so disarmingly, saying in effect, "I am not a diplomatist struggling after an advantage. I am an honest man arguing for his rights. Whether I have the right depends upon my case. If I have no case I have no claim and I ask for nothing in that event. Whether therefore I am entitled to anything or to nothing depends upon my case. I ask you to do me justice and nothing more, and I even place my case in your own hands. How can you refuse to con-

---

[1] C.O. 48/477, F.O. to C.O., 31 Aug. 1875: "...in view of the Delagoa Bay arbitration, I feel satisfied that the best course is to avoid arbitration altogether. I strongly suspect that...the award would be against us."

sider my case unless you mean to deny me justice?"[1] It would not be the last time that the Republics would approach the British Government and public opinion with the same artless prayer that Great Britain forego the advantage of her might and do them simple justice. Brand, with the firm and proud temperament that was his, did not endeavour to make sentimental propaganda for his state. What he did he ever did scrupulously. And yet he had fashioned a powerful weapon. The state of British public opinion on South African questions during the Midlothian campaign in 1880 and of world opinion during the Great Boer War showed how great was the sentimental disadvantage of England's complex policy, constantly and profoundly influenced by the events of the whole world, when opposed by the relatively simple and direct demands of local communities.

In 1876 Brand was unquestionably the ablest political figure in South Africa. If he could be won for confederation Carnarvon's policy would gain a valuable and probably a definitive victory. He was, like Kruger twenty years later, the patriotic centre of the Dutch throughout the entire country. He was their state, and attachment to him was their strongest corporate feeling. *Cui adhaereo praeest.*

When he arrived in England on 6 May 1876 the Colonial Office was prepared to make concessions in order to win his support. "If he would confederate", ventured Herbert, "there would be a possibility of putting Griqualand back into the Orange State, without surrendering the territory from under the British flag."[2] Malcolm urged that the selection of Bloemfontein as the federal capital would have "a most material effect in inducing the O. F. State to come in". Even the unprecedented proposal that Brand should be made the first Governor General of the Confederation with Burgers as Lieutenant-Governor was received sympathetically as "a bold but not absolutely inadmissible proposal".[3] It was vain.

On his arrival in England Brand ostentatiously announced his arrival to Lord Derby at the Foreign Office. Informed that he

---

[1] G.D. 6/49, pp. 247–54.
[2] C.O. 48/477, F.O. to C.O., 31 Aug. 1875, Minutes.
[3] C.O. 48/481, Glanville to C.O., 1 Feb. 1876, Minutes.

G

would have to deal with the Secretary of State for the Colonies he affected to regard him as a special plenipotentiary, so that Carnarvon inquired nervously of the Law Officers whether he needed a commission from the Queen in order to talk to Brand. Not once during his sojourn in England would Brand admit that the Free State was other than a sovereign foreign power.

On 15 May he presented himself to the Colonial Office. He came loaded with documents and maps and bore the air of a man deeply wronged. Carnarvon must look at his papers and maps and admit there and then the full justice of the Free State claim. Dismayed by the mass of papers Carnarvon tried to wave them away. He had no desire to match documents with documents. He knew the dangers of such a procedure. Let bygones be bygones. The question at issue was no longer legal but political. Each side had something to ask and something to give. Did Brand require some territorial adjustment? He could have it, if he would agree to confederation. Did he want a share of the customs duties? Customs duties would be federal revenue, and a share would properly belong to each member of the confederation. But Carnarvon did not know Brand's capacity for moral obstinacy. He had brought his documents at Carnarvon's request and Carnarvon was going to look at them. Hastily Malcolm was summoned to stand by his superior's side, and together they listened politely to the President's lengthy explanations and pretended to follow his maps. Nothing could have been more embarrassing to Carnarvon. What Brand claimed he claimed as the Free State's right. He could not prejudice that right by making concessions. He could not sell that right. If it was to be given land, it must be given the entire diamond fields; if it was to have money it must be given the loss of revenue sustained since the annexation.

Carnarvon sought desperately for some agreement. He successively proposed confederation, an alliance without confederation, and joint action on native affairs. In return the British Government would make a money payment to the Orange Free State and place the salary of a British Resident at Bloemfontein on the estimates for the following year. But Brand with stubborn patience would not budge. To Carnarvon's request for confederation he replied that he had no authority to discuss it. To the request for co-operation on native affairs he replied in a phrase that explained republican native policy more effectively than a volume of discussion: "We have no native question; we have settled that already. The whites are to the natives as two to one."

At last Carnarvon's patience broke. He threatened to refer the whole issue back to the Cape. That, Brand knew, meant Barkly. *Il vaut toujours mieux avoir affaire à Dieu qu'à ses anges.* The moment had come to compromise. Of course he did not want the diamond fields. Having witnessed the trials of Southey as Lieutenant-Governor he knew that the Free State could not possibly control the fields. Indeed, a bolder Secretary of State than Carnarvon might well have compelled the Republic to take over the fields; for the British element would certainly have dominated the politics of the Free State.

Two months after landing in England Brand finally agreed to waive his claim to the diamond fields for a money payment of ninety thousand pounds. Carnarvon could afford a break of negotiations as little as Brand. If the Free State would not give a definite promise on confederation a money payment might at least predispose it to friendliness. It was not to be. Brand had exploited his tactical and moral advantage brilliantly. By asking for everything he had received very satisfactory compensation and in return had given nothing, not even a promise. Carnarvon had failed to win the support of the stronger colony and of the stronger Republic. He had already overwhelmed the weaker colony. It seemed logical that he would overwhelm the weaker Republic.

The dispute over the diamond fields was settled. But its settlement wrecked the conference. Molteno, following Brand to England at an interval of three months, came prepared at long last to discuss the incorporation of the fields. When Carnarvon somewhat shamefacedly revealed that the debt of Griqualand had been swollen by £90,000, all desire to co-operate with the Imperial Government left Molteno. Though Carnarvon urged him earnestly to attend the conference on his own terms, discuss what he wished, as unofficially as he wished, with the liberty of withdrawing when he wished, he refused to appear even as a witness. At his meeting with the Secretary of State he shook his head in turn at every proposal that was made, at incorporation, at confederation, at payment of customs dues to the Government of Griqualand West.[1] The arrangement with the President of the Free State had "changed the question". Taking refuge behind the distance and the time that separated him from his colleagues he insisted that he could do nothing without consulting them. And all Carnarvon's urgency thereafter availed nothing.

The Conference which met at Downing Street on 3 August, 1876 represented only two of the five communities. Almost pathetically Carnarvon strove to win support from a gathering that had no power and no desire to decide or to bind. The grant of a K.C.M.G. to Shepstone was paraded before the delegates as an augury of the honours Her Majesty might bestow upon other deserving colonial statesmen.[2] There was entreaty in Carnarvon's tone as he addressed the truncated Conference. Even the loosest bond would be acceptable to the British Government. Individual states would be all but autonomous; they could retain their local customs and laws; they could even have much freedom in native affairs. "The bundle of sticks may be tied together very loosely or very tightly, but, provided that there is common action, the object is secured." For all answer the group listlessly traversed the questions of gunrunning and native affairs. Their discussion was formal and their expressions of agreement non-committal. Brand nonchalantly admitted that the natives "may have supposed grievances or something of that sort and they may think that they ought to be in a higher position than what they are",[3] but, like Molteno outside the meeting, abated nothing in his refusal to discuss confederation or in any way to bind his Government.

Meanwhile Carnarvon was not hiding his anxious disappointment in another part of the Colonial Office. The South African states must be succoured against themselves. The less their dis-

---

[1] G.D. 6/23, conversations with Molteno.
[2] Wolseley had advised Carnarvon to do this for this very reason. G.D. 6/38, Wolseley to Carnarvon, 31 July 1876.
[3] C.O. 48/484, Conference.

position to find strength in common action, the greater the need for an energetic imperial presence. When there were rumours of unrest on the Cape Eastern Frontier in August, 1875, and again in 1876; when there was a threatening of Zulus on the Tugela, or when in the midst of the conference news arrived of ugly doings in the north-eastern corner of the Transvaal, the minutes in the Colonial Office no longer carried protests against the retention of imperial troops in South Africa. "For Imperial reasons", remarked Herbert, the British Government could not cease to keep a considerable force in South Africa. It would even be expedient to increase that force.[1] Such a decision inevitably had its effect upon the political atmosphere. In former days when the British Government had been concerned with an early withdrawal of troops it was disposed to make every concession to colonial desires. But now it was natural that the British Government should demand a greater liberty of action as the price for the presence of its troops. It was still more natural that it should incline to policies that could appeal if necessary to the force and prestige of military authority. Its respect for local privileges was lessened and it was less ready to accept as final the failure of simple negotiations.

Towards Molteno the Colonial Office now held a curt and almost minatory language. He was asked to state without evasion whether he would or would not agree to the incorporation of Griqualand West. If he would, the Home Government would engage itself to override any objection by the Griqualand West population. In insisting upon the " distinction between Imperial and purely colonial objects ", the Colonial Office quite ignored the fact that it was forcing upon the Cape Colony a territory so depressed that the Lieutenant-Governor could not both keep a horse and entertain his friends, and could not, in spite of the special loyalty of British military Governments in small and remote places, hold the Queen's annual birthday ball. Molteno did not waver. His answer rapped the Secretary of State over the knuckles. The incorporation of Griqualand West was a matter to be agreed upon in the first place by the legislatures of the colonies themselves. Whatever doubt may be cast upon the

[1] C.O. 48/481, Draft of secret Despatch, 22 Sept. 1876.

wisdom of his opposition to the Home Government, he cannot be denied high ranking amongst the colonial statesmen who gave life and growth to responsible government by their readiness to challenge imperial authority and their refusal to bow their heads before the wishes of Downing Street.

"Profoundly unsatisfactory", ejaculated Herbert on reading Molteno's reply.[1] The Colonial Office had been too patient. It too could refuse its co-operation. The Cape desired to annex Tembuland and territory in South-west Africa. The Cape could have Tembuland and Walfisch Bay if it took Griqualand West as well. Otherwise it could have nothing at all. Her Majesty's Government might even join Griqualand West to Walfisch Bay and place a British colony across the road to the interior. More serious yet, it might conclude that it could no longer "continue to hold at a distance" an Eastern Province which was willing to co-operate with Her Majesty's Government.[2] Here was threatening indeed. The dread spectre of separation would raise its head again. Molteno took fright and hurriedly agreed to urge incorporation upon the Cape Legislature. But now as he prepared to return to South Africa other rumours more alarming still reached him. Was it true that the British Government was about to annex the Transvaal? It was with feelings of the deepest disquiet that he left England.

Meanwhile Carnarvon set to work to prepare a Permissive Federation Act to be the constitutional basis of political union between the South African communities. He sent a draft of the Bill for the consideration of Ministers in the Cape Colony and Natal. He would do all he could to meet their criticisms, he promised. But which was uppermost in Carnarvon's mind—diplomacy or coercion?

[1] C.O. 48/481, Molteno to C.O., 15 Sept. 1876.
[2] *Ibid.*

CHAPTER V

THE ANNEXATION OF THE TRANSVAAL

THE judgment of most historians upon the annexation of the Transvaal has been summary: the restoration of the Transvaal was a tardy act of justice forced upon a country that had sought to ravish the independence of a weak neighbour. The problem of the Transvaal before 1877 cannot be properly grasped if the claims of the more indignant critics of British policy are accepted. They put forward claims that made the Transvaal rank as a nation state. Though their claims be legally defensible, they are historically misleading and illusory. The political, economic, and social life of no community could be separate from that of the other communities save in an artificial manner.

The Dutch were the first colonists. But they were followed by English who were colonists too, although greatly outnumbered. English and Dutch names could be found freely intermingled on the disturbed Western Frontier. Natal colonists held land in the Transvaal and Transvaal cattle grazed on the pastures of the Natal uplands. The Hollander invasion of the republican civil service had begun, but the quota of officials from the British colonies was by far the strongest. English churches were active in Bloemfontein, Pretoria, and the larger towns. English schools and the English language were being cultivated by an increasing number of the sons of progressive republicans. Lacking enough patriotic holidays the Transvaal unofficially adopted the Queen's birthday as a holiday. Neither Republic made any real attempt to exclude British subjects from office. Brand and Burgers both came from the Cape. The wife and child of Burgers lived in Scotland and he himself looked upon the Cape as his real home. Brand remained a member of the Cape Bar. Informed opinion in Cape Town long considered that he would ultimately return to become Chief Justice. When the Transvaal president led his forces against Sekukuni in 1876 he found it necessary to address his followers in both English and Dutch. For the redcoat the Boer had a generous respect and admiration. Nothing is more mistaken than to suppose that the Dutch of the Republics were filled with a strong racial bitterness before 1877. Racial antipathies gained more strength in the last twenty years of the nineteenth century than in the entire previous period. The discontent that prevailed was with the Wodehouses, Barklys and Southeys; it was a discontent which the Boers shared with many an Australian and many a descendant of the 1820 British settlers on the Cape Eastern Frontier. The return of the Transvaal to political community with the rest of South Africa was looked upon by most South African opinion as certain. A united South Africa was an ideal that was quite as much Dutch as it was English. What was uncertain was the time and manner of its return.

The conviction that the dangers of disunion would brook no delay led the British Government to bring the Transvaal abruptly under its flag. It was not a greed of dominion. The annexation was the arbitrary action of a Government faced with failure. The question that confronts the historian is not so much whether the annexation was right or wrong, but whether it was an act that could possibly have achieved its end. The answer would seem to be clearly given in Gladstone's Midlothian campaign and in the British defeats at Bronkhorstspruit and Majuba. Actually, however, there is something to be said for the contention that the blunder that led to Carnarvon's undoing was not the annexation, but the years of mischievous administration that followed it.

The career of Burgers, the scapegoat of the annexation, as President of the Transvaal ended in humiliation. Yet he had done more than any of his predecessors to overcome the formlessness of the Republic's political life. The Voortrekkers had not sought to establish a new society but to maintain an old. Far more enlightened than most of the local leaders Burgers tried to draw the Transvaal out of its political and economic backwardness. That in the effort he dissipated his own private fortune is evidence both of his sincerity and of the inadequate means with which he laboured. During his presidency men of more liberal views in religion and education entered the country and progress was made towards a central control of native policy. It was he who attempted to bring to a head the struggle between the forces of a uniform and central control and the localism that had threatened to split the country into separate republics.

The Dutch of both Republics had strangely forgotten the time, only two generations removed, when they all lived in one colony as subjects of the King of Holland. They most damagingly impeached the rule of Holland by forgetting it. Even in the days of their worst trial their imagination never escaped back to the time before the coming of the English. Instead their instincts turned towards a parochial self-rule. Their political thought was uncomplex and immature. The informal regional groups, corresponding to the voluntary units of the Great Trek, were still the strongest and most self-conscious elements in their political life. They had quarrelled their way into the understandings that held the Republic together, but the menace of division was not dispelled. Their destiny was unity, but it was a destiny deferred by a dragging tradition of disunion. Both the groups that thrust outwards against the western and south-eastern borders had it in them to split off into separate republics, not rebelliously, but naturally, as if it were a principle of their growth. Of the greater claims of the entire Republic, and of all South Africa beyond it, these groups were not fully conscious.

In such a land the law did not run powerfully. Men defended their property with their person and their own arms. Often they made war upon their native neighbours upon their own responsibility. Such men could be casual and elastic in their respect for the law. Custom and self-made pacts ruled more strongly than resolutions and enactments that came from Pretoria. Yet they had a passion for politics as strong as their devotion to religious observance. Their passion expressed itself in an unrestrained freedom of speech, which made them a true democracy though a weak one. Their constitutional history had been an alternation of quarrelling and spasmodic compromise. Their unity, when it finally came, was not really proof of a slow cementing into consistency and durability of their opinions and practice, but a more rapid fusing in the heat of the clash with the British Government.

The economic situation of the Transvaal during the first years of Burgers' presidency seemed promising. There were men digging at the Lydenburg gold fields. Further and more profitable discoveries of gold were confidently anticipated, so that many who had failed to pick up fortunes on the diamond fields moved into the Transvaal rather than return to the "overcrowded" Cape. The existence of gold was of international importance. In the 'seventies Germany, France, Holland, and the United States went on the gold standard one after another, creating a sudden demand for a vast amount of gold at a time when the Californian and Australian deposits were all but exhausted. The drain on the world's gold supply unsettled prices, and made the call for gold still more urgent. England and South Africa eyed the Republic as a potential gold-producing country with new interest. Coal, iron and copper were known to be plentiful. The land was fertile. Maize, tobacco and fruits thrived well. Sheep were profitable. The varied climate was as suitable for European settlement as any other part of South Africa. But the Republic lacked communications. In 1875 Burgers decided that the Transvaal should have a railway, and departed for Europe to raise a loan.

It was a decade of active railway construction in all the larger British colonies. The Cape and Natal had extensive projects. Between 1870 and 1878 New Zealand built a thousand miles of railway. It is still a matter of speculation what the political and economic effects were of the heavy financial burden which the colonies thus suddenly assumed. In New Zealand the public debt mounted between 1872 and 1881 from ten million to twenty-eight million pounds. Reckless spending in New Zealand and the heavy losses of investment in the Canadian Grand Trunk Railway created a prejudice in England against investment in colonial railways without adequate guarantees. The most adequate guarantee was an imperial guarantee. The refusal, however, to grant imperial guarantees for railway construction was almost an unbroken rule of British colonial policy. The London financial market was certain to look all the more coldly upon the venture of a colonial community which was not even under the British flag. Burgers, moreover, chose as the moment for floating his railway loan a time of international financial confusion when defaulted republican loans stank in the nostrils of every European

Exchange. The disclosures before the Parliamentary foreign loans committee made the very word republic, South American or South African, the worst of recommendations.

In July 1875 the President of the French Republic realized for the Transvaal its dream—a seaport outside the sphere of British influence. Delagoa Bay, now Portuguese territory, was appreciably closer to Pretoria and the gold fields than Durban. In spite of the tsetse fly that killed the oxen and the summer torrents that washed away the roads, trade had prospered enough to alarm the rival port of Durban. Exports to Natal from Delagoa Bay had risen from £3600 in 1872 to nearly £21,000 in 1875, while imports from Natal had risen from £6900 to £22,000. In Portugal itself Macmahon's favourable decision excited a renaissance of colonial interest which defeated the efforts made by the British Government to acquire Delagoa Bay.

The hostility of Cape and Natal commercial interests to Delagoa Bay was not simply due to a fear of competition from a foreign port. A railway would place upon the uncertain credit of the Transvaal a load of such magnitude that its South African creditors could not but fear for the safety of their placements. It has no small bearing on the final annexation of the Transvaal that the President's premature and ill-considered ambition earned for him the animosity of all South African commercial and banking interests. It was a foregone conclusion that they would lift not a finger to make his task easier. Rather would they be concerned with withdrawing the credit they had given him.

At best Burgers' expedition to Europe was a bold effort to save his state from dependence upon British interests. Actually his every step was inspired by the poorest financial wisdom. In January 1876 the Insinger Bank of Amsterdam offered at 88 a loan of 3,600,000 guilders in debentures of one thousand guilders each, paying interest at 5 per cent., repayable in twenty-five annual drawings and secured by 3,000,000 acres of land upon which the loan was a first mortgage. The Republic, Burgers insisted, could bear the tax burden for the loan with ease; the cheapness of the new route would create a profitable volume of trade; best of all securities was the "good faith and honesty of the population and the old Dutch virtues which, with the language of their fathers, they have retained ". The assurance availed but little. Of 3600 debentures only 1076 had been sold by the end of the year. The coupon of June was met out of subscribed capital. Before he left Europe Burgers had spent the entire proceeds of the loan. After the bankers' commission had been paid the bulk of the money[1] was spent as a gesture to investors on carriages, engines and wagons. Forty employees sent from Holland arrived at Delagoa Bay only to be immediately discharged for want of money. And all the while there was not even a tolerably competent survey of the line. Burgers had no real proof that the line was feasible and no guarantee that the outlay would not have to be twice the estimates.

To build his railway Burgers hoped for the material assistance of the Portuguese Government. In January 1876 the *Diario do Governo* of Lisbon published the articles of a treaty between the Transvaal and Portugal. Under the treaty there was to be reciprocal exemption from import duties of the products of the Republic and the Province of Mozambique. A duty of 3 per cent. was to be laid on all goods imported through Delagoa Bay for Transvaal consumption.[2] The Portuguese Government agreed to subsidize half the cost of the line to be built from the coast to the Transvaal border. In return the Transvaal pledged itself to continue the line from the border.

The Portuguese Government was a broken reed. Although it signed a contract with George Moodie, a dishonest promoter, promising to pay a subsidy in accordance with the treaty, it cautiously refused to pay any money until the railway should be an accomplished fact. Within six months Moodie unloaded his concession on to the luckless shoulders of the Transvaal Government. The Lebombo Company was thereupon formed with a nominal capital of £100,000 divided into four thousand four hundred shares. Of these the Transvaal took three thousand three hundred and sold exactly twenty-four. In November the firm of Cockerill, ironmasters of Liège, accepted a provisional contract by which it assumed the assets and liabilities of the Lebombo Company. But it was an arrangement that merely increased the embarrassment of the Transvaal, for the contract

---

[1] Some £70,000.   [2] The Natal duty was 6 per cent.

called for concessions of land, extensive mining rights and worst of all for subsidies. By the end of 1876 the economic collapse of the state was merely a matter of time.

For the economic collapse of the Transvaal the ignominious failure to turn even a single sod was only in part responsible. For some years land prices had been steadily driven upward partly by speculation and partly through the absorption of much of the most desirable land. Formerly every burgher's son on coming of age had become entitled to burgher rights and a free grant of a six thousand acre farm. Farms of such size soon made heavy inroads upon the land supply of the Republic, the more so since it was not unusual for farms represented as containing six thousand acres to contain in fact nine thousand and twelve thousand acres. According to Sir Arthur Cunynghame one tract stated to be 160,000 was found upon measurement to be 240,000 acres. A critical shortage of land was already threatening. The earmarking of three million acres of land as security for the railway loan precipitated a crisis. At the end of 1875 and the beginning of the following year free grants and sales of public lands almost abruptly ceased. It seemed the moment for which the speculators had been waiting. The connection between the dislocation of the land market and the financial plight of the Government is not clear in all its aspects. What is clear, however, is that the President, by calling upon the farmers to pay increased taxes for a railway and a native war at the very time that he restricted the supply of cheap land, imposed a serious financial strain on the population.

The outward and visible signs of a land crisis were strikingly seen in the increasingly insistent pressure of the farmers upon the land of the natives on the various borders. In August 1875 Acting President Joubert issued a proclamation defining a new line well within the area which the Keate Award had assigned to the natives.[1] The previous May he had already annexed the disputed territory on the Zulu border. His act was followed by uneasy stirrings in Zululand and a fingering of guns and assagais.[2] On each frontier the Dutch could point to one or more treaties

[1] C.O. 48/476, D. 123, Barkly to Carnarvon, 20 Sept. 1875.
[2] C.O. 179/118, Bulwer to Carnarvon, 26 Oct. 1875.

with native chiefs which justified their encroachment. Actually these treaties are valueless in any attempt to understand the urgent competition for land between whites and blacks. Given a restless pastoral community, accustomed to extensive land holdings, it was impossible for the native tribes to maintain their independence. It was inevitable that the tribes, whether on British or Dutch frontiers, should be subjected to European rule. The indictment against the colonists was not that they deprived the native tribes of their independence but that under the guise of treaties and legal forms they crowded them into congestion, or reduced them to the position of rightless squatters and labourers. It was in the Transvaal that this *refoulement* went on most vigorously. Speaking of the fateful lands of the Bapedi chief Sekukuni, the Resident Magistrate of Newcastle wrote that the Boers "encroached by degrees upon Native territory, commencing by obtaining permission to graze stock upon portions of it at certain seasons of the year, followed by individual grazers obtaining from Native headmen a sort of right or license to squat upon certain defined portions". After a few years of occupation the licences were construed as titles and permanent occupation ensued. Natives that had never known a surveyor's beacon or seen a title deed were turned into trespassers and breakers of the law of private property.[1] Inevitably the commingled habitation of natives and farmers led to friction and a cry from aggrieved Europeans that the land "be cleaned".

When Burgers returned from Europe he found the Lydenburg district asimmer with discontent. Sekukuni's Bapedi were of a mind to do some cleaning themselves. His land was Transvaal land, "legally" ceded by the Amaswazi in 1846.[2] His land, Burgers could not fail to note, lay across the line of the projected railway. Indeed, part of it had been pledged as security for the railway loan. Hence the war that commenced against him was not altogether punitive; it was really a war for the ownership of his land. With the aid of the Swazis who had come with black

---

[1] C.O. 179/121, D. 194, Bulwer to Carnarvon, 12 Oct. 1876, Minutes.

[2] Maps published by Petermann's *Geographische Mittheilungen* and drawn by Jeppe and Merensky leave the territory outside the Transvaal. A map published in 1875 in Amsterdam included the territory for the first time. C.O. 48/478, Conf., Barkly to Carnarvon, 14 July 1876.

plumes flying and their knees drumming against their war shields, Burgers did not fear failure.

The war revealed the infirmity of the structure upon which Burgers was planning to build. Considering the hilly nature of the country the only warfare capable of success was one of raids, burnings and harryings carried on over a lengthy period. The attempt to subdue the natives by a frontal attack was poor strategy. Not afraid of native bullets themselves the Boers refused to risk their horses which made easy marks. A horse, like a broken waggon, was a heavy personal loss. In the final analysis, however, the failure of the expedition was the failure to capture native cattle. The average burgher on commando expected his patriotism to bring him profit. Otherwise he was not satisfied. When the Swazi allies had the good fortune to sweep off a few herds they were confiscated by the whites. Thereupon the Swazis returned home incensed and the manner of their returning was such that the farmers ruefully wondered whether their allies were not worse than their enemies. Farmers and store keepers were grumbling at the shortage of waggons and draught animals. Soon the frontier farmers were deserted by those who saw no benefit to themselves in the war. Having obeyed the call without enthusiasm they returned home to refuse the special war tax. Burgers stormed at the departing commandos, and as though unlimited resources were his to command, offered horses, farms and money to volunteers. It was useless. His prestige was gone. The farmers did not like his imported Hollanders, and were shocked by the gold coins which bore his far from Augustan head. Burgers, like all minters of South African coins, forgot that the splendid stepping ox would be even more appropriate on the coins of South Africa than it was on the standard of the children of Israel. Men resented the bodyguard which he placed at the door of his tent. Some of the younger bloods made lewd remarks about them in his hearing. All that remained finally were a few hundred local frontiersmen and a band of adventurers and desperadoes seeking booty.

The initial reverses were in themselves not serious. The war had not been irretrievably lost. Even the ragged force that remained could in the course of time humble the tribesmen. But

Burgers' need had been for a quick victory. His setback let a
storm loose upon his head within and without the Transvaal.
The protests of the humanitarian element, and of those like
Shepstone who were fearful lest the Transvaal be victorious,
were swollen by a roar of fear and disapproval. White men had
been humiliated by blacks! What disastrous encouragement for
Zulus, Basuto, Pondos and Xosas. Men flinched, or pretended
to flinch, before the prospect of a general uprising. The rumour
ran that Cetywayo's emissaries were seen everywhere in Kaffir-
land and Basutoland. Nor were these terrors without point.
The conditions on the Zulu border were dangerously tense.
Most of the Dutch population there was in laager. In the face of
such weakness the Zulus grew more braggart and their blood
hotter. From Natal Bulwer wrote of the danger of a Zulu onslaught upon the Transvaal. In Basutoland on the other side of
Natal there arose prophets and prophetesses, the harbingers of
war. The talk of confederation, reaching the kraals, caused the
opposite rumour to spread that the whites were planning to
unite against the tribes. From Pondoland came tales of meetings
and drillings, and the lackland Basuto chief Nehemiah Moshesh,
"connoisseur" of books on Napoleon, was accused of preparing
another descent upon the Griqua country. On the Eastern
Frontier the whites were swept by a sudden gust of panic. The
Queenstown Tembus were sullen and ill-tempered. The crowded
tribes were trampling on each other's toes and the frontiersmen
believed that they were about to sweep into the Colony. Sending
out a call for gatlings and police the citizens of Wodehouse drilled
in the daytime and did sentry-go at night. Farms were abandoned.
The panic, although the Minister for Native Affairs declared it
to be unreasonable, was the measure of the anxiety of the
Europeans throughout the country.

Whatever Barkly said concerning the Republics was usually
touched with prejudice. But what he now wrote was most fair
and dispassionate by the side of the flood of hostile misstate-
ments and exaggerations which the opponents of the Transvaal
caused to flow. Barkly and Lanyon in Griqualand West gladly
forwarded letters and newspaper cuttings to Downing Street.
As of one accord all South Africa turned its gaze upon the Trans-

vaal. Europeans and natives seemed to understand that the issue
was unusual. The war was the most important news the newspapers could publish. Some papers had a "Special War Correspondent", and published the latest telegrams in extras with
spectacular headlines. The worse the confusion the more virulent
the attack. Slavery, the butchery of prisoners, no accusation
seemed too violent. "There is no doubt", said the Special Correspondent of the *Cape Argus*, "that what Turkey is to the rest
of Europe, the Transvaal is to the remainder of South Africa."
Thousands of slaves were held there. The details were so
searching and revolting that if they were true, and "if every
offender were punished, according to the measure of his crimes,
the Transvaal would be turned into a penal settlement". "The
only thing", said the same correspondent, "that can save it from
a still lower social degradation, and a deeper depth of crime, is
that it shall be taken under the authority and tutelage of a
stronger and wiser people, and be taught, *ab initio*, as a child is
taught, its duty as an integral part of the great commonwealth of
nations."[1] Even the Dutch paper, the *Zuid Afrikaan*, admitted
that Burgers was "carrying our independence by steam to Cape
Town".[2] Small wonder that Mr Evelyn Ashley complained in
the House of Commons that the Transvaal was the region in the
whole world where it was most difficult to get at the truth,[3] and
that no less a person than Fairfield perpetrated the Babuism that
"the aggregate of complexity is on the increase".

The indictment against these popgun imperialists and dingy
letter writers was only partly that they inspired a deep prejudice
against the Transvaal. Their atrocity-mongering was objectionable enough, although, to give the devil his due, the conduct of
the pack of freebooters who continued the war against Sekukuni
was far from squeamish. But incidents offensive to a sentimental
humanitarianism were easy to find outside the Transvaal on the
diamond diggings or in Natal. The greatest sinning of the Transvaal's enemies was that their propaganda acted like so much dust
in the eyes of public opinion, blinding men to the truth that the
central problem of the Transvaal's native policy was not slavery,

[1] *Argus*, 12 Dec. 1876.　　　　[2] 16 Dec. 1876.
[3] Hansard, vol. 273, col. 790.

H

which did not exist, nor cruelty, which was occasional and insignificant, but the more subtly dangerous struggle between Europeans and natives for land and the mode of existence which possession of land could alone insure. Worse yet, British policy was tricked into using arguments in defence of its action towards the Transvaal that were misleading and false, and that, as their falsity was revealed, were used to build up the view that Great Britain's position in the Transvaal had been from the beginning wholly based upon a detestable lie.

The war gave the creditors of the Transvaal their opportunity too. The chief role in destroying what remained of Transvaal credit was played by the Cape Commercial Bank and its agents in the Transvaal. Towards the latter part of August the directors of the bank, who were for the most part Dutch, held a meeting to consider the state of affairs in the Transvaal. Their decision was to use all the influence they could to bring the Republic under British rule.[1] One of their number waited upon the High Commissioner and from him Barkly heard a strange story of intrigue and jobbery. When Burgers had first gone to the Transvaal he had gone, it seemed, as the agent of the "clique" in order to undermine President Pretorius and "upset" the Keate arbitration. After the appointment of Burgers to the presidency he had continued to accept instructions from Cape Town, and in return the bank had advanced him £60,000 with which to redeem the depreciated greenbacks of the state.[2] According to Sir Bartle Frere the bank had continued to lend money to Burgers at rates of interest much lower than those which it might have obtained elsewhere on far better security. The inducement was political and not financial.

In going to Europe in search of credit Burgers had kicked over the traces. Either because he over-estimated the success of the loan he had floated or because he felt that the bank was so deeply involved that it must continue to uphold him, he had "fairly broken loose from all control and lost his head in his undisguised hatred of everything English". The bank was trapped in a net of its own weaving. Not to endanger its credit it had kept its ad-

[1] G.D. 6/32, Barkly to Carnarvon, 1 Sept. 1876.
[2] G.D. 6/33, Frere to Carnarvon, 14 Aug. 1877.

vances to the Transvaal Government a secret. Fearful that the bank's agents would be put under forced contribution and appalled by the reckless expenditure into which their creature was plunging the "clique", it decided to "wind him up". To its agents were sent positive instructions noi to advance another penny, not even at 12 per cent., and to call upon the Government for security for the loans already made. More effectively yet it was arranged that certain friendly members of the Volksraad should move for statements of accounts in order to disclose the utterly bankrupt condition of the administration.[1] Since a public appeal for British intervention would reveal the bank's own embarrassed financial position, it was more politic that a move should be made by those on the spot and that the bank should do all in its power privately "to turn the scale in favour of British rule".[2] It is clear that as far as South Africa is concerned the annexation of the Transvaal was an act desired and encouraged by strong elements from both racial groups. It cannot be said that it was the result of a conspiracy of British interests against the political rights and ambitions of the Dutch group. The annexation of the Transvaal had its roots in South Africa as well as in England.

In England the frustration of the London Conference brought Carnarvon to the crossroads of his policy, where he had to choose between the opposite beckonings of Molteno and Wolseley. His choice was clear. He could not abandon the position that Great Britain held as paramount power. But how was that power to be further exercised? Could he abrogate the Cape constitution, or should he force the hand of one of the Republics? It was Hobson's choice. All fingers pointed to the Transvaal. The Free State could be touched as little as the Cape. The British Government could hardly admit its wrongful annexation of the diamond fields, and then proceed against the independence of the Free State. Moreover Brand's Government was stable and prosperous. Government was inexpensive; revenues were in excess of expenditure and direct taxation was light. Finally, as long as the Eastern Province competed with the Western Province for

[1] Cp. G.D. 6/36, F. Wetherley to Lanyon, 27 Sept. 1876.
[2] G.D. 6/32, Barkly to Carnarvon, 16 Sept. 1876.

Free State trade, and Durban strove with the Cape ports the Free State held a privileged position. The natural defects of its landlocked position were counteracted by the rivalry for its trade. Railways to several points on its frontier promised to increase its advantage. While the British colonies were engaged in cut-throat competition, the Free State saw no reason for closer union.

That one or the other of the Republics should accept or be brought to accept British policy was of the logic of Carnarvon's planning. The possibility of establishing British authority over the Transvaal had been considered as early as April 1874. At the time Carnarvon had entertained the idea unwillingly.[1] Convinced that the British Government had already sinned enough against one Republic Carnarvon turned a deaf ear to the importunities of Barkly and Southey. A year later Wolseley and his staff again emphatically pointed to the Transvaal. Once it was British, they said, the Free State would find it impossible to stand aloof.[2] The British connection was popular with two-thirds of the Transvaal population. In most of the towns the English already outnumbered the Dutch. Along the main roads enterprise was chiefly in English hands. Only a minority led by the "Hollanders", the most active and influential class, was irreconcilably opposed to the British flag. To hold them in check the British Government must not allow even the first sod of a railway to Delagoa Bay to be turned, nor permit Portugal to retain the Bay. "So long as Delagoa Bay remains in the possession of the Portuguese", warned Colonel Colley, "the 'Hollander' party will continue to hold out hope to the Boers of ultimately obtaining it by purchase or cession, perhaps with the assistance of Germany, and so becoming a great and rich state, with its own seaboard and harbour, independent of and perhaps eclipsing the hated 'Englander'."

Since 1843, when it had annexed Natal rather than allow the establishment of a maritime Republic, the British Government had opposed every move of either of the Republics towards the sea. When Marshal Macmahon's decision in the Delagoa Bay arbitration was given in favour of Portugal, the British Govern-

---

[1] G.D. 6/32, Carnarvon to Barkly, 24 April 1874.
[2] G.D. 6/38, Wolseley to Carnarvon, 16 Aug. 1875.

ment did not need Wolseley's warnings to realize that the Transvaal would now be released from the handicap of its landlocked position, and that the British monopoly of the South African coastline was broken. The Colonial Office would gladly have acquired not merely Delagoa Bay but as much of the East African coastline as was not already unequivocally Portuguese. But it was helpless. A suggestion that the harbour be acquired in return for a slight reduction of duty on port wine was plaintively dismissed by Herbert because those departments which were interested in the wine duties "could not be made to understand the value of Delagoa Bay".[1] To another suggestion that the British Government should take steps to destroy the prosperity of Delagoa Bay by calling on Portugal to check the gun trade the answer was simply that the hands of the British colonies were also unclean. Nobody dared mention the impossibility of asking the British Parliament for money with which to buy the port, although Herbert with unconscious humour remarked that "we could afford a great deal of Natal money".

There were two ways of safeguarding the British monopoly of the coastline. The first was to prevent the construction of a railway line between the Transvaal and Delagoa Bay; the second was to turn the independent Republic into a British possession. The second had the advantage that it promised to do far more than control the Transvaal's relations with Delagoa Bay.

It is clear that the policy which ended in the annexation of the Transvaal was in its beginnings influenced much more by a sense of the Transvaal's strength than its weakness. The Colonial Office was originally disturbed not by the fear of a Transvaal collapse but by the opposite fear that it might become so strong by extension of territory and access to an independent port that it would be beyond the reach of confederation and the British flag. It is equally clear that the British Government, as late as August 1876, knew little of an impending bankruptcy. It was the wealth of the Transvaal that it saw as the obstacle to its policy, not its poverty. "It was not then supposed", wrote Fairfield in December 1875 of the Conventions of 1852 and 1854, "that any political importance would attach to the small and isolated com-

---

[1] C.O. 179/119, Thompson to Herbert, 10 June 1875, Minutes.

munities thus contemptuously abandoned in the interior.... Since that time mineral wealth of unprecedented and indeed untold extent has been discovered in the interior...showing that the most active field of industry, and the centre of political importance are no longer to be sought in the southern country. The contemplated opening of an easy line of communication between this quarter and the splendid harbour of Delagoa Bay threatens to deprive the southern ports of much of their mercantile importance."

The annexation of the Transvaal could only be carried out on certain conditions. It would have been difficult to explain to any Parliament of the Gladstonian era that Great Britain had extinguished the independence of a state at peace with its neighbours because that state was thinking of building a railway to a foreign port. Nor would it have been possible to force an independent state into confederation, even on the ground that confederation was in the best interests of South Africa. But when the Transvaal made war upon its natives it affronted humanitarian sentiments; when its forces were defeated it gave point to the fears of those in South Africa and England who dreaded a general conflagration; and when the state became utterly bankrupt and it was confidently asserted that a majority of the population desired British intervention, there could be no difficulty in justifying the annexation. The war against Sekukuni was the opportunity of the British Government. It remains to be seen how it actually used its opportunity.

What transpired within the Colonial Office between the arrival in August of the first full account of the war in the Transvaal and Shepstone's departure for South Africa is far from clear. It is not even altogether clear that when Shepstone left England on 23 September annexation of the Transvaal was a foregone conclusion, whatever the conditions he might find on reaching South Africa. At the end of July when the Colonial Office already knew that a commando had been called out against Sekukuni, Herbert still wondered whether a protectorate might not be established over the country between Walfisch Bay and the Limpopo, or whether the British Government should merely give the Republic yet another warning that it would not recognize any extensions of territory the Transvaal might make.[1] There can be very little doubt that both Shepstone and Wolseley, who were in London during and after the meetings of the London Conference, impressed upon Carnarvon the dangers of a Transvaal war and the need for resolute British action. Shepstone excited the humanitarian sentiment of the Colonial Office by raising the cry of Bulgarian atrocities in the Transvaal.[2] When Barkly's telegram arrived on 14 September announcing that the rout of the commando against Sekukuni had led to a movement in the Transvaal favouring a cession of the country to Great Britain,[3] Carnarvon saw that a critical moment had been reached. The telegram announced an opportunity of obtaining control of the Transvaal. Shepstone hurriedly returned to South Africa. The most reasonable interpretation of Carnarvon's private letters to Disraeli, Wolseley, Shepstone and of his several secret despatches is that Shepstone left England as the man who was most likely by his knowledge of the Dutch either to influence opinion in favour of the British flag or so to present annexation that they would readily accept it. To Carnarvon the attitude of the Dutch was of much importance. "One point, of course", he earnestly impressed upon Shepstone not once but several times, "requires very great attention, and indeed one of no small difficulty. On the one hand it is of great consequence to secure the Transvaal, and on the other it is most desirable to make cession as far as possible the act of the Dutch part of the population. If they think they have it in their power to say that they have been coerced into union much of the good of the annexation will be lost; for they will remain a discontented element in the body politic, allying themselves with everything that is factious, troublesome and anti-English. You will, of course, remember that in South Africa we have to deal not only with the Dutch in the Dutch states but outside of them, and that any real feeling of anger within is likely to communicate itself to those without, especially at the Cape. There is a limit to this consideration, for we cannot please everyone and if we attempt to provide for every

[1] C.O. 179/119, G. Thompson to C.O., 25 July 1876, Minutes.
[2] C.O. 48/481, Shepstone to C.O., 9 Sept. 1876, Minute.
[3] See Uys, *In the Era of Shepstone*, p. 173.

possible contingency, we may lose the real substance, which is perhaps for the first time within reach. But the question is one, I am sure, of the highest importance; it is certainly desirable to have the consent of the Volksraad to the cession of the state and it would be dangerous to take over the country *against* their desire except under circumstances so grave as to justify us on the ground of unquestionable general safety."[1] Even Wolseley, "long arm of the British Empire" though he was, admitted that Shepstone could hardly enter the Transvaal unless invited by a "very strong party in the Dutch population".[2] An unprejudiced mind must admit that Carnarvon's instructions and letters, taken all together, were tantamount to the declaration: annex the Transvaal with the consent of the population if possible; in any event annex the Transvaal.[3] "I attach to a cession the greatest importance", he privately informed Barkly. "It solves a legion of difficult questions; it relieves us from many real and pressing dangers and it puts us as regards African politics in a position more favourable than any which we have as yet occupied."[4] He was even afraid that President Brand might make the cause of the Transvaal his own, and, by sending money to Burgers, succour the Transvaal and thus shrewdly safeguard the independence of his own state. As a precaution Barkly was instructed to warn Brand that any untimely move could cause him to lose the £90,000 promised him in London.[5] As weeks and then months passed the tone of his letters grew more urgent and anxious, till they were really nothing more than commands to Barkly and Shepstone to wait no more and seize the Transvaal forthwith. "We can never hope that the opportunity will, if now lost, recur."[6] Thus what had been a possibility eagerly canvassed in September 1876 became a necessity in the months that followed. "We have to secure, if possible, the Transvaal", he wrote to Bulwer,[7] "with the fewest conditions and with the greatest amount of good will on the part of the Dutch people. Remember

---

[1] G.D. 6/23, Carnarvon to Shepstone, 4 Oct. 1876.   [2] *Ibid.*
[3] For a capable presentation of this view see Uys, *op. cit.* chap. VII.
[4] G.D. 6/32, Carnarvon to Barkly, 20 Sept. 1876.
[5] *Ibid.* Carnarvon to Barkly, 22 Sept. 1876.
[6] G.D. 6/23, Carnarvon to Shepstone, 11 Oct. 1876.
[7] G.D. 6/38, Carnarvon to Bulwer, 17 Oct. 1876.

always that a discontented and aggrieved nation would hereafter be a troublesome element in the midst of our general system. But such an opportunity as is now presented may—probably will— never recur and therefore it must not be lost. Where we cannot get all we want, we must take as much as we can get, and much may be done in softening any irritation by the manner in which a measure is carried out. Under no circumstances does it seem possible or right that we should revert to the *status quo*." It was a difficult responsibility that rested upon the shoulders of Her Majesty's Special Commissioner, Sir Theophilus Shepstone.

Shepstone returned to a South Africa in which the inevitability of an annexation of the Transvaal was accepted, whether regretfully or triumphantly. An empty treasury, a dragging war, a total loss of credit, an obstinate President and a dispirited people left little room for confidence in the future of an independent Transvaal. The revenues of the British colonies themselves began to suffer. At the very moment that it had need of an expanding revenue Natal's customs receipts for 1876 were diminished by nearly £18,000. The service for present loans and the credit for future loans were in danger. In the Transvaal accounts against the Government remained unpaid. Many accounts which were unpaid but certified as correct by the auditor floated amongst the people as a sort of depreciated paper money. Since this paper was tendered in payment of taxes, it meant that the Government's only reliable income was its own bad debts. Landdrosts accounted for their funds many months after collection, and used their own discretion in making payments without the authority of a central officer. The banks in the Transvaal and Griqualand West refused to discount bills at any price. The postal service to Kimberley would have been discontinued if Lanyon had not paid the contractor's subsidy. Worst of all was a slump in land prices. The Government, shopkeepers, farmers and speculators were all in the same straits. When every fresh disclosure of his incompetent financial policy merely drew the purse strings of the farmers tighter and made the banks more obdurate, Burgers' call for fresh taxes and loans was a vain and desperate optimism. Authority ebbed away from the central Government, and the state drifted into chaos.

December was the month for native wars. Already in November it was told that a Zulu attack upon the Transvaal was imminent. That Cetywayo and his young spears were fidgety needed no proof. That they were determined to attack the Transvaal or their Swazi allies is less certain, since it is impossible to see clearly through the misrepresentations and exaggerations of those, amongst whom must be counted Shepstone himself, who sought to raise the spectre of another native war in order to arouse a deeper panic in the Transvaal and vindicate the need for British intervention. Yet Bulwer was convinced that a war was likely. There was something shrewd, dispassionate and independent in his temper that commands respect for his evidence. Together with outspoken good sense he had a gift for being in touch with the situation itself and not with its appearances that distinguished him from more undiscriminating and patriotic observers whose only desire was to embarrass the Transvaal.[1] Of the despatches that reached Carnarvon his were the most sober. Though he appreciated the seriousness of the crisis[2] he forbore from passing on uncriticized the confused and wild accounts of defeat and atrocity that poured in upon him. Oppressed by the climate of Natal and anxious to see his aged father before he died he had no ambition to distinguish himself in South Africa. Until he was disheartened by the death of his father he did not cease to hunger for release from office. That his cautious and reasonable mind agreed that trouble with the Zulus was probable is testimony that cannot be lightly dismissed.

Whether a war was imminent or not the Transvaal's independence was doomed. Both Shepstone and Barkly were impatient at any further delay lest the opportunity be lost. Barkly was especially afraid that the presidential elections which were to be held on 15 February might result in a verdict opposed to British intervention. If a new President were elected, he could reasonably ask the British Government to stay its hand and give him a fair trial. It was even conceivable that Burgers might be re-elected. Or an unrepentant " Boerdom " might triumph in the

---

[1] C.O. 179/121, D. 156, Bulwer to Carnarvon, 9 Aug. 1876.
[2] G.D. 6/38, Bulwer to Carnarvon, 3 Nov. 1876.

person of Paul Kruger who suddenly became a strong candidate in January 1877.[1] Meanwhile in England Carnarvon himself grew impatient. Although he was still anxious that an abrupt move should not engender "fresh difficulties and animosities in the Dutch population", the mails from Cape Town gave such desperate accounts of the state of the Transvaal that he grew alarmed lest the fruit be rotten ere it be ripe and the Republic be "so wasted and beggared as to be, for years to come, worthless".[2] Herbert was more hopeful. Believing that confederation was at last within reach, he advised that consideration of a charter for the new university at Cape Town be postponed in order that the new institution could more appropriately be named the University of South Africa.

At the end of December after some two months of waiting Shepstone decided to enter the Transvaal. Few acts in South African history have caused greater controversy. What was the attitude of the population towards Shepstone's mission and its consequences? Of the British section of the population little need be said. They heartily favoured annexation; they had worked for it and it was their huzzas that acclaimed Shepstone on his way to the capital. It would, therefore, be vain to quote Shepstone in support of his own contention that the bulk of Dutch opinion welcomed him. His information came from prejudiced sources and his pretence to know the state of popular feeling must be dismissed. What information he had came from half a dozen men whom he paid £1356 from Secret Service funds to travel through the country and report upon the political sentiment of the different districts. A careful examination of the vouchers showed that except for a payment of £20 to a poor but influential farmer for wheat and tobacco on political grounds Shepstone did not resort to bribery, unless the baubles he gave to children, and the subscriptions to churches and sports funds can be so interpreted. Chosen by Lord Carnarvon as a colonist who understood the workings of the Boer mind he nevertheless proved himself not merely disastrously ignorant of rural sentiment but while actually

[1] G.D. 6/32, Barkly to Carnarvon, 23 Jan. 1877. "But for my action an election for president would have very soon taken place with Burgers and Kruger the only candidates."
[2] Ibid. Carnarvon to Barkly, 30 Nov. 1876.

living in their midst incapable of judging the elusive and impalpable ways of Boer thought.

It does not follow, however, that the majority of Dutch opinion had never desired the British connection. The conclusion has been too readily drawn from the final failure of the annexation and the disillusionment caused by the humiliation of British arms that the Boer population had been opposed to the annexation from the beginning, so that only a momentary helplessness and the menacing presence of the 3rd Buffs on the borders kept them from defending their freedom the moment it was imperilled. The conclusion is only partly true. The unalterable attachment of a number to the Republic and its independence cannot be denied. Later they became the rallying point for discontent and rebellion. But when Shepstone arrived at Pretoria their protests did not carry the will of the entire people behind them. It was not a united people upon whom Shepstone brutally inflicted a British yoke; it was a people rudderless through the failure of their Government, angry at the mismanagement of their President, perplexed by the quarrels and helplessness of their leaders, and nervous of Zulu attack. In the Orange Free State during the desperate months of 1858 men had turned to the British Government and were ready to welcome a closer connection with the British colonies. So now in the Transvaal, greatly more distraught than the Free State had ever been, many men saw in confederation and the British name a promise of help and relief. The £90,000 promised to Brand had impressed many. Amongst some there was even a shrugging of shoulders at the inevitable. Thus the coming of Shepstone was not altogether unpopular, more especially because the Dutch could not deny their respect to a man whose power of "managing" the natives was legendary. But Shepstone and through him the British Government misunderstood, and misunderstood to their own undoing, the explanation of the generally forbearing and mild reception accorded them, misunderstood the housewives who readily baked bread for soldiers on march, and the officials who signified their willingness to continue to hold office. The explanation was that the annexation was not regarded as a conquest that gave the victors any rights over Boer liberties and privileges.

How many times in his public despatches and in his conversations with Molteno and the two Presidents had Carnarvon not insisted that under confederation the greatest latitude would be given to local traditions and institutions? That the Transvaal should become British soil only to have its institutions suppressed and an autocracy of Natal and Cape officials who snubbed its leaders placed over it was unexpected and intolerable. Yet this is precisely what the British annexation did. Later pages will seek to explain how small-hearted economy and pitiful tactlessness ruined the British chances of holding the Transvaal.

The opposition which did exist in the Transvaal was far from insignificant. Try as he might Shepstone could not close his eyes to it. But he made no effort to mitigate it or win its tolerance, receiving his adversaries with a cold and offending formality, and treating them as obstructionists and almost as rebels. "All of the intelligence of the country is with us," he wrote to Bulwer, "but there is a class, and a large one, that must see the strong arm before they will yield."[1]

Two members of the Transvaal Executive, Paul Kruger and Jorissen the Attorney General, were appointed to confer with Shepstone. After the first interview in which he informed them that nothing could save the independence of the state, he abandoned them to the rude mercy of Osborne, the magistrate of Newcastle, and Henderson, father-in-law of one of his sons. The selection of Henderson was nothing less than a cynical rebuff of the very man who was destined to become one of the greatest figures of South African history. The presence of Henderson in Shepstone's intimate entourage can only serve to cast a doubt upon his good faith; for Henderson, originally a banker, was one of the prime movers in Natal's railway construction, and therefore opposed to the scheme of a rival Transvaal railway. He was intelligent, industrious and very capable in financial matters. His devotion however was rather to Shepstone than to the Transvaal, and to himself rather than to Shepstone. In the language of American political life he was a lobbyist, one of those men who are ever ready to inveigle themselves into, or if they are powerful and well connected, impose themselves upon the counsels and

[1] G.D. 6/38, Shepstone to Bulwer, 7 Feb. 1877.

activities of Governments; one of those men born of a business civilization who seek to make the Government of the people serve the prosperity and success of their own undertakings. Of Henderson's meetings with Kruger the only result could be deadlock and irritation.

It was more valuable, however, that Shepstone should secure the support or the good will of the Volksraad. Having made up his mind that nothing would deter him from declaring the Transvaal British territory, it would only have been in accordance with his private and official instructions if he could either have provided the Volksraad with a formula permitting it to accept the inevitable, or have given such assurances as might have enabled the Boer leaders to accept the future with honour and dignity. Instead he sat stolidly by while the Volksraad formed itself into a *concilium de emendanda ecclesia* and floundered towards its own extinction. To protests he replied that the country had proved its inability to govern itself and had gambled away its independence. To impress them still further with their helplessness he grimly warned them that the Zulus were massed on the frontier and that he might not be able to hold them back.

Burgers' speeches before the Volksraad, passionately and brilliantly delivered, were models of evasiveness. Dexterously and almost in the same breath he presented himself as the advocate of confederation with the British colonies and of continued independence. Beneath the cloak of a stirring appeal to the honour and patriotism of the Volksraad and the people, which the members could not forbear to applaud, there lay concealed an insincerity that bordered on duplicity. In laying before the legislature a project for wide reforms which were at the same time a Declaration of Independence, a Bill of Rights and a Reform Bill, he was merely trying to blend enough of defiance —*belli simulacra cientes*—with enough of co-operation to reconcile himself with Kruger and Shepstone alike, and to give the burghers the impression that he would only go down to defeat honourably. It is almost certain that there was a secret understanding between the President and the Special Commissioner. "I had thought", reported Shepstone to Frere, "that I should be ready to annex the Transvaal in a few days from this date, but last night I found to my surprise that Mr Burgers, who has been all along, so far as his conversation and professions to me went, in full accord with me, had suddenly taken alarm."[1] More than a year later Sir Bartle Frere wrote to Sir Michael Hicks Beach that at the time of the annexation Mr Philip Watermeyer, a member of the Cape Assembly, was a guest in Burgers' house. Through him Shepstone assured the President that if he gave up all idea of resistance his personal interests would not suffer from the annexation, and that he would be recommended to Her Majesty's Government for a life pension of £1000 per year.[2] The language of certain minutes in the Colonial Office and the subsequent remarks and fears of Burgers show that the President had placed the British Government under a definite obligation to him. When accounts reached England of his resistance to Shepstone Carnarvon spoke of a "treachery" that obviously did not mean treachery towards the Transvaal. The relations between Burgers and Shepstone almost certainly were prearranged. Shepstone entering the Transvaal was therefore a little like a mediaeval bishop entering a church that was about to be consecrated. To his knocking upon the outer doors of the Transvaal and the cry of *tollite portas* Burgers, like the priest lurking within the church who represented the forces of evil, made a show of resistance, and then as Shepstone advanced forward with reassuring promises that the British Government meant well by the Transvaal, slipped unobtrusively away to Cape Town to protest tearfully to the High Commissioner his innocence and his need of a pension.[3]

One cannot follow the deliberations of the Transvaal Volksraad without commiseration. Dazzled and yet bewildered by the

---

[1] G.D. 6/33, Shepstone to Frere, 3 April 1877.
[2] The reader is referred to the emphatic pages of Professor Uys, *op. cit.* on this point.
[3] C.O. 291/1, Conf., Shepstone to Hicks Beach, 16 Jan. 1878. It was decided in the Colonial Office to give him a temporary allowance of £500. "He is deserving", minuted Herbert, "of high praise, and placed H.M. Govt. under a great obligation in that he prevailed upon the Boers who were only too ready to fight to accept the inevitable and to protest peacefully. I consider that he saved us from a very serious collision with the Boers, the memory of which would never have passed out of their pugnacious minds. I think it impossible in any case to repudiate Sir T. Shepstone's promise of a pension, but in this case I think the man whatever his faults (and they are great) has deserved one."

President's oratory, intimidated by Kruger's armed followers, agitated by rumours of British regiments and Zulu impis, they threw out the President's scheme for reforms and only at the end of the session in a mood of stunned pessimism did they desperately and blindly pass a Treason Act, conferring large powers on the President as if in the futile hope that the strength of their resolution might possibly stay Shepstone's hand. Thereupon they disbanded and, as a last cutting reminder of the depth to which the state had fallen, found that there was not even money enough to pay their travelling expenses. The Transvaal, none could deny after the disclosures of the session, had not the resources nor the power to maintain its independence.

The formal annexation proclaimed on 12 April 1877 was received without disturbance and without acclaim. At such a turn of events Shepstone was not simply glad; he was relieved. His grim manner was a mask for doubt. But he had insight enough to know that the doubt of the Boer leaders was greater than his own. He waited as long as he did in the hope that the leaders would offer him the Transvaal, or admit the necessity of annexation. They did nothing, and thereby virtually admitted failure.

The Transvaal had lost its independence. The all-important question was now what the British Government planned to do. Upon the answer to that question depended the real decision of the Transvaal people upon the extinction of their independence. The protest signed by the Executive Council was formal, as Burgers took care to indicate to Shepstone. With a single exception the republican officials signified their gladness to serve under the new administration. The exception was Paul Kruger, the new man of destiny. Of him it may be said that he achieved greatness in his old age, yet in truth he also had greatness thrust upon him. He had a body that would have been gross and an expression that would have been heavy but for that craggy head and those eyes filled with an unflinching light. The countenance which his pictures show indicates a sombre mood, a taciturn and unyielding spirit. He possessed the unshrinking and courageous temper of the Puritan, American or South African, who had withdrawn into the wilderness with a resolution as unlimited as his faith in God. He was stubborn. His powers of obstinacy outran his vision. He became the tragic figure he was because in the last resort he failed to impose his exclusive and narrow ideals upon an epoch that had changed too fast and too completely to be resisted by a personality who was but the last bulwark of an antiquated society. Yet his stubbornness was not blind or un-reasonable. Though he had the pioneer Boer's deep suspicion of outlandish and unsettling English ways, he did not object in his old age to being photographed with his arm leaning on a massive King James' version, and he had a thoroughly English respect for law and order, even when it was imposed by an English Government. Though he had a commando of 400 men at his back his manner towards Shepstone was mild. Instead of the forthright and gruff rebuttal of his opponent's contentions that might have come from a man of such small schooling, rustic life and set views, he freely admitted the collapse of the administration and actually pleaded that the Transvaal be given an opportunity of re-establishing its credit and reorganizing its Government. But to Shepstone and his entourage Kruger was a man to be re-strained and not placated. There were not many at the time who succeeded in distinguishing the singular force behind his un-couth and, to some people, offensive exterior. "Mr Paul Kruger", wrote Frere in June 1877, "is a rough and plain likeness of Mr Edwin Chadwick.... I am assured by those who know him well that he is a very shrewd fellow, who veils under an assumed clownish manner and affectation of ignorance considerable ability, that he has great natural eloquence and powers of persuasion. There is certainly nothing in what is visible to strangers to indi-cate a possible regenerator of the Transvaal."[1] There can hardly be any doubt that the British officers and officials, obedient to the precision and orderliness of their training, the polite usages of the table and the ballroom, and the conventional decorum of social intercourse, were apt to regard the conduct for example of a Boer camp, with its undisciplined procedures, as indicating the absence of other and more important qualities. It is quite clear that Shepstone and Carnarvon allowed the misfortunes of Burgers' regime to impress them too easily with the political incapacity of the new British subjects. Of the Boer character, his political

---

[1] G.D. 6/33, Frere to Carnarvon, 5 June 1877.

I

thought and ideals there was much misunderstanding. Men fashioned by a society in which class differences were both pronounced and easily distinguishable, in which proprieties of dress, habits of personal cleanliness and good manners tend to be accepted as reliable symbols of deeper and more essential qualities, are in danger of failing to penetrate understandingly behind the less decorous, less elaborate and more ungracious mode of life of a society such as that of the Transvaal with its sluggish social and intellectual life and its weaker economic development. Gazing upon the well known picture of Paul Kruger as President clumsily wearing his high hat and morning clothes, the citizen of a modern and prosperous South African city can scarcely suppress the embarrassing query how such a man could ever have left an indelible mark on the history of the British Empire. Shepstone and his associates, and later Carnarvon as well, were altogether misled by his unprepossessing appearance. "Paul Kruger", wrote Morcom, the lawyer of Shepstone's mission, "is an elderly man, decidedly ugly, with a countenance denoting extreme obstinacy, and also great cruelty. His conduct at the public luncheon on Tuesday was as the Belgian Consul described it 'gigantically horrible'. His dirty wooden pipe was visible, for it stuck out of his breast pocket; his scanty hair was in such a condition of greasiness that it lay in streaks across his head, the drops of rancid coconut oil gathering at the ends of each streak of hair, and thus rendering necessary the use of his pocket comb during lunch. The napkin was turned to strange uses during lunch."[1] It was a comment that described nothing. Boer leaders owed their position to character and accomplishment rather than to rank and wealth or table manners. No man was followed gladly if he lived and acted unlike other men. Therein Burgers had erred. Almost to the last man the Boer leaders with whom the British administration had to deal were unprepossessing ordinary looking men whose services it did not seem important to win. There is much reason for suggesting that the inability or unwillingness to recognize the intrinsic qualities of the Boer temperament, and the failure to understand the nature of their political experience and ideals, contributed to a carelessness and

[1] G.D. 6/38, Shepstone to Bulwer, 7 Feb. 1877.

short-sightedness that was punished by political failure and military humiliation. No great civilization has ever displayed in comparable measure Great Britain's political genius for developing and giving successful life to self-governing institutions, or for inspiring the officials in its dependencies with an enlightened desire to govern efficiently, generously and justly. Yet, even though it must be admitted that the British flag flew over the Transvaal for only four short and stormy years, it may well be asked whether the British administration of the Transvaal did not belie these qualities.

A last effort was made by those who opposed Shepstone to appeal to Downing Street. After great difficulty a sum of money was raised to pay the expenses of Kruger and Jorissen. It would seem only consistent with the career of a man who later became the hero of Dutch racial pride, to maintain that his mission to England betokened an invincible opposition to the British connection. Yet the evidence suggests that as a member of the Executive Council Kruger was too well aware of the conditions which had led to annexation not to appreciate the possible advantages of the British regime. Only an unreasonable tactfulness or an undiscriminating patriotism would insist on representing Paul Kruger as the unrepentant leader of those who would never under any circumstances accept the British flag. True, he would never love the "Englander", and he would prefer independence to British rule, but if that rule were acceptable he was undoubtedly prepared to come to terms with it. Paul Kruger was no sentimental visionary. He was hard-bitten and a realist. In spite of their mission of protest both Kruger and Jorissen felt it wise to make friends with the mammon of unrighteousness before leaving. Both delegates asked for an understanding that their salaries should be paid in their absence by the new administration, and Jorissen asked for an assurance that he would not forfeit his position as Attorney General.

Upon Jorissen's words little significance can be placed. Inferior to his companion in everything but his ability to speak English and write "High Dutch", he was a clerkish figure, scanty in his knowledge of the law, as bankrupt as the administration he had served, so that his wife and children had to live on a pound a week while he was abroad. In taking leave of Shepstone both delegates were careful to explain that they were going to England "to discharge an obligation which had been imposed upon them". They were performing a reasonable duty and if they failed, said Kruger, "with the frankness which has always characterized his intercourse with me", he would be as faithful a subject under the British regime as he had been under the old. With yet greater frankness Jorissen admitted that the change was inevitable and even ventured the belief that a return to the old order would be calamitous.

The interview between Carnarvon and Kruger in August 1877 tends to confirm the view that Kruger could have been reconciled to the annexation, provided no violence was done to the Transvaal's institutions and customs. The policy which Carnarvon had announced had been a policy of incorporation; in the new South African confederation which he planned it had been promised that each community would lose only that part of its identity that was claimed by the common interest. The abruptness of the annexation and the manner assumed by Shepstone gave Kruger to fear that what had been intended as a policy of incorporation might be turned into an act of confiscation, and that the British officials would enter the Transvaal as reformers and remain and act as its conquerors. The questions he asked of Carnarvon show his concern. What was to be the fate of the Dutch language under the British Government? In what manner did the British Government intend to treat the native population? The questions reveal what were amongst the leading preoccupations of Kruger's mind. In reply Carnarvon assured him that the Transvaal would have to submit to no sudden or rash changes, and that far from having to fear the effects of British annexation it would soon have ample cause for satisfaction. Before the eyes of Kruger he dangled a vision of a country with telegraphs, roads, railways, a share in the customs dues, and union with its neighbours. Kruger was not blind to these advantages. But what mattered, he replied to Carnarvon, was the popular vote. Would Lord Carnarvon permit the Transvaal people to "speak out their mind" on the annexation? It was the most embarrassing question he could possibly have asked. It disclosed the blunder that the British Government had committed in failing to base its authority upon some expression of opinion, either by the people or its Government. Not all the memorials that Shepstone had received, nor the numerous private visits from sympathetic Boer leaders could ever be a substitute. Whatever mistakes the new Government might commit, all the difficulties it could not help but encounter would strengthen the hands of its opponents. Until this omission had been made good the odour of injustice and oppression would cling to British acts. Kruger admitted the failings of the old administration with candour; he agreed that what was done could not be undone, and once again promised his loyal co-operation. But still he urged that a vote be taken. Carnarvon was willing that the Transvaal should vote upon any large constitutional question such as confederation with Natal, as long as approval or disapproval of the annexation was not involved. It was clear of course, as Kruger himself was bound to admit, that the British Government could not undo the annexation. But it was equally obvious that such opinion as Kruger represented could never, in spite of assurances of loyalty, be reconciled to the annexation unless it could find under the British Government a place that was consistent with Boer traditions and customs. In other words, the British Government was accepted by the Transvaal population on trial. Throughout the interview Kruger's manner and speech carried the suggestion that his expressions of loyalty were conditional upon the acceptability of the new regime. When he left his last words once more expressed the wish that Carnarvon should not "forget the very important point of the vote". Carnarvon had no reason to feel that the words of such a man might convey a threat.

Not the least regrettable outcome of the method in which the annexation had been carried out was its effect upon public opinion in Europe. A growing resentment in France, Germany and Holland towards British colonial policy saw in the annexation and the subsequent rebellion of the Dutch an opportunity for hostile criticism. The British Government had annexed an independent foreign state. Nor could such criticism be easily refuted, especially since the opponents of British policy were permitted to introduce into the debate all the powerful and popular vocabulary of self-determination, self-government and, what was in 1877 still a new-fangled phrase, the autonomy of peoples. The earliest blows were struck by professors in the universities of Holland, who represented the Boers as modern Pilgrim Fathers who had fled vainly into a dangerous interior in order to shake a monarchical and imperial dust from their feet. And because it was true that public opinion in the Transvaal had not been consulted, and because Great Britain had replaced their self-governing institutions by an almost military autocracy it was difficult to reply that the language of European nationalism could not be made to apply to the special conditions of South Africa.

It is a natural tendency to conclude that the withdrawal of British authority from the Transvaal in 1881 was a belated atone-ment for a wrongful and unwarranted act. But the weight of evidence is still on the side of the belief that in 1877 the Trans-vaal could no longer stand of its own strength, and that the general attitude to the annexation was such that if Shepstone had had the courage to submit his act to the Volksraad it would most probably have been ratified. It is one of the anomalies of history that an act so audacious as the annexation of the Trans-vaal should have been followed by a policy so dismally lacking in intuition, constructiveness and the same quality of audacity. Hence it is not enough to maintain that the single blunder of the annexation led to the undoing of Carnarvon's entire policy. Nor can the Boer uprising that brought the British occupation to an inglorious end be explained by speaking glibly of the attachment of the Transvaal Boers to their independent and republican insti-tutions. Granting the full magnitude of the original mistake, it was a mistake that could have been repaired without the lowering of the British flag, had there not been added to it such an un-bearable accumulation of misunderstanding, error and misfortune that the best conceived and most popular of policies must have collapsed beneath the strain.

CHAPTER VI

SIR BARTLE FRERE

THE annexation and its aftermath offended a sentiment that was unfathomable by men like Wolseley and Frere whose love was for a cool green country, lush of grass and gentle of climate, and who therefore never really understood the deep attachment of the Boers to a country subject to long searing droughts when for months the dust that rose from the cracked soil almost obscured the setting sun, a country without real rivers, save when the thundering and flaming sky deluged the earth and swept away its richness in those innumerable gullies and watercourses that made roadbuilding in some parts of the country almost impossible. Yet this land, in which the Boers owned farms sprawling each of them over ten or a dozen square miles, inspired an affection fully as profound as that of the French peasant for an equal number of acres. The natural tendency, especially in England, to see behind the misleading word " Boers " a poor and ignorant peasantry, hid the truth that many of them were large proprietors, of exceeding self-respect, keenly aware of their superior race in the midst of the native population, and on the whole well fitted to the land they lived in. They were mindful, as a result of the isolation and slender immigration of the eighteenth century, of their family connections which were so wide and numerous that at the time of the British annexation it was claimed that the population of the Transvaal was mainly composed of thirty family groups. Just as the French peasant naturally asks after the *pays* of the stranger whom he meets, so was it the Dutch farmer's normal mode of greeting to ask after the family name of the stranger.

With their faces turned inland and away from the sea they knew little of European or imperial exigencies. Sincere and punctilious in their devotions, they had a deep respect for legally constituted authority. They were easy to govern, except for an irreducible dislike of direct taxation, and although not to be driven without exciting the most obstinate resistance, easily swayed by the talent or the eloquence of their leaders. In a day when there were no modern industrial towns, rich and poor lived on their farms the undifferentiated lives of frontiersmen, free of the discipline of fashion, expert at breaking in an ox or a horse, good shots and eager hunters, able to tan leather, make bricks, work in wood and stone, and withal hospitable and kind to strangers. Although there were already apparent significant differences in wealth beneath the uniformity of dress, speech and behaviour, poverty in the sense that poverty was known in an English industrial town was absent. Marriage came early and children were welcome. When a boy was born his parents gave him a mare, a cow and some sheep. When he reached marriageable age he might have two hundred sheep, forty head of cattle and a dozen horses, enough to stock the new farm which was the height of his ambition. It was this passion for the individual ownership of great acreages that caused the constant pressure upon the land of the natives, and which was the mainspring of the Boer's political thought and conduct.

The annexation had found a new Governor and High Commissioner in Cape Town. The name of Sir Bartle Frere is intimately connected with these difficult years. When he arrived at Cape Town at the end of March 1877, it was the Home Government that trusted him and the Cape colonists who feared him. When he left Cape Town three and a half years later he left under the cloud of censure from the Home Government, but with the admiration and esteem of the colonists. The story of his governorship could not be more concisely told, for according to the special logic of South African governorships he could not both have won the affection of the colonists and carried out his instructions from Downing Street.

When Lord Carnarvon asked him to succeed Barkly he thought of him as a personage considerable enough to be the first Governor General of a confederated South Africa. Only a year younger than Molteno, Frere had reached an age when men who had spent onerous and profitable years in Her Majesty's service in tropical climates were usually content with their honours and happy to return finally to the coolness of England. To such a man the offer of a mere governorship could have no attractions.

But to his eager imagination the wide ambition of leading a notoriously intractable country into harmony had an instant appeal. Leaving England against his own convenience and at no small self-sacrifice he nevertheless went gladly in the hope of crowning his work by what he recognized would be an imperial and historic achievement.

No South African Governor had come so rich in a varied experience. For nine years he had been Chief Commissioner in Scinde; he had been Governor of Bombay, and a member both of the Viceroy's Council and of the Council for India. The Geographical Society had made him its President and he had been honoured by both Oxford and Cambridge. In 1872 he had been sent to Zanzibar to negotiate the suppression of the slave trade. He belonged to the new generation of imperialists announced by Livingstone and realized by Chamberlain. He was one of the really original band of African imperialists who discovered to themselves and to the world that Africa was more than a *terra incognita* lying between alternative routes to India. He was of those that used their influence to build a more coherent and powerful Empire in which the parts should be more conscious of their common attachment. While he was willing to recognize, for example, the right of the Cape colonists to self-government, he felt that the soil they occupied was as British as their essential allegiance. The guiding principle of his Empire was not the loose and voluntary bond of free and self-governing states but the more disciplined association of colonies and possessions about the superior and protective might of the Mother Country. To Frere Colony and Mother Country were bound together so that neither could forgo its relationship or escape its responsibility. Without this knowledge of Frere's thought it is difficult to understand his handling of such controversial issues as his historic dismissal of Molteno's Ministry in 1878 and his readiness to make war upon the Zulus upon his own responsibility. He dismissed Molteno because the Cape Ministry had in his judgment lost sight of imperial interests; he waged the Zulu War because he conceived it to be the proper duty of the British Government to protect its subjects, even if they were unwilling ones like the Transvaal Boers.

It was natural that on reaching South Africa he should endeavour to see beyond even the achievement of confederation
and see South Africa in a still wider imperial setting. His vision
reached easily and naturally to a distance that even Boer expansiveness had hitherto hardly envisaged. Because of his experience
in India and on the east coast of Africa he could see the continent's southernmost tip in a proportion and in a light in which
few South Africans had as yet learned to see their own country.
More than anybody else did he become the link between Sir John
Kirk and Cecil Rhodes. Expansion into the unannexed native
regions, the firm delimitation of Portuguese claims and annexation of the east and west coasts as far north as possible, the
control, if not the annexation, of the interior territory as far as
the Zambesi and beyond—such were the proposals that reached
Downing Street within the year. To read Frere is to discover the
essential unoriginality of Rhodes. Rhodes did not discover African
imperialism. His task was to set it on high like an oriflamme.

On imperial defence he naturally had much to say. The Cape
Colony was an important link in the system of imperial defences.
Within three months of his arrival he had examined the state of
its defences and read through the recorded correspondence with
the War Office. His despatches and private letters struck a note
of indignation and alarm. For years past the replies of the War
Office to "reasonable and well considered requests" for means
of defending Her Majesty's flag at the Cape had been little more
than repetitions of Mr Lowe's famous dictum, that if "British
subjects *will* go abroad for their own profit or pleasure, they must
defend themselves". He had left an England where men talked
of war with Russia. Here at Cape Town people were talking
still of the visit a few years before of the Grand Duke Alexis
himself. What reports had the smart young Russian officers with
him sent to the Russian Foreign Office about the defencelessness
of this British possession? He discerned a sinister wit in their
waggish threat to requisition a million or two in cash and carry
off Sir Henry Barkly and Mr Molteno. And then there were the
German men-of-war that had recently so leisurely refitted in
Simon's Bay, the Emperor of Brazil's two men-of-war and the
tramps that brought sugar and coffee from Rio and mules from

Montevideo, dangerous testimony all of them to a rich and easy prize that must prove tempting, especially to "American skippers with a turn for filibustering".[1]

The prose of colonial Governors and even of Secretaries of State and their subordinates is commonly so dull that in retrospect the historian feels that he has mumbled his way through their tens of thousands of pages. Yet, like friendly islands in a monotonous sea, there occasionally appear the phrases of Bulwer Lytton, vivid and entertaining when they are decipherable, the lucidity and wittiness of Fairfield, or the literary skill and vivacity of Frere. The plain letters that Sir Henry Barkly wrote in his inelegant hand to a Secretary of State who did not always trouble to answer them, become now the graceful hand and easy sentences of a keen and rich mind. It is Frere's civilized pen that first does justice to the unholy marriage of a rich Bantu skin and the dirty, ragged garments that were the outward sign of the new social status of the natives; that saw illuminating resemblances between Dutch and Welsh farmers, and between Cape politics and the politics of the Thirteen Colonies. His educated mind enlightened and enriched whatever he recorded. His exuberant intelligence, his clear ringing style, and the spate of his phrases, ideas, images and arguments were a headier draught for the colonists than the gallantry of Sir Harry Smith or the transient splendour of a Grand Duke. Small wonder certainly that the caution of Molteno should fit ill with the Governor's impulsive and ambitious mentality. The difference between the two men was the greater because Frere had a certain recklessness, strange perhaps in so experienced an administrator, and yet the natural defect of his strongest qualities. In consequence he lacked the judicial habit of mind, the mild and conciliatory courtesy that had made Molteno love Barkly, which would have made him an umpire in a land of disputes rather than what he really was—a man too experienced in action, too eager to arrive at success to co-operate easily with men whose inexperience was natural, whose independence was fettered by party and locality, and whose vision penetrated the future with more of concern and less of boldness —perhaps because that future was their responsibility. To the

[1] G.D. 6/33, Frere to Carnarvon, 11 June 1877.

Colonial Office the conviction and ardour of his address made him a somewhat uncertain guide to the affairs of South Africa. Precisely because of their urgency his despatches and his letters became inadequate sources of official information. He bethumped Downing Street with words and there was perhaps real design in the abnormally large number of despatches by Sir Michael Hicks Beach merely "acknowledging" the receipt of his communications.

The coming of such a man was viewed in Cape Town with not a little apprehension. Those who wished Molteno and his cabinet little good caused the rumour to spread that the new Governor was coming out with extraordinary power to override all opposition, send Molteno packing and revolutionize South Africa.[1] Molteno himself was suspicious of what Frere might do. Shortly after Frere's arrival he declared by way of warning that the Governor of the Cape Colony took advice from his Ministers, but that Ministers did not take advice from the Governor. "Any memoranda", Molteno wrote, "of their final opinion on important subjects were generally submitted in draft to the Governor as a matter of convenience to avoid taking him by surprise, but not with any view to further discussion."[2]

It was at this point that there commenced the struggle between imperial exigencies and the constitutional sufficiency of the Colony. It was a struggle in which the oppugnant elements were destined never really to come to grips, for no Governor had ever been so belaboured by unforeseen blows or so diverted from his premeditated aims by necessities for which he had not prepared himself. In measuring Frere's success or his failure the pressure of simultaneous crises falling upon him and the responsibility for problems which he had not been led to anticipate need constantly to be remembered.

It was with keen interest that he looked upon the scene of his coming labours. As befitted one who had been president of the Royal Geographical Society he travelled gladly. "The scenery is very striking", he noted, "but the people are still more than half asleep. They put me much in mind of the Welsh in the most re-

[1] G.D. 6/33, Frere to Carnarvon, 4 April 1877.
[2] C.O. 48/482, D. 5, Frere to Carnarvon, 17 April 1877.

mote parts of Wales. But the Railway is stirring them up wonderfully. We saw something of some of the Boers, and Wine producing Farmers, and I think we may make more of them than I had expected. They were very friendly but like most people here, seemed rather to expect a snubbing, and to be a little agreeably surprised if one seems pleased and glad to see them."[2] Most of all was he impressed with the manner in which South Africa turned its eyes away from the sea, gazing inwards and upon itself. The isolation of the previous century had left its mark in the peculiarly South African tendency to look upon itself as a world apart and thus to permit its own problems to take on those dimensions that made South African thought often seem so parochial and limited.

He had arrived in Cape Town just a fortnight before the annexation of the Transvaal. He found Cape Town aware of the probable outcome of Shepstone's mission. Molteno himself was in favour of annexation, provided it received the support of the Transvaal population. The prospects for confederation seemed distinctly brighter. Molteno had returned in a mood less intractably opposed to the policy of the Home Government. Chastened by the coldness with which Downing Street had wished him godspeed, and impressed by Carnarvon's determination to advance against all odds, he now expressed to Frere his readiness to annex the diamond fields. A sensible and shrewd man, thought Frere, and wondered whether a K.C.M.G. given as a reward for past services might not capture his fuller loyalty. Molteno was not indifferent to "monarchical gewgaws". But he was not greedy of the honour and did not permit his views to be influenced by the temptation. He insisted still that it would be the more generally acceptable and easier plan to advance the Cape Parliament to the dignity of the Union Parliament, adding to it a fair proportion of representatives for each province, and increasing the powers of the divisional councils to meet the wants of the more remote provinces. But he now also spoke of retirement[1] to facilitate the changes the near future might hold, and seemed to be ready to adopt or support whatever scheme might have the best chance of being carried.

[1] G.D. 6/33, Frere to Carnarvon, 9 April 1877.

Then came the news of the Transvaal annexation. Hard upon its heels arrived the revised draft of Carnarvon's Permissive Bill. Frere was exultant. But the faces of those about him were blank and unhappy, even though they had known that Shepstone had gone up to the Transvaal with the British flag in his baggage. Shepstone had been too precipitate, they declared. The Home Government would certainly reverse the annexation. No attempt had been made to enlist the support of the Cape Government. Almost brutally the Home Government had tried to force its hand. If any proof were needed of the complicity of Downing Street there was the Permissive Bill which arrived with revealing opportuneness immediately after the annexation. Molteno shook his head. Upon the Permissive Bill he looked sourly and sunk into an obstinate silence that Frere could not break. Frere complained of such confused and oblique vision. "You must not think I am unduly depreciating my fellow workmen", he excused himself. "I merely wish to remind you that administration in Radnorshire is very different from government in Middlesex, and that I am at present in Wales."[1] But he was not bitter. There was no need. The resistance of Molteno and his colleagues would be vain. The ground had been cut from beneath their feet; they had no choice left and confederate they must. In the Transvaal Carnarvon now had an irresistible lever. To it could be joined Natal, Griqualand West and, added Frere significantly, to it could also be added the Cape Eastern Province. In other words, Molteno was to be compelled to yield or else definite encouragement would be given to the East to renew its former separatist agitation.

Actually both this scheme and the suggestion that a union of Natal and the Transvaal would give the nucleus of confederation were of the most illusory nature. A confederation which excluded the richer of the two Republics and the richest of the British colonies was a vain hope. Without the inclusion of the Cape there could not possibly be any acceptable political arrangement. Only under its leadership could the full self-government be achieved which would permit Great Britain to withdraw from an active participation in South African affairs.

[1] G.D. 6/33, Frere to Carnarvon, 12 May 1877.

Carnarvon himself was fully aware of the importance of winning the Cape. During the anxious weeks in July and August 1877, while the Permissive Bill was the sport of Great Britain's troubles in Eastern Europe and Ireland, he wrote frequently to Frere asking him to tell the Cape Ministry that opinion on both sides of the House favoured the measure. When, after hearing of the success of Shepstone's mission, he introduced an amendment to the bill permitting the annexation of the Transvaal to Natal, he hastened to assure the Cape Ministry that it now provided equally for a "confederated or a unified form of government",[1] and sent fair copies of his speech in the House of Lords to the Cape press lest they receive a misleading impression from the London papers. He actually welcomed the battered and vague form in which the bill finally emerged, hoping that its very want of definition would leave room for compromise with the Cape. After all, he told Frere, "between a Union composed of members elected to the Cape Parliament by the Cape, Natal and the Transvaal with subsidiary municipal governments and a Union composed of members elected to a federal Parliament by the Cape, Natal and the Transvaal with subsidiary provincial governments there *may* be no difference but one of name".[2]

Carnarvon's South Africa Act did not receive the royal consent until 10 August 1877.[3] It is usually lightly dismissed as a vague, mutilated and impractical instrument. The very manner of its passing had seemed an omen of its ultimate fate. Parliament stumbled impatiently over the bill as it hastened to consider the near Eastern crisis. O'Donnell, Parnell and the Irish members struck a blow for Ireland by showering seventy amendments on to the paper, and by plunging into such obstruction that the decorous Mother of Parliaments was for a while the hubbub of imperial institutions.

The Act bore upon its face the signs of its own fruitlessness. Belying its title it revealed British policy in the very act of abandoning the calm channels of diplomacy and debate in order to enter the swifter and more dangerous currents that swept to-

[1] *Ibid.* Carnarvon to Frere, 23 May 1877.
[2] *Ibid.* Carnarvon to Frere, 11 Sept. 1877.
[3] 40 and 41 Victoria, c. 47.

wards annexation. It revealed British policy, to change the figure, with its feet in two camps, hoping that its benevolence would not be doubted though it had raised its hand to strike. An Act that was described to Parliament as a tentative framework, a convenience of which the colonists might avail themselves in designing their common political life, could also be described as an instrument of constraint. The number of "quasi Crown Colonies" would, by the annexation of the Transvaal, be increased to the number of three, not one of them self-governing, all of them subject to the will of Her Majesty's Secretary of State. With these bound into a preliminary federation, the Home Government hoped more easily to force the hand of Brand and Molteno. It was as if Carnarvon's hand, after feeling vainly for the heart of the problem, had closed tightly on a limb in the desperate and unreasoning hope that he might thereby capture and work his will with the entire body.

Nevertheless the critic who reads carefully the provisions of the Act cannot fail to discover the evidence they give of a deeper and more vital purpose than the constraining of unwilling colonial communities. It is a temptation not easily resisted to follow the noise and tumult of the misunderstanding between Boer and Briton, and to allow the dust of their altercations to obscure what was at the same time the chief problem of South African life and the most important preoccupation of British policy—that native question which, as Carnarvon informed the House of Lords, "long has been, and must be for many years to come, the hinge upon which South African policy must turn".[1] In an Act that was otherwise vague and wanting in detail the only emphatic note was concerned with the native policy of the new confederation.

It was of moment for the British Government to know whether it was fashioning in South Africa a new Canada or a new India; whether the white race should prevail entirely over the black, or whether the Mother Country should hold an even hand between them. That the white colonists, English and Dutch, should be permitted to govern themselves was of the logic of British policy, and the annexation of the Transvaal and the appearance of Jamaican government in Natal could only be a temporary check

Hansard, vol. 233, cols. 1645–6.

to ultimate self-government. But did it follow that the white community should govern not merely itself but the black population as well? The language of the Act showed that Carnarvon intended to reserve to the Home Government the surveillance of native affairs. In evaluating the success or failure of British policy it is not enough, therefore, to point to Majuba and the restoration of the Transvaal. It is equally important to know firstly what the British Government desired to do, and secondly what it was able to do in protecting the natives from the violent and demoralizing assault of European land greed and ignorance. Its failure was announced less by the restoration of the Transvaal to independence and the gulf of resentment that was rent between Dutch and English, than by its failure to do anything to stem the torrent that was rushing the native population into political helplessness and economic hopelessness. The paramount justification for imperial intervention was to reconcile the self-government of the Europeans with the protection of the natives. Therein lay the justification and also the failure of British policy; for it suffered its principal damage between the Scylla and Charybdis of oppugnant native and European interests.

The Act, in other words, merely brought out more clearly how long and difficult the road was to compromise between imperial responsibility and local self-government. In the last resort not confederation but this compromise was the Imperial Government's chief problem. The road to such a compromise was not merely long; above all it was expensive. It could be achieved only if the British Government were willing to assume the financial responsibilities of partnership in South African affairs. It was not enough to seek to create a confederation that would assume the entire burden. The policy of *laissez-faire* against which Carnarvon was in rebellion had sought inexpensive forms of colonial Government. It had hated native wars not because of the harm the natives always received from them, but because native wars were expensive. An opposite policy was impossible without financial sacrifice. By the very justification he had given for the annexation of the Transvaal, namely its bankruptcy, and by the explanation he had given of Southey's dismissal, namely the impending bankruptcy of Griqualand West, Carnarvon had

K

shown how discerning had been the refusal of the Cape to
assume the arduous leadership of the subcontinent. By its own
words and actions the British Government had demonstrated
how much South Africa had need of its continued presence and
support. That support to be really efficacious had to be given, not
in the hour of disaster or crisis when British treasure always
flowed generously and unstintingly, but in the hour of peace,
conscious of its purpose and with calm deliberation.

The hoisting of the British flag in the Transvaal soon showed
that confederation could not be hurried. Carnarvon did continue to speak of it as nigh at hand. It was not so. In vain Frere
assured Molteno that it had become easier and more imperative
to co-operate with the Home Government. The "Old Dutch
Party" looked askance upon the solicitude for native affairs expressed in the Act, and feared the return to South Africa of what
after forty years they still called an "Exeter Hall Policy". Even
liberal thought in the Cape was suspicious, fearing that a too
close connection with the Transvaal would favour a "Boer
policy of severity and repression" towards the natives. Molteno
found Cape public sentiment in agreement that the Cape could
not take upon itself the bankrupt Transvaal of British propaganda. Confederation was indefinitely postponed. How indefinitely it was postponed and by what disasters not even its
strongest opponents realized.

In preparation for the "great and general settlement" that
was to bring all communities within the same constitution and
under the same flag, Carnarvon had to provide for the Government of the newly annexed province. It was when he considered
the form of Government to be given to the Transvaal that he became aware of the quicksand into which he had wilfully stepped.
What had seemed so clear and evident a few months before the
annexation was now uncertain and perplexed. He knew, if he
had not known it before, that the majority of Transvaal opinion
was not unreservedly in favour of the new regime, and that its
essential loyalty was still to be won. That loyalty could not be
won by reducing the Transvaal to the standing of a Crown
Colony. Shepstone's proclamation of annexation had spoken of
a Government with its own laws and institutions. Yet to invest

the Transvaal with an independent legislature meant the untimely creation of another parliament like the Cape Parliament with constitutional powers to obstruct imperial policies. Both within and without South Africa the British Government had learned that constitutions once given could not easily be amended, and still less easily be taken away. In Jamaica after emancipation, in British Guiana after free trade in sugar and in the Ionian Islands in the later years of the Protectorate, the British Government had had full experience of what happened when dissatisfied elements were endowed with a measure of political freedom. Hence in the words of Meade the Transvaal could only be given "a Crown colony constitution of the severest type".[1] In the Transvaal Shepstone, although of the opinion that the promise of the proclamation should be redeemed as soon as practicable, nodded in agreement.

This decision made possible the later accusation that the British Government had acted in bad faith and forced an illegal form of Government upon the Transvaal.[2] It was the tragedy of the short-lived British administration of the Transvaal that its autocratic institutions became the vehicle not for a vigorous and effective policy, but for a policy that was unenterprising and weak. In the four unhappy years that followed the annexation the more uncertain the British administration became the more severe and autocratic was its temper. What caused a policy conceived in such boldness to degenerate into such a stiff and unimaginative autocracy? The causes are not altogether to be found within South Africa. They lie in part in world conditions that directly affected British colonial policy.

Properly speaking there is no such thing as a colonial policy distinct from domestic or foreign policy. The possessions and colonies of a great commercial and industrial power like Great Britain are influenced constantly by very many of the same considerations that influence the other great interests of the nation. It is wise to remember that the attitude of the Home Government towards the Transvaal was not single but compound, influenced in

[1] C.O. 291/1, Conf., Shepstone to Carnarvon, 31 July 1877, Minutes.
[2] The Law Officers were of the opinion that the Transvaal was to be regarded as "conquered or ceded" territory, and that the Crown therefore had the power of legislation by Order in Council.

a direct manner, for example, by British relations with Russia, just as in the following decade it was most certainly influenced by relations with Germany. The Empire at large affected each of its parts. The expensiveness of Canadian and New Zealand railway building made it difficult for Natal to receive an imperial guarantee for its railways; the history of Jamaican institutions had an immediate bearing upon those of Natal; the imperial subsidies given to the Fiji Islands and the Gold Coast affected the finances of the Transvaal. Above all did the world wide depression of the 'seventies and 'eighties leave its mark upon the conduct of imperial relations.

In May 1873 the Austrian Bourse collapsed. There followed harrowing months in which depression crept from one financial centre to another. The French luxury trade collapsed; then broke the American market in which British capital was heavily invested; the German hopes that were built high on victory and French indemnities were pricked also. In England, because she was widely interested in American and European countries, the effects were worst. Prices fell and continued to fall. In the midst of what Alfred Marshall called a "depression of prices, a depression of interest, and a depression of profit", the United States, France and Germany began to build tariff walls which intensified competition and challenged British industrial supremacy. The great mid-Victorian flood of British goods and capital was forced to abate its volume, and the press of the nation wrote familiarly of the adverse balance of British trade, while the man in the street began to grow alarmed at the rising tide of foreign imports and hostile dumping. In January 1878 Beaconsfield wrote to the Queen that the Cabinet was "much affected by the depressed state of trade and the great fall in revenue", and took "a dark view of the condition and prospects of the country".[1]

Shaken in the sense of untouchable security that two generations had enjoyed, men looked apprehensively at the problems of British foreign policy and grew more sensitive than they could have been in the previous decade to the maintenance of British

[1] Monypenny and Buckle, vol. VI p. 217. Beaconsfield to the Queen, 9 Jan. 1878.

prestige. Disraeli's purchase of the Suez Canal shares in 1875 and his conduct at the Berlin Congress in 1878 were popular largely because they were spectacular and singular moments in a period of doubt and anxiety. It is evident that public opinion had already begun instinctively to recognize that the duty of British foreign policy had become as never before the duty of protecting the vital economic and commercial interests of the nation. The confident tone in which Palmerston had browbeaten the chancelleries of Europe gave way now to those anxious letters to colonial Governors asking questions about colonial defences, and to a feeling that any European war in which England was involved would call upon the strength of the entire nation. In one manner of speaking the new imperialism inaugurated by the purchase of the Suez Canal shares was defensive and not aggressive. It was less aggrandizement than an unconscious appreciation of the exigencies of Great Britain's lessened stature amongst the powers that caused even Gladstone unwillingly to become imperialist and enter Egypt. Jingoism—the doggerel tune that first contained the word *Jingo* was the Cockney response to Tchaikowsky's *Marche Slave*—was, in spite of its bombastic language, the result of a feeling of discomfort in the face first of Russia and later of Germany. Never before had Free Trade England been so aware of the dangers of war and the blessings of peace. Hence it had been more important in the English mind that Beaconsfield had returned from Berlin in 1878 with peace than with Cyprus.

The bulk of British exports went to nations outside the Empire and the most valuable imports also came from outside the Empire. It was but natural that British policy should rather direct its attention beyond the Empire and overlook even during years of *malaise* the truth that the Empire's trade was valuable and expansive and had kept pace throughout with foreign trade. For over twenty years the Empire had never absorbed less than one-third of the entire British exports, and yet as late even as 1886 the hundreds of questions and answers in the evidence of the Royal Commission concerned themselves overwhelmingly with foreign rather than imperial trade. It is true that colonial tariffs had little effect upon the wide range of commodities from coal to the choicest products of Lancashire and Staffordshire. It is evident that because imperial trade was not hindered by colonial tariffs and because colonial markets were a British preserve upon which foreign trade had not as yet made dangerous inroads, British policy was not inclined to give special consideration to the economic interests of the colonies.

It was against this unwillingness that Carnarvon struggled in insisting, as he did in and out of season, upon the need of an improved system of imperial defence. "I entirely sympathize with you", he wrote to Frere after reading his strictures upon the defencelessness of Table Bay. "In the extraordinary difficulty of getting the simplest and absolutely necessary precautions taken as regards military and naval defence, I have often of late been in despair; and I believe that if we ever go to war and our enemies have the slightest energy and 'dash' we shall suffer terribly from the marvellous 'incuria' of the last few years. The real vice of the situation is that it is impossible to persuade the Treasury to sanction any expense which is not at the moment popular with Parliament: and as Parliament cannot know what is necessary, the ordinary and often essential precautions are neglected."[1]

Thus in part did it come about that the most urgent instructions which the new administration in the Transvaal received concerned the need for careful economy. Local revenue must suffice as far as possible to secure effective government and order. An unforgettable remark by Fairfield shows that the Colonial Office knew full well how seriously limited were the resources of the new colony. The Colonial Office had decided to send to Sir Theophilus Shepstone a small legal library. Fairfield brightly suggested that a book on the poor law should be added because "possibly the local government might be soon called on to consider some measure for the relief of loafers who may come to what is supposed to be an *el dorado*, but is really more in the nature of a howling wilderness".[2] The book was never sent, and Fairfield never knew how nearly he had provided for the coming, not of loafers, but of South Africa's poor whites.

[1] G.D. 6/33, Carnarvon to Frere, 23 July 1877
[2] C.O. 291/1.

It was logical that a colony submitted to a strict economy could not be given liberal institutions. The idea of entrusting power to an elective body, Frere admitted, was now a "wild and impractical suggestion". Shepstone, to do him justice, did recognize the dangers of a narrow and short-sighted economy. He urged that the Home Government be liberal rather than stinting.[1] But his actions were governed by that warning from Carnarvon which said: "I need not remind you how very desirable it is not to come upon Imperial assistance in point of view of money more than is necessary. The feeling of Parliament is now, I believe, very favourable to the whole policy; but Parliament does not like to be made to pay even for what it approves."[2]

The imperial grant made to the Transvaal of £100,000 was not ungenerous. Nor, however, was it munificent; for the debt of the Transvaal was close to £300,000 and the revenue during at least the first year could not be otherwise than uncertain. The attempt to rush an impoverished and bankrupt community into premature solvency undeniably did more than the annexation itself to alienate the sympathies of the population. It was far from the least of the blunders committed by British policy that it permitted a comprehensive scheme, such as Carnarvon entertained for the whole country, to be carried out with an utter insufficiency of means. The annexation had been an imperial act. The conduct of the new Government was forcibly an imperial responsibility.

That the new administration found that it had to continue to levy the very railway tax which had damaged the prestige of the republican Government is enough to indicate the unfavourable auspices under which Shepstone's regime began. Economy meant not merely inferior officials and bad government; it meant also too few officials and too little government. This was especially true for the natives. For four years it was the fate of the administration to be unable to pay any serious attention to a native population larger by far than that of Natal and the Orange Free State combined. The Transvaal suffered grievously from the common fault of colonial Governments of undermanning their

[1] G.D. 6/33, Shepstone to Frere, 20 June 1877.
[2] G.D. 6/23, Carnarvon to Shepstone, 20 May 1877.

departments and underpaying their officials. It was forgotten
that nothing is so likely to breed a narrow, autocratic and unenterprising officialdom as the false economy of insufficient
salaries and overworked departments. For want of magistrates
and commissioners native taxes could not be collected. For want
of regular and loyal officials the duty of maintaining order in the
Transvaal became finally the unhappy responsibility of British
regiments.

In the territory Shepstone had to govern credit was frozen and
specie had disappeared, much of it hoarded by the farmers and
the bankers. The new administration quickly saw that if taxes
were to be paid and if it were to have the confidence of the population, the frozen credit of the country had to become liquid so
that specie and trade might flow again. It was Shepstone's
feeling that nothing would succeed in influencing the population in its favour so much as a generous attitude in financial
matters. Where people were naturally inclined to see the weaknesses of British rule it could not be wise to begin that rule with
a cheeseparing attitude. The decision Shepstone reached therefore was to pay not simply the most pressing debts but all legiti-
mate debts. The volunteers of the Sekukuni campaign who had
been paid in "good-fors" were numerous, so that the payment of
these debts would affect a large number of the population. Moreover, a generous settlement would make possible their disband-
ment and prevent a possible organized expression of discontent.

The immediate claims upon the Government exceeded the
amount of the Parliamentary grant. Together with interest on
loans and debentures they totalled £134,000. To borrow money
from the local banks was possible only at high rates of interest.
Yet the money had to be found. The Cape Commercial Bank
seemed determined on prompt repayment of its loans, if possible
before any other creditor. Whatever the sympathy in which the
Government was held, all of those throughout the country who
felt that they had the slightest claim, held aloft their folded and
creased "good-fors" and clamoured for the golden sovereigns
with which the credulous believed Shepstone's waggons had
been laden.

If Shepstone's intentions were good his financial management

was distinctly bad.[1] It could hardly be otherwise. Skilled financial assistance he had practically none. He did not even have the
outworn officials whom Molteno craftily offered to send him in
order to save the Cape Treasury their pensions. He depended
almost wholly upon Henderson, the honorary financial Commissioner, and Treasurer General Breda who was already a very
sick man. It was a deeply regrettable necessity. Henderson, it is
true, laboured day and night. He even lent money to the Government out of his own resources. In reviewing the claims of the
farmers he saved thousands of pounds, rendering himself unpopular and going far to defeat the purpose Shepstone had had in
mind. His honesty was uncertain. Whilst he was giving the
Government the gratuitous benefit of his financial skill, he was
engaged in organizing one of those land-jobbing companies—
The Transvaal Board of Executors and Trust Company—which
were the bane of the whole land. Amongst his associates were
Mr Swart, the Government Secretary, who had suspiciously
urged upon Shepstone the necessity of strict Crown Colony
Government and a vigorous policy of British immigration, two
managing officials of the Cape Commercial Bank which had
played a part in undermining the credit of the Republic, and
Mr George Moodie, the entirely dishonest promoter of the
Lebombo Railway Company, who had exultantly hailed annexation because there were "millions in it".[2]

With the Cape Commercial Bank Henderson was as accommodating as he had been severe with the petty claims of the

[1] Shepstone's handling of the finances of the Special Commission before
the annexation had already revealed him as an execrably bad manager. His
accounts were so wretchedly kept that their publication would have ruined
his reputation, even though they were thoroughly honest. For years he was
the best hated man in the Treasury. The Treasury's aversion to Shepstone
actually affected their attitude towards South African financial questions.
Even the Colonial Office which always admired him, had to admit that his
accounts were "disgraceful". It was not till 1883 that the accounts of his
Mission could be reviewed by the Treasury. That short-tempered department
gasped with indignation to find that an item for forage contained a concertina,
a great coat and a set of vases. "My Lords feel sure", the Colonial Office was
told, "that the Secretary of State will not wish them to charge the Consolidated
Fund with the cost of Sir Theophilus Shepstone's hat, Mr H. C. Shepstone's
hairbrushes, Mr Fynney's cricket bat, or Mr Thresh's fishing rod." C.O.
179/150, Treasury to C.O., 2 Feb. 1883.
[2] G.D. 6/33, Frere to Carnarvon, 16 Aug. 1877.

farmers. Neither he nor the Treasurer General, Breda, had any authority to sign money warrants or drafts. Yet Shepstone permitted them to sign financial papers which he himself did not countersign. Frere only discovered what was happening at Pretoria when large drafts began casually to arrive in Cape Town without warning or any explanation. He gasped at such dangerous irregularities. As some of the larger drafts had been used as negotiable commercial paper by different individuals before they reached Cape Town it was difficult to refuse them without undermining the credit of the new administration. But it was obvious that the Cape Commerical Bank was cheerfully and rapidly realizing its old and none too secure debts. "Mr Henderson", reported Frere to Carnarvon, "has exercised his power more with a view to the advantage of the Cape Commerical Bank than with any reference to the amount of cash available from your loan."[1] The actions and motives of the Cape Commercial Bank, he explained, "in whose favour most of the money seems to have been drawn, are plain enough. The Bank has always been as much a political as a banking institution".[2] Within a very few months it had secured possession of drafts totalling over £31,000. To Frere's ingrained careful financial habits it was shocking to learn that somebody at Pretoria had authorized the withdrawal of £75,000 from the military chest, a sum so staggering to Lord Carnarvon that he sent an agitated telegram calling for particulars.

Frere acted peremptorily. The imperial grant, he told Shepstone, was for civil and military purposes and none other. In haste he gave the Transvaal Government a long disquisition on the rudiments of finance and sent Shepstone copies of the Standing Orders on the subject of drafts by colonies, together with explanations how drafts should be made out.

Considering the necessarily slow resumption of tax payments the transfer of nearly a third of the imperial grant to a banking institution was most unwise. The activity of Henderson and the means employed by the Cape Commerical Bank to secure such preferential treatment were open to the most serious question. By the end of December, when the Government had to meet a

[1] G.D. 6/33, Frere to Carnarvon, 16 Aug. 1877.
[2] *Ibid.* Frere to Carnarvon, 14 Aug. 1877.

payment of £15,000 on the railway debentures, the imperial grant would be entirely exhausted. In other words after but six months of British rule the financial affairs were in such a state of chaos that years afterwards Treasury officials were still vainly and angrily trying to discover in what manner and to what ends Shepstone had spent much of his money. Whether it be said that the imperial grant had proved too small for the needs of the Transvaal, or that it had been recklessly and unwisely squandered, it remained true that by the end of 1877 the Government was forced into premature dependence upon the limited local resources. Too early Shepstone found himself compelled to exalt the power of mere British presence in the Transvaal, and in reliance upon his personal prestige to negate the influence of the Boer leaders and to ignore the habits of two generations of self-government. An administration that was military and fiscal, obsessed with the narrow duties of economy, a regime of barren achievement stubbornly defending its failures was the result. It became finally a timorous despotism, without consent, without tradition, without enlightenment and without strength. During the first critical and formative months, during the very period when the most fruitful efforts could have been made to extend and strengthen the basis of popular support, the administration made the first mistakes that were ultimately to lead to disaster.

That much and significant support could have been won cannot be fairly denied. In the first months there was far more of uncertainty than of hostility. What there was of hostility was balanced, in part at least, by some genuine optimism that was not altogether confined to British shopkeepers and speculators. It is certain that where the Boers faced native border tribes they welcomed the protection which the new Government might afford them. Would Shepstone have the tact to discern and the wit to guide the silent undercurrents of feeling and action which, if ignored or roughly disturbed, might erupt in a flood? Would he be able to gauge the real depth and the actual direction of feeling amongst the Boers and encourage them in that co-operation without which the administration could hardly hope to continue in existence? Above all, could he persuade the population to pay its taxes fully and regularly? For in the Transvaal the fiscal problem was inseparable from the political problem. If the farmers could be persuaded to pay the taxes which they had refused to the republican Government, salvation might yet be won. While financial aid from the Home Government either as a grant or as a guarantee for a loan was valuable and necessary, in the last resort the Transvaal had to assert its own financial independence. Unless it did so its ultimate abandonment was a foregone conclusion.

In England Carnarvon was determined that there should be economy in the Transvaal. Sargeaunt, one of the Crown Agents and therefore skilled in all matters of colonial finance, was selected to go to the Transvaal to pull "Shepstone up on the 'road to ruin' in time to prevent serious mischief being done".[1] Ostensibly he went to assist Shepstone; actually he was sent to supersede him in a quiet and unobtrusive manner. Herbert informed him that no important matter whether political or economic, whether connected with the present or future government of the Transvaal, was to be excluded from his enquiry. He was especially instructed to report upon the financial condition of the country, the feasibility of the Delagoa Bay railway, and its future administrative establishments.

The coming of Sargeaunt was the coming of the Treasury official. With him there entered into the Transvaal the grim solvency of the Gladstonian budget. Taxes must be paid and the country itself must be bound in its undertakings by the limits of its income and credit. Sargeaunt's discipline in finance foreboded a greater strictness of Government as well. Privately because his love for the Boers was small, and officially because his duty to efficiency was great, he felt that economy was best served by autocracy. In the end it was his mission that made the Government of the Transvaal an alien government, with the taxgatherer and the British soldier as the chief symbols of its authority.

The British administration in the Transvaal was the victim of far more than its own blunders. If South Africa had been reasonably prosperous and undisturbed, if there had not descended upon the land the worst drought in more than a generation, and a succession of desperate and costly native wars, the

[1] G.D. 6/33, Carnarvon to Frere, 22 and 30 Aug. 1877.

history of the annexation of the Transvaal would almost certainly
have been otherwise. It seemed like the very perverseness of fate
that the forces which during the course of the century had
been working towards the very disasters which British policy
was anxious to avoid, should inopportunely precipitate a series
of crises by which all other questions were eclipsed. When the
storm finally lifted, Carnarvon was gone; his policy had been dis-
credited, and there was a general disillusionment over South
Africa.

CHAPTER VII

THE ECONOMICS OF WAR

IN 1877 the Cape Eastern Frontier had enjoyed more than twenty-five years of peace. There had been ugly moments of disquiet when, as in 1872, a sudden movement of unrest amongst the tribes raised the spectre of another native war. But in 1873 a commission laid down lines between the chafing tribes and wrote a treaty of peace.[1] The commission insisted that the unrest had been due to little more than the natural quarrelsomeness of native tribes. Once the government had raised its voice against the stocklifting Kafir McGregors, and reshuffled the handful of magistrates and residents amongst the tribes, there would again be peace and respect for "treaty obligations". In the following year Brownlee, Minister for Native Affairs, declared that the condition of the frontier was "satisfactory beyond the most sanguine expectations". Both the optimism of the Minister for Native Affairs and the entirely superficial report of the Frontier Commission testify to the real ignorance of native conditions that obtained in the Cape Colony. After half a century of the closest contact with the natives the chief responsibility of Government was still considered to be the military problem of maintaining peace and quiet.

Yet in common with the entire great native world the Eastern Frontier had been undergoing changes which the years of peace had but goaded faster onwards. At the time of the last war in 1851 the Cape Government had still been concerned mainly with the tribes on its immediate frontier. By 1877 a remarkable consolidation had taken place amongst the natives everywhere. This consolidation was not the universal conspiracy to rise in concert and drive the white man into the sea—the favourite fear of alarmed frontiersmen. It was rather an unpremeditated community of affliction that related the natives to one another in spite of traditional tribal feuds. White South Africa in 1877 was

[1] C.O. 48/464, Barkly to Kimberley, 15 Jan. 1873.

not dealing any longer with merely primitive communities, but with communities driven out of their savagery and drawn deeply into the mechanism of colonial society. Within South Africa there was not to be found a single tribe that was sufficient unto itself. The natives bought, they sold, they worked. The racial separation of white and black could not obscure how much they were part of one another. The distinction drawn between the civilization of the European and the barbarism of the native no longer corresponded in an adequate manner to the difference in their relative economic and social positions. Their contact, and ultimately their conflict, were caused not by different but by similar interests. The problems on the Cape Eastern Frontier were therefore no different from those in Basutoland or even the Northern Transvaal. Out of the melting pot which was Kimberley a contractor of native labour to the Cape railway construction works drew a haphazard group of one hundred and twenty labourers, and found that it contained Kafirs and Fingos from the Eastern Province, Mashonas from the Zambesi, Zulus from Natal, Amaswazi from the Transvaal border and natives from Delagoa Bay. Tribe was linked to tribe in a subtle bond, welded not by the natives themselves, but by the European; for everywhere the stronger pressed upon the land and the life of the weaker, appropriating the one and transforming the other. The time of isolated native wars was thus past. Once war flamed at any point on the long frontier, the danger was great that the uniformity of grievance and discontent would cause the conflagration to spread far and wide.

The Cape Eastern Frontier and the territories beyond were entangled in a political and legal confusion that bore witness to the inconsistent policies of past generations. Some territories had been entirely annexed; some were partly dependent, and others were entirely independent. The greatest disorder existed in the manner in which the natives within the colony held their land. Tribal tenure and private ownership existed side by side with squatting and utter landlessness. Even beyond the frontier in the more spacious Transkei there was hardly a district in which the dispersive force of intertribal conflict and European pressure had not caused numerous splinters of tribes to become imbedded in larger and more homogeneous groups. Even of the bigger groups there were few that had inhabited the same territory for a considerable number of years.

The effects of European expansiveness were most evident in the dense congestion of the population on both sides of the immediate border. From Fort Beaufort to the Bashee the country was quite definitely overpeopled, overstocked and over-cultivated. There was scarcely a location in the Eastern Province or a district in Basutoland in which complaints and quarrels about cattle and trespass were not of the most frequent occurrence.[1] In April 1875 Civil Commissioner Rose Innes of King-williamstown complained that his district was already so over-crowded and overstocked, and land adapted for cultivation so scarce, that disputes over the right to arable land during the planting season were common. It was once again the contentious-ness of the confined mediaeval villager, who held that his neigh-bour was holding unrighteously and more than he ought. Indis-putably the natives had too little land. "It is not too much to say", reported Rose Innes two years later, "that the time is not distant when the overcrowding of the native population...will require in some manner to be provided for and reduced".[2]

Much of the land was poor, or stony and unfit for cultivation. Even the better land was becoming impoverished and less pro-ductive. Mediaeval agriculture, poor as it was, gave more rest to its soil than did the tilling of the Eastern Frontier.[3] The un-scientific and wasteful methods of the natives and the heavy demands which their gardens and their cattle made upon the fertility of the countryside were manifesting themselves in the erosion which washed away the topsoil, and in the disappearance in some parts of all larger vegetation. In Tembuland there were

---

[1] Cp. G. 16, 1876, Report by E. S. Rolland.   [2] G. 12, 1877.

[3] The following illuminating remark was made by an experienced frontier magistrate: "It is an indisputable fact that comparing them with Europeans, taking man for man, and acre for acre, the native produces more from a smaller extent of ground, and with more primitive appliances, than the Europeans. Any farmer in this division cannot say otherwise than that the native cultivates land that he would not, and I have been myself surprised at the out of the way places in which I have found growing crops. There is not a spot of ground neglected by the native that can be cultivated." John Hemming to Secretary for Native Affairs, 1 Dec. 1879.

large tracts of country in which there was not a tree or a bush to be seen, so that the natives, like the Greeks of fifth-century Athens, had to go long distances to find wood.[1] Using the dried dung of their animals for fuel they deprived their land of the only manure they had. In areas like Bomvanaland where the soil was already poor and rocky the practice of burning the grass and the trees had so reduced the natural humus of the land that the pockets and scattered patches of arable land were generally too small and shallow to be cultivated with a plough. In the district of Kingwilliamstown the Civil Commissioner complained that the soil was so thin and unprotected that heavy rains washed away the humus, exposing the underlying rock and gravel. The amount of arable land, he asserted, was barely sufficient for the immediate requirements of the people.[2]

Greatly worse than the crowding of human beings was the excess of livestock which placed a heavy strain upon the pasture of a country that was subject to periodic and severe droughts, and encouraged the ruinous grass burning which prematurely hastened the growth of the spring shoots. In areas like Herschel the overstocking was so great, and the natural protection given to the topsoil by the vegetation so weakened, that the country was seamed with the big dongas and ditches which were the despair of roadbuilders in the entire Basutoland area.[3] Into the over-stocked districts there were nevertheless imported every year large numbers of cattle, sheep and goats which had been earned as wages by returning labourers. In consequence the circum-scribed grazing grounds were unable to accommodate both the natural increase and the imported stock. Every importation quite simply meant that a roughly equivalent number of cattle or sheep died each winter of undernourishment and cold, or were re-exported as draught animals or for slaughter.[4] The crowding also did much to increase the severity of disease. Lungsickness was the scourge of the entire land from the Cape to Zululand and beyond; its ravages gnawed incessantly at the vitals of the native economic order, deepening their discontent, and swelling the pressure that drove them abroad to labour for their European neighbours.

[1] G. 33, 1879. [2] G. 21, 1875.
[3] G. 13, 1880. [4] G. 27, 1874; G. 12, 1877.

L

In all regions of the world where soil subject to drought is intensively worked it becomes powdery, and is easily blown into the dust that sifts down upon the South African landscape in the brilliant sunsets of winter. The common assumption that natives live by preference in areas where the soil is loose and easily worked must be qualified by the fact that only unusually favourable conditions could save the soil from being drained of its virtue by the demands made upon it. Where the residues of the crops were eaten by the cattle, and there was no knowledge of cover crops to anchor the soil, where terracing and tree planting were impracticable or too expensive, the damage that drought and a heavy population of human beings and animals could do in a few years was immense. The natives of the Cape Eastern Frontier had done to their soil under the force of necessity what the American farmer two generations later did when he ruthlessly exhausted millions of semi-arid acres in Kansas, Wyoming and New Mexico. Under his plough the desert soil, which had been covered and bound against the wind and the elements by sagebrush and the natural drought-resistant foliage of the region, crumbled finally into dust. The result was a series of wheat failures, and the great bronze sunsets unforgettably revealed the scattering of untold millions of tons of precious dust over the Great Central Plains. In South Africa the erosion by wind and rain was not caused by men eager to wrest a swift fortune from their soil but by men seeking but to fill their bellies.

The entire native population of Basutoland, the Cape Eastern Province and an indefinite but almost certainly large proportion of the Transkeian population was unable to produce enough wealth to satisfy its needs, which contact with the Europeans had served to increase. European clothing was widely worn. The use of waggons and ploughs was slowly increasing. There was much drinking of the raw "Cape smoke", and canteens were numerous and apparently profitable. But the relatively expensive waggons and ploughs were not, as settlers and even magistrates and missionaries were prone to believe, a reliable indication of any really general increase in wealth. Fingoland was by all odds the most prosperous of the native districts, yet its magistrate calculated in 1874 there was but one waggon to every hundred of population. The moderately prosperous native was then no better off than a mediaeval serf who was very well to do with a two-wheeled waggon and a harness of thongs. In the district of Idutywa, a poorer district but far from being the poorest, there was one waggon to every three hundred and fifty of population. While it is wise to discount the value of the figures given by missionaries and magistrates, it is nevertheless possible to derive from them indications of considerable value. It is of some significance at least that figures derived from small districts, where a magistrate might achieve a fair accuracy, corresponded very acceptably with the figures given for larger and less manageable areas. It is certain beyond a peradventure that the average native was poor in livestock. This was contrary to popular European belief. But if there was any truth in the teeming herds that the colonists claimed to see in the native areas, it was because these areas were even more teeming with natives. A native herd was not the possession of a single man like a European herd but was the sum of a large number of separate individual holdings. In the Idutywa district the individual possessed on an average one head of cattle, one goat and three sheep. In the location of Victoria East he possessed on an average half a head of cattle, one goat and two sheep. Since possessions in cattle were not equally distributed it must follow that numbers of natives were poor indeed. What was true of cattle was true also of gardens and crops. Native gardens scattered over a location easily gave a deceptive impression of both the amount of grain that was produced and the amount that might be produced.

The number of trading stations (there were thirty in the Herschel district) cannot be taken as any indication of a prosperous condition amongst the natives. There is indeed every reason to believe that the balance of trade was normally against them.[1] In times of good harvests trade could be brisk enough. But good harvests meant low prices, especially for native grain. That the market value of native grown grain was usually lower than that of European grown grain is easily enough seen in the fact that districts like the Free State conquered territory which

[1] See G. 16, 1876, Report on Victoria East; G. 12, 1877, Report on Emigrant Tembuland.

produced a large surplus of grain were active importers of the
cheaper Basuto grain. It was however an unusual year in which
the natives did not buy back some part of their own grain at enhanced prices. The natives, reported R. H. Dugmore, the super-
intendent of the Healdtown location, "are unfortunately very
ready to sell their crops in a good season, without keeping a stock
to fall back upon in time of scarcity, and consequently have at
times to buy back the grain they sold at double or treble the
price they received for it...".[1] Contrary to popular belief the
native stores were not the source of enormous profits. Their
profits were limited by the real poverty of their customers. It is
improbable that the average individual spent over £1. 10s. per
annum at the stores. The stores, unless they were canteens as
well, performed a valuable service. In periods of distress and
shortage, periods that were all too frequent, they were usually
accommodating, and by serving as reservoirs of grain helped to
protect the natives against the too serious effects of their own
improvidence.

What the tribes exported and sold was not really their agricultural produce. They had an exportable commodity more important than their grain and their hides. It was their principal
defence against drought, low selling prices, high buying prices
and overcrowding. That commodity was their own labour. It
can confidently be said that by 1877 the bulk of the able-bodied
men of Basutoland and the native districts of the Cape Eastern
Province depended upon wages in money or kind as an important source of income, without which indeed they could not
expect to uphold even the low level on which they existed. On
this the evidence is emphatic and will not brook any denial.
From this dependence not even the Fingos, the favoured of the
frontier, were absolved. In such small areas as the district of

[1] G. 17, 1878, 15 Feb. 1878. The following figures are not accurate but they
may be suggestive. The magistrate of Victoria East calculated that a population of 13,000 natives had sold produce to Alice traders to a value of £19,273
in 1875, and had purchased goods to a total value of £21,074. If rents in
money or kind paid by the squatters on European land, and hut taxes be
added, the suggestion is strong that the natives of the district had a large
deficit to make up by means of their exports of labour. And indeed Victoria
East was one of the districts in which the majority of the able-bodied male
population worked for Europeans.

Umzimkulu where counting was not altogether guess-work, the magistrate calculated that one-third of a population of three thousand was continually away in the Cape Colony at labour. Of the twenty thousand natives of the Tambookie location of Queenstown many were reported by their magistrate to be too busy to spend more than a few days a month in the location.[1] From the Basutoland district of Maseru at least half of the total population was reported to be always absent at work in the European areas. In Thaba Bosigo there was hardly a single able-bodied man who did not spend some time of the year in European service. Rolland even affirmed that as much as three-quarters of the able-bodied male population of Basutoland annually were given passes to go to work at the diamond fields, in the Free State or the Cape Colony.

The guns in the hands of the furtive knots of Basuto who scurried through the Free State to Basutoland on their way from the diamond fields gave the impression that it was solely the temptation to possess the arms of the Europeans that drew the natives out to labour. The fear that the tribes were deliberately arming themselves against the whites was thus easily born, so that the only topic that could draw together the unwilling heads at the London Conference in 1876 was the traffic in arms and ammunition. Yet it was the improvident competition of the British colonies for revenue that fomented the dangerous traffic, while the existence of the traffic itself was a more convincing demonstration than any other that could be found of the manner in which European opinion misunderstood the unrest that agitated the tribes. Far greater than the attraction of guns was the compulsion of what Rolland called the "utter necessity" caused by the loss in 1869 of the best arable land in Basutoland. A far greater incentive to war than the possession of guns was the harsh pressure of economic circumstances upon every aspect of native life.

The reason that the Eastern Province had enjoyed a quarter of a century of peace was probably partly due to the restraining influence of magistrates, but much more obviously to the insurance against too abject destitution which wage earning afforded

[1] G. 27, 1874

the natives. The ability to buy food from the traders, even at exorbitant prices, and above all the developing habit of depending upon the sale of their labour to make good the insufficient productivity of the native areas, tempered the misery of adverse harvests and prevented the natives from descending too easily to those desperate straits that invariably had preceded earlier native wars. Hence it must follow that if the Eastern Frontier were to witness another outbreak it could only possibly be the result of the pressure of unprecedented hardship.

Money could do very little to supply the greatest want of all, which was land. On occasion natives did succeed in purchasing or renting European farms. But such land, being immediately filled to suffocation, did nothing to appease the violent land hunger, and merely threw into greater relief the pressure of the population upon every available inch. In the district of Victoria East European landlords with ground for rent were never at a loss for native tenants willing to pay in cash and in kind. Against the insufficiency of land and the compulsion to labour the best of seasons was an inadequate protection. Poor seasons, and they came not rarely, were a lash that drove the natives out in increasing numbers.

The Cape Colony itself greedily absorbed labour. Capital it could secure easily, and on the whole cheaply. But so great was the need for labour on farms and on public works that colonist opinion was inclined to welcome and not to criticize measures which hastened the flow or increased the reliability of native labour. Neither the introduction of the 1820 settlers nor Sir George Grey's scheme of German immigration had done anything to satisfy the need for inexpensive labour. The sudden and uneconomical expansion of the Cape Colony's small population over an immensely wide area during the Great Trek resulted in much more than extensive appropriations of native land. It is one of the neglected yet important effects of the Great Trek that it imposed a serious strain on the labour supply of the country by creating a demand for an unusual amount of cheap native labour to work upon the vastly increased holdings of the European population. Ever since the Great Trek there had been a demand for labourers in every section of the country. Their scarcity was not caused by the emancipation of the slaves in 1834, nor even by the absence in the Cape Colony after 1828 of vagrancy laws of sufficient severity to force "idle" natives into service; for in the Transvaal and the Free State where vagrancy laws could be applied the call for labour was equally insistent.

A knowledge of the problems of native land and labour explains much that is confused in South African political life. At the diamond fields the state of public and political sentiment tended to fluctuate with the labour market. What were brought forward as serious grievances during 1875 when labour was scarce were borne more lightly in the following year when labour was more plentiful, although the actual state of the market for diamonds had not improved. Behind the outcry against the Transvaal in 1876 there lurked the conviction that the time had come for the European population to subject the native world more conclusively to itself, so that its labour could be more fully and dependably exploited, and its taxes be made to bear more of the weight of the heavy increase in public charges that the decade had brought. It cannot be seriously disputed that in the native policies of the two major British colonies the desire to tap more profitably the reservoirs of labour and revenue played a leading role.

With the discovery of diamonds and the efforts to remedy an exceedingly poor transport system it was principally to the native population that the Cape and Natal looked to provide the labour and part of the additional revenue for which a more active industrial policy called. For the diamond industry the destruction of the economic power of the Basuto had therefore been a timely and fortunate occurrence. In Natal, Basutoland, on the Cape Eastern Frontier, and to some extent in the Republics, officials with power over the natives used their influence to force them out of their areas to seek work. Even those magistrates whose devotion to native interests was whole-hearted and sincere saw it to be their duty to hasten the movement. Some of them already realized that unless the income derived from the sale of stock and produce were supplemented by the proceeds of labour, taxes could not be paid, and that in the recurrent seasons of food shortage there would be suffering in the land. Or they felt that if the native population were ever to become civilized it must be taught the virtues of diligence and labour. "While industry", wrote Acting Government Agent Rolland,[1] "is in all cases at the outset aroused by necessity, such utter necessity as that in which the Basutos found themselves in 1869, it can only be sustained by a continuation of that necessity." The manner in which the forces that bequeathed to modern South Africa its unique black proletariat were welcomed in the nineteenth century as forces of reform and civilization is one of the most amazing chapters in the country's social history.

South Africa, and the older and more liberal Cape Colony in particular, were not wanting in minds that were well disposed to the natives. Yet on the eve of an astounding series of native wars that paralysed the country during almost four years, even this liberal thought was apparently too weak or too befogged by misleading moral and religious notions to be capable of a calm appreciation of the true plight of the native population. That missionary sentiment in Natal ranged itself behind Pine and public opinion at the time of Langalibalele's uprising was almost entirely due to the belief that the tribal organization and the consequent indolence of the natives were the chief obstacles to their civilization and christianization. Not merely missionaries but the colonists themselves commonly justified their attitude in native matters on moral and religious grounds. An official resolution of the Cape Legislative Council insisted that it was desirable "in the interests of the Agriculturists and other Employers of Labour in this Colony, as well as in the interests of the Native Tribes upon and beyond our Borders, to encourage in every practical way such Natives to engage in Agricultural and other Labour".[2] It would be difficult to find a debate on native matters in the Natal Legislature in which some of the speeches were not cast in the language of moral necessity or obligation. A bill introduced on 6 January 1880 into the Natal Legislature to oblige natives to wear European clothing in certain localities, was welcomed because it would at the same time promote civilized decency, and increase the labour supply by forcing the natives to earn money to buy clothes. Underlying all native policy there was a great confusion

[1] G. 16, 1876.   [2] C. 8, 1881.

of ideas. Side by side with the belief of the Dutch and English frontiersmen, forthrightly expressed, in the racial and intellectual inferiority of the natives which condemned them to serfdom, there echoed the mingled notes of unhistorical Evangelicalism and a romantic belief in the natural and simple man. But however conflicting the language in which native problems were debated, the conclusions were similar. The contention on the one hand that the natives would derive great benefit from a more intimate and regular contact with the Europeans, became an excuse for squeezing them out of their unimproved simplicity into the fruitful contact with European civilization that was found at railway construction works and diamond diggings. On the other hand the doctrine of the "simple wants" of the natives became an excuse for seriously underpaying them, or, what was really equivalent, for taxing them in a manner disproportionate to their wealth, their income or the benefit they derived from government expenditure.

Nowhere can the unintentional collusion between the genuine humanitarian desire to improve the condition of the natives and the selfish motive of exploitation be more interestingly observed than in the policy of substituting individual tenure for tribal land tenure. Those whose concern was with the moral and economic improvement of the natives were convinced that the traditional authority of the chiefs and the customs of the tribes were a hindrance to their efforts. A system of individual land tenure would in their judgment do more than any other single innovation to disrupt the reactionary power of chief and tribe, and free the individual to expand the latent moral and economic powers which tribal discipline had held in thraldom. Only a smallhearted prejudice would refuse to recognize the liberal thought and generous intention that sponsored the system of individual landholding in the Cape Colony. Yet the policy was not incompatible with a determination that as a reform it should not obstruct the flow of native labour. It was such a determination that ultimately robbed the policy of much of its value by withholding from it the additional land without which it could not be truly successful. In a location like that of Healdtown the two morgen lots into which it had been surveyed were never intended to give an entire support to the families that occupied them. The lots were kept small of set purpose so that the women should cultivate the land while the men earned money by their labour outside the location. It was not in the Healdtown location alone that many even of these small lots were found upon trial to be valueless, with the result that from its very beginning the purpose of the system of individual tenure was defeated by the heaping of natives upon the more fertile land. In Glen Grey, although that district ultimately gave its name to the system of individual land tenure, most of the individual tenants in 1877 had other natives squatting upon their properties in return for payments generally equivalent to the government hut tax.[1] Of the land shortage from which the natives suffered the most convincing proof could be seen in the manner in which they spilled over as squatters upon the neighbouring land. Of the natives under his care the magistrate of Bedford reported in January 1877 that all were resident upon European farms as labourers and tenants.[2] They paid rent for pasture land, or, dividing the produce with the European landowner, cultivated a portion of his farm. In addition such tenants also might work for wages. Where the Europeans were themselves resident upon their farms they were in a position to limit the number of natives upon their land. But farms upon which the owner was not himself resident were often jammed with native squatters. The Kafir tenant or squatter system was more profitable to many landowners than was farming. "These native money producing machines", wrote the Civil Commissioner of Victoria East,[3] "are encouraged on all sides" with the result that there was in his district a kraal on almost every farm.[4] The attempts that were made to curb the squatting system were uniformly unsuccessful. Even the imposition of taxes upon farmers who let their land to native squatters met with little success, as the taxes simply tended, in the language of the frontier, to "raise the niggers' rent".

The squatting system was a serious evil. The farmers were disinclined to pay any attention to the interests of their tenants provided they received rent and labour from them. Kraals placed

[1] G. 12, 1877.   [2] G. 12, 1877.
     G. 17, 1878.   [4] Cp. also G. 27, 1874; G. 21, 1875; G. 16, 1876.

upon private land were more inaccessible to the authority of magistrates and the influence of missionaries than many a village beyond the pale of colonial law. "As a rule," complained the Civil Commissioner of Victoria East,[1] "if one wishes to behold a thoroughly savage Kafir kraal such as those which existed in the land long before a white man's face was seen in South Africa a visit to almost any farm in this or in the neighbouring districts will gratify one's curiosity." And yet the absentee farmer, like the storekeeper, was not an unmixed evil. Even if he caused the native upon his land to pay excessive rents, and gave him in return no security of tenure, he afforded relief to the crowded areas, and actually gave to the natives some protection against the pressure that bore upon them.

The real seriousness of the economic condition of the natives was not immediately evident. Their level of subsistence was naturally low. When seasons were normal and the farmers stood in need of labourers there was not apt to be any suffering or serious shortage of food. But against serious adversity the weak structure of native economic life could not prevail. And it came about that in 1877 a great area which included much of the Transvaal, Zululand, Natal and the entire area down to the Cape border was afflicted by a cruel and ruinous drought. South Africa was used to droughts, even though men did speak of a special South African Golden Age when the seasons came as they ought and the ground was never dry. But such a drought as oppressed natives and Europeans in month after month of unbroken tyranny was beyond the experience of all. Upon the native tribes on both sides of the colonial frontier it fell with especial bitterness.

The drought started in Fingoland, Emigrant Tambookieland, Herschel and parts of Basutoland in 1875; it grew in extent during the following year. In 1877 and until the beginning of 1878 it raged most fiercely; in 1880 it still lingered here and there like a disease. Its first effect was to cause an expansion and scattering of the tribes in search of work or pasture. Into more favoured areas like Gatberg and Matatiele there was a steady influx of natives and cattle from Basutoland, Herschel, Fingoland

[1] G. 17, 1878.

and the Colony.[1] Through the movement of diseased herds the dread lungsickness spread more widely and did more harm. Locations like Oxkraal and Kamastone had been unable to feed themselves since the harvest of 1876, and depended upon imports from more fortunate areas. The harvests of 1877 and 1878 were almost complete failures. All the effects of overcrowded locations, of overstocked pastures and of overworked soil became glaringly apparent. From his central position at Kingwilliamstown the Civil Commissioner could survey the entire frontier.[2] His full and solemn warning in January 1877 echoed the fears of the whole frontier. "The present season is one of severe drought, and the extent of land laid under crop is very far below the general average of ordinary seasons. Across the Kei food is becoming scarce, and not readily procurable, while mealies and Kafir corn can only be had at exceptionally high prices. Traders in the Transkei assure me that natives are taking food instead of money in payment for what they sell. Along the coast they are subsisting upon roots and shellfish. This scarcity of food will require to be watched in order that supplies may be obtained from abroad...to meet the exigencies of the case which will become still more pressing and complicated, if rain does not shortly fall...."

The conditions and the tradition of the frontier did not permit the European population to look upon its native neighbours with a calm and unprejudiced eye. The English farmer on the frontier was no more of a negrophilist than the Dutch farmer in the Republics. But upon the frontier there were nevertheless men whose interests did not oppose them to the natives or whose position made them authentic witnesses. Even in the ranks of the overworked, underpaid and poorly selected frontier officials there were several to whose minds the drought brought home the tragic seriousness of conditions. They knew how great was the need to destroy on the one hand the pessimism that denied the native the capacity or the will to improve his condition, and on the other hand, the equally dangerous optimism that was undisturbed by the ravages of lungsickness, or by the sight of the

[1] G. 21, 1875; G. 12, 1877; G. 17, 1878; G. 33, 1879.
[2] G. 12, 1877.

natives huddled in their inadequate areas. They had long since foreseen that a civilized Government could not safely tolerate the wastefulness of native agriculture, the vicious ignorance of witchcraft or the authority of unprogressive chiefs. In the achievements of some of these officials there were already the fruitful beginnings of a systematic and progressive native policy. These men knew that the natives who could no longer move on to virgin land when they had prematurely exhausted the old, who worked for Europeans, spent money at European stores and rented land of their neighbours, could not simply be treated as a military problem. The most serious problem was not defence but the encouragment of activities that would adapt the natives to their changed condition and enable them to find relief from the economic discomfort into which their contact with the advancing European frontier had plunged them.

Popular opinion was inclined to insist even during the drought that the natives had their own indolence and shiftlessness to thank for their plight. "What can we do with such a people", complained no less a person than George McCall Theal, the Government Agent with the unhappy chief Oba. "They break their promise without the slightest sense of shame; they profess to be starving, yet they find means to purchase brandy; they have seen the effects of irrigation elsewhere, yet they will not expend a little labour in repairing a watercourse, though seed, tools to work with and food for the labourers are offered free of cost."[1] More reflective minds however were beginning to see the dangers of continued neglect, and to grope towards practical reforms. To the popular assertion that the native had merely to learn the virtues of regular and constant labour in order to extricate himself from his poverty it was replied that an insufficiency of land and wasteful agricultural methods were also barriers to improvement. If measures were adopted to force the natives to work, then there should at least be added measures to teach them to make more efficient use of the resources they already had. If it was inevitable that the native should earn money as a labourer it was still necessary that he should produce more as a farmer. A satisfactory relationship to the land was the

[1] A. 31, 1878, Theal to Civil Commissioner of Victoria East, 2 Jan. 1877.

secret of any successful native policy. Otherwise crowding and insecurity could only be the constant cause of unrest and fear.

Unfortunately both men and seasons conspired against the maintenance of peace. In 1876 the nervousness of both Europeans and natives was seen in a sudden "war scare" and a feeling of insecurity that caused a stagnation of trade and much financial loss. As the drought continued and it became evident that the harvest of 1877 would be a failure for Europeans as well, the rumours and suspicions of the previous year flared up anew. When missionaries speak with more than usual bitterness of the vileness of native practices, when the colonists accuse the natives of trespass and theft, when trading posts retail war talk, when the newspapers are full of alarming reports by that anonymous but always positive gentleman who signed himself "Our Own Correspondent", and when there is amongst the tribes a rising up of prophets and prophetesses, then those who have experience of South Africa look first to the rainfall for an explanation. In South African farming communities, whether they be white or black, a protracted and depressing drought has ever been a frequent cause of political unrest and sometimes of violence. The normal irritations of life during busy and profitable seasons become galling; petty discontents swell until they become unendurable grievances. And under the tyrannous sun men on both sides of the frontier looked upon their neighbours with hard eyes, reading peril in one another's discontent. Cattle and sheep died by the thousand; stock thefts reached a height unprecedented in frontier annals. "The country is spoken of by the Natives as 'dead' which means in point of fact that restraint is cast off, and that people may do anything they please with impunity. This idea pervades all classes more or less; it exhibits itself amongst the Europeans in various ways, one being general discord."[1] Fed by the same vicious brew of gossip and false reports the natives and Europeans each feared an attack from the other, and it was not always the natives who were most afraid.

[1] G. 17, 1878.

CHAPTER VIII

POLITICIANS IN UNIFORM

UPON the frontier it was a common complaint that the British Government was too remote and too inexperienced to appreciate the problem with which the colonists upon the spot had to deal. Yet the special expertness of the colonists was itself oppositely compounded of experience and prejudice, of assurance and fear, so that the native policies of both British colonies and Republics were inextricably involved with the ideas and modes of feeling of the colonists.

It was fear above all else that deterred the colonists from lending a readier ear than they did to schemes for the economic and social improvement of the natives. By 1877 the conviction was widespread that the natives increased in number more rapidly than the Europeans. The congestion of the native areas could therefore be looked upon as a natural condition, for which the fecundity of the natives was more to blame than European expansion and confiscation. In such a mode of thought it was not easy to disabuse men's minds of the fear that any effort to relieve the congestion by granting more land to the natives would simply bequeath to the future an overwhelming and unmanageable population. It was a clearly Malthusian assumption which felt that concessions could only in the end increase the pressure of the population upon their subsistence, and, by aggravating their poverty, enhance the menace of their excessive numbers. Hence it was natural that the answer of hardbitten farmers and even frontier commissions to the recurrent unrest amongst the tribes should be a call to military and repressive measures, in ignorance of the truth that the social misery which was destroying the life of the tribes was also destroying the peace of the land.

Out of the frontier scares came frontier commissions. The war scare of 1876 led to the appointment of a frontier defence commission under John Gordon Sprigg, one of the prominent leaders of the Eastern group in the Cape Parliament. The title of the commission revealed the purpose and the nature of its inquiry. It was with the problem of defence that its report was primarily concerned. "Early and provident fear", it quoted, "is the mother of safety."[1] The first need of the frontier was an increase in the strength of its police. An additional expenditure of £150,000 per year was necessary for defensive purposes. Such proposals were timely and necessary. But like other frontier commissions Sprigg's commission was inclined to believe that its problem was largely solved if the Europeans were protected by a strong defensive wall.

Such safety could only be an illusion. The time was long past when the two races could live in separateness on either side of a wall or treaty line. In reality the physical and political frontier had disappeared. Still there persisted the policy of treating the natives as if they confronted the Europeans behind the barriers of a hostile independence. Thus it was that while the commission was not unaware of the anomalies of native settlement it was chiefly impressed with the fact that they outnumbered the Europeans. Its recommendation that the land be more fully reserved for European settlement was dictated by a fear of the disproportionate numbers of the two races, and was therefore no different from the policy of the past two generations.

Only a sentimental and impractical view could pretend, in the manner of Godwin, that the poverty and all the ills of the native population were due to the malignity of European colonial methods. To believe that contentment and progress, especially in the backward communities, can be achieved simply by administrative reforms, however extensive, is the illusion of an uncritical liberalism. Nevertheless it was true that all that stood between peace and war in 1877 was a light and flimsy rule. The administration was occasionally highhanded and habitually aimless. Extreme misdemeanours did not go unpunished, but the daily life of the population was largely unheeded. Under such conditions native policy became desultory and a chapter of accidents.

The efforts to remedy the inescapable evils of contact were without plan or power. Actually they were, with the exception of a handful of magistrates, almost wholly confined to the activity

[1] G. 1, 1877.

of the sparse missionary stations whose perseverance in the face of discouragements and misunderstanding was remarkable. The police that had once been a crack corps were now poorly trained and badly equipped. Because they were but indifferently paid their discipline was irregular and their enthusiasm half-hearted. It was small wonder that on the frontier the law notoriously left every vendor of strong drink to his own conscience, to decide whether he should adulterate the " Cape smoke" with tobacco, vitriol or not. Disturbance and maladjustment which the immediate action of a smart body of police could have controlled were left to grow and to warp. Kreli, who was the most restless and disgruntled chief on the entire frontier, was also the least subjected to restraint. The want of efficient means of enforcing the law was itself a reflection of an absence of unity and a dispersal of authority.

On 18 August 1877 Sir Bartle Frere left Cape Town for the Eastern Frontier. Just twenty years ago he had passed through the Indian Mutiny and its innumerable "scares". Yet what he saw now on the frontier filled even him with amazement. "I cannot attempt to give you any idea", he exclaimed to Lord Carnarvon, "of the helpless headlessness of almost everything. There is much excellent material of every kind, and endless capabilities but a sad want of organization, authority and co-operation."[1] Confused and alarmist accounts by the ubiquitous but always "reliable witnesses with unusual experience and unequalled powers of observation" stampeded the farmers into still greater fears. The frontier vindicated Lord Palmerston's observation that if you wish to be misinformed about a country you should consult a man who has lived there thirty years and speaks the language. A clamour of complaint, accusation and advice assailed the High Commissioner's ears. "Everyone", he protested, "seems more or less infected with the Kaffir tendency to endless talk and discussion and with a vague want of accuracy which seems another local failure." Because of his own ignorance and local inexperience Frere underestimated the seriousness of the crisis. He was inclined to look upon the scuffle between the Fingos and the Galekas out of which the war was developing as

[1] G.D. 6/33, Frere to Carnarvon, 5 Sept. 1877.

M

little more than an Irish faction fight. Yet his experience in India and elsewhere did permit him to lay his finger unerringly upon the serious administrative defects of the frontier. He was not long in discovering that "energetic, well trained officials, who were good office men, active administrators, sound hearted and high spirited gentlemen, who knew the Natives and their habits and language, but who retain their European turn of mind, and thought, and standards of conduct, are certainly very rare. ...But the present mode of selecting, treating and paying public servants here is not such as would attract men of the kind I have described." In other words what one magistrate called a "zigzag, do nothing, Kaffir speech regime" was the inevitable outcome of a public opinion that asked for little more than peace and a plentiful supply of labour properly controlled, and an administration that, however excellent its intentions, financially starved its native policy in favour of railways and public works projects.

The Galekas had taken the first step that led to war by raiding the Fingos. Their hostility pointed to more than tribal jealousies. The Fingos were living upon land from which Kreli had been expelled. It was a land war. What was really happening could best be seen in the Idutywa district in which Galekas, Fingos, Tembus and other broken fragments of tribes had been gathered; for at the first sign of hostilities they began fighting and plundering amongst themselves, each man's hand raised against every other, his land and his cattle. The Galekas and the Fingos represented the opposite poles of frontier policy. That the Fingos were the favourites of the Government, praised for their prosperity and industry, and the Galekas were despised for their surliness and indolence was due in no small measure to the opposite systems of treatment that had been meted out to them. Such good officials as there were on the frontier were to be found with the tribes that were well treated and well disposed. To Captain Blyth, an energetic, firm and just magistrate, a man whom the natives trusted and respected, with a real genius for the most difficult forms of leadership, the Fingos owed their special position on the frontier. The disappearance of canteens in Fingoland, the agricultural shows, the lawful behaviour and political adaptability of the natives under his care were at the same time monuments to his ability and a demonstration of the capacity of the natives for moderate progressive changes when under the guidance of a sympathetic and thoughtful leadership. That Kreli and his forty thousand Galekas had a Resident without a clerk, poorly paid and with Kafir huts for living quarters, is some indication of the neglect of one of the most numerous and important groups upon the frontier. It is true that the charges of neglect that may be preferred against the government and the administration of the frontier must take into consideration the existence of excellent officials with successful records. It is not possible to neglect the scope and number of their duties which choked their initiative and baulked their imagination. A governor who had had the experience of Sir Bartle Frere was not necessarily the fairest judge of the conditions he found. Like army officers with Indian experience he was too much inclined to judge the frontier by the standards of the Indian and English civil services. Such comparisons could only be unfair.

Between October 1877 and November the war was confined to Kreli's Galekas, and the military operations took place across the frontier. In the usual manner of native wars the volunteers and the Fingo allies harried the enemy, destroyed their supplies of grain and burnt their huts. After a short campaign aglow with the usual "brilliant affairs" the war came to a seeming end. In November the war was reported as over. The volunteers returned home driving their booty before them. The Bashee was left unguarded. Senior officers were bringing the services of their subordinates to the attention of colonial and imperial authorities, and the Government was preparing to divide part of Galekaland into European farms in the time-honoured fashion of the frontier, when suddenly the Galekas came streaming back. All was to be done over again. Worse yet, the war spread into the colony itself.

Only now did it become properly clear that the war was not simply the result of intertribal quarrelsomeness. The unrest seethed in every location and upon every farm. Europeans and the squatters upon their own land faced each other waiting for the first blow to fall. The sudden occurrence of a war apparently so causeless, so purposeless and in the end so hopeless seems proof that it was a war into which the frontier population felt itself helplessly swept.

Behind it all the drought burned on. Another sowing season had come and another crop failure was at hand. Only a deluge, reported the *Cape Argus* of 22 January, could soften the ground which after two years of drought was too hard for the plough, and which even if it could be turned would produce no crops. Cattle died in their tens of thousands; the most resistant vegetation withered; streams and fountains dried at their sources, and the Bashee itself was fordable almost as far as the sea. Well-to-do farmers felt themselves forced close to poverty and poor farmers sank into distress. The more profligate, those who were already but little removed from the poor whites of the next generation and therefore economically very close to the natives, had even eaten their seed. Less eager for war now that he looked upon the gaunt face of a suffering countryside, "War Horse" Cunynghame wrote: "From what I have seen in this war, I have no doubt that a dreadful famine, which indeed has already commenced, will follow in the footsteps of this war." Deputy Commissary General Strickland felt himself compelled to abandon the ways of a strict and unbending economy and distributed grain from the military stores to starving natives, begging that more grain be imported from Adelaide and Buenos Ayres "in the cause of humanity, without delay, not alone for Imperial wants, but to meet those of a coming famine in the Colony".

The new year opened with violence. It opened also with political discord. What a Stuart publicist called a rot amongst the Bishops set in. The return of the Galekas set Frere, Merriman, Molteno and the "War Horse" quarrelling. It was all the fault of the lumbering imperial forces that two months of expensive campaigning had been wasted. The colonial commandos were more mobile, less expensive and more skilled in the ways of the frontier Kafirs. The rebellion was now upon colonial soil. The war was a colonial responsibility, and it should not any longer be conducted by forces that were not under the direct control of the responsible Government of the colony. Thus spoke Molteno, all unmindful of the positive services the troops had already rendered to a frontier that had neglected its own defences.

From a military point of view the attitude taken by Molteno and Merriman was open to the most serious objection. The appointment of a Commandant General of the colonial forces to act independently of the officer in command of the imperial forces created an office unknown to law. It ignored the legal authority of the Governor as Commander in Chief of Her Majesty's forces, imperial and colonial, and created an anomalous dual command. The attempt to create a separate colonial commissariat raised prices. The inexperienced colonial commissariat broke down, and came humbly back to Commissary General Strickland, who in the defence of economy and efficiency feared no man and quarrelled with most. There was real danger in the disjointed operations of separate imperial and colonial forces. The eagerness of poorly disciplined volunteers to go galloping off after cattle promoted desultory operations, and widened the area of disturbance. The colonists swore at Commandant Griffiths when he passed by opportunities for capturing cattle, till that sorely tried officer spluttered: "I wish that there were not a cow in South Africa." The warfare beloved of colonial irregulars, with the burnings and raidings and the deep sense of grudge against the enemy, was a method of inflicting especially heavy losses upon the natives at comparatively little risk, especially if there were native allies to sleep protectively round the camps at night and to be the first to beat the enemy's fastnesses. As a method of thoroughly crushing a native enemy it was unexcelled. It brought hostilities to a close not by defeating the natives in a military sense, but by ruining their economic existence. The peace it brought came at the price of the exhaustion and desolation of the vanquished.

That Frere strenuously opposed the military policy of the Ministry was due partly to his objection to the illegal and inconvenient creation of a dual command and to Merriman's unconstitutional assumption of the duties of a Minister for War. But the Governor was also uneasy at the striking bitterness of both the frontiersmen and the Ministry. Molteno lost his temper in interviews. Frere complained of the studied discourtesy of

Merriman who acted in open disregard of both Governor and Commander of the Forces. It was as if tempers had seriously broken under the strain of weather and alarms. The farmers had grown stronger in the feeling that there was wisdom in striking the first blow with all swiftness and power. The magistrates complained that the Europeans obstructed their efforts to keep the natives quiet. There can be no doubt that the rebellion of colonial natives was precipitated in part at least, as its extent was certainly widened, by the provocative and violent conduct of the farmers who felt that the infection of unrest should be stamped out rigorously, and a thrashing administered to the natives so complete that there would be an end evermore to their disgruntlement and their lawlessness. *Cessante ratione cessat etiam lex.* The Kafirs, said Merriman, were like the Irish. The more you do for them, and the more you apply the rules of abstract justice, the more turbulent they become. It is therefore with little surprise that one reads of the boast of some volunteers that they took no prisoners. The Ministers themselves spoke of drum-head justice and the summary execution of those caught in rebellion. When Frere, remembering the storm of resentment that Governor Eyre had drawn upon his head, expostulated, Attorney General Stockenstrom mocked him for his humanity.

The drought gave the colonial forces a great advantage. The emaciated herds of the natives could not be quickly moved, and were easily captured. In numbers of natives killed the war was also probably more deadly than any previous war in spite of the colonial habit of "potting" the scrambling natives from a distance and breaking in pursuit of the cattle as soon as the natives had fled. The colonial forces behaved very like the Scots Army in the north of England during the Civil War, whose conduct called forth the remark of Lord Hollis that unpaid and volunteer forces took and plundered greatly more "than would have sufficed for their pay and entertainment if it had been orderly raised and provided by the authority and care of the State which was to pay them".[1]

Frere's dismissal of the Ministry was an act almost unique in

[1] Quoted in M. James, *Social Policy during the Puritan Revolution*, pp. 37–38.

the constitutional history of the British Empire. In the light of the subsequent growth and practice of parliamentary government his action stands condemned as unconstitutional and a threat to some of the most important principles of colonial responsible government. Technically and legally a Governor could unmake a ministry. In times of crisis and under great provocation he might be justified in thus acting. Yet even then such power could only be used with the assurance that parliamentary and public opinion would endorse or condone his action. As a precedent to which governors of self-governing colonies might regularly have recourse, Frere's action was unacceptable. Its final effect could only be to plunge parliamentary Government back again into the quarrels and the deadlock that had wrecked earlier representative institutions, and from which government could only emerge either by the abrogation of responsible institutions or by the surrender of the Governor. Under a system of responsible government, whatever its vicissitudes, it must always in the last resort be Parliament that determines policy and settles the constitution of the Cabinet, just as it must in a practical manner be the Cabinet that gives advice to the Crown or its representative. The weight of constitutional opinion was therefore quite properly on the side of Molteno.

But if strict principle were with Molteno the judgment of history has come more and more to see excuses for Frere. He had no alternative but the most emphatic protest against such radical changes introduced in the midst of a war in which heavy burdens and charges had already been borne by imperial troops and the imperial war chest. Any Governor, he vigorously declared, who consented to withdraw troops from the scene of war and to refuse military aid would be "fit for a lunatic asylum". His conduct was far from unpopular. It is of constitutional significance that he won the approval not only of the frontier population, but of the Cape Parliament and the Press as well. The resolution of the Cape House of Assembly that the dismissal of ministers had been unavoidable was carried by thirty-seven votes to twenty-one. It is a fair conclusion therefore that the Ministry was dismissed at a moment that was unusual, when its parliamentary and public prestige was greatly weakened, when it was torn by internal differences and thoroughly unpopular with the Home Government whose views still exercised a much more important influence upon colonial opinion than came to be the case in later years. In brief the circumstances were so special that the constitutional precedent could only be of very limited application.

The new Prime Minister was the Kaffrarian Sprigg. His co-operation with the Governor was facilitated by the departure of Cunynghame who was replaced in the very beginning of March by Sir Frederic Thesiger. In departing the "War Horse" sniffed wistfully at the frontier and beyond. War was brewing on all sides. There was still so much for a soldier to do. In the space of two years there would be fighting in Griqualand West, Pondo-land, the Transvaal, Basutoland, and a great and disastrous war in Zululand. He gave Frere parting advice. Now that the General was finally going nobody seemed to pay any attention to what he said. Yet the wars that he scented were really close at hand. The war on the Eastern Frontier was but the first of them.

The war was over at last in June 1878. The peace that followed is of especial interest in the history of native policy. It laid the basis of all future Cape native policy. Out of it grew ultimately the Transkeian Territories and the well-known system of native government developed there.

Under the influence of Frere, Sprigg undertook a general settlement more constructive than the naïve expulsions and annexations that had ended former wars. Cape policy now en-visaged the early annexation and integration of all the independent territory up to the borders of Natal. There was to be an adequate system of defence. A general disarmament was to be enforced upon all the natives including the Basuto, and the natives were to be brought under the control of an active European adminis-tration. The war had conclusively taught the Cape Government how small and ill-organized its power had been.

During the war Frere had perforce been brought face to face with the chaos and the neglect that had preceded the conflict. Although he made no original or important contribution to native policy he nevertheless did use his influence on the side of the more liberal and farsighted tendencies in native policy. He agreed with the view that the natives were by no means "disinclined to settle down into more civilized habits", and urged such reforms as the substitution of individual for communal tenure, better housing, and the replacement of wasteful pastoral habits by more intensive and profitable agricultural methods. In answer to the numerous addresses of congratulation that were submitted to him at the end of the war he reminded the colonists that the war had taught the need for a reliable and permanent system of defence, and for a policy that would not neglect the energy and the intelligence of the natives, so that they might haply become "valuable elements in the future population of South Africa". It was true that the Gaika location within the colony was in time-honoured fashion divided up into European farms, but beyond the Kei River at least there were no confiscations of land, and this alone was the greatest boon the peace settlement could have conferred upon the native population. The creation of a great native reservation which was not broken up by European settlement rescued the large native population to the east of the Kei River from the fate of the natives within the borders of the Cape, where conditions had been made incurably worse by the confiscation of the Gaika location.

There were naturally mutterings against the "mistaken humanity" of the Governor. Yet even though fingers itched to take possession of some of the country beyond the Kei, it was beginning at long last to be evident that stagnant neglect and crowded living had been a potent cause of restlessness. There was more willingness to believe that the cause of peace might find effective allies in improved native agriculture, a more economical system of land holding, a greater security of property, good police, effective magistrates, and a system of native education. Moreover the war had brought the Western Province and its more liberal mode of thought in native matters into a valuable contact with the problems of the frontier. In native policy Molteno's refusal to consider the separation of East and West was justified.

It was, of course, inconceivable that a peace settlement following upon a war that had been fought with so much feeling should be concerned only with reforms and the amelioration of the condition of the natives. In the locations within the colony the punishment meted out to the rebels was severe indeed. The confiscation of the Gaika location had the most desperate effects, which were spectacularly revealed in the fate of a further project to settle Europeans in the districts of Kentani and Willowvale. Before the land could be given out, wrote Theal, "the pressure of the Bantu for greater space was so strong that the project of white settlement there had to be abandoned". It was clear that the crowding of population had reached a point of such intensity that it was impossible to find any ground that could be taken away. The natives had been punished till they could be punished no more. In Victoria East the tenant and squatting system, which before the war was general, had been almost entirely destroyed. The population thus dispersed either found its way into locations already full to suffocation, or like the bulk of Oba's followers, went into service. The story of the sheer hopelessness of social and economic conditions in the Ciskei may be read in the reports of magistrates in the following years, in the accounts and complaints of locations that were too small, or too stony, or too sandy,[1] in the incessant disputes over cattle encroachment that compelled some magistrates to have recourse to the mediaeval device of forbidding planting at any but certain times.

In spite of the real promise which the settlement contained, the feeling of the colonists continued in the main to be opposed to any policy that did not satisfy their demand for security and labour, and of these the greater was labour. Colonial opinion still insisted that reforms such as the introduction of individual tenure should not seriously affect the market for native labour or its cheapness. "The real civilizer of the natives", wrote the *Standard and Mail*,[2] "is the farmer who teaches them to work." The average colonist therefore welcomed the system of individual tenure and the abolition of the chieftainship, not because the natives might find within the new system the room for a more expansive life, unrestricted by the obscurantism of chiefs and the hostility of tribal customs, but because these reforms promised to put an end to what was called "the give and take protective system" of tribal life. In such a point of view the system

---

[1] Cp. A. 16, 1881.   [2] 2 Sept. 1879.

of individual tenure was seen not as a means necessarily of improving the condition of the natives but as a means of putting an end to their independence and coherence as tribes. There were, of course, those who felt that the natives could become adapted to the altered circumstances which European contact had brought, provided the power of the chiefs and the strength of tribal organizations was broken. But the real strength of popular opinion insisted that the aim of native policy was principally to give to the Europeans labour, peace and freedom from native pressure on their land. "Still it cannot be denied", again wrote the *Standard and Mail*, "that the land question is, with reference to native affairs at the Cape, one on which the position of the Colonists depends. When tribal tenure is allowed to exist in extensive territories occupied by a numerous native population that population may attain a certain degree of prosperity and make some advance in civilization, but they will soon multiply, find their lands too narrow, and get in between the Colonists in such numbers as ultimately to get the better of them and push them back, whereas the Colonists are debarred from getting any of the lands held by native tribes. This is not an imaginary state of affairs, but one which shortly before the war had become a reality in part of our Frontier districts. The introduction of individual tenure...is the remedy for this evil."[1] The colonist, it is not difficult to see, looked upon his native neighbours very much as did the encloser of sixteenth and seventeenth-century England who was sure that "the insolent, prooling, pilfering cottier" would be better off at work for wages than if he were to live in idleness on unenclosed common land. The average colonist found it difficult to be impressed by the poverty of the natives, for it was so evident that they could relieve their poverty by labour. It was in the end this point of view that continued to rule even in Cape native policy.

As far as confederation was concerned the war was the beginning of the end. The shock of the war undermined its strength still further and began the long agony of its collapse. It seemed the very perversity of fate that a South African war should break out just at the time when Parliament and public opinion in

[1] *Ibid.*

England had their attention fixed upon far more engrossing and critical things. Plevna had fallen in December 1877. With its fall Great Britain felt itself drawn dangerously closer to a war with Russia. Spreading colossally from the Baltic to the China seas, athwart the very approaches that India's invaders had always used, Russia had broken its way in 1871 back into the Black Sea, and now she threatened to emerge into the Mediterranean opposite Egypt and the Suez Canal. At the beginning of the age of conflicting imperialisms it was of Russia that Great Britain was first afraid.

When official reports and humanitarian complaints began to arrive of the burnings and raidings on the Cape Eastern Frontier Carnarvon read them with dislike. The Colonial Office had its cold and noncommittal formulas for replying to the complaints about the treatment of natives which the Aborigines Protection Society sent periodically and by force of habit. The annual memorials of the society were an institution that was treated with a sort of formal respect. But when there was a war between the colonists and the natives it was different. People who complained about atrocities joined hands with others who complained about expense. It was an alliance of heart and purse that no Parliament could ignore. Thus when requests for reinforcements came from the Cape, Natal and the Transvaal at the same time Carnarvon received them with irritation. How could he justify before his colleagues and Parliament the sending of British regiments to fight Kreli when they might be needed against the Czar? It was not to assume such responsibilities and expenses that the British Government had entered into the politics of South Africa. By deferring confederation these native wars conspired to defeat it. In the condition of English political life it was almost certain that a policy which had received its support from the Cabinet and Parliament largely because it was economical could only retain its popularity if it remained inexpensive.

In the midst of the war Carnarvon left the Cabinet. With his resignation his South African policy lost the protection which his conviction and purpose had given it, and became exposed to the indifference and hostility of opinion in England and South Africa.

As it emerged from the ninth of its Kafir wars and looked beyond its borders the Cape saw there nothing but justification
for its earlier doubts about confederation. The Diamond Fields
Horse,the crack volunteer force on the frontier, had just had time to
fight one good engagement with the Kafirs before it had to hurry
back to defend the peace of Griqualand West. In the direction
of the Transvaal the Batlapin had risen against the Europeans
who were carting away their precious firewood and jumping their
land. Closer still to Kimberley the unthrifty Griquas, in the
clutches of land speculators, blamed their poverty upon the
Government and rose in arms too. When they were joined by the
Korannas, hard drinkers, great thieves and objectionable neighbours, there stretched from the Transvaal to the Northern border
of the Cape Colony a long thin line of rebellion in difficult
country that took almost a year to pacify.

In the Transvaal and Natal the prospect was still less reassuring. That there would be a Zulu war none could doubt; the
only uncertainty was whether the Transvaal or Natal would bear
the brunt. Shepstone hardly knew where he needed help most,
at Lydenburg to hold the Bapedi in check, at Utrecht to prevent
Cetywayo from falling upon the farmers, or at Pretoria to over-
awe the Boers who were muttering sedition and contemplating
violence against the British regime. The drought that had inflamed the Eastern Frontier burned as far as the Bapedi country.
In the mountains to which the farmers wanted to confine the
natives there was no pasture. What grass there was, grew in the
flat country where was also the arable land desired by natives and
Europeans. Descending from the mountains and finding the
farmers fearful and unorganized, the Bapedi commenced plundering and raiding in defiance of the British administration.
From the optimism of the annexation the British administration
had fallen into deep anxiety. Be it the fault of the drought or of
discontent the taxes that had entered remarkably well during the
first six months now dwindled into a sluggish and reluctant
trickle. One thing, however, was certain. The greatest need of
the Transvaal was quiet. Yet it was of war and not quiet that
Shepstone began to speak. He hoped for war against Cetywayo
and Sekukuni because he was too weak and too poor to afford

the luxury and the risks of a liberal and constructive native policy. The British administration which had entered the Transvaal crying out aloud against the native policy of the Republic had within a year learned to speak the language of its predecessors. Nothing so signally proves its weakness. Already under Shepstone, in other words, did there commence the series of attempts to mollify and win the Boers that finally ended in the restoration of their independence. And yet this *volte face* was neither illogical nor strange.

The outbreak of war on the Cape Eastern Frontier had suddenly dispelled the smug pretence that there had ever been any important difference between the native policies of the Republics and the British colonies. Before 1877 the Transvaal had been accused by its neighbours of fomenting native unrest. Now quite suddenly the Transvaal found itself exonerated, and the Boers were solicited for help as allies against the common foe. Not the Boers but the natives were made the real enemy of peace. Thus did it come about that the British Government annexed the Transvaal to protect the natives, and then found that it had to fight the natives to protect the Transvaal.

In September Sargeaunt sent his report on the administration and the finances of the Transvaal.[1] It was a disillusioning revelation of the Transvaal's extreme financial weakness. Its revenue was adequate to meet only the most rigidly controlled expenditures. It was totally inadequate to pay for the garrison that was becoming increasingly necessary to the maintenance of British authority. The debt of the country had grown greater by an overdraft of £150,000 with the Standard Bank, and the expenditure of £54,592 for the luckless expedition against Sekukuni in the late autumn of 1878.[2]

Sargeaunt's report raised in an acute manner the question of

---

[1] C.O. 291/1, W. C. Sargeaunt to Hicks Beach, Sept. 1878.
[2] The debt of the Transvaal on 1 Jan. 1878 was £253,096. The 6 per cent. loan from the Standard Bank was actually a consolidation of the Transvaal's various debts to banks. As also roughly £27,600 of other debts were paid during the year, the indebtedness on 1 Jan. 1879 was £274,044. This did not include £100,000 parliamentary grant, nor the expenses of the Sekukuni expedition, nor any military charges. C.O. 291/2, Shepstone to Hicks Beach, 6 Feb. 1879. No figures on Transvaal finances, whatever their source, are strictly reliable.

imperial responsibility for the Transvaal. To what extent should the Home Government be responsible for its new acquisition? Hicks Beach admitted readily enough that until confederation had been achieved the Transvaal remained an imperial responsibility. He saw, perhaps, even more clearly than Carnarvon, the depressing effect of the country's debt, and the dangers of a narrow economy. To the Treasury accordingly went a direct request for a further grant of £100,000, and a hint that it might be wise to get rid at once of the whole of the Transvaal's floating debt to the banks.[1]

Unfortunately the Transvaal was not alone in its demands upon the Imperial Treasury. Had it been alone it might not have experienced any insuperable difficulty in obtaining financial assistance. It is an important observation that British policy in the Transvaal was closely affected by events that can only remotely be connected with the annexation. Lest it be too readily assumed that the destiny of the Transvaal was altogether governed by what transpired within its borders, it is well to remember that from the middle of 1878 the British Government grew increasingly anxious over the financial condition of South Africa as a whole. When Hicks Beach asked for further financial help for the Transvaal he received a reply which showed that My Lords of the Treasury had little desire to cast any more British pounds upon the ungrateful South African waters. The war on the Eastern Frontier had cost the imperial chest the sum of £800,000 for which the Cape has as yet assumed no responsibility, although Hicks Beach had written in August insisting that the Cape Colony was bound to bear the expenses of proceedings taken with the "sole object of maintaining the security of the Colony". Griqualand West owed £90,000 to the Bank of England, and had overdrawn its account with the Crown Agents by £12,500. Natal had been much encouraged by the unnaturally high revenues of 1877 and 1878. In its eagerness to outdistance the Cape in the race for the interior trade, it embarked upon an ambitious and expensive plan of public works that filled the Colonial Office with anxiety lest, mistaking its strength, Natal should finally be compelled to unload its burden

[1] Cp. C.O. 291/1, W. C. Sargeaunt to Hicks Beach, Sept. 1878, Minutes.

upon the Imperial Government.[1] Small wonder that the Treasury wrote peremptorily to the Colonial Office. Instead of endeavouring to tide over immediate difficulties by a grant the Colonial Office would act more wisely if it settled "on some definite basis the financial relations of the Imperial Government and the South African Colonies". The Treasury curmudgeon was beginning to look askance at the whole policy of confederation. Of the future of that policy it was doubtful, for it advised the Colonial Office to agree upon the relative proportions in which the costs of the "further complications in the Transvaal" were to be borne. It was prophetic language.

In the meantime the Treasury agreed to defray the military expenditure of the Transvaal. The burden which the Treasury assumed was real enough. Few military stations in the Empire were as expensive as the Transvaal. But an expenditure on soldiers and warlike stores was of no direct assistance to the budget. It established no schools, built no roads, increased no salaries and added no clerks to understaffed departments. It left the administration unaided to struggle under its load of obligations and debts, and forced it to impose a stringent financial discipline upon the Boer at a time when the shadow of an impending Zulu war deepened the gloom.

[1] The Natal estimates for 1879 provided an increase in expenditure of £100,000 over the previous year, meaning a deficit of £51,000, and proposed a Public Works Loan of £300,000.

CHAPTER IX

LAND AND LANDLESSNESS

THE ZULU WAR annihilated an entire British regiment; it killed the Prince Imperial, and gave the death blow to Carnarvon's South African policy. Of the war the immediate causes can be simply told, but the war was itself the climax in a swelling crisis of unrest.

The war marked the moment when the best and most accessible land in Natal and the Transvaal had been taken up by Europeans. Native independence was a hindrance to their free expansion, and a restraint upon the exercise of their authority. The repeated allusions in the newspapers, despatches and speeches of these years to an impending war between the races planted in the minds of the Europeans the conviction that until the native population had been violently and forcefully subordinated to European influence and power there could be no peace. Thus it was that in the Cape Colony, which had just emerged from an expensive and exhausting native war, the administration could decide to disarm the native population and draw upon its head a war with the Basuto.

The land policy in each of the different communities lies at the heart of their native policies. Everywhere the system of landholding explains many of the worst anomalies of native policy. The prosperity that had come with Barkly in 1872 had been followed by a widespread speculation in land. In the Cape Colony land changed hands at enhanced prices. Bank stocks sold at high premiums. There was no one in South Africa to fight, as did Sir George Grey in contemporary New Zealand, against the illusion of a prosperity founded upon the lavish expenditure of borrowed capital. Such a prosperity, when it collapsed, tended to throw the land into the hands of a few monopolists. The unhealthy system of credit did its worst harm to the Transvaal, Griqualand West, and Natal.

In all the territories the system of landholding was exceedingly

N

unfavourable to the natives, although it was in the Transvaal that the natives were in worst case. When Shepstone became Administrator he could not fail to observe the remarkable fact that "notwithstanding the enormous native population which the Boers found in the Transvaal and which continues to reside there, the Government of the Republic never thought it necessary, even as a matter of mere prudence, to set apart land for the occupation of the natives; on the contrary the land occupied by the latter was, without reference to the occupants, granted to private individuals; and there are instances in which the residencies of chiefs of tribes, with thousands of inhabitants living in one spot, have been so granted to individuals without reference to or even the knowledge of the chief and people concerned."[1] That the Republic had not been blind to the vast inroads made upon native settlement was shown by the recurrent debates on the need for native locations in 1868, 1871, 1873 and 1874, even though the debates were uniformly without practical result. Natives, if they held land at all, held it not as of right but during good behaviour, or else, like the natives in parts of the Northern Transvaal, because they had thus far been able to resist European penetration. Under the laws of the Republic only a burgher could hold land. If the natives became possessed of land by purchase, they could not acquire legal title to the land. The title was commonly acquired in the name of some European missionary.

Upon the Transvaal no less than elsewhere in South Africa there had descended the speculator. The normal hunger of the farmer combined with the rapacity of speculators to produce by 1877 an artificial state of overpopulation. So careless had been the largesse of the Republic that there was little valuable land left in its hands. Immense tracts of the best land had passed into the hands of those who hoped ultimately to profit by an advance in prices. There were many who owned between two and three hundred thousand acres. The inhabitants of Lydenburg complained to Shepstone in 1877 that non-occupation was "one of the greatest evils from which this district in common with districts in this, as well as in other colonies suffer. The land is owned in most part by men who neither cultivate nor utilize it in any way. Some are

[1] C.O. 179/136, Shepstone to C.O., 17 Jan. 1880.

utter absentees." It was the acute and artificial shortage of land in the Transvaal that sharpened the competition for the border-lands and the unannexed territories. And even there upon the outskirts of settlement the speculator was active. The Water-berg district, heavily peopled by natives, was a favourite field for the operations of the traffickers in land, whose selling and reselling finally produced such a tangled web of conflicting claims and interests, that the only certainty was the rightlessness of the natives themselves.

Only a constant vigilance exercised by an unprejudiced ad-ministration could safeguard the landed interests of the native population. Even in Griqualand West, which had ostensibly been annexed in the interest of the natives, the administration proved powerless to prevent the extensive expropriation of land by Europeans. The Land Court, presided over by Judge Stocken-strom, assigned to the natives all land that had not been speci-fically disposed of by judgment of the court. Between the Harts and the Vaal rivers, for example, Judge Stockenstrom awarded about 150,000 acres of land to European claimants, and the rest to natives. By the beginning of 1878, when Griqualand entered upon a year of native disturbances, Europeans had possessed themselves of some 420,000 acres in that region. Less than 100,000 acres were left to the natives.

It was actually in the interest of speculators and others greedy for land that as much territory as possible should be awarded to the natives. Many who cried out most loudly against the oppres-sion of the natives actually did most to ruin them. Some of the most appealing letters in defence of the tribes were written by agents who were also in the employ of landjobbers. Land was signed away and grants were made; yet rarely was the native the gainer. Too frequently was it true that the documents which deeded away large tracts bore upon them half a dozen crosses witnessed solely by the friends of the European grantee. It was with a pile of such grants before him that Judge Stockenstrom was provoked to the ironic outburst that "all who have watched the evidence during the proceedings must have been struck with the marvellous facility with which those who have gained the confidence of these natives can induce them to append their signatures to any document upon a mere statement of its alleged contents". Some four years afterwards Colonel Moysey made a detailed and expert examination of the system of landholding in the Keate Award area. When he beheld the inroads that the Europeans had made upon the territory of the tribes, he too expressed his amazement that any chief, styled paramount or not, could have had "the will, the intention or the power to alienate the land of his tribe, and by a formal document to enable an individual and a stranger to dispose of his holdings with its human load to another yet more strange".

During the Republic titles to farms were acquired under conditions that could only result in confusion. When a burgher wished to establish his claim to a farm he first registered the land with the nearest landdrost. After giving a merely general description of the land he received an extract (*uittreksel*). He thus obtained a preliminary title without any legal scrutiny of his claim, even though the same land could be registered under varying general descriptions by other claimants. When a sufficient number of claims to land in a district had accumulated, it became a settled district, and a commission of inspection proceeded to mark out the ground by the rude and confusing process of noting trees, ant heaps, and estimating distances and areas by the time it took to cover them on horseback. No Domesday Book hide could have been more unreliably measured. A few months after such a survey the holders of the *uittreksels* acquired final and legal title to their property. Of such summary inspections irregularity was the result. In the frontier districts especially no effort was made to enforce either the law that no farm could exceed 3000 morgen in extent, or the law that non-occupancy of a farm for a period of eighteen months should be visited by confiscation. In such outlying districts it was easy for individuals to acquire official recognition of farms covering an acreage far beyond the limits permitted by law.

The refusal of the British Government between 1871 and 1877 to extend its authority to the Keate Award area handed the natives over completely to landjobbers, farmers, adventurers, and to the anarchy of tribal disputes. The annexation of the Transvaal came too late for the natives, but most opportunely for the Europeans. They had reached a position where they could advance no farther without the serious risk of a native war. To them the British annexation was a welcome event, providing only that it protected them in the possession of their land and did not seek to prevent further encroachment. Through the annexation many a worthless title deed was elevated to the status of a negotiable certificate of possession; many farms were occupied for the first time, and the frontier commenced again to march against the weakening resistance of independent native settlement.

It was a common rejoinder on the Transvaal western border that there was land enough for all. But in a country where rainfall is scanty and irregular land is useless without water. Maps of Africa and especially South Africa are misleading; for what are indicated as streams and rivers are often dry beds during the greater part of the year. Much of the land assigned to the natives of Griqualand West that looked so plentiful and attractive on paper was in fact composed of the table lands to the west of the Vaal River which break down towards the river in a long line of bluffs and ravines, so inhospitable that to call them hunger lands was not too expressive. A leading source of complaint against the encroaching Europeans was that literally enormous areas of land were rendered practically useless by the white man's monopoly of the few but invaluable sources of water supply. In some parts the native cattle took a whole day to reach drinking water and could therefore be watered only three times a week. The absence of abundant water was often the secret of the incredible acreages which the Europeans claimed. It was almost a rule that when either the Europeans or the natives put forward what on paper appeared to be monstrous claims, they were stretching their boundaries so as to include some water supply essential for their cattle. Most of the claims of the natives could have been greatly modified could they only have been given sufficient water. As it was, the loss of a single fountain destroyed the value of thousands of acres. It happened not rarely that European owners of springs deliberately isolated themselves and drove away the natives of the district by using dams and furrows to divert the water from its natural course, or by allowing the excess to run to waste. The difficulty of creating reserves for the native population was due therefore not to any insufficiency of area, but to the uniformity with which the advancing European line absorbed the sources of water supply.

Shepstone had come from Natal to cure the native ills of the Transvaal. But the ills he left behind him were almost fully as serious. The natives and Europeans of Natal were both the victims of a vicious land system. Out of a total acreage of more than 12,000,000 acres the natives held some 2,000,000 acres. They numbered at the lowest reckoning more than three hundred thousand. The Europeans who were less than twenty thousand owned most of the best land. The natives owned much of the worst. It followed that a large proportion of the native population was forced to live upon land to which it had no legal claim. Where the natives lived upon private or Crown lands they lived there entirely upon sufferance and without legal title. The first of native disabilities, therefore, was the legal weakness and insecurity of their tenure.

In Natal the natives and the colonists lived together more closely than elsewhere in South Africa. No community more signally belied the delusion that white and black interests were separate. It is in Natal that it can most clearly be seen how much the economic existence of the two races had become intertwined. The tradition that saw the natives as a military menace, and the policy that was the consequence, were in conflict with the real truth, that in an economic sense the two races were sensitive to the same forces. The very conditions that were disadvantageous to the natives had unfavourable effects upon the Europeans as well.

The Europeans had a land problem no less than the natives. They too suffered from its insufficiency. So mistakenly had Natal regulated the disposal of public lands, and so wantonly had it squandered this wealth, that it was actually unable to encourage immigration because the inducement of good and cheap land was gone. Although a vast space of waste and unoccupied land formed the most common feature of the country, there was a serious land shortage.

In the first years of the colony's life after British annexation a real effort had been made to encourage the growth of a thrifty population that would plough and sow and build upon its own land. In the new dispensation which Sir Harry Smith brought in 1848 it was the aim of the Government to encourage the industry of the farmer who really occupied his land, and to discourage to the uttermost the "desolating traffic in waste lands by the land jobbers, who have so frequently deprived the farmers of their neighbours, and the country of its inhabitants". Every man who was without land and desired to live under the Government of the Queen, could have a farm of 6000 acres to "settle and occupy". Lest the intention of this land settlement be perverted and men solicit farms merely to sell them to their own profit, it was stipulated that certain classes of grants should not be alienable, without the consent of the Lieutenant-Governor, for a period of seven years. The history of colonization and settlement in the Empire proves the wisdom of such provisions. In Natal, however, they could not be applied.

Sir Harry Smith himself had come to Natal to prevent an exodus of its Boer population. It was one of the most impressive effects of the Great Trek that it gave to the Europeans access to vast acreages of land. If a colony like Natal, which in the eyes of the Boers already had the serious disadvantage of being British, were not to lose its population to the interior, it must offer the same liberal and unrestricted conditions of land tenure as were obtainable elsewhere. The colony was too young, and its Government too eager to win the good will of the disaffected Boers to attempt to carry out the provisions of Sir Harry Smith's land policy. In order that all possible grounds of complaint and of grievance might be removed the practice of granting large farms was introduced, and the attempt to enforce occupation and prevent speculative buying was relaxed. Such generosity, however, failed to stimulate immigration beyond the merest trickle. In 1857 Lieutenant-Governor Sir John Scott tried to encourage immigration by a system of assisted passages. There followed a wild period of optimism during which rumours of gold discoveries and the temporary prosperity of the inland trade gave a misleading impression of solidity to a speculative bubble in land and goods. There was a rush to accumulate large holdings. Land changed hands rapidly and heavy inroads were made upon the Crown lands. Between 1857 and 1860 less than three hundred immigrants entered the country. Yet by a system of almost promiscuous largesse more than 1,360,000 acres were alienated. Before the colony had been in existence a quarter of a century, it had no land left sufficiently attractive to encourage immigration on a scale commensurate with its needs and ambition. A country as large as Scotland only had the population of a third-rate English town. What Crown lands there still remained were remote from centres of population, roadless and unsuited for occupation by inexperienced settlers. As early as 1864 the Immigration Board sorrowfully complained that immigration was handicapped by a scarcity of land.

After 1864 came the inevitable slump. Land values fell. The market was glutted with cheap land. In the absence of any regulation upon landholding, the land became concentrated in the hands of still fewer individuals. Immigration virtually ceased. After active efforts to promote immigration only forty-five people entered the colony in 1874. Out of an area of 12,000,000 acres two-thirds had been alienated. Of these 2,000,000 acres had been set aside for native locations. Since fully one-half of the European population lived in the two towns of Durban and Pietermaritzburg 6,000,000 acres[1] were in the possession of a population of 8000 individuals, including women and children. That nearly a million acres of the best land in the colony had become the property of a single company still more conspicuously revealed the nature of Natal's land distribution, and suggests that there were many white men in the scanty rural population who were without enough land.[2]

From the system of land distribution could be deduced Natal's most urgent problems. Held as it was, the land could not be rationally taxed. South Africa's inordinately large landholdings never bore a reasonable share of taxation. The story of native taxation cannot be fully understood without remembering this, for in part native taxation was a device to avoid heavier land taxes. The wasteful distribution of land was a restraint upon a prosperous and expanding European settlement. The lack of an industrious and prosperous farming population handicapped

[1] According to Wolseley 8,000,000 acres.
[2] C.O. 179/123, D. 41, Bulwer to Carnarvon, 17 Feb. 1877.

economic development. A scattered and sparse European settlement induced a sense of weakness in the face of the large native population, which helps to explain why the politically powerful Europeans were so prone to resort to restrictive and repressive measures against the natives.

Natal's population was primarily a population of merchants, middlemen and transport drivers. Its roads were bustling while its countryside was stagnant. The discovery of diamonds caused the port of Durban to hum, and filled the roads with waggons and cracking whips. But in the country itself "a vast waste of wilderness meets the traveller's eye wherever he turns his step over the great uplands of Natal and year by year the blue sky of winter is darkened by the smoke, and the nights are reddened by the glare of unnumbered fires which carry again into the atmosphere the wealth that the summer's rain and sun had quickened upon the soil". These vast tracts of land, complained Wolseley, were held "by private speculators and others in the close proximity of towns and along the main road of commerce; these desirable sites of settlement are not only kept from the hands of those who could turn them to advantage under a system of small culture, but they are also kept as barriers against the occupation of more remote districts, drawing round such districts wide cordons of desolation". It is one of the most familiar paradoxes of South African life that the same process which produced an exaggerated and uneconomical sparseness of European settlement was responsible for an equally exaggerated condensation of the native population. European underpopulation and native overpopulation were phenomena with similar causes. Out of this truth flows much of the history of native policy and of the relations between the races.

It was easy and popular to blame the native reserves for Natal's artificial land shortage. Although the Europeans held in excess of 6,000,000 acres they sought to make inroads upon the 2,000,000 acres upon which lived a much denser native population. So well aware was Shepstone of the gravity of this problem that in 1875 he did not dare to press a Squatters on Crown Land Bill for fear of a worse and wider uprising, which Natal might be unable to put down.[1] Natal was afraid of its own native population.

[1] G.D. 6/38, Broome to Carnarvon, 17 Dec. 1875.

Profitless to the community, the speculative holdings were profitable enough to their owners. It was estimated in 1874 that 5,000,000 acres of land belonging to private individuals or companies were occupied by natives.[1] These squatters provided a rental sufficient to permit the owners to hold the land profitably, and thus to keep it securely locked up for a future market. Although Law 2 of 1855 contained provisions against squatting on Crown lands and unoccupied private lands without permission of the government, the law was almost uniformly ignored. The rental from squatters was not seldom the sole profit from a farm, and, as the rental after 1876 was sometimes as high as £5 per hut, the profit could be handsome. The foremost offender was a company euphemistically named The Natal Land and Colonization Company, which deliberately held its enormous territory containing some of the most fertile and accessible land in the country, until the railways, roads, bridges, and new markets should have caused all land values to rise.

While the provision of land for the natives in Natal was not ungenerous compared with the Cape Eastern Province, they were manifestly in need of larger reserves. The land which they already legally owned was used poorly and wastefully. Yet some of the locations were poor and unproductive. The tangled country of "baboon rocks" and boulders in the Inanda location, for example, greatly reduced the area of arable land and added nothing to the pasture land. The locations were so crowded, that in districts like Ixopo and Klip River, the great majority of the native population dwelt upon Crown lands and private property. When Wolseley proposed to tax those who cluttered up the Crown lands and prevented, as he believed, the free settlement of Europeans, Shepstone answered quite simply and dryly: "There is no land for them to go to in the Colony; the locations are full and private owners cannot accommodate them; they must, therefore, either pay or resist."[2]

Sometimes the natives could neither pay nor resist. Because they had no legal tenure, their expulsion from private lands or even Crown lands was easily undertaken. A favourite excuse for

---

[1] C.O. 179/116, Shepstone to Carnarvon, 22 Sept. 1874.
[2] C.O. 179/117, D. 131, Wolseley to Carnarvon, 14 June 1875.

clearing farms of squatting natives was that native cattle were increasing beyond all measure. Actually it was in European herds that there was the greatest increase. The collapse of the land boom, the absence of intense cultivation, the profitable character of transport riding, and a heavier infiltration of Transvaal and Free State trekboers caused an increase in European cattle after 1868. The result was a greater inclination to drive the natives from the private lands so as to make room for cattle.

Only exceptionally could the natives add to their holdings. The location originally assigned to Langalibalele was 90,000 acres in extent. After his rebellion it was surveyed again. The startling discovery that the tribe had, in the best European fashion, quietly absorbed 55,000 acres of adjoining Crown lands, threw an interesting light on Langalibalele's reputation as a sly dog amongst the natives, and the special dislike in which he was held by his European neighbours. Elsewhere the efforts of the natives to acquire land were not so successful. The purchase of land was legally possible. But cash purchases were beyond their means. The fluctuation in native income due to seasons and market prices, their own feckless ways and the relatively high cost of land, made it difficult for them to keep up the instalments over any period of years. "Several attempts have been made by natives to hire Crown Lands," wrote the Magistrate of the Newcastle Division, "but up to the present only one has succeeded, and he has been obliged to sell his right to a neighbouring Boer, on account of the manner in which the land was already surrounded by that in the hands of the Boer. It is probable that all natives endeavouring to become possessed of land in this division will have to share the same fate, as to raise means sufficient to purchase or lease a very small piece of land, a number of kraals have to club together, and the land they get is too small to carry them and their stock. Their only hope for some time to come is to be tenants to private owners, or by finding cheap labour."[1]

Natal looked to its natives for cheap labour. It also looked to them for revenue. The chief virtue of Shepstone's reign of peace was that it permitted Natal to draw a relatively large and growing

[1] Magistrates' Reports, 1882.

income from its natives, without ever being forced by war into heavy expenditures. Of the income obtained from native sources only the smallest part was devoted to purposes of native development. "The native population of Natal", Shepstone candidly admitted, "contributes to the revenue annually a sum equal, at least, to that necessary to maintain the whole fixed establishment of the Colony for the government of the whites as well as themselves." Like the rest of South Africa Natal was struggling hard after 1870 to achieve the benefits of the industrial revolution. In order to keep pace with its expensive requirements the government was compelled to increase its income. Of the country's resources the subject population was more important than either crops or minerals. To tax the native population, to release the labour force imprisoned in the tribal organization, and to encourage the natives to increase their consumption of dutiable goods—these ends were not the whole of native policy, but they were nevertheless a great part. It was an openly admitted principle of Natal taxation that cheap goods imported mainly for native consumption should be taxed more heavily than the more highly priced goods intended for the European market.[1] In countries such as Natal, where customs duties are the principal sources of revenue, the burden inevitably rests heavily upon the poorer and politically powerless elements of the population. The exceptional customs tariff enacted in 1863 was designed especially to affect articles consumed by the native population. Cotton and cheap woollen blankets paid a levy of 15 per cent., although the general tax on goods for European consumption was 6 per cent. *ad valorem*. Agricultural implements for the farmers were imported free of duty. But on the cheaper and inferior Kafir hoes the duty was a shilling. In such goods, which were an important item in the customs revenue, Natal had a natural monopoly; for being bulky they could not be profitably imported through the ports to the north or the south of Durban, where the duty was lower but transportation charges higher. Upon Kafir beads the rate was actually so high that for a while the taste for beads in Natal almost died away, and the not unprofitable bead trade with the interior fell into other hands. The duty of one shilling on

[1] C.O. 179/136, Shepstone to Hicks Beach, 23 Jan. 1880.

each Kafir hoe was also so high that it was actually found profitable to manufacture them locally and escape the duty. The Government was hoist with its own petard, although the natives, in the terse words of Shepstone, "paid just the same".

Langalibalele's rebellion revealed a native government that had become frankly insufficient. Upon the simple responsibility of keeping the peace which Shepstone had discharged so well, pressed the necessity of reform. Yet it was in the same decade that Natal entered upon a period of active expansion. During Langalibalele's rebellion Natal lost its faith in the lumbering ox. The rebellion precipitated a crisis in transportation. Redwater sickness was everywhere. Prices of transport were high and getting higher. High rates and insufficient transport hindered trade in bulky commodities for which there was a demand in the interior. Thousands of bales of wool of the previous year's growth could not be moved from the Free State. Natal feared for her trade and her customs duties. The time had come for steam to displace the ox.

Railways and roads, bridges and harbours imposed a heavy contingent burden upon the community. Present and future were pledged to the new enterprises. Any native policy calling for meaningful reforms in landholding, administration and law, must be expensive. Such expense was an obstacle to the early achievement of Natal's ambitious designs. For a native policy that would impose additional charges on the revenue there was no enthusiasm and no place. A new lease of life was therefore given to the unenterprising policy of peace, and relations continued to be conducted through negations and restrictions.

In the financial history of Natal the effects of South African disunion can be clearly discerned. Natal was forced to make efforts dangerously close to the limits of its strength, in order not to be outdistanced by the stronger Cape in the race for the trade with the interior. From the beginning the conflicting and unco-ordinated railway schemes threatened to place a difficult burden upon the resources of the country. It is important to remember that Natal's railways were originally built, not to tap rich agricultural resources within the colony, nor to open up otherwise inaccessible regions to settlement, but chiefly to win for its small merchant community an import trade in goods that would for the most part be consumed outside the colony.

The history of the rivalry between the Cape and Natal reveals that the problem of confederation was not simply one of inducing the Dutch Republics to co-operate with the British colonies, but also of getting the British colonies themselves to compose the bitter commercial and political rivalries that were responsible, just as much as the separatism of republican politics, for the fatal disharmony that marked the last quarter of the nineteenth century. Railways that were hailed as the iron bonds that would link up the subcontinent into a single system of economic interdependence were actually guilty of increasing competition and illwill. Every sod that was turned in the Cape, every sleeper that was laid in Natal, and every whisper that ran in the Transvaal about the Delagoa Railway, only served to show that interests and enterprises that were unharnessed by a common political co-operation would not cease to be jarring and opposed. To balance their uncertain budgets, and to carry their heavy accumulation of indebtedness, the Cape and Natal were forced into a cut-throat rivalry for the trade of the interior, and forced to rebuff the interior communities in their demands for a share of the revenue collected at the British ports.

Expenditure in Natal rose sharply during the 'seventies. The rise was met in part by an increase in the Colony's revenue. But the revenue of Natal was subject, as such revenues commonly are, to fluctuation. Any disturbance in the interior immediately made itself felt in the customs returns. The decision to build railways brought with it the need quickly to expand the Colony's income. In the Colonial Office the leaping expenditures were viewed with alarm.[1] In the 'seventies there was hardly a year in which Natal was not urgently warned against expanding too indiscreetly and beyond its strength. "The fact is", wrote Meade, "that Natal finances have suffered from the demoralization which spread over the Colony when they were determined to embark in a huge railway expenditure".[2] A greater virtue than ambition in the eyes of

---

[1] C.O. 179/126, D. 12, Bulwer to Carnarvon, 22 Jan. 1878.

[2] C.O. 179/130, D. 143, Bulwer to Hicks Beach, 30 Aug. 1879, Minutes. On the estimates of 1879 the sum for interest charges was £82,021. It meant that more than 25 per cent. of the revenue would be absorbed by interest charges on railway loans.

the Colonial Office was solvency. Between the eager and venture-some colonial attitude that was willing to speculate upon its future, and the fastidious and scrupulous financial thought of the Colonial Office, there lies that gulf which has so frequently been taken by the more adverse critics of British colonial policy to prove the short-sighted and selfish vision of Downing Street. That the Colonial Office was over cautious and anxious to avoid calls upon the British Treasury, and that it would rather see Natal's money spent on a scheme of defence to relieve British regiments cannot be doubted. Amongst the cardinal sins of British colonial policy is false economy. And yet it was much sound and mature advice that such a colony as Natal received from England, advice that was frequently needed and that was not without its effect upon the repute of the colony in the financial markets of London.

The colonists of Natal and their able editors were prone to accuse the Secretary of State of writing and acting without proper knowledge of the special problems of the colony. Lord Carnarvon's comments upon Langalibalele's rebellion and trial mortified them. Yet at the height of this controversy the Colonial Office was engaged in saving Natal from doing itself a lasting and insidious harm. The Colonial Office vindicated its watchfulness by preventing Natal from buying its railway by the dissipation of its remaining landed wealth and the sacrifice of a considerable native population. In its eagerness to have its railway, the Legislature passed a number of bills in 1874[1] that proposed to subsidize the railway construction company by surrendering to it two and a half million acres of the waste lands that still remained. The grant was striking because it came close to exhausting the land reserves of the colony. It was startling because the Legislative Council proposed to surrender to the company large powers to deal with the natives living upon the grant; for the value of the grant did not consist in the market value of the land, much of which lay far removed from towns and roads, but in the power to exact a subsidy from the natives.

It was a foolhardy step of which the Legislative Council was itself apprehensive. To submit a large population to the self-interest of a single company could only imperil the peace of the

[1] Laws 3, 6, 11 of 1874.

entire colony. The division of land occupied by the natives amongst a number of owners afforded some guarantee that untoward action would not be simultaneous or concerted, whereas the action of a powerful company obedient to orders from directors in England might very easily endanger the prestige of Government. But the Natal Legislative Council felt that it must choose between two evils; and it was more willing to run the risk of native unrest than fail to obtain railway communications.[1]

The danger of relaxing the control of Government over any question connected with the native population was immediately clear to the Colonial Office. To Shepstone, who was in England, Carnarvon turned for information and advice. In Natal Shepstone had publicly supported the bills, although he had not failed to indicate to the Legislative Council the peril that they were incurring. But he was prepared himself to incur the risk if the prosperity of Natal were thereby advanced. A railway, he believed, would help to increase the proportion of "white sinews", and correct the unhealthy preponderance of black over white. The natives, after all, had no legal right to the land which they occupied. The Government was free to use the land in the interests of the colony's progress. Now that the Secretary of State, however, was clearly unsympathetic with the measure, Shepstone changed his mind. He eagerly pleaded for the disallowance of the bills. "The Secretary of State", he urged, "has more than once stood between us and the harm we wished to do ourselves, and the colonists have lived to thank him for the exercise of such a parental function".[2]

To pay for its public works Natal finally decided to have recourse to loans and an increase in native taxation. Since 1849 the hut tax, which was the principal tax, had been seven shillings per hut. Out of a total revenue in 1850 of £39,112, the native contribution by direct taxation was £9521. In 1875 the general revenue had grown to £260,271. In that year the proceeds of the native hut tax and the marriage fees amounted to £42,308. From such figures the conclusion was drawn in Natal that native contributions to the revenue had not expanded in the same ratio as the

---

[1] C.O. 179/115, D. 187, Shepstone to Carnarvon, 22 Sept. 1874.
[2] *Ibid.*

general revenue. Since 1868 there had therefore been an insistent call that the natives should be taxed more heavily. The roads and railways which the Government planned to build, the police it maintained, and the magistrates it appointed were as much in the native as in the European interest. An increase in taxation was only fair and could not possibly be too onerous. After all, the natives had only to come out and work for the Europeans, in order to earn the needed money. In 1876 the marriage tax was abolished and the hut tax was doubled. In the interests of the revenue the argument that the marriage tax would undermine polygamy and make the native a more civilized being was conveniently forgotten.

The apparent disproportion in the tax burden assumed by the European and native population becomes less when it is remembered that a very considerable amount of Natal's increased revenue came from the duties upon goods intended for the Republics and the interior. Writing to Carnarvon in October 1874, Froude remarked that the total amount paid by the natives of Natal was £60,000, and that of the rest of the revenue two-thirds came from taxes on goods re-exported to the Republics.

In itself the doubling of the hut tax was not unbearable, even though direct native taxes rose from £42,308 in 1875 to £59,100 in 1877, £62,638 in 1880, and £70,042 in 1884. But to these figures there should be added such items as £3687 in 1872 for import duties on "apparel and slops", £240 for duty on beads, the native fines paid in the courts which amounted to £2233 in 1878, and the dog tax which in 1881 amounted to £964 in the division of Newcastle alone. The available evidence suggests that the direct and indirect native contribution to the Colonial Treasury was at least doubled in the decade after 1875. Although there is no way of determining the effect of increased taxation upon the natives, it is at least certain that the same period does not show even a remotely comparable improvement in their economic condition.

Corresponding to the steep rise in native taxation was an equally abrupt increase in the rentals paid by squatters on private lands. In districts where a large proportion lived upon European land it was not the Government hut tax of fourteen

O

shillings, but the heavy rent exacted by private landowners that more adequately measured the demands made upon the natives. In some well-favoured districts that received their rains from the Drakensberg Mountains the natives were spared the worst effect of climate and season, and could usually depend upon regular and plentiful crops. Close to towns like Newcastle and the capital, and in the Klip River district where the majority of the white population were pastoralists, the natives could sell produce to the European population at fair prices, but natives thus privileged were a minority. In the remoter districts, beneath the eyries and amongst the " baboon rocks " of the Inanda location, for example, much lower prices prevailed, and it is certain that profits from the sale of produce were totally inadequate to meet the demands placed upon their resources. Where the average price for draught oxen was reported to be £7 in 1872, the price in the districts of Alfred, Tugela and Alexandria ranged between £5. 10s. and £5. 15s.; hides averaging 5¼d. per pound were bought in Alexandria for 2¼d. per pound; maize selling at an average price of 18s. 3d. per muid was as low as 7s. 6d. in the Tugela district.

More serious were the sharp fluctuations in food prices that only in the rarest cases were of advantage to the natives. In Natal, as in the Cape, magistrates constantly reported the low prices at which the natives sold and the high prices at which they bought. Too frequently did it occur that maize, sold at harvest time for as little as 5s. per muid, had to be repurchased later in the year for 20s.; in bad seasons prices were as high as 40s. and 50s. Although the annual returns made by the magistrates of the acreage which the natives had under cultivation, and the quantities of maize, kafir corn and other crops were fuller and more detailed than in any other colony, they could still be little more than approximations. And yet the story they tell is very definitely the same as was told by the more casual evidence available for the Cape. At the moment that the Natal native population was required to assume larger burdens, it enjoyed only a very low standard of existence, even though that standard was still higher than that of the Eastern districts of the Cape. The favourite contention of the Europeans that the natives had too much land, that they were wealthy in cattle and were rapidly becoming more wealthy, cannot be accepted as true. Labour, Shepstone admitted, was the main source that must supply the money for their taxes. Crops might be poor or they might be plentiful, yet taxes came as regularly as the seasons.

At an early moment in the 'seventies a considerable proportion of the able-bodied males of Natal's native population laboured during at least part of each year for the colonists. Such a resolution as was passed by the Legislative Council on 5 December 1872, calling for the more active introduction of native labour from beyond the colony, did not at all prove the contention that Natal's own natives would not come out and labour. Rather did it mean, as the evidence tends most strongly to show, that Natal used the labour of its own subjects wastefully and uneconomically. "I believe", wrote Lieutenant-Governor Musgrave in January 1873, "that in fact a very fair proportion of the able-bodied male Natives of the Colony are engaged in the service of their white fellow subjects, although it is not very willingly admitted by the European population among whom it is the fashion to complain that the Kafirs will not work. I think I am right in regarding one in seven as the general ratio in most populations of the adult males capable of bearing arms. Assuming this proportion, from a total population of 300,000 we only have 43,000 adult males; and it is my firm conviction that many more than half of these are always employed in the service of the Whites in some capacity. Statistics are difficult to procure in a Colony like this; but ordinary observation may be trusted to some extent, and it is obvious to the casual observer that none of the most common domestic occupations of life could proceed among the European population for a day without the assistance of Kafirs. The contrast in this respect between South Africa and British North America is very striking to one who has the opportunity to compare the two places. In North America the population is obliged in all things to be self reliant; they have no servile race to help them. Here, the Europeans of whatever rank of life, are served by Kafirs; who cook for them, wash for them, wait upon them, act as Nurse maids for their children; in short do all the manifold services required by those who do little or nothing for themselves. A mechanic going to execute any little job of work; it may be a Blacksmith or a Carpenter, will have one or two Kafirs to carry his tools for him and generally to render him assistance. A farmer coming into Maritzburg with his Ox Wagon will have two or three in attendance as 'Foreloupers' and Drivers. The total number so employed in Domestic Service on Farms and in Trades, must be very large, without counting those who work on the Sugar Plantations. Computing it from the numbers of the Whites, I have no doubt that it would be found not far short of 25,000. If these are already withdrawn from the adult males; and if it be remembered that the Native population are themselves Cultivators of the soil, being in some cases indeed the employers of paid labourers, and the producers of their own food, which is not imported and not grown for them by the European population—then I think the matter wears a different appearance, and it is seen that notwithstanding the large number of natives already in Natal, there may be a demand for more labour for large agricultural enterprises without imputing any very unusual amount of laziness to our own black population."[1]

Beneath the constant complaints about the scarcity of native labour was the tacit assumption that it was as a labourer that the native could best serve the Colony. This assumption may be most clearly discerned in the provisions made for native education and improvement, and in the standing of the native before the law and the magistrates. Beyond the efforts of the missionaries which, though devoted, were utterly inadequate, and the casual undisciplined effects of contact with the whites, Natal had really no policy of education that actively sought to better native manners of living. It was one thing to hold out such theoretic privileges as the franchise; it was yet another to provide the money, build the institutions and appoint the officers in a scheme of native improvement. Obviously it was difficult to urge improvements in either the system of landholding or in native agricultural methods, when it was the conviction of the average colonist that it was only by increasing the sphere of European ownership and enterprise that the colony could advance in prosperity and wealth. Thus, paradoxically, continued

[1] C.O. 179/111, D. 9, Musgrave to Kimberley, 6 Jan. 1873.

pressure upon the natives seemed to be essential if the colony were to progress. It is most revealing to remark how closely the language in which the colonists objected to the indolence and improvidence of the natives resembled the language of the opponents in England during the eighteenth century of the "barbarous" methods and "immoral" laziness of the small English farmer whose lands they desired to enclose. In nineteenth-century South Africa there was the same tendency to see in dispossession rather than education the proper treatment of the backward agricultural methods and the idleness of the reserves, the same tendency to force upon the natives the status of labourers.

He who would acquaint himself more thoroughly with the position which the native held in Natal, must go to the records of the magistrates' courts where they still exist, and study the cases under the Masters and Servants Law and the litigation between Europeans and natives over grazing rights, complaints of trespass and disputes on the ownership of land. He will find magistrates devoted to their office, and understanding of the difficult needs of their charges, men upon whose shoulders rested the grave responsibility of piloting the natives through those indefinite borderlands where native and white interests and customs met and clashed. Yet whatever the merit of individual magistrates, and however great the personal prestige of their chief, Shepstone, the native administration of Natal was poor. Being indifferently paid, some of the magistrates traded with those under their care. The majority spoke the native language badly or not at all; their defects were hardly bettered by the average poorness of the court interpreters. In every district the magistrate's staff and the police force were insufficient, so that in districts where large numbers of natives lived upon European land a considerable measure of authority and power fell into the hands of minor officials like the field cornet. In parts of the upland districts the natives were much at the mercy of the white farmers. The sympathies of most of the magistrates were incontestably with the labour-hungry farmers.

Natal's Masters and Servants Act had been passed in 1850. Its operation casts a revealing light upon an important phase of native government. Since Natal had made as little provision for jails as it had for police, the difficulty of sending offenders to prison encouraged magistrates to avail themselves of their power to flog. It was a short and ready way of dealing with offenders that was popular with the colonists. These resisted every effort of the Colonial Office to secure the removal of the flogging clause from the Act of 1850. In the rural districts of Natal flogging was prescribed as a matter of course in a very large proportion of sentences. In the Tugela district every servant convicted in 1872 was flogged.[1]

The number of natives flogged was really not high. Between 1870 and 1873 the number of floggings administered amounted to 633 for the whole of Natal. What was significant was the inordinately large number of convictions in proportion to the complaints of European masters and,[2] in the words of the Attorney General of Natal himself, "the indiscriminate way in which the lash is used against all classes of servants, and for any offence, however trifling". The punishment of servants on such recorded grounds as "misconduct", "disobedience", "neglect of duty", "impertinence", "absence", and "desertion" suggests most strongly that frequently the mere complaint of the European employer was sufficient to obtain a conviction. Although the Attorney General condemned flogging as an obnoxious punishment and a "stain upon the Statute Book of the Colony",[3] it can at least be explained by the special circumstances of the Colony. It was simply true that the generality of Natal's magistrates were not only too busy and understaffed to perform much more than their routine duties, but they also stood closer to the employers of labour than to their servants. In the courts of Natal to work badly for the white man, or to arouse an employer to anger, was listed equally with drunkenness and the other punishable failings over which missionaries shook their heads and magistrates their lashes.

Between the uprising of Langalibalele and the Zulu War lay a period of unusual tribulation for Natal. Like the Cape Eastern

[1] C.O. 179/111, D. 40, Musgrave to Kimberley, 25 Feb. 1873, Enclosures. By the end of the decade the lash was no longer used in Natal.
[2] *Ibid*. D. 59, Musgrave to Kimberley, 7 April 1873, Minutes and Enclosures.
[3] C.O. 179/117, D. 50, Pine to Carnarvon, 17 Feb. 1875, Enclosures.

Frontier and a great area of the Transvaal, it suffered from a prolonged and devastating drought. The magistrates of Umgeni, Newcastle, Inanda, Weenen, and Umsinga reported a succession of partial or complete crop failures in their districts for each year from 1875 to 1879; until 1880 there were in all Natal no reports of really good crops at all, although the Klip River district seems to have enjoyed normal seasons for every year except 1878. In the Tugela valley there was a continual crop failure until the outbreak of the Zulu War, so that large numbers of the natives entirely abandoned the district. The first effect of the drought was to drive an increasing number of natives to work for their food and their taxes. Maize and kafir corn became scarce; prices rose sharply. Through want of grass and the consequent high mortality amongst the overworked draught animals, transport costs were more than trebled in 1878.[1] In 1878 a sack of grain had become equal in value to a cow in the Weenen district; the natives became heavily indebted to local storekeepers and the Resident Magistrate was finally forced to proceed to relief measures. The Buffalo River and other streams of the Newcastle district almost ceased to run in 1878. Where the natives were forced to drink heavy stagnant water there was much sickness and death.

The cattle suffered above all. Drought and fire destroyed the grass, so that to the ravages of lungsickness and redwater was added an unusual death rate from starvation. In the worst districts the natives were ready to part with their stock at the lowest prices. In the light soils of the Alexandria district the scarcity of food drove the natives to live on shell fish and wild roots. To the unhappy natives of Umgeni the havoc of the seasons was made more desperate by a plague of myriads of caterpillars.[2] At the end of 1878 the price of maize was fully four times as high in Durban as it was in London, and the Colonial Office received an urgent telegram from Sir Henry Bulwer asking that 2000 tons of maize be sent to Durban.[3] The first sowing of the early summer

[1] Magistrates' Reports, Weenen, 1878.
[2] Magistrates' Reports, 1876 to 1879 *passim*.
[3] C.O. 179/127, Tel., Bulwer to Hicks Beach, received Colonial Office, 23 Nov. 1878.

of 1878 was a general failure; the second crop, if it succeeded, could not be harvested before June 1879.[1]

Happily the famine never came. The more fortunate natives in districts where there was food shared with the needy; the country's inefficient and sorely tested transport system did succeed in relieving the distress of the worst areas. Storekeepers and magistrates, the white man's roads and his ox waggons had served the natives well.

Severe conditions of drought in Zululand were an essential part of the events that led to the Zulu War. Colonists looking upon Zululand from without easily received an impression of ample space, and even Shepstone concluded that Zululand could afford to resign a large area of its territory without serious inconvenience. The relationship of a people to the territory which it occupies is at all times difficult to determine. An area that will reward abundantly the skill of a resourceful race may yet provide only a bare living for a more primitive race, unable to oppose to the rigours of climate and season the tools and devices of civilization. In Zululand, areas that were well watered tended to be rocky and broken. Other parts were unhealthy for horses and cattle. Large extents of bush in the chief Somkeli's land were uninhabited by man or beast, indicating clearly enough the presence of the dread tsetse fly and probably the malarial mosquito. The bush at the junction of the two Umfolosi rivers, once inhabited and cultivated, was entirely abandoned at the time of the Zulu War. As a result the country, where it was healthier, was thickly peopled, while the rest lay deserted. Ulundi, the royal kraal, lay in healthy country, relatively cool, and providing good grazing for cattle. What mattered in Zululand were the elevated flats and grassy slopes, freer from fly and malaria, suitable for pasturage, and healthy for men and cattle. Hence it was that in the midst of an apparent spaciousness the lands of Zulu chiefs were often interlaced, so that like mediaeval barons they owned kraals in one another's territory. Where the ground was good and healthy, kraals jostled one another in rivalry; elsewhere there was no encroachment and little quarrelling.

[1] C.O. 179/129, Bulwer to Hicks Beach, 4 Jan. 1879.

Amongst the causes of the great restlessness in the Zulu country at the end of 1876 and of the tension upon the Transvaal border that preceded the annexation was a serious scarcity of food which followed the drought of the summer of 1876–7. Already wasted by lungsickness, the herds of cattle were more severely scourged yet. Compared to what it had been in the 'sixties the country was destitute of cattle. "The Zulu country", wrote F. B. Fynney, "is very poor in cattle; as both lungsickness and redwater have made great ravages amongst the herds...and the only way now for a poor Zulu to obtain a beast is to assist in the 'smelling out' and killing of some richer neighbour".[1] Seldom or never did a Zulu who was poor get killed. Much of the internal discord that observers outside Zululand took to be proof of the innate and dangerous quarrelsomeness of the Zulus could be traced back to the different effects of drought and cattle disease. Chiefs claimed a share of the property of anybody convicted of witchcraft. There was a constant temptation, therefore, for men to impeach their fellows, and, by betraying them, to obtain part of their wealth. It was natural that the natives on some of the mission stations should be "smelled out", either because they had more cattle, or because the natives believed that the lungsickness was a spell which the converts had cast upon the pagans. Actually very few missionary natives were touched, but those Christian natives who were "smelled out" became, in the missionary letters that found their way to Natal and England, martyrs who had died upon their knees praying for Cetywayo and the Zulu nation.

British intervention in Zululand was inevitable. Sooner or later the territory would be annexed. The frontiers of Zululand marched with the frontiers of two European communities; its inhabitants were appearing in Natal and at the diamond fields as labourers. Only a sentimental and uncritical temper could question the necessity of including Zululand, as Basutoland and much of Kaffraria had already been included, in the political system of the Europeans. What mattered was not that the Europeans in their power would finally move upon Zululand and seize it, but rather the manner and the conditions of its seizing. It was Sir

[1] C.O. 179/124, Bulwer to Carnarvon, 19 July 1877, Enclosures.

Bartle Frere who decided to bring Zululand under the Crown. His effort led to war.

To the question of Frere's responsibility for the Zulu War there can be no clear answer. The causes of the war lie hidden in the devastation of drought and disease, in the irritations produced by the jostling contacts of Boers and Zulus on fertile border lands, in the rivalries between chiefs within Zululand itself, in the clamouring of missionaries that Cetywayo was a very tool of Satan, in an exaggerated European nervousness of native attack, and last but not least in the uneasy tossing of Shepstone's Transvaal Government in an effort to find comfort in the midst of Boer discontent, financial instability, and native unrest.

Sir Henry Bulwer had long complained of the unguarded talk by responsible men of war with the Zulus, and the impending conquest of their country. It was not only the Europeans who were alarmed by rumours from Zululand. The Zulus themselves were no less agitated by rumours of marchings and armings and drillings directed against them. Some of the missionaries in Zululand deliberately excited the feeling of alarm in the colony. The Zulu country was stocked with arms and ammunition, and the sun set daily on murder and brutality. In the breasts of forty thousand warriors there burned a wild confidence in victory. If ever they carried out the threats they sang in their songs, there would be such a slaughter as the country had never seen. To the missionaries the destruction of Cetywayo's power would open the way to the Evangel, for as long as he ruled they could make no headway against the "godlessness" of the Zulus. Their aims were lofty and they lived their lives arduously in the service of their calling, yet they pressed upon the native tribal system as a hostile and disruptive agency. Missionaries, though their designs be ever so well meaning, came with an alien culture. Like colonists, traders, and magistrates they adhered to moral attitudes, social principles and economic motives that were completely alien to native modes of thought. Whatever the intention of the agencies of European culture that came into contact with native life, whether to "benefit" it by "improving" native moral or economic conditions, or to weaken and destroy their economic strength, their common basis was a disapproval of the native mode of life. It was not strange that to Cetywayo, whose heart yearned to return to the heroic days of Chaka, a Zulu converted was a Zulu spoiled. His was the attitude of the unrepentant Indian in Parkman who exclaimed, "Heaven is a good place for Frenchmen, but I wish to be among Indians...."

The life of the missionaries in Zululand was made difficult. But they in their turn took revenge by deluging the Natal Government with letters, wondering when the "blessed day" of annexation would come. Their statements were exaggerated, so that it was sometimes difficult not to receive from them the impression that their stations were crowded with converts eagerly welcoming the martyr's crown at the hands of pagan hate. They were frequently guilty of interference in the internal affairs of Zululand, and it was only the wisdom and tact of Bulwer that on several occasions prevented the actions and words of missionaries from leading to a serious crisis. "Between ourselves", wrote Bulwer to Carnarvon, "I think the missionaries would not have been sorry if such a crisis had arisen."[1]

Prominent amongst the missionaries of Zululand was one Robertson of the English Church Mission, a friend of Shepstone of twenty-four years standing, the informant of the *Natal Colonist*, and the ally of all that wanted to annex Zululand. It was upon him that Shepstone largely relied for information about the happenings within Zululand, for in matters of which he was held to be the best informed man in the land Shepstone's judgment was strangely influenced by hearsay, and by personal and official representations. Whereas Bulwer in Natal was of an extreme calmness, exasperating to a more volatile temperament like that of Frere, weighing carefully and soberly what was told him, urging inquiry and an impartial arbitration, and never to the end of the crisis that preceded the Zulu War entirely convinced that a war was necessary, Shepstone in the Transvaal came increasingly to feel that Cetywayo lay athwart the road to the success of the British annexation. An independent Zululand was his Carthage and had to be destroyed. The story of the Zulu War is in large measure the story of Shepstone's intractable problems in the Transvaal. The story is unfolded not so much in Natal as in the Transvaal.

[1] G.D. 6/38, Bulwer to Carnarvon, 14 Sept. 1877.

CHAPTER X

THE ZULU WAR

PAUL KRUGER returned from his unsuccessful mission to England to find such a stirring in the Transvaal as he had not expected. The drought, the menace of frontier native troubles, and the unpopularity of the Government provided a congenial soil for agitation. The irreconcilables already spoke openly of revolt. Looking upon the British garrison and finding it small they discussed the ease with which it might be overwhelmed, and declared that if there were to be any further memorials they must be written with guns and signed in blood. At first Kruger was disposed to frown upon the discontent which he found. He had gone to England with little enthusiasm, and had returned with no definite hope for the future. His manner was such that in spite of his great personal prestige he was even accused of defending the British Government and accepting its bribes. Popular opinion, Kruger could not fail to see, was stronger than he had thought. He harkened to the outcry, but not because men accused him of treachery. Here was the very expression of public opinion of which he had spoken in the Colonial Office. The Secretary of State had refused to allow a plebiscite, and yet here the people were taking it upon themselves to express their will in a memorial that finally bore close to seven thousand signatures.

The People. Kruger used the word time and time again in the months that followed his return. If the people spoke, he had no alternative but to follow, and it could mean nothing that he had spoken of co-operation to Administrator Shepstone or Lord Carnarvon. His strong democratic sense and his deep, almost mystical attachment to the traditions of the Boers, made him give to the people a force that placed its wish above the power of an alien government.

On 4 April 1878 a meeting of delegates was held at Doornfontein. Before the meeting there was so much talk of violence that Shepstone thought it necessary to issue a proclamation warning the leaders and pointing out that such gatherings were illegal. The final outcome of the meeting was a distinct personal triumph for the moderating views of Kruger. Contrary to much mistaken popular assumption he was not a man of violence. Even though he now maintained that the British Government owed its existence to injustice and untruth, he was not prepared to act in defiance of the existing order. " I do not wish to go beyond the law ", he said. He was not a ringleader. Yet if the people believed that Her Majesty's Government had annexed the Transvaal against its wishes, then let the people declare themselves. " If there exists a majority for independence then I am Vice-President ", he declared; and if he were Vice-President the British Government of the Transvaal no longer had any legal existence for him. He was convinced now that there was such a majority. Therefore he could in all freedom of conscience work to restore the Transvaal to its independence.

In the middle of May Kruger left Pretoria on his way again to England. Shepstone thrust him more utterly into opposition by dismissing him from the Executive Council. As his term of office had expired in November 1877, the dismissal was legal enough, but it marked the end of even the very little effort that Shepstone had made to win the support of the most important man on the Boer side. With Kruger went Joubert and the Hollander, Bok, who acted as secretary to the deputation. They were received in Cape Town by the Governor, who spoke to Kruger, tempting him, and invited him to go up with him to see the Cape Parliament at work. Such institutions and such autonomy were the high reward that the Transvaal might win if it desisted from disloyal and factious conduct. But Kruger would not be tempted, and did not turn from his path.

On 10 July the deputation was received by Sir Michael Hicks Beach in Downing Street. The atmosphere of the meeting was stiff. Carnarvon a year before had been much more friendly and gracious. The Secretary of State briefly reminded the deputation of the answer which his predecessor had already given, accepted the address they brought with them, and bowed them out. The correspondence between the Colonial Office and the deputation was equally curt. The Transvaal's sense of wrong, Kruger pleaded and warned, might be one of sentiment, but its effects were none the less real. Unless the Boers were given satisfaction their rancour would continue to fester. It was in vain. The correspondence was brought to an abrupt close, and the deputation was informed that the sovereignty of the Queen could in no circumstances be withdrawn from the Transvaal. Kruger and Joubert left England. But their last words were still of an injustice that could only be undone by the independence of the Transvaal.

An understanding with the Transvaal had become urgent. Even while he was confronted by the delegates Hicks Beach knew that the Crown Colony Government of the Transvaal must be tempered. Writing to Frere on Kruger's birthday, he agreed that the time had come to give to the Transvaal a more generous constitution, in which, however, the civil list and native policy would be reserved. "I am disposed to think", he wrote, "that the entry of the Transvaal into confederation will be much facilitated if, after full consideration of the present state of the Province, you should feel able to recommend that its Legislature should in the first instance be empowered to act freely in such matters as would continue after confederation to remain within its jurisdiction." Upon the policy of confederation which he was eager to consummate the state of affairs in the Transvaal had a direct bearing. Molteno had gone and with him there had gone the most convinced opponent of British policy. But as long as the Transvaal Government was at odds with the Boers, as long as there was no assurance of stability or peace in the Transvaal and upon its borders, the Cape Colony shrank from any intimacy with its neighbours. The debate held in the Cape House of Assembly on 16 August 1878 made it clear that however well disposed sentiment had generally become towards confederation in principle, there was the greatest unwillingness to embark upon a road so uncertain and so beset with danger. To a Parliament in which the Dutch vote was strong the disaffection of the Transvaal population was a serious obstacle. If confederation was to make any progress, the Transvaal must be given a more advanced form of government. "Some sort of constitution for the Transvaal seems to me essential", Frere reported after the debate. "It cannot with safety be delayed and it ought, I think, to be discussed, and the leading features made known to the Boers before the Transvaal delegates, Messrs. Kruger and Joubert, return to this country."[1]

The impolicy of the peremptory dismissal of the delegates now becomes clear. The Secretary of State had before him two of the most important men in the Transvaal. To the more liberal institutions intended for the Transvaal their services or their support would be invaluable. By making no serious effort to find a possible basis of understanding or discussion with them the Colonial Office deepened their feeling of resentment, and made it difficult for any concession or change of policy, however well intentioned and generous, to appear as other than arbitrary, and imposed without the consent of the people. It was now evident, too, how grievously British policy had erred in choosing the facile but precarious path of autocracy, for the longer the popular institutions of the country were in abeyance and the leaders estranged from the Government, the steeper was the way back to self-government.

The absence of a representative body and the abolition of Boer institutions made it all the more necessary that the administration should endeavour to keep the Boer leaders as close to it as possible. In this the failure of the British administration was abject. Admitted that the peculiar circumstances of the Transvaal made an autocratic Government easier than a popular form, and that the stiffness of Shepstone made friendly relations with the leaders difficult, it is still true that within even the narrow limits of Crown Colony Government Shepstone and his successors showed a fatal lack of elasticity and tolerance. It is not surprising that the first real discussions between the Boer leaders and the British authorities came when the intractable and armed camps of the Boers forced attention to views that had hitherto been practically voiceless. The British Government discovered, in other words, that it was easier to take away than to restore. Could Shepstone only have annexed the Transvaal with the same genial dexterity that Wolseley had used to juggle Natal

[1] C.O. 48/486, D. 184, Frere to Hicks Beach, 22 July 1878.

out of its liberties he might have persuaded the Volksraad to accept the new regime. But the belated concessions that the British Government now proposed, because they were concessions, encouraged the Boers to ask for more, and because as concessions they were insufficient convinced the farmers that the British Government had had no change of heart and was acting ungenerously towards them.

In the Transvaal itself Shepstone's administration realized too that a *rapprochement* with the Boers had become essential. To win the tolerance of the Boers the administration was ready to pay a price. The price was the abandonment of the native policy heralded at the time of the annexation.

It was an abandonment that Shepstone undertook without reluctance. He hoped not merely to remove the cause of much misunderstanding, but also to alleviate the hated pressure of taxation upon the whites. Without any feeling of inconsistency he adopted that very republican policy which he had done most to discredit. The defeat of Sekukuni and the overthrow of Cetywayo became necessities of his policy. A general subordination of the native population would open a "mine of wealth". Native taxation would tap "the most valuable resources of the country", and produce a happier economic condition that would coax the dissenting and dissident population into loyalty. Thus it was that the British administration abandoned any sincere effort to carry out the reforms that had bulked so large at the time of the annexation. The worst result of the annexation was that it created a "Boer question" that obscured the "native question", and imposed upon the British Government the duty of assuaging the outraged feelings of the Dutch patriots and gave it no freedom to carry out, however slowly, a policy that took some favourable account of the natives. Instead of reforms Shepstone came to counsel a policy of force that would ease the minds of the Boers and permit the collection of native taxes. Aware that the Home Government was strongly disinclined to any further subsidies or loans and that the Boers would resent taxation or even a sterner collection of existing imposts, Shepstone turned, as Natal had turned, to the native population. To break them to an unaccustomed fiscal yoke there must be peace in the land, and the authority of Government must be unquestioned. That meant the subjection of Sekukuni and the crushing of the Zulu power. Before the end of his first year in the Transvaal Shepstone had come to the conclusion that a successful Zulu war would be the quickest way of putting an end to his difficulties in the Transvaal. The defeat of Cetywayo, he hoped, would be rewarded by the loyalty of the Dutch and the submission of the natives. "Should we be fortunate enough to get safely, and with credit in the eyes of the natives, through this Zulu business, then I feel no apprehension regarding anything else." Frere reached the same conclusion, telling Thesiger that "till our difficulties with the Zulus and Secoecoeni are ended, we can hardly expect much revenue to come into the Transvaal Exchequer".

Shepstone confronted the spectre of a Zulu war without qualms, assured that the annexation of Zululand could be achieved with comparative ease. "I see", he roundly declared, "that incongruous, perhaps antagonistic elements are daily approaching each other, and that they must sooner or later produce the inevitable result; if we were prepared the sooner this result is produced the better...[and] the sooner the root of the evil, which I consider to be the Zulu power and military organization, is dealt with the easier our task will be."[1] When Bulwer, in his concern to avoid war, proposed arbitration and a clearly defined boundary, he objected that Cetywayo was after all a savage, who could not be expected to yield, as might a civilized ruler, to diplomatic suasion. Formal treaties with uncivilized tribes involved an incongruity that must sooner or later prove fatal to peaceful relations. In the thinking of the colonists it came to be assumed with little debate that the peace of South Africa was incompatible with the further independence of Cetywayo, and that he was the hope of every chief in the land that would welcome an uprising of the blacks against the whites. Even in England, those like Carnarvon who shrank from all idea of a native war felt guiltily that a war with Cetywayo would serve the cause of civilization against a "bloodthirsty savage" whose rule was a course of murder organized by treachery and conducted by witchcraft.

[1] G.D. 6/23, Shepstone to Carnarvon, 11 Dec. 1877.

P

The disasters of the Zulu War no doubt point accusingly at those whose words and deeds helped to bring on the outbreak. These tragedies, so important in their consequences that Zululand achieved an abrupt and unforgettable notoriety in England and Europe, were nevertheless imprevisible, illogical, and accidental. From them certainly can come no true or just criticism of the war. In defence of Shepstone and those who thought like him, it must be said that both the Transvaal and Natal were bound to come to grips with Zululand. What Shepstone and later Sir Bartle Frere reported to England about the subversive comings and goings of Zulu emissaries among the surrounding tribes, the turbulence and the truculence on the borders, was all essentially true. With their facts Sir Henry Bulwer preferred not to quarrel. He did, however, question the counsel they gave and the violent course they took.

By the side of Shepstone the Lieutenant-Governor of Natal was, as Carnarvon was swift to observe, a mere child in native diplomacy. Wilting and unhappy under the swift sun of a dry Natal summer that brought the heat of noon before the morning was well begun, he looked less for honour and achievement in his office than for rest and a return to England. Yet on that account he was freer from the partisanships, and less embarrassed by the partialities of local feeling upon native questions. To nervousness he opposed calmness, and scepticism to clamant rumour. A policy of the scope of Shepstone's he had none, and his views cannot be made to confront those of Shepstone as right against wrong. Rather did he essay to seat himself judicially between the contestants, seeking to restrain the one, and to reason with the other. "Have you any good reasons to believe", he asked Shepstone, "that they want to quarrel with us?"[1] What had provoked the cry of war? Was it a European fear of the Zulus, or rather, perhaps, a Zulu fear of the Europeans? Was it at least not true that the territorial dispute was originally of Dutch making? Must it not inevitably prove bewildering to the Zulu mind that the British Government, which had formerly opposed all Boer claims upon Zululand, should now espouse them? And granted that Cetywayo would listen to no reason, and accept no impartial

[1] G.D. 6/38, Bulwer to Shepstone, 14 Nov. 1877.

decision, was Shepstone prepared for war? Would the disunion that prevailed in Zululand cause it to fall easily into the hands of its white conquerors, or might it not become dangerously and formidably united in the face of European aggression?

In reply Shepstone shook his head.[1] The dispute with the Zulus could no longer be settled by the judicial means possible between two equal and consenting parties. Cetywayo, he complained, was taking aim at his head with a loaded gun. It was too much to ask of even a good Christian that he should not defend himself. In every circumstance of life, Bulwer was told a little testily, prevention was always better than cure. What was more, the Zulus did not have the slightest claim to the land in dispute with the Transvaal. Not injustice but kindness would be done to the Zulu nation by the destruction of Cetywayo's tyranny.

From England the Colonial Office had watched events with anxiety and breathed Lord Melbourne's question: "Can't you leave it alone?" It had already been a shock to Carnarvon that the man upon whom he leaned so heavily in the furtherance of his South African policies should have taken counsel with poor financial advisers. Now Bulwer was accusing Shepstone of listening to equally poor advice in the field of his own greatest competence and in such an explosive matter as native policy. It was incredible, and yet Bulwer's good faith and his belief in what he wrote could not be doubted. A warning was imperative. Carnarvon underlined the peremptory words which he sent privately to Shepstone, admonishing him that "*a native war is just now impossible and that you must avoid it*".[2] He also wrote to Bulwer. "I have told Shepstone", he said, "that if the worst comes to the worst, he must temporize and avoid a collision, for which the present time is entirely and absolutely inopportune."[3] His command was unequivocal, yet men and the circumstances that governed them conspired to circumvent it.

The boundary between Natal and Zululand was a natural boundary formed by the Tugela River and its tributary the

[1] G.D. 6/38, Shepstone to Bulwer, 26 Nov. 1877.
[2] G.D. 6/23, Carnarvon to Shepstone, 3 Jan. 1878.
[3] G.D. 6/38, Carnarvon to Bulwer, 2 Jan. 1878.

Buffalo. But between the Transvaal and Zululand the rivers ran across the boundary at right angles, tempting the Boers to follow them more deeply into Zululand. Whereas the unhealthy, low-lying land through which ran the Natal boundary acted as some sort of buffer between the whites and the blacks, the country on the Transvaal side was high, healthy, well watered and excellent pastureland. The Pongolo bush was the chief source of timber for the indispensable waggons used in the poorly wooded Transvaal hinterland. Close on three score sawyers were constantly busy there. In this attractive area Zulus and Boers met. The story of their meeting is the familiar story of every South African frontier line. Provisional concessions to the advancing Europeans by the natives grew swiftly into vested interests, and qualified agreements became indefeasible private rights. In 1861 the pressure of the Boers received "legal" recognition by Cetywayo's "cession" of the Blood River Territory, bounded by a vague line between Rorke's Drift and the Pongolo River. Both because the Boers had no intention that the treaty should set a term to their desire for more land, and because the ceded territory contained a native population that had suddenly become landless and rightless under the law of the white man, the entire frontier became the scene of dispute, and knew no more rest. Henceforth the Boers based their claims upon the cession of 1861. Their further encroachments and a disconcerting tendency for the original line to drift and wander in search of yet more land, received a sort of remanded and prospective sanction from the original grant. Six different maps of the Transvaal published between 1870 and 1877, all of them at least semi-official, showed no agreement whatever in either the western or the eastern Transvaal boundaries, varying sometimes as much as one hundred and fifty miles. "In a little while", grumbled the old chief Panda, "the Boers will not leave me room enough in which to stretch my legs."

The sense of injury and resentment felt by the native population provoked a nagging and irritated relationship that rose and fell in intensity with the seasons. In July 1877 Lieutenant-Colonel A. W. Durnford reported on what he had seen and heard during a visit to the Zulu border. "It seems very prob-

able that many of the frontier Boers have worried the Zulus a
great deal, encroaching on their land and scaring their cattle.
There seem to have been frequent seiz res of cattle upon various
and frivolous pretexts, under the apparent authority of Government; the assistant field cornets being the commanders of parties
of farmers, and when the class of man holding such an appointment is considered, it is very evident that the Zulu has very little
chance of redress at such hands. The weakness of the late
Government has been shown in this border land, cattle having
been seized because the hut tax was not paid when demanded,
taken away and returned again." In revenge the Zulus gave as
good as they got. Both Zulus and farmers were victims of one
another.

In the last months of 1877 there was an ominous drift towards
collision on the frontier. The eddies from deeper within Zululand washed their unrest against the frontier and spilled agitation amongst the settlers. The Zulus were aggressive; Cetywayo
through his emissaries held a high language, and the farmers in
fear called upon the new Government to show its worth. It
seemed probable that a Zulu war would break out before the
war on the Cape Eastern Frontier was over. Already officers of
the troops in Natal were calculating the number of infantry and
cavalry a Zulu campaign would require.

It was 18 October 1877 before Shepstone had been able to
visit the disturbed area. He came with the earlier opinion which
he had formed in Natal that justice would be on the side of the
Zulus. Examining the crosses of Zulu indunas and the signatures
of Boer leaders upon the documents in the one-sided archives
of nearly twenty years of dispute and compromise, shocked at the
ravaged orchards and deserted farmhouses with their broken
windows and shattered doors, mortified to find that the erstwhile
respectful tone of the indunas had turned to a vaunting and an
overbearing manner, he experienced a comprehensive change.
As if the scales had fallen from his eyes he suddenly found himself impressed, as for the first time, by the legal force of the Boer
claim, and by the clear duty that his Government had to protect
a civilized settlement against a brutal invasion of established
rights. He had come in the belief that he might have to sacrifice

territory. Now he spoke of an "explosion that must come", and declared both wishfully and prophetically that "had Cetywayo's 30,000 warriors been in time changed to labourers working for wages, Zululand would have been a prosperous peaceful country instead of what it now is, a source of perpetual danger to itself and its neighbours". But before Zululand could achieve the distinction of a nation of labourers working for the white man's wages, the spirit of tyranny had to be violently exorcized.

Bulwer could not or would not follow Shepstone's reasoning. But in Cape Town Shepstone's words fell upon the readier ears of Sir Bartle Frere. His critics have made Frere the principal scapegoat of the Zulu War, and his apologists have absolved him of all serious blame. To the perpetual question of responsibility for the war there can be no simple answer. Frere was an imperialist. His experience and temperament predisposed him to an expansive policy. He had been sent to achieve confederation. It was his view that if ever confederation were to be firmly established, South Africa must absorb its enclaves, round out its frontiers, and see to it that no enemy or rival pressed too closely upon these frontiers. A policy that called for the more adequate defence of Cape Town, called equally for the annexation of Zululand and the extension of an insulating British influence over the coastline to the north of the new confederation.

In September 1878 Frere wrote to Hicks Beach urging upon him the declaration of British sovereignty over the entire seaboard from the Cape Colony to the limits of Portuguese possession on both the east and west coasts. Also did he urge the establishment of the general sovereignty of the British Government over all the chiefs and rulers between the west coast and the Transvaal on the east, and between the boundary of the Cape Colony to the south and the Portuguese boundary to the north. If that could be done, and if the Transvaal could be reconciled to British rule, there would be an end "to schemes such as are now being discussed for introducing one of the great military powers of Europe and America as a counterpoise to the British influence and supremacy in South Africa".[1]

British agents and administrators throughout Africa were, like

---

[1] C.O. 48/485, Conf. B., Frere to Hicks Beach, 5 Sept. 1878.

Kirk and Frere, nervous of a foreign encroachment upon what they defined as British interests. They assumed that such interests, being British, were inherently stronger than all ·other interests, so that the mere documentary annexation in Whitehall of an entire coastline up to points removed by a thousand miles from established colonial boundaries was enough to set the British seal indelibly upon a million square miles of hinterland, and to throw a cloak of British influence over millions of natives. Small wonder that Mr R. B. D. Morier, the forthright British ambassador in Lisbon, who was accused of bullying the entire Portuguese Ministry to do his will, complained to Lord Salisbury that the Colonial Office would do well to enforce a new imperial decalogue upon the "exuberant manhood of our young colonies", requiring them to "keep the commandments, remove not your neighbour's landmarks; covet not that which is not yours; but if you do, don't do it in public". There were in other words being sown in South Africa the seeds of a diplomatic ill will in colonial matters that the British Government was destined to reap for twenty years to come.

The attitude of the Colonial Office to the proposals of the High Commissioner was ambiguous. On the one hand Hicks Beach informed Frere that as long as no provision was made for the government of such territories the Home Government was not prepared to assume the imprevisible burdens of annexation. Nor did he see the value of such sweeping declarations of sovereignty when the nature of the African coast was such as to afford "no temptation whatever" to occupation by another European power. And yet office minutes, and general correspondence, showed that the Colonial Office was stirred by the same feelings of uneasiness that led Frere to urge the British Government to forestall or frustrate while there was yet time any challenge of the British position in South Africa.

Precisely because the Colonial Office was divided by equivocal and indecisive counsels it could enjoin no clear policy upon Frere. To visit the sin of deliberate disobedience upon his memory is quite useless as well as unfair. In his mind a Zulu war did not mean simply the overthrow of Cetywayo and his regiments; it was also an act of imperial expansion. "It will be found necessary", Frere remarked in May 1878, "sooner or later, to extend the British Protectorate in some form or other over all the tribes...between the sea and the present Transvaal frontier, and the longer it is deferred the more troublesome will the operation become."[1]

In the month of May, when the South African winter sets in, the farmers were in the habit of moving with their flocks to warmer pastures. Their movement in 1878 in a year of unusual shortage of grass and water touched off the resentment of the border Zulus. War talk grew more insistent than ever. The rumours in the Transvaal and Natal that Cetywayo was planning to attack the whites fed upon the rumours among the natives that the whites were preparing an invasion of Zululand, and these became in their vicious turn food for the fear of a general conflagration. Addressing the Cape Parliament in August, as might a European ruler surrounded by enemies, Frere pointed to disturbances in Griqualand West, disquietude in the Transvaal, and the imminent danger of a Zulu war, and wondered whither to direct his attention first. As if in answer, Shepstone wrote four days later calling upon the High Commissioner to act against the Zulus. The British Government had allowed the idea of European supremacy to become obscured in the native mind. It had sought to halt the natural and necessary advance of European influence until now it was bound in the interests of the general safety to reassert that supremacy by the firm suppression of native unrest. "There is at this moment", he urged, "a process of political fermentation going on among all the native tribes from the colonial seaboard to the Zambesi River. The war and rebellion on the Cape Frontier, the attitude of Cetywayo, the risings in Griqualand West, the aggression of Sekukuni, and the complaints made by the interior traders of the treatment they have met with from such chiefs as Lobengula show this." Frere's letters show that what Shepstone said had a marked influence upon his thought and action.

Fresh from his experience on the Cape Eastern Frontier and disturbed at the unmistakable moodiness and fits of temper of

[1] C. 2220, p. 35, Dec. 1878, Frere to Hicks Beach, 13 May 1878; sent 30 July 1878.

the native population, Frere was ready to believe that there was more than mere coincidence in such universal unrest. In the India which he knew so well one undisciplined frontier after another was being suppressed by the advance of the British Raj. In South Africa, too, he felt that the paramount power was compelled to erase every frontier and subordinate every tribe that diminished its authority or refused to admit its discipline. The disarmament of the Zulus captured Frere's imagination. He spoke of it as if it involved the disbanding of territorial regiments, and the emancipation of the natives from an unnatural restraint upon their freedom to be labourers. The natives within and on the borders of European settlement, he agreed with Shepstone, should all be brought under the discipline of a closer contact with the Europeans. Large masses of uncivilized natives, he said, "must not be left within our own dominions to fester in idleness". For it could not be denied that "tamed and civilized individuals", be they elephants, horses, or men, were in the long run stronger than the "untutored, unbroken, untamed, uncivilized". The question why Natal's natives were so good, and their brethren just across the Tugela so bad, he answered in the same manner as the Natal colonist: Natal owed its internal peace, and its native subjects owed their contentment, to the benefits of contact between savages and industrious, civilized people. The happy necessity of working for a subsistence had in his view wrought a comprehensive change in their original Zulu character, showing that they were not unregenerate and that Zulus might well be changed from a "man-slaying human military machine", to a "useful class of native labourers".[1]

In February 1878 had been appointed the Commission to inquire into the Transvaal-Zulu boundary dispute. It was composed of J. W. Shepstone, Acting Secretary of Native Affairs in Natal, Lieutenant-Colonel Durnford, R.E., already well acquainted with the disputed area, and the Attorney General of Natal, M. H. Gallwey. The Commission was appointed quite evidently because Bulwer had willed it, and not because either Shepstone or Frere expected its findings to lessen in any way the hazards of war. Its labours were therefore beset from the beginning

[1] C.O. 48/489, Frere to Hicks Beach, 12 Feb. 1879.

by doubt and prejudice. Frere did not receive its report till July. Yet as early as May his correspondence revealed how he would receive the report when it came. "I do not see", he wrote to Hicks Beach, "how these Zulu claims can be admitted without the Transvaal giving up portions of territory which have for years been unquestioned as belonging to the Transvaal Republic." Any such surrender would be "inconsistent with the pledges given by Sir Theophilus Shepstone to the inhabitants of the Transvaal that in taking them over the British Government would maintain the integrity of their state". Concessions would not make the frontier any more secure. The Zulu border must be made to yield, as the Eastern Frontier had yielded, to the discipline and determination of European troops.

It was unfortunate that two of the members of the Commission should have been members of the Government of Natal, which was notoriously jealous of Transvaal claims to Zulu territory. Yet a better commissioner than Gallwey could hardly have been chosen. A capable lawyer, he was also a man of independent mind and forthright speech, who would subject the documents and treaties of the frontier dispute to a strict legal scrutiny. Indeed, the work of the Commission was valuable chiefly on account of its legal findings. It did not attempt to decide problems of policy, whether Zululand should be annexed, whether the peace of South Africa called for the destruction of Cetywayo's impis, or whether it would be expedient to win Dutch good will by a report sympathetic to their claims. It disclosed, as no other inquiry had disclosed, how little the rights and claims of South African frontier settlement really depended upon legal acts and procedures, and how much treaties and concessions were mere cloaks devised to cover an earlier and arbitrary encroachment. For these reasons the Commission was a hindrance to Frere and not a help; for he had made up his mind that it would be expedient to apply any other rule than that of *uti possidetis*. Whatever the original and legal rights of the Zulus, the settlers were there on the frontier, and were entitled to be secured against loss. South African policy would be ill served by an expulsion of Boers.

The Commission found the extremest confusion regarding the disputed territory. Boundaries, even where they were defined on paper, could not be followed upon the terrain itself. Documents and witnesses contradicted one another. At least one forgery was exposed. On another vital document the purported signature of Panda himself had not been witnessed. Still another instrument that was put forward as an official treaty was shown to be nothing more than a grazing concession to a group of farmers. Upon the important concession of 1861 itself the Commission looked with "grave suspicion", and asserted indeed that "no cession of territory was ever made by the Zulu nation". In short, the Commission brought to light the entire irregular and haphazard expansion of a characteristic frontier line.

The report was emphatic and unanimous. "The evidence shows", it said, "that this so-called 'disputed territory' has never been occupied by the Boers, but has always been inhabited by the border clans, who have never moved their kraals, and that the only use ever made of the land by the Boers has been for grazing purposes, which in itself proves nothing...." The Transvaal Government had never exercised any jurisdiction, civil or criminal, nor had they ever governed any of the natives resident on the land. They had never received taxes or land rent from the Zulu inhabitants, and had never appointed any Government officer there.[1] It was drastic language. The report was all the more drastic because it recommended a boundary line that lost to the Transvaal the entire Blood River Territory.

Frere was quick to seize upon the weakness of the Commission's findings. The "disputed territory" of its report was not the entire Transvaal-Zulu border, but only the Blood River Territory. With the other disputed area to the North of the Pongolo River where the town of Luneburg was situated it had hardly concerned itself at all. Had the Commission extended its inquiry to cover the entire frontier line, including the territory on the left bank of the Pongolo River, its conclusions must of necessity have been less severe. There were on the entire frontier three areas of settlement. There was first of all an area of indisputable Boer settlement. In the district of Utrecht, for example, Boers were too firmly established to be evicted. Then there

[1] C.O. 179/127, D. 104, Bulwer to Hicks Beach, 16 July 1878. Report of Commission, dated 20 June 1878, and sent to Frere by Bulwer, 8 July 1878.

was an indeterminate region of intermingled white and black settlement, round the town of Luneburg, for example, and finally the area in which there were many claims but few Europeans. It was with this area that the Commission had primarily concerned itself.

It can readily be understood why such a report should have been embarrassing and unacceptable to Frere. For a harassed politician who had to devise means to suit ends, and who was hoping to bring some order into the confusion of the Transvaal and South-Eastern Africa, the report was too emphatic, too inflexible, and too narrow. Its execution would be too direct an affront to the population of the Transvaal, and too signal a victory for the natives.

At the Lieutenant-Governor of Natal the High Commissioner shot a quiver of questions.[1] Would either the Boers or the Zulus acquiesce in the report? he asked incredulously. If they did not, how was it to be enforced? Could the British Government afford to offend the Boer population? Was it not likely that the Dutch frontiersmen would take the law into their own hands and kindle the flames of a war that would burn far beyond their own frontiers? Even if they accepted an adverse award they would do so with a surly bad grace that would give to agitation proof of the charges of ill faith against the British Government. The British Government had promised the Transvaal a secure frontier and protection against native aggression. That promise must be kept. Bulwer, on the other hand, protested that the award provided the basis for a settlement without recourse to war.[2] Let the High Commissioner avoid all appearance of coercion. Let him give his decision as arbitrator fairly and firmly. Thereafter the action of the British Government could be guided by the manner in which that decision was received. Between the opinions of the two men there could be no reconciliation. While Bulwer argued that if the Transvaal upon fair enquiry had been found in the wrong it was the duty of the Government to give effect to the award, Frere retorted that the pacification of the whole frontier was not achieved by a settlement reached at

---

[1] C.O. 179/127, D. 120, Bulwer to Hicks Beach, 13 Aug. 1878, Enclosures.
[2] *Ibid.* Bulwer to Frere, 18 July 1878.

one point. His vision was wider than that of Bulwer, even as his temperament was more audacious. Bulwer blamed the restlessness of the Zulus on a generation of Transvaal encroachment; Frere as strongly insisted that the Zulus were intent upon war, and that the British Government must be prepared for war.

Frere reached Durban by R.M.S. *Courland* on 23 September 1878. Ostensibly he had come on a tour of inspection, with an open mind, to examine, to enquire, and to learn. Actually he had already advanced close to a definite decision. What he saw and heard in Natal turned the scales. He found the colony in the grip of a violent war scare. The colony had lost its composure. It was full of hysterical nervousness, apprehensive of invasion, and resounding with the call that something drastic be done, preferably by the British Government. The High Commissioner encountered much ignorance on matters concerning the Zulus. He himself had to admit that much of what he heard came from men who judged all issues by the simple virtue of their residence in the country, and a vaguely expert "knowing of the Kafir". He took a serious view of the military kraals that the Zulus had built in the Blood River Territory or close to the settlement at Luneburg. Even more seriously did he look upon a raid that a band of Zulus had conducted upon Natal soil in pursuit of the two wives of Sirayo, a petty chief. When the women were carried back into Zululand and killed, he declared that the affront to British soil could only be made good by the surrender of the murderers to British justice. In reply Cetywayo sent a perfunctory offer of compensation and his regrets. The High Commissioner concluded that Cetywayo was acting in bad faith, and that Natal was in imminent danger. Natal he judged to be so defenceless that there was nothing "but the forbearance or incapacity of the Zulus to prevent the whole country being devastated". General Thesiger agreed. To the professional soldier there is a war on every poorly defended frontier. He had submitted to the War Office months previously his own plans for an invasion of Zululand. In August Commodore Sullivan had examined the Zulu coast to reconnoitre possible landing places for troops and army stores.

When Frere agreed with General Thesiger that the condition

of South Africa called for a Zulu war, he felt, as did public opinion generally, that all political progress would be halted until the natives had been forced to acknowledge the superiority of the British Government. It was quite impossible to hope for a solution of the difficulties in the Transvaal until its inhabitants were assured that the British Government had some better reason to abstain from fighting the Zulus than a sense of "inferiority and weakness". The war that was about to be fought was intended to win the loyalty that the annexation had failed to win, and to resuscitate the failing spirit of confederation.

Carnarvon had forbidden a Zulu war. His successor, Sir Michael Hicks Beach, did not have Carnarvon's original interest in the affairs of South Africa. Where Carnarvon had watched every event, writing numerous minutes and private letters in his unformed and scrawling hand, pasting newspaper cuttings in his book of memoranda, and often rewriting entire despatches, the despatches of Hicks Beach were as a rule more perfunctory, often shrinking to simple official acknowledgments. He sought to pursue the same general policy as his predecessor, but without the same conviction or vigilance or attention to detail. His unfamiliarity with South Africa inclined him to put his faith in the men on the spot. Even where he felt himself in disagreement with their judgment, he was still inclined to yield to their greater familiarity with local conditions. For several months after his accession to office he was content to stand by, placing no restraint upon the development of events. *Nec scit qua sit iter nec si sciat imperat illis.* There seemed little else to do. Every despatch and newspaper told a uniform tale of the cruelty of Cetywayo, of the bellicose spirit of his subjects, and the indignities which the Transvaal frontiersmen had to endure at the hands of the Zulus. It was taken for granted in the Colonial Office that the report of the Boundary Commission would be against the Zulus, and that the British Government would have to support it. Both Malcolm and Herbert looked upon the Commission as little more than an expedient that might defer but could not prevent a war. Malcolm even seemed to look upon war with composure. "We have", he declared, "now gained time, and have sent out to S. Africa a force sufficient to deal with the Zulus.

The authorities will therefore now probably hasten on the crisis."[1]
This attitude of *laissez-aller* within the Colonial Office lasted
until August. Then their mood changed to one of alarm. Disraeli
had returned from Berlin with peace and Cyprus, but even
then England was still uneasy. From India came reports of a
forward policy that threatened to substitute Afghanistan for
Turkey as a *casus belli* with Russia. There arrived from the
Treasury a letter written in great alarm, and written privately,
presumably lest an official letter be received by the Colonial
Office as merely another complaint about these expensive South
African colonists. Not unwisely the officer in charge of the
Military Chest had written betimes to warn My Lords of the
Treasury of the imminence of a Zulu campaign, and these,
knowing from the recent war in the Cape that South African
wars were both expensive and succeeded by a quarrelsome pro-
cess of apportioning the cost, were urgent that the Colonial
Office do everything to prevent a war.

On 4 September the report of the Boundary Commission
arrived in Downing Street. Unexpectedly it proved to be in
favour of the Zulus. If the Zulus had not been in the wrong,
could they be blamed for a war? Could a war not be staved off?
Actually the Colonial Office knew that the report would do
nothing to stave off a conflict. "But", sighed Fairfield, "it
appears to be a foregone conclusion that there is to be a war."
The officers on the spot, he continued, with a civilian's distrust
of the army, would welcome it "because a war means plenty of
decorations for the chiefs and 'brevets' for the lesser officers,
and without a 'brevet' early in his career an officer is almost
certain to find himself compulsorily retired in middle life".[2] His
superior, Herbert, was no less pessimistic. "I fear", he agreed,
"we are in for (if not already in) a war with the Zulus."

The eyes of the Colonial Office were upon Frere. He alone
could avert a war and resist the military element that surrounded
him. The Colonial Office was soon undeceived, for on 10 September Frere wrote asking for reinforcements. Those reinforcements were required not for defence but for an attack. He was

---

[1] C.O. 179/126, D. 32, Bulwer to Hicks Beach, 2 Feb. 1878, Minutes.
[2] C.O. 179/127, D. 108, Bulwer to Hicks Beach, 24 July 1878, Minutes.

committed to war. A carefully edited series of the despatches which Hicks Beach wrote to Sir Bartle Frere on Zulu matters could very easily give the impression that the Colonial Office had to the last set its face against war. It is true that the Secretary of State repeatedly urged Frere to place himself on the defensive, and do nothing to bring on a conflict. On 17 October he wrote refusing Frere's request for reinforcements, and on the following day a telegram from the War Office informed Thesiger that looking to the position of affairs in Europe it would be impossible to despatch any more troops to South Africa. But behind these peremptory messages there lurked indecision and doubt. It was as if the British Government were afraid of war, and afraid at the same time of a febrile peace that would encourage Cetywayo and what Frere called his "celibate man-destroying gladiators" to continue their threats and provocations. A week after the refusal to send reinforcements the Colonial Office asked the Foreign Office to obtain from the Portuguese Government permission for British troops to use Delagoa Bay in case of war. In reply to a suggestion that the troops that had taken part in the war on the Eastern Frontier should be given medals, Hicks Beach economically hinted that if there was to be fighting in Zululand it would be wise to defer the award, so that the one medal could be struck for both the Kafir and Zulu wars. It was plain to see that the British Government did not know which road to follow, so that in its embarrassment it was constrained to place its reliance on the man on the spot. There was more than mockery in the imaginary letter which Sir William Harcourt later declared had passed between the Secretary of State and Sir Bartle Frere:

"My dear Sir Bartle Frere,

I cannot think you are right. Indeed I think you are very wrong; but after all, I feel you know a great deal better than I do. I hope you won't do what you are going to do; but if you do I hope it will turn out well."[1]

Frere kept the indigestible report of the Boundary Commission unpublished for nearly six months. Its promulgation in Decem-

---

[1] Hansard, vol. 245, cols. 84–85.

ber 1878, when its secret had long since leaked out, was purely formal. It was useless to carry out the award when Zululand was about to lose its real independence. Virtually repudiating the verdict of the Commission, Frere demanded compensation for the Transvaal farmers who had suffered losses at the hands of the frontier clans. For the Sirayo incident and the violation of Natal soil he imposed a fine of cattle. Cetywayo was to give assurance of a future conduct acceptable to the British Government, break up his "frightfully efficient man-slaying machine", and accept the advice and guidance of a British resident.

Among savages with no government save the intermittent one of councils the party of action and violence must always prevail. In spite even of the ponderous warnings of missionaries that his fate might well be that of Charles I or Abraham Lincoln, Cetywayo did little to hold his more restless followers in check. A Zulu of Zulus, he spoke grandiloquently of his power and the number of his followers. They were like the grass, he said, and wherever they went the hills would burn. The war party cried that it must bathe its assagais in blood, a phrase, as Frere may have observed, not unlike that employed by Indian officers when they spoke of "keeping the Bombay army in wind". On the other side of the Tugela Frere was making arrangements with Thesiger to forestall an irruption and to fight a war upon his own terms. His preparations were made openly so that the Zulus might see and hear and be afraid, and those that loved not Cetywayo might at the proper moment turn against him. The attack was planned to avoid the winter, and take place during what was normally the rainy season, when there would be water and pasture for the indispensable draught animals. It would also be the season when the maize crops had not yet been harvested, and when Cetywayo might find it difficult to collect an army and keep it in the field. Frere expected an easy and swift ending to a Zulu campaign. Thesiger and his military staff were confident. Zululand was a house divided against itself, and would collapse at the first assault. These calculations could not have been more mistaken. Even had there been no disaster at Isandhlwana the Zulu campaign would still have been arduous, dangerous and costly.

Q

The growing crops did not keep the Zulus in the fields, as Frere had hoped. The rains did not come till the middle of December, and as the first planting had therefore failed, there was no harvest to keep the natives from joining their impis. From the Transvaal Frere could expect little help. In October 1878 Colonel Rowlands had led an ill-timed expedition against Sekukuni which, returning with its tail between its legs, did nothing to inspire confidence in the British arms. Obedient to the precept of King Solomon that "he that meddleth with the strife that belongs not to him takes a dog by the ear", the Dutch leaders refused their co-operation, and unhelpfully called a great meeting at Wonderfontein in December to pledge themselves solemnly to regain their independence. The farmers of the frontier district of Utrecht alone under Dirk Uys, most gallant of a gallant family of Zulu fighters, agreed to join the British forces. He was a great-hearted man, if ever there was one, but his little following only accentuated the aloofness of the rest of the country.

Chief of the obstacles that upset the general's most careful calculations were the drought, the collapse of Natal's transportation system, and bitter quarrelling between the military and the civil authorities in Natal. The Commissariat was the first to feel the effects of a number of bad seasons in high prices for food and services, and above all in the poor quality and extreme dearness of draught animals. The doubling of the European population by the addition of the forces, and the sudden strain put upon the resources of the colony by the complicated demands of an army in movement, caused prices to advance. As the costs of the campaign soared the Commissariat staff were beside themselves with concern. Even Bulwer, thoroughly out of sympathy with the military as he was, felt constrained to ask the colonists to remember that the British taxpayer was pouring out money for a war in which he had no direct concern. More pointedly yet did the Colonial Secretary, Mr C. B. H. Mitchell, exclaim that "modern mercantile morality does not regard as unpatriotic the obtaining, under any circumstances whatever, the highest possible prices for its goods". The Commissariat bid desperately in the open market against merchants, and these bid against the Commissariat which, turning angrily to Bulwer, clamoured for martial law, and the right to commandeer supplies and equipment at fixed prices. Waggon hire was £80 per month, so that the saying that was supposed to have run on the Cape frontier during the war of 1851, that the war would never end till the price of waggons fell, seemed to apply to Natal as well. Enough draught animals could not be obtained even at exorbitant prices, till the movements of men, waggons and horses were so embarrassed for want of supplies and forage that at times the forces were almost on the point of coming to a standstill.

The great difficulties of Commissary General Strickland were not altogether of the colonists' making. That many of them profited greatly was seen clearly enough in the incredible multiplication of trading stores close to army headquarters. Weenen had never known such prosperity. The boast of one profiteer that "war beat sugar cultivation into fits" was probably fully justified. But the crisis was not originally due to the rapacity of the traders. The truth was that Natal's transportation system had collapsed under the double strain of drought and war. Cattle, in the absence of railways still the only means of transport, had been decimated and weakened by the protracted drought. Overladen waggons and long hauls wrought further havoc; the promiscuous movement of diseased animals spread redwater and lungsickness. The diseased cattle captured in Zululand contaminated healthy stock until lungsickness in Natal took on the proportions of an epidemic. The scanty pasture near the roads was over-grazed; there were no relays, and artificial feeding was out of the question. Small wonder that farmers hesitated to abandon their animals and their waggons to the rough mercy of Her Majesty's forces. As it was, the Commissariat probably had two-thirds of Natal's transport in its hands, and still the port of Durban and the warehouses in the Free State were choked with goods that could not be moved. Ever since 1874 Natal had suffered from a scarcity of transport, and the prices of which Strickland complained had actually been rising since the beginning of 1876. In many cases the prices of 1879 were twice those of 1876 and 1877.

Until the stunning disaster of Isandhlwana bowed Thesiger's head it was upon Bulwer that the wrath of Frere and the General

Staff fell. Months before the first columns crossed into Zululand Thesiger had already written angrily of his ignorance and obstructiveness. When Thesiger received on 26 October the unexpected news of his father's death he burst forth that it made him "doubly anxious to leave this detestable country".[1] He had been in South Africa less than a year. Unmoved by the general's urgent and peremptory manner Bulwer hastened but slowly in preparing for war, refining and distinguishing and "spinning minutes", as if in the hope that by hindering the preparations he might cause war to be deferred altogether. He strongly opposed Chelmsford's desire to be given entire command over the Natal native levies, lest the native population be subjected to military government and be exposed too intimately, like Natal's cattle, to the dangerous infection across the Tugela. Until 26 May 1879, nearly four months after Isandhlwana, he refused to declare martial law, and even the Colonial Office accused him of having caused a delay of two months and the loss of a million pounds. Bulwer was trying to serve two masters. He was trying to safeguard Natal against military law, and at the same time perform his bounden duty to ensure the speedy triumph of Great Britain over its enemy. He earned the resentment of Lord Chelmsford. But at the end of the war Natal was still at peace with its own native population.

At dead of night on 11 February 1879, a messenger knocked at the door of Hicks Beach's house in Portman Square. He bore a telegram with the dreadful news of the disaster at Isandhlwana,[2] where there had fallen as many officers as at the battle of Inkerman. It was a disaster and like most disasters can never be fully explained, although it is clear that cavalry and more expert scouting would have preserved the force against the surprise that overwhelmed it. In strange surroundings and amongst savage enemies overconfidence and carelessness can defeat the greatest courage.

Isandhlwana marks a definite turning point in British South African policy. A policy that in straining after confederation had not hesitated to annex an independent republic, and that

---

[1] C.O. 179/128, War Office to Colonial Office, 4 Dec. 1878.
[2] Lady Victoria Beach, *Life of Sir Michael Hicks Beach*, vol. I, p. 123.

would certainly have annexed Zululand and other territories, now turned about and began to slip down the arduous path it had steeply trodden, back again finally to abandonment and non-interference. The Zulu War was on every tongue, and personages ignorant of colonial matters and unknown in colonial history arose from their seats in Parliament and gave their emphatic views on imperial policies. The debate was nation-wide. In public house and Parliament, the men and institutions that could be blamed—Frere, Hicks Beach, Chelmsford, Sandhurst, and the Colonial Office—were duly blamed. One voice attributed the disaster to the unmilitary and perverted education of British army officers, and to competitive examinations in Chaucer and Spenser. Other and more numerous voices demanded that England leave the colonists to make their own terms with the natives. Since Carnarvon's resignation important members of the Government's following had looked ever more coldly upon a policy that was extending Great Britain's responsibilities not merely in a single colony but throughout the entire Empire. The enthusiasm that had acclaimed Disraeli upon his return from Berlin as suddenly waned.

On 7 March 1879 there was a meeting of the Cabinet. Since the beginning of the year no more urgent meeting had been held. The heavy guns in Parliament, Blachford, Chamberlain, Dilke, and others, were trained on Frere and the Government. The life of the Government was in danger. Its action therefore was swift and drastic. The day following the meeting of the Cabinet Frere's censure was made public. A censure so severe that men wondered that it had not been accompanied by his immediate recall undoubtedly dulled the edge of the attack upon the administration in Parliament. In the debate which followed Hicks Beach presented an apologetic, uncomfortable and evasive defence that denied none of the major charges against him. The Government saved itself at the expense of its subordinate. Sacrificed to the exigencies of party, virtually censured by the Cabinet itself, his usefulness compromised, Frere had received a rebuke whose sting lay less in the publicity of the debate than in the acquiescent attitude of his own superiors.

What time Parliament and Press and public opinion were

awaiting further news from Chelmsford's columns in Zululand, Frere himself had gone up to the Transvaal. He was long over-due. His visit had been delayed for almost half a year by the war. In February Brand had pleaded with him to go up to the Trans-vaal. The grievances of the leaders had too long been ignored. There was need of a more attentive ear, and a yielding manner, especially towards the demands for the liberal constitution which had now been delayed for two years.

A morose and defiant Boer laager only sixteen miles from Pretoria showed indeed that the affairs of the Transvaal would brook no further delay. A group already loudly proclaimed its intention of blockading Pretoria and hauling down the British flag. As yet the majority still hearkened to Kruger, and while he counselled calm there was little danger of an outbreak. Frere's own belief that the agitators were few and the faint-hearted many seemed to be vindicated by the calm dispersal of the camp upon his promise to send home to England the memorandum which the Boer Committee had drawn up. Some of the Boers returned home in the apparent belief that Frere had engaged himself to support their demand for independence. When their belief was later belied by his published despatches, what trust they had in him was destroyed and their disposition to listen to the more ardent and extreme grew. Hardly had the camp broken up when Reuter's telegram arrived with the news that the Zulu policy of the High Commissioner had been censured by the Ministry at home and that, even though Cetywayo were utterly crushed, Zululand would not be annexed. Military engineers had built the telegraph in the Transvaal; the Transvaal was now as sensitive to the news of the outside world as Cape Town, and received it as quickly. Frere's censure was significant news. In it the Boer leaders discerned tell-tale signs. Her Majesty's Government disapproved of Frere, and it disapproved of further expansion. If it could be convinced of the burdensome and un-profitable nature of its acquisition, the Transvaal might be abandoned, even as the Orange River Sovereignty had been abandoned nearly a quarter of a century before. In the Press of Natal, the Orange Free State, and the Cape Colony the possi-bility of restoring the Transvaal to independence was henceforth freely discussed. A change of Government in England suddenly became a matter of vital concern to the Boer leaders, for they assumed that an opposition that attacked the errors of the party in power would signal its own arrival to power by correcting those errors.

There had elapsed just two years of British rule. Shepstone had gone "on leave" in January. The administration that he surrendered into the hands of Lanyon enjoyed neither power nor any popularity. The hopes, confessed Frere himself, of firm, vigorous and progressive government which were entertained at the time of the annexation had been but imperfectly fulfilled. For want of money the various departments of Government were still understaffed and underpaid. Upon Shepstone there had accordingly devolved an unusual responsibility and authority. Of the Boer leaders not one held important office. Since the majority of the Boers could not read English it was from the lips of those that loved not the Government nor the British connection that they heard of the doings of the Government. Sargeaunt's financial reforms were still on paper. The irregular system of taxation of the Republic had been in effect continued. Frere complained that there was no official inquiry as to who was liable to pay taxes, or who had paid his legal quota. "Men pay when and how and pretty much what they please."[1] Those who omitted to pay their taxes were not necessarily called to account. Neither the landdrosts nor the other officials liked the unpopular duty of tax gathering, so that even under active and well disposed land-drosts the revenues were much in arrear and imperfectly collected. At the first breath of discontent they desisted from any pressure at all.

In actual figures the imperial expenditure in the Transvaal seemed unimportant by the side of the outpouring of imperial funds that would not cease till Ulundi and the capture of Cety-wayo. Yet from Downing Street it must have seemed as if all South Africa were in a conspiracy in 1879 to drain the Imperial Chest. The Imperial Chest was in practice a limited fund of £1,000,000 which had to meet in the first instance the demands of Her Majesty's service throughout the world. The Zulu War

[1] C.O. 291/2, D. 40, Frere to Hicks Beach, 6 May 1879.

alone was well on the way to exhausting the fund, thus bringing closer the unpleasant moment when a fidgety Parliament would have to be asked to vote further supplies. Suddenly and without a word of excuse or explanation Griqualand West, the smallest of the colonies in this voracious subcontinent, drew upon the Imperial Chest for £220,000. The Treasury could not conceal its annoyance, and came hammering at the door of the Colonial Office. "It can hardly be anticipated", querulously declared an important Treasury official, "that Parliament will grant a quarter of a million...on the statement that the Cape authorities thought it necessary." Even Hicks Beach gasped when he heard from Frere that a rough and tumble in the Keate Award area had caused all that expense. When he learned that Frere had airily telegraphed Warren, the Administrator of Griqualand West, that "all war services are on account of the Imperial Government", he knew that he could not quarrel with the strictures of the Treasury.

The end was not yet. First there came news that the Basuto chief Morosi, impoverished by drought and galled by a determined magistrate's assault upon his jurisdiction, had risen in arms; from the Transvaal was announced a bigger and better, and more expensive expedition against Sekukuni; a scrambling for land between Pondos and Xesibes and an epidemic of cattle-stealing threatened to light a conflagration on the other side of Natal; in Natal itself weatherwise and provident men began to grumble in advance that Natal had not caused the Zulu War and would not pay for it.

The only true cure for overexpenditure of imperial money was local self-government. On 12 June 1879 Hicks Beach sent to Frere an emphatic despatch on confederation. Compared with Carnarvon's despatch sent just four years before, it was stiffer and more exacting. The Secretary of State was at little pains to hide his feeling that Great Britain had paid enough and endured enough for its South African dependencies, and could no longer "be expected to undertake the responsibility of their future government and defence". Sprigg, the Prime Minister, was pledged to confederation by his victory over Molteno. The time had come for the Cape Colony to take up the problem of co-operation and leadership. Hicks Beach requested Frere to con-

sider whether general proposals for the establishment of a South
African union or confederation might not be submitted to the
Cape Parliament. Her Majesty's Government was willing to
allow five years for the consolidation of the union. During this
period Great Britain and South Africa would contribute in equal
proportions to the cost of general defence. Thereafter South
Africa would be left to its own resources, Her Majesty's troops
being withdrawn to the Cape Peninsula. Carnarvon had never
spoken so bluntly. To him confederation had sincerely been more
than a means of beating a retreat. His policy had been winged
by an audacity and a sincerity which compelled the respect of
his opponents. Not because Hicks Beach's shoulders were less
fit to bear his burden, but because circumstances oppressed him
more, did British policy flutter down to a lower level, where it
was narrower, less ambitious, and, in the face of adversity, less
courageous.

Carnarvon had offended Cape sentiment by an aggressive
assertion of imperial primacy; Hicks Beach offended sentiment
by insisting on the British Government's determination to abandon that leadership. To his despatch there could only be one
answer. It was Molteno's familiar answer that confederation
was for the moment impracticable. It was impracticable chiefly
because Cape public opinion feared the withdrawal of British
power. The Zulu War had not laid the spectre of native uprising; it had only served to make it more real in colonial eyes.
Indeed Sprigg was already preparing to go up to Basutoland to
address the chiefs on the explosive question of Basuto disarmament. With Morosi still defiant on top of his hill, Sprigg's
mission would be of the utmost delicacy. No policy aimed at the
withdrawal of British troops could be popular in the Cape
Colony. An inspired Press absolved the Ministry of its election
promises. "The millenniary theory of South African Union is
plainly not yet exploded", jibed the Cape Times.[1] In a phrase
that would have shot Cobden to his feet, the same paper declared
that the colonist paid his share towards the maintenance of
British regiments just as truly as the British taxpayer himself.
Troops were more useful in the colonies than guarding the iron

[1] 12 July 1879.

and stone of Government offices in Whitehall. The colonist had
as good a right to protection as the inhabitants of Liverpool and
Manchester, and a far better right than the "unspeakable Turk".

Cape opinion knew also that as long as confederation was
deferred the Transvaal, together with Natal and Zululand,
remained the responsibility of the British Empire. It was
frankly glad to take shelter behind British influence. The Cape
Argus would even have gladly given to the Empire the care of
the Transkeian territories as well.

"The great question of the union of the South African communities has been postponed for a time." With this sentence Frere
closed the session of the Cape Parliament. The words were un-
assuming but the meaning was drastic. Confederation was not
postponed; it was dead. But like the body of the dead Patroclus
it remained still the subject of contention and strife.

In refusing once again to enter into partnership with outnumbered Natalians, disaffected Boers, and a "horde of actively
hostile natives", the Cape brought the British Government face
to face with its own dilemma. Would the British Government go
forward or back? To go forward needed effort and a spirit of
confidence which it had lost. To go back meant the return of the
Transvaal to independence and a confession of failure that would
make the name of confederation a mockery for a generation to
come.

As early as March 1879 there were asked in the Colonial Office
the questions: Should the Transvaal be held any longer? If it
were restored to independence what would the effect upon South
Africa be? "The withdrawal of our Sovereignty from the Orange
Free State", suggested Fairfield, "did us no harm that I know
of. It was followed by 24 years of peace as far as we were concerned." Her Majesty's Government had had its fill once more
of native wars, and there was again the disposition to see in the
independent republics a breakwater between British interests
and the tides of native unrest. It was not that Downing Street
loved the Boers more but that it loved the natives less. Herbert
was as pessimistic as his subordinates.[1] "There is, I fear," he
moodily observed, "no great prospect of our being able to carry

[1] C.O. 48/489, Frere to Hicks Beach, 20 Feb. 1879, Minutes.

on the Queen's Government in the Transvaal, unless some considerable despotic powers are reserved to the Crown. It is a fairly open question whether the Transvaal should not after all be 'retroceded'." Remarks such as these made at such a moment are significant illustrations of the temper in which the British Government approached the problems of the Transvaal after the Zulu War. The inclination it had to hold on to the Transvaal was born rather of obstinacy than any clear policy. "Parliament has", said Herbert, "very rarely the courage to part with undesirable possessions."[1]

Even less did the Colonial Office have the conviction now to endow its undesirable possession with a truly liberal constitution. In January Brand had written to Frere that with a liberal constitution there would be a greater possibility of conciliating the Boers. After his reception by the surly Boer camp in April, Frere saw that a constitution liberal in its elements could not be wisely deferred. The Colonial Office did not deny the desirability of conciliation. But which had the greater claim: law, order and solvency, or a liberal constitution and the slaking of Boer anger? The answer was in effect that the Transvaal could have a liberal constitution under confederation, when its budget and its debt would no longer be the direct concern of the Home Government. In the meantime the form of Government must be adapted to financial and political exigencies. If the Boers would not pay taxes and held seditious meetings, Government must become more severe. "The machine of Government", said Herbert, "must be put steadily in motion under the protection of a sufficient military force and will probably after being once so started work fairly well." In the Transvaal Administrator Lanyon echoed Herbert's sentiment.[2] He did not share Frere's hope that new institutions would capture the sympathy of the Boer leaders by giving them some voice in the Government, or that in a year or eighteen months they could be expanded to make room for a Volksraad and self-government. He was fearful lest the Transvaal should stumble under the weight of too much liberty. The real bond of union amongst the Boers, Lanyon asserted, was a

[1] Ibid.
[2] C.O. 291/3, D. 67, Lanyon to Wolseley, 15 July 1879, Minutes.

cordon of agitators and place seekers. A country that would dissolve into anarchy and a scramble for power the moment that British authority was withdrawn was not fit for self-government. Such a country called for rigid Crown Colony Government.[1] "All that is necessary to place the Transvaal upon a secure and solvent financial basis is a Government strong enough to ensure obedience to its laws and peace within its borders."[2]

The answer to Frere's contention that the Transvaal should no longer be treated as a Crown Colony was the appointment as High Commissioner of South-Eastern Africa and Commander of the Forces of Sir Garnet Wolseley, hero of Coomassie, lion of Pietermaritzburg and, but for Chelmsford, conqueror of Zululand. It was a perverse judgment that sought the road to confederation by setting up rival British jurisdictions under men who disliked one another intensely. The appointment of a man whose last visit to South Africa had been to abrogate a constitution, not to build one, and the appointment of Lanyon, chosen to succeed Shepstone because he had pared and disciplined the wayward finances of Griqualand West, left no doubt at all that in the Transvaal there would be no relaxing or relenting, but a binding and a hardening.

It would be perverse to condemn British policy merely because it insisted upon efficiency and economy where disorder and wastefulness had hitherto prevailed. Many of the administrative reforms that were introduced were admirable and necessary. Yet the very virtues of the new administration conspired in some cases to make it unpopular. What was practically a revolution took place in the management of Government offices, especially those of the landdrosts and magistrates. Accounts, salaries, and office expenses were subjected to an inspection more like the normal severe scrutiny of a British Treasury Department. In the course of these changes it was sufficiently revealed how much the inefficiency and the venality of the lesser republican officials had done to corrupt the financial security of the administration. But the new reforms were a "vexatious puzzle" to most of the untrained and unsystematic landdrosts. The same

---

[1] Frere to Hicks Beach, 23 July 1879.
[2] C.O. 291/3, D. 74, Lanyon to Hicks Beach, 17 Aug. 1879.

reforms sought to enforce a greater strictness in the collection of taxes from a population that was notoriously averse to taxation. The embarrassment of the landdrosts under the new system was therefore keen. With interests that attached them to the people rather than the administration, they were called upon to perform an unpopular function amongst a doubtfully loyal people. It is a tribute to their respect for law and order that many of them carried out their duties with zeal. Yet it was certain that the greater part of those who formed the lesser officialdom would fall away from the Government and cling to the people at the first breath of rebellion.

Lanyon's work, as Fairfield described it, was repressing outbreak after outbreak of sedition, breaking down resistance to the process of the Law Courts and making the Boers pay their taxes and arrears. His administration was bound to become a fiscal and police despotism. His every action was calculated to pique the population. He was like the Irish drummer boy: "Hit the man high, hit the man low, I could not please him anyway." Either because of a natural swarthiness of complexion or because of his life in the West Indies, it was whispered that he was a man of "colour". In South Africa with hundreds of thousands of men of "colour" of its own breeding, this was nevertheless a most damaging assertion. That a rumour so palpably false should have been current at all was evidence of the prejudice which he roused.

Not even to help in the final defeat of Cetywayo could he obtain assistance. He approached Marthinus Wessel Pretorius, who was, because of his father and because he had been president, one of the most influential of the Boer leaders. Would he accept the rank of Commandant General and raise a force of five hundred men to patrol the Transvaal-Zulu border? A sum of £500 was deposited in the bank in his name. But there were words between Pretorius and the other leaders. Pretorius suddenly vanished, to reappear at the diamond fields whither pressing matters had called him. Alone of the Boers, Piet Uys continued to fight the Zulus, and fighting against them like his father tragically died. With his death there was lost to the Boers and the British alike, for he belonged to them both, a high-minded and heroic man, with an authentic nobility of character that added distinction to an illustrious name. He had opposed the annexation of the Transvaal, but once it had been accomplished, worked loyally for its success. When the Zulu War began he armed and equipped a numerous family at his own expense, even bringing into the field two young sons, the elder but fifteen years old, each as brave as his father. Although he was pressed to accept a Commandant's pay of thirty shillings per day, he refused any pay for himself and his family; when his own property was injured he refused to report his loss, and in settling claims for compensation for damage of property of others he acted with a scrupulous fairness that illustrated, as did his entire life, an order of patriotism that raised him high above any of his contemporaries.

Wolseley's appointment meant that British policy in the Transvaal could not be truly conciliatory. It meant that if ever the Boers desisted in their agitation it would be because the new administration had compelled them to yield to its authority, to accept the rule of law, and to recognize that neither sedition nor violence could prevail against its determination to hold the Transvaal. It was characteristic of the uncertainty of the British Government that to so unconvinced a policy it gave so decisive an agent. Had the British Government, the Liberal opposition, and public opinion shared Wolseley's conviction, it is possible that he could have browbeaten or dazzled all but the fighting minority to desist. The cessation of native disturbance and the return of better seasons would in time do much to allay irritation and grievance. But unhappily for Wolseley the days of Disraeli's government were clearly numbered. In censuring Frere it had done public penance for its South African policy. It had been defeated in its effort to bring any nearer the confederation that might have been its best protection against its opponents in the coming elections. Now, however, as it drew closer to its trial at the polls its only wish was to be absolved of further commitments. Against such pessimism the local administration in the Transvaal could not contend. The more energetic it became the more timid and nervous was support of the Home Government. Under Wolseley therefore the Boers lost none of their hope and their leaders none of their determination.

Wolseley made his first serious mistake in alienating Frere and the Cape Colony. In doing so he made more hopeless yet the cause of confederation which the division of South Africa into two exclusive High Commissionerships had already fatally harmed. Frere was deeply hurt by Wolseley's appointment, the more so as Hicks Beach had not even taken care to tell him in what way his authority and powers were to be curtailed. Loyal and spirited even in the period immediately following his censure, his attitude now changed. Despatches that had been eager and colourful became taciturn, sombre and listless. From Wolseley, whose behaviour was like that of a naughty but clever young person misbehaving himself before his betters, he received an uncavalier treatment. Until he asked for it he received only scanty information on the settlement of Zululand and the conduct of affairs in Natal and the Transvaal. Whether by accident or by design Wolseley even sent one despatch to Frere by way of the War Office in Whitehall. When he did write, his pen sought a language that might have been used to a not very intelligent subordinate. In *The Times* of 3 December 1879 appeared an article, obviously inspired by Wolseley, and written by a member of his staff. It spoke so slightingly of Frere that the Colonial Office grew afraid lest friends of Frere drag South Africa again into another damaging Parliamentary debate. "South Africa", smiled Herbert, "is a small place, and cannot contain two such portentously great men at one time." The manner of Wolseley's appointment and his bearing were a needless humiliation of a superior and finer temperament. Because of the estrangement between the two men the difference between the communities came more acutely to the fore, obscured their common needs, and gave force to the feeling that the confusion in South Africa was such that it were better to be done with it altogether.

CHAPTER XI

MIDLOTHIAN AND MAJUBA

BEFORE WOLSELEY HAD arrived in South Africa, Chelmsford had deprived him of the laurels of a Zulu victory by finally crushing Cetywayo at Ulundi in July 1879. Cetywayo was sent a prisoner to Cape Town, where he arrived in a silk hat, grey tweeds and bare feet.

The post-war settlement, however, was entrusted to Wolseley. Zululand was not to be annexed. No decision could more convincingly demonstrate the wish of the Home Government to be done with its South African adventure. For a generation the ultimate annexation of Zululand had been looked upon as the ineluctable outcome of British presence in Natal. As late as May 1879 opinion in the Colonial Office still agreed with Frere that the annexation of Zululand was a necessary consequence of Zulu defeat. But British policy had lost its momentum. In its hesitation retreat seemed safer and more attractive than advance. Wolseley must, Hicks Beach enjoined, "carefully bear in mind that the object of Her Majesty's Government is not to add to the extent of British possessions". Even though Cetywayo languished in the old fort at Cape Town the British Government was not prepared "to sanction any further interference with the internal Government of the country than may be necessary for securing the peace and safety of the adjacent colonies".

Wolseley's settlement of Zululand aimed in the first place to break up the cohesion of the country, so that the despotisms of Chaka, Dingaan and Cetywayo would no longer be possible. With a light-hearted ignorance of native mentality he divided the country into thirteen parts, and over each unlucky part he placed a chief drawn from houses that had ruled before the coming of Chaka. Each chief signed a formal agreement solemnly undertaking to abolish the Zulu military system, not to import arms, not to make war, to govern justly and not to alienate any land. The most important frontier territory was given to John Dunn, the father of a very large number of Cetywayo's subjects. He was a renegade Englishman and a gunrunner, who lived, in the euphemistic words of Wolseley, a Mormonlike mode of life, with the habits of a Zulu and yet able to take his place in an officers' mess.

The settlement of Zululand was an act of scuttle. The refusal to establish even a protectorate contained a logic that was plain to see. Even as the Sand River Convention of 1852 had preceded the abandonment of the Orange River Sovereignty two years later, so did the virtual abandonment of Zululand point to a dereliction of British control over the Transvaal. Shocked by the costs of war and peace, bewildered by the confusion that two years of striving had been unable to resolve, the British Government began once again to withdraw, unmindful of the avowed failure of its withdrawal in 1852 and 1854. But in 1879, as twenty-five years earlier, the British Government could only withdraw temporarily to an untenable position. It was folly to suppose that a Zululand ruled by thirteen weak nobodies with as much cohesion as dry sand, could really remain independent or at peace. The unlucky device of nominating thirteen unpopular *rois fainéants* was an encouragement to unprincipled whites who, acting as the agents of the chiefs, were an immediate source of discord and malpractice. In trying to avoid the dangers of annexation the British Government had simply sacrificed the advantages and the prestige of real power without seriously lessening its obligations.

The Zulu War had been fought to secure the allegiance of the Transvaal and remove the serious obstacles of native unrest from the path to confederation. It achieved neither end. Wolseley's settlement, perverse and ignorant in colonial eyes, did little to set men's fears about the natives at rest. When Wolseley crossed the border into the Transvaal in September he knew at once that peace in Zululand had brought no rest to the Transvaal.

Lanyon had taken his cue from the capture of Cetywayo. The regiments were free; it seemed the obvious moment for inaugurating a stronger rule. He decided to assure himself of the loyalty of officials and landdrosts by requiring them to take an oath of allegiance.[1] To the common man he sent tax notices.

---

[1] C.O. 291/3, D. 67, Lanyon to Wolseley, 15 July 1879.

R

The Transvaal Government had reached that dangerous moment mentioned by Tocqueville when it was trying to reform itself. The compulsory oath of allegiance was a common device of Governments forced by weakness, distraction and unpopularity to be harsh. The non-jurors, a little surprisingly, were few. Those who refused the oath, including Piet Joubert, quietly relinquished their offices. The tax notices produced more excitement. In the Middelburg, Heidelberg, Standerton and Potchefstroom districts determined groups of farmers suddenly appeared in some of the stores, seized the stocks of ammunition, and paying for them in hard cash, grimly left. Although the culprits, after so brazen an act, meekly paid their fines, the meaning of their gesture was plain. They did not like tax notices.

The worst blow at the rule of law was struck by the Chief Justice himself. Chief Justice Kotze's decision[1] given on 17 May 1879 in the case of *White and Tucker* vs *Rudolph* was a warrant and an encouragement for all those who refused to swear, to pay taxes or to recognize the British Government at all.

To check drunkenness amongst the troops at Utrecht Lanyon had ordered the landdrost to seize some offending stores of liquor. The case came before Kotze. He ordered the liquor to be given up, and then in his judgment declared that neither Her Majesty in Council nor her officers administering the government in the Transvaal had any power to legislate for the territory.[2] He held that the Transvaal had become British territory neither by conquest, occupancy nor cession. Its case was *sui generis*, and the basis of the new order was therefore to be found specifically in Shepstone's proclamation of annexation of April 12, 1877. "This proclamation", ran the judgment, "is a solemn treaty entered into by the Crown and the people of this country.... Every stipulation contained in that proclamation has a binding effect, and must be strictly observed.... It is provided by this proclamation that the Transvaal will *remain* a separate Government, with its own laws and *its own legislature*, and that the laws now in force in the State will be retained until altered by

[1] Kotze, *Biographical Memoirs and Reminiscences*, ch. XIX, for a full statement.
[2] C.O. 291/3, D. 72, Wolseley to Hicks Beach, 12 Dec. 1879.

competent *legislative authority*. At the time of the annexation the Transvaal had a legislature of its own, and the Proclamation expressly guaranteed the continuance of the local legislature.... The Crown cannot exercise the right of legislation over this country, although of course the Transvaal being a portion of the British Empire is subject to legislation by the Imperial Parliament...."[1]

For Lanyon the decision was most unfortunate. It touched his every move with illegality and arbitrariness, and while it did not deny British Sovereignty over the Transvaal, affirmed that if there were any legislative authority in the Transvaal it was the old Volksraad. Henceforth the opposition could assume that both justice and the law were on their side.

Wolseley strode into the Transvaal in September declaring that the Union Jack would fly over the Transvaal as long as the sun shone, and that the Vaal would flow backwards ere the British would withdraw. He continued to say it on every occasion to every man he met. He asked Lanyon to say it, even Frere to say it. He wrote to Hicks Beach asking him to write it in despatches, to cable it, to declare it in Parliament, and not to falter in making it known that nothing could ever affect the permanency of the British occupation. The talk in and out of Parliament of hauling down the British flag and doing belated justice to an oppressed nationality must be given the lie direct. Until then the Transvaal Government would live as upon a quicksand.

The answer to Boer discontent, Wolseley decided, must not be concessions, but force. Admitting that the majority of the population was " disaffected to our rule ", and that " a close form of government such as that enjoyed by our Crown Colonies " would never be willingly accepted by them,[2] he nevertheless insisted that no political reforms could be affected " as long as armed

---

[1] The opinions of both the Law Officers, given on 12 May 1877 immediately after the annexation, and of the Lord Chancellor, given on 6 May 1881, just before the retrocession, were diametrically opposed to Kotze's judgment. Both the Law Officers and Lord Selbourne maintained that the Transvaal had become British territory by conquest or cession, and that therefore Her Majesty in Council was competent to legislate for them. See C.O. 291/3, D. 72, Wolseley to Hicks Beach, 12 Dec. 1879, for both opinions.

[2] C.O. 291/3, Conf., Wolseley to Hicks Beach, 13 Nov. 1879.

bands of men roam about the country talking nonsense about fighting the British troops". As if forsooth their "big talk" would frighten the Government "as well as the women and children". A strong and determined Government bred loyalty. Once the Boers had laid aside their rebelliousness they could have a free constitution. "To give them back now, however, a Volksraad similar to that they had before annexation would be simply impossible, as it would be merely handing over the country to the anarchy which existed in it prior to annexation with a great deal of vested passion against the British Government, added to the folly which ordered their councils formerly." It is clear how utterly he stood outside the Dutch. His efforts to insinuate himself into their confidence were clumsy. Because he saw their faults and their unconformity before their virtues and their affinity, his every step became a chafing and a fretting. He had the devotion to duty of a soldier, the concentration of an egoist and the quick energy of a braggart.

The new Executive Council which he proclaimed within a week of his arrival in the Transvaal was in no sense a liberal body. Although it conformed to Frere's proposals, its spirit ignored Frere's liberal phrase that the "Boers were, like all mankind, well able to manage their own affairs". It seems clear that the sudden establishment of the Executive Council was somewhat of a stratagem.[1] Some such move had become necessary after Kotze's judgment. Because the new body was to have three unofficial nominee members it had a vaguely representative character, and might therefore be put forward as the successor to that Volksraad which, according to Kotze, had not been extinguished by the annexation. Such a view was certainly held by the Colonial Office. "It seems necessary", wrote Herbert, "that something should be done at once, as not only must the old Volksraad be prevented from meeting and acting, but an amended legislature can no longer be dispensed with."[2] Hicks

[1] Since the Letters Patent were promulgated at Westminster on 8 Nov. 1879 more than a month later, it seems obvious that Wolseley acted on his own responsibility. The Letters Patent provided for a Legislative Council as well, which would however be in function composed of the same members as the Executive Legislature.

[2] C.O. 291/4, Lord Chancellor to C.O., 9 Aug. 1879, Minutes.

Beach himself agreed to the constitution in the full knowledge that it was insufficient, and, in itself, unacceptable to the Boers.[1] A formal constitution of some sort was also necessary to satisfy the requirements of the South Africa Act of 1877. The Act stipulated that the legislature of each colony should agree to confederation. As Hicks Beach still clung in forlorn hope to confederation it was necessary to call into being a body that could legally accept confederation for the Transvaal. Such a body was therefore a device and not in a true sense a constitution.

The Boer reply to Wolseley's constitution was given in yet another meeting of Boers in December 1879. Wolseley concentrated troops at Pretoria, built redoubts at Heidelberg and declared again that the Boers, one and all, were "ignorant of the first principle of governing". In return he received resolutions passed by the meeting breathing a spirit as contentious and ardent as his own. Demanding the restoration of their republican institutions they denied allegiance to Her Majesty and swore to defend their Government to the death.

Here was sedition and even treason. Wolseley raised his hand to strike.[2] He arrested Pretorius, Chairman of the People's Committee, and Bok, the Secretary. Having arrested them he saw how helpless he really was. He might by punishing the Hollander Bok strike terror into the small band of Hollanders whose entire influence was against the British Government. But with Pretorius he was helpless. It was not merely that the old man was sick and had only occupied the chair twice at the meetings. He simply could not be punished. Kotze was still on the Bench, and firmly refused to be removed or reduced. None but possibly a jury of Wolseley's own soldiers would find the old man guilty. There was not a tumbledown prison in the land fit to hold Pretorius; and to give the opposition a martyr would be the height of folly. Wolseley stayed his hand.

Having first arrested Pretorius Wolseley tried to suborn him.[3] He spoke sternly, hiding his weakness. The Boers must know

---

[1] C.O. 291/4, Shepstone to Herbert, 31 July 1879, Minutes. "...in the absence of authority to act it is scarcely an Executive Council, though the name had better be employed."
[2] C.O. 291/5, Tel., Wolseley to Hicks Beach, 21 Jan. 1880.
[3] *Ibid.* Conf., Wolseley to Hicks Beach, 8 March 1880.

that agitation was useless. Her Majesty's Government would never, never give up the Transvaal. In front of his prisoner Wolseley laid a Dutch translation of the Secretary of State's despatch of 20 November 1879, reaffirming the British Government's complete unwillingness to restore the Transvaal to an isolated independence. Pretorius read and his face fell. Yes, Wolseley was right. No, it was useless to try to overcome such obvious determination. Then, asked the High Commissioner, would he take the oath of allegiance, and would he become a member of the Executive Council? It was a soldier's way of pleading: to arrest a rebel, clap him in prison, and offer him high Government office. Wolseley's strategy was plain. The arrest and the subsequent proposal would show that the Government was determined to end indiscipline yet anxious to reach an understanding. If Pretorius accepted his offer, there would be added a well-known Boer to the representative nobodies on his Executive Council. Unfortunately for Wolseley Pretorius would not eat of the Government's bread and salt.

In Pretorius Wolseley was confronted by that evasive device of speech, idiomatic of the South African Dutch tongue, which consists in qualifying agreement by disagreement, by combining acceptance and refusal in the same sentence, so that affirmation is ruled out by denial, and the result is perfectly non-committal. Yes, answered Pretorius, he would do what the High Commissioner asked him, but no, not at that exact moment. Would the High Commissioner first give him a waggon so that he could travel amongst the people, explaining to them the attractive new constitution, and reading to them that very determined despatch? Then when the people were persuaded of the folly of resistance he would gladly join the Executive Council. Pretorius rode away a free man on a Government mule waggon. He did not return. Wolseley had failed to remedy what had been the great failing of nearly three years of British rule: the total estrangement of the Boer leaders. They had refused to be awed by the empty terrors of his threats or led astray by his promises.

In other directions the Government was more successful. In the all-important matter of finance the Government had turned over an entirely new leaf. Both Lanyon and Wolseley knew that law and order alone without economy would be unpleasing in the eyes of the Home Government. When Lanyon had assumed office he found that to some of his subordinates the preparation of statements necessary in drawing up the estimates was an entirely new experience. Now, a year later, the estimates actually left the Transvaal in time to be of some use to the Colonial Office. And they were for the first time heartening estimates. The estimated surplus for 1880 was nearly £6000.[1]

The Transvaal budget was balanced by its native population. In 1879 both Lanyon and Wolseley had claimed that the subjection of Sekukuni would open up the great resources of native taxation. Sekukuni had been defeated; Wolseley's Legislative Council had obediently imposed a ten shilling hut tax.[2] Lanyon confidently expected a return of at least £35,000. The Transvaal Government had a native policy at last.

In the pursuit of solvency Wolseley turned to Natal also. He had witnessed the booming trade that the Zulu War expenditure had caused, and asked Bulwer the question that Transvaal and Orange Free State Presidents had asked for a generation in vain. Were not the interior communities entitled to a share of the customs duties collected at the British ports? Wolseley's request was at the same time a condemnation of past British policy towards the Republics. Since their inception they had been starved of credit, denied financial assistance and mulcted by high prices. Their weakness was not wholly the result of their incompetence; some of it at least was imposed by their neighbours. The financial collapse of Burgers' Government had not been unconnected, for example, with the breakdown of Natal's transport system. The period covered by the regimes of Burgers and Shepstone had witnessed a rise in transport costs and prices that reached a peak during the Zulu War. It is certain that the Transvaal suffered acutely from a disadvantageous dependence on Natal. Step by step the British Government in the Transvaal had been forced to commit these very acts of republican policy against which it had fought most strongly. Like the republican administration it

[1] C.O. 291/5, D. 21, Lanyon to Hicks Beach, 14 Feb. 1880.
[2] Ord. 6 of 1880. Law 4 of 1873, and Law 3 of 1876, had imposed taxes but had been virtually inoperative.

had been bankrupt; it had quarrelled with its native neighbours; its first expedition against Sekukuni had been quite as disastrous as that conducted by Burgers; now it asked Natal for financial assistance, and like the Republic was repulsed.

A resolution of the Natal Executive Council of 5 December 1879 refused to pay the Transvaal a penny. In the elections of 1880 almost every candidate made the refusal to share the customs dues with the Transvaal a prominent plank in his election platform. Hicks Beach was indignant. "The reply of Natal to Sir Garnet Wolseley's request", he sneered, "is worthy of the Natal Govt. and Legislature. Nothing could be more narrow or selfish."[1] Narrow and selfish it might be, yet quite inevitable. It cannot be stressed too often or too strongly how much the South African communities were the victims of their own and of one another's problems. They were all so very poor; the territory containing the greatest diamond deposits in the world was actually the poorest; and they were all trying to achieve so much. Because the same begrudging land had to nourish their high ambitions they were forced into competitiveness, jealousy and selfishness. There, after all, lies the principal cause of the failure of more political schemes and ideals than confederation alone. It was poverty that had caused a handful of men to wander forth into such a wide land. Poverty brought rival groups of blacks and whites to face one another in hostility across fertile borderlands. Poverty caused the coastal colonies to fight for trade, and deny assistance to yet poorer neighbours. To persuade such a land to yield a harvest, not in corn alone, men must be prepared to invest heavily. That modern South Africa ranks prominently amongst the great dominions of the British Empire must not obscure the truth that for the greater part of its history it was disconnected, struggling and poor. Not in its recent wealth but in two meagre and stinted centuries lie the origins of much South African political thinking and action.

By the beginning of 1880 the prosperous tide of the Zulu War had ebbed as suddenly as it had risen. Over Natal's head the British Treasury held suspended an indebtedness for the Zulu War of at least £500,000. From its natives it could expect little

[1] C.O. 291/5, D. 21, Wolseley to Hicks Beach, 16 Jan. 1880, Minutes.

addition of revenue. On all articles for native use the duties were already too high. The costs of railway construction were greatly exceeding all estimates. Further loans were inevitable to cover past deficits and contingent liabilities.[1]

If Natal would not give the Transvaal any money willingly, then perhaps it could be compelled to do so. Wolseley revived Burgers' ill-fated plans for a railway to Delagoa Bay. The Transvaal would earn the money it needed at Natal's expense. Only two years previously the British Government had been so opposed to the railway as a "reckless and hopeless" scheme that the Portuguese Minister for the Colonies, Senhor Gonveia, had declared that "it would be about as easy to persuade the Imperial Parliament to find the required funds for such an undertaking as to induce the Portuguese Cortes to vote money for the St Gothard tunnel". Now Wolseley was as convinced of the Transvaal's need of a railway as Carnarvon had been of its absurdity. A railway to Delagoa Bay was, he optimistically declared, "the cheapest and most effectual solution of all our difficulties in the Transvaal".[2] It would end the Transvaal's financial worries. The railway would also be the "means of putting an end very shortly to all the political troubles which press upon us here". Proud to have its own railway and port, Boer opinion would be mollified; and anyhow the introduction of British labourers, artisans, and agricultural emigrants would transfer political power into "the hands of more intelligent and better educated men than the Boers". It was all so simple if the Imperial Government would only guarantee a loan of £1,000,000. There unhappily was the rub.

The one hundred and twenty miles from the Portuguese border to New Scotland would be inexpensively built at £689,000. With the necessary rolling stock the cost could not be less than £884,500. If the experience of Natal meant anything, even such a sum was far too moderate. Then there would still remain the stretch of railway in Portuguese territory, and Lourenço Marques itself. The one needed building and the other needed rebuilding

[1] Bill 24 of 1879 authorized railway extension from Pietermaritzburg to Ladysmith at a cost of £912,606.
[2] C.O. 291/5, D. 21, Wolseley to Hicks Beach, 16 Jan. 1880.

before Wolseley's railway could be practicable. The town was surrounded by a swamp, and was notoriously lacking in even a single water closet. The houses drained into the streets; even the soldiers were without healthy sanitary provision. The wells were seething with corruption. Down at the bay there were no jetties, wharves or docks to take care of coal or steamers or immigrants.

The real problem raised by Wolseley was not whether he had underestimated the cost and the difficulties of the undertaking, although there could be no doubt that he was too sanguine. The real problem was one of principle. He declared to the British Government in effect that it was no use writing despatches on confederation, pleading with one colony and upbraiding another, unless the British Government was prepared to remove one of the worst obstacles to closer union. The whole country needed credit. Of the five communities only one, the Cape Colony, enjoyed a really substantial credit. True the Free State had known no deficit for years. But its credit was passive. Brand had not put it to any real test. He built no railways, maintained no harbours, profited from the competition between Natal and Cape traders, traded profitably with Basuto and diamond diggers, and fought no native wars. For years the financial experts in the Colonial Office had shaken their heads and worried over the financial standing of Natal, the Transvaal and Griqualand West. An imperial guarantee such as Wolseley requested was an affirmation of faith in the Transvaal. It would be an unmistakable expression of the British Government's will to lead South Africa, not with the exhortations of a spectator, but with the active ministrations of a collaborator. The refusal of a guarantee —Natal needed it as badly as the Transvaal—could only mean sooner or later the abandonment of practical direction and an active stewardship.

The answer that Wolseley received was not given by Hicks Beach alone; it came from the circumstances that were shortly to drive him from office. "A guarantee for railways", he himself admitted, "would seem likely to go a long way, whether with the Cape, Natal, or the Transvaal, in promoting confederation. And in the last case there are specially strong reasons in favour of it...." But from Treasury, or Parliament, or public he could depend on no real support.[1] Convinced apparently that silence was both golden and cheap, the Treasury had completely ignored the Transvaal estimates for 1879. "The Treasury", fumed Hemming, "clearly pays no attention to our letters. Some times they do not answer them at all; and at other times...they write as if they had not read them."[2] Even Lanyon's optimistic estimate of a surplus for 1880 apparently failed to warm the heart of the Treasury. "All our efforts", sighed Antrobus, "to induce the Treasury to consider whether anything can be done to lighten the burden of the debts have failed...."[3] That was in March 1880. The day of reckoning had come; and already Gladstone was in Midlothian denouncing the Government's sin.

On 18 March 1880 Hicks Beach sent a telegram to Frere: "If your ministers will at once annex Griqualand West, assuming all the other liabilities of the Province, and undertaking to remit its debt to the Cape Province, we will not require the repayment of the £220,000 due to the Treasury Chest. Early action is necessary."[4] The telegram was a general declaration of policy. It really contained the answer to Wolseley's request. Like Wolseley in the Transvaal, Frere had asked Hicks Beach for money to consolidate the provincial debt of Griqualand West and build a railway line to Kimberley. Help from England or the Cape was imperative. Warren, the Administrator, had been forced to raise the postage rate from one penny to four pence for half an ounce, and to place a tax upon "the very poisonous Cape brandy", even though for public decency he had closed fifty canteens. As the individual diamond claims continued to fall into the hands of the larger companies, the revenue decreased. Having already swallowed up the petty claim holders, the companies were now rapidly absorbing the more substantial men who had been Kimberley's most important taxpayers. Warren's Government, only thinly veiling its insolvency, was too weak to come to terms with them.

[1] C.O. 291/5, D. 21, Wolseley to Hicks Beach, 16 Jan. 1880, Minutes.
[2] C.O. 291/4, Treasury to C.O., 5 Nov. 1879, Minutes.
[3] C.O. 291/5, D. 21, Lanyon to Hicks Beach, 14 Feb. 1880, Minutes.
[4] Hicks Beach to Frere, 18 March 1880.

It seemed entirely logical that the first duty of Lord Kimberley, Hicks Beach's successor at the Colonial Office after Midlothian, would be to continue the liquidation of Conservative policy. That had seemed the clearest promise of Gladstone's Midlothian campaign. Gladstone's attitude to the Transvaal was certainly part of his peculiar and energetic sympathy with submerged or unemancipated nationalities. To him the struggle of a people to free itself of foreign control was so appealing that he extended to it an instant sympathy. But it is misleading to suppose that the bitterness of the electoral campaign was provoked wholly or even largely by South African events. It had accumulated since 1876. The fierceness of Gladstone's attack upon the "worst and most immoral minister since Castlereagh" was excited much more by resentment over the Bulgarian atrocities and the Tory conduct of those Near Eastern questions that had brought the country to the verge of war.

But upon South Africa and especially upon the Transvaal the campaign had decidedly made another impression. On the hustings Gladstone had repented of Carnarvon's sin; in power he surely could not continue to cling to it. On 10 May 1880 Kruger and Joubert therefore wrote to Gladstone from Cape Town, appealing to him to restore the Transvaal's independence. Their letter had an undertone of menace. The Boers were quiet not because they were satisfied, but because, being resolved on independence, they could wait. But in the end truth would prevail.

The appeal was denied before it had been heard. On 20 May the Speech from the Throne announced that the Transvaal would remain British territory. To the Boer leaders, in their single-minded devotion to their cause, the Speech seemed a breach of faith. After having used the Transvaal as a bludgeon against his political opponents Gladstone's disposition was to lay it aside. The elections were over and government had begun. It was difficult to overcome the inertia of prevailing conditions, and difficult to turn back the current of events, which his predecessors had set in motion, whether in Egypt, Afghanistan or South Africa. It is moreover one of the marks of nineteenth-century liberal and radical thought in England that it contained within it so many motives that chafed or even militated against each other. Hume and Cobbett had stood at opposite poles on the Poor Law question; Cobden and Bright had differed on education; there was always the irreducible antagonism between the generous spirit that called for reform and liberty at home and abroad, and the shrewder spirit that embraced economy and abjured all enterprise that was expensive and unremunerative. After Midlothian the conscience of the Liberal Government suddenly grew uneasy at the opposite appeals of the Boers and the natives. In the heat of his sympathy for unemancipated nationalities Gladstone easily lost the power of appreciating the real political dangers that arise when small communities in the Balkans and in South Africa live independently side by side. But after the campaign the Liberal Government experienced, almost conveniently, a recrudescence of humanitarian feeling. Such promise of redress to the Boers as had been implicit in the opposition speeches of the Liberal party were now qualified by twinges of a humanitarian conscience.

Amongst the influences that led the new administration to place itself exactly in the position of its predecessors, two documents that were presented to the Cabinet in its meeting on 12 May are of importance. The first was a minute by Fairfield on the Transvaal, prepared especially for the Cabinet meeting; the second was Wolseley's confidential despatch to Hicks Beach of 13 November 1879. Nobody after reading these documents in their entirety can doubt the very great influence which they unquestionably had upon the Cabinet. Fairfield's brief memorandum was an excellent introduction to Wolseley's much longer despatch. It set out to be little more than a résumé of Transvaal history. Its tone was impartial. "There is no doubt", admitted Fairfield, "that up to a certain point their dislike has been growing more and more intense...." Yet it voiced certain doubts and asked certain questions. Wolseley's despatch read as if it had been specially written to answer the questions and set at rest the doubts. Wolseley's despatch was such an unsympathetic and damaging analysis of the Boer character, and such a grim warning against the dangers of British withdrawal from the Transvaal, that only a Cabinet with its mind firmly made up could have remained indifferent to it. Extensive quotation is imperative.

The mass of Boers were the victims of the agitators and men of violence whom a vacillating British policy had encouraged. "The Boers", he wrote, "are essentially the most ignorant of people, easily led by the few designing men who appeal to their instinctive dislike to English rule and the English race generally." What the Boer resented was not so much the British Government as any government at all. "They resent all and any form of constitution which restricts their individual power to do as each man lists. Each individual wishes to govern, I might say to bully, the natives in his immediate neighbourhood as he thinks fit, and hates the establishment of a strong government over him such as we are endeavouring to inaugurate, by which the natives will be protected from violence, and by means of which order will be maintained and taxes collected." The Imperial Government had won a victory over bankruptcy and disorder and must not throw it away. Outstanding liabilities had been discharged; public credit had been revived and a new impetus given to trade. Yet without the confidence inspired by the annexation these things could not have come to pass. What if the majority were in favour of independence? It was a majority that included most of the ignorant and illiterate elements of the population. Most of the men of intelligence and substance who were the real force of the country, were in the numerical minority. "There can be little doubt in the minds of men who knew the Boers that they are in their present ignorant state utterly incapable of governing themselves." An independent Transvaal meant a weak Transvaal, and a weak Transvaal "may eventually reverse the relative positions occupied by the white man and the native generally throughout Africa, a result that might prove fatal to British interests by giving rise to further native wars". The country moreover was no desert. It was known to be rich in gold and other minerals. Large discoveries were toward. "Any such discovery", prophesied Wolseley, "would soon bring a large British population here. The time must eventually arrive when the Boers will be in a small minority...." Confederation would be altogether impossible if the British flag abandoned the

Transvaal. His advice prevailed. The Liberal Government qualified the promise of reparation to the Boers by the claims of other interests. In the Speech opening Parliament there accordingly appeared side by side two opposite obligations: to make provision for the security of the indigenous races, and to extend to the European settlers institutions based on large and liberal principles of government.

In the Transvaal itself liberalism grew narrower and beautifully less. After the failure to win Pretorius Wolseley and Lanyon deliberately tried to mould merchants, civil servants, farmers committed to the British cause, and a few renegades and *arrivistes* into a Government party—the "party of progress"—who would encourage confederation and hold themselves in readiness to assume power as soon as self-government should come, forestalling any flux of the Dutch elements into a single powerful party. The effort of Wolseley was to tame the Transvaal by discipline, awe it by soldiers and arms, flatter it by the prospect of a railway, rescue it by economy and prosperity, dilute its Dutch blood by immigrants, and when it could no longer be kept as a Crown Colony ensure its government by the "party of progress".[1] Thus it was that a constitution advocated by Frere to win Dutch support was used to alienate it and wound it. It was a policy that provoked its own ultimate defeat. The fellow ship of the Government's supporters came too much from selfishness and sycophancy; it had no patriotism and no genuine conviction, so that even its privileged position in the shadow of the Government was rendered barren; it was ungenerous and utterly without basis in any of the authentic traditions of British colonial Government.

Lanyon was conscious of the unpopularity of his rule. Because it makes reconciliation harder, unpopularity condones autocracy and makes it easier. During the year 1880 Lanyon's rule was a race between the growing hostility of the population and the solvency which his arbitrary Government could wring out of them. Whichever came first, rebellion or solvency—such solvency as the Treasury could accept—would probably decide the fate of the Transvaal.

[1] C.O. 291/6, D. 91, Lanyon to Kimberley, 10 June 1880.

In his desperate bid for solvency Lanyon was not without success. Delinquent taxes were paid in excess of the estimates. Between January and August the total receipts were £146,000. The gathering of the native hut tax had begun late in the year, yet had already yielded £20,000 out of the £35,000 estimated. The revenue entered faster as the year grew older. For the first fifteen days of September it totalled nearly £14,000. The contention that the majority of the Boers could be brought to accept the authority of the British Government seemed justified. Yet many Boers paid their taxes with resentment in their hearts, both because the British Government was under "protest" and because the Government so strictly and systematically collected taxes from all alike. Towards the end of the year there was left a residue of men delinquent in their payments, not out of poverty but because they were unsubmissive. They were the chief forces of unrest. If ever they could be forced to recognize the power of Government, the battle would be won.

Wolseley's successor as High Commissioner, Sir George Colley, was a soldier too. He realized the mutinous temper of the people but did not fear it. At the end of August he actually recommended a reduction of the Transvaal garrison to five hundred infantry, with four guns and sixty mounted infantry at Pretoria, and with ten companies of infantry and sixty mounted men in the different outstations.[1]

Colley disastrously misunderstood the Transvaal. That he had had his back virtually turned on it since August was due to the presence of another and apparently more acute crisis. His attention strained anxiously in the direction of Pondoland and Basutoland. Could the Cape disarm the Basuto? His soldier's eye discerned the poor discipline and poorer preparation of all the Cape forces, the certainty of a long drawn out and difficult campaign, the expense of a difficult line of communications, above all the disadvantage of a war against a mobile enemy that had its strongholds in the parts of Basutoland farthest removed from the Cape. For the Transvaal it was full of meaning that the Cape should become involved in war, for the war was both an encouragement to rebellion in the Transvaal and the utter de-

[1] C.O. 291/6, Colley to Kimberley, 24 Aug. 1880.

struction of the faint hope there still was that the Cape might still confederate South Africa and salvage the Transvaal.

The Cape had enjoyed the profit of the trade in guns and ammunition with the natives. It now suffered the punishment. The overt cause of the Basuto War was the attempt to disarm the Basuto in terms of the Peace Preservation Act. If that were the only cause the story of the war could be simply told. The disarmament was part of the process of extending the control of the Cape Colony over all tribes and all territories as far as the Natal border. To govern a large area so filled with quarrelsomeness the Cape felt that it had to have the most positive guarantees of peace. Arms in the hands of the tribes, especially in the hands of the strongest and most self-conscious tribe of them all, were an incentive to war and rebellion. South Africa, and not the Cape Colony alone, had chosen as the most important immediate aim of its native policy the complete subordination of the native population to European control. The Cape forced war on the Basuto much in the same way that war had been forced on the Zulus.

The hard times that helped to provoke or exasperate conflict on the Eastern Frontier, in Zululand and the Eastern Transvaal, played their part in Basutoland as well. Of the area of Basutoland as given by a map but a very small portion was inhabited. The region of settlement was a strip of territory, unequally fertile, varying in width from one to twenty miles, with a length of one hundred and fifty miles. The remainder of the country was a confused tangle of mountain chains, of bush, precipice and torrent, untenanted and inhospitable. Never happy in their cramped land the Basuto felt the same stirring of the tribes that had led to that astonishing series of wars all over South Africa. As early as 1876 Basutoland manifested much of the same emotional disturbance that had preceded the self-destruction of the Eastern Frontier tribes in 1857. In a great many villages a kind of hysterical mania became epidemic. Those possessed were said in the native idiom to be "taken", and were subject to trances. In their trances they brought messages from Moshesh and the spirits. The spirits revealed what weighed upon many Basuto

S

hearts. They abhorred clothing, Christianity and hut tax receipts; for until they were removed they would stand in the way of a blessed millennium of unlimited cattle, extensive land, and of European non-interference. Manifestly Basutoland was finding difficult the enforced adjustment to the rule of law, to a want of land and the long periods of absence at labour with the Europeans.

It was the want of land that Basutoland found most oppressive. The "loyalists" of the war were those with most land. For years before 1880 the complaint was constant that there was not enough land. "I see many people", said Molapo's councillor Ntsana at the annual Pitso in 1874,[1] "moving out of the country because it is too small and they are too crowded." Letcala agreed: "Our greatest want is space, room to live in. At present our cattle herds have to stand all day huddled close together round the gardens; there is no room for the stock—no open pasturage." Out of such pressure upon the land for gardens and pasturage there inevitably came chronic discord. The collapse after the war with the Free State had permitted petty chiefs to cut up the country by a series of irritating boundaries which exaggerated still more an uneconomical scattering of villages. The complaint of Sofonia Moshesh that he found the chiefs "nowadays oppressing the people about their garden lands" and exacting fines for the trespass of cattle, was general. At one time or another almost every magistrate lamented the squabbling and the snarling of men in competition for garden space and pasture. In December 1878 the magistrate of Berea reported conditions in his district that could be found all over the country.[2] Pasture lands were getting more limited every year. In many villages land disputes were of daily occurrence, and pasturage was so scarce that the people could only keep a few milch cows in the village. Large numbers of Basuto had no cattle at all. In the less fortunate parts of Basutoland as in certain French villages of the eighteenth century, cattle depended for their main nourishment upon the gardens, so that if reaping was unduly delayed the stock suffered because it could not get into the stubble. As in

---

[1] G. 21, 1875.
[2] G. 33, 1879. Report by C. G. H. Bell, 31 Dec. 1878. See the same official's report of 29 Dec. 1879 in G. 13, 1880.

the neighbouring Kafir country an overstocked and overculti-
vated land was still further impoverished by grassburning and
the destruction of timber for building and firewood, the worst
effects of which were visible in the disastrous erosion that seamed
the country with great watercourses or dongas.

For a native territory Basutoland exported vast quantities of
grain in good seasons. Not enough, however, could be grown to
feed the population, pay its taxes and fines, buy its ploughs,
saddles, blankets and brandy, or pay for the imported merchan-
dize that in 1872 was estimated to be worth £150,000. Basutoland had also to export its labour, and perhaps from no other
native territory did the labourers go forth in greater numbers.
Over 6500 was the number of passes issued at a single office in
1874. "Many who come home to us from the Colony", exclaimed one chief at the Pitso of 1874, "will be obliged to go back
again; I think even now there must be more Basutos in the Free
State than there are in the Lesuto. There is no room for them
here."[1] There was not a magistrate in all Basutoland who could
disagree. Upon Basutoland fell also in these years the scourge
of drought, that laid the land in dust, and the plague of cattle
disease that decimated the herds. The decision of the Cape
Government to disarm the Basuto affected a people shaken by an
economic revolution and whipped by intemperate seasons. Disarmament was a provocation; the causes of war were deeper.

During the growing season of 1879 upon which the people
depended for their food supply for 1880 all Basutoland suffered
severely from drought. Maize sold at £2 to £3 per bag. "The
chief characteristic of the year 1879", wrote the magistrate
stationed at Maseru in the Thaba Bosigo district, "is the protracted and severe drought which has prevailed throughout the
land, the effects of which are only too plainly visible in the
parched up country and withering crops, and nowhere are they
more keenly felt than at Maseru, where our wells and springs are
drying up and the water supply, already inadequate for our
arrangements, is daily decreasing."[2]

In October 1879, Sprigg, the Prime Minister, went to Basutoland to explain the Government's policy. He came to explain

[1] G. 2, 1875, Pitso, 2 Oct. 1874.   [2] G. 13, 1880.

rather than to listen. The Basuto were the Government's children, and the Government knew better than they what was good for them. They must give up their arms. In reply the Basuto admitted that they were the Government's children. But unlike children they spoke more wisely than their father; for they had entirely the better of the discussion. The account of the Pitso, even in its abbreviated official version, was a discomfiture for Sprigg; for had he listened and, having listened, asked questions of the magistrates, he could not have left Basutoland with his decision to carry out a summary disarmament unchanged.

Sir Benjamin D'Urban had spoken of the natives as irreclaimable savages. There was a greater disposition now to speak of them as children. This new status, no more correct than the old, was nevertheless more hopeful for the future relations between the natives and the Government. Since it is of the nature of parenthood to feel solicitude as well as to practise discipline, Sprigg's fatherly posture at the Pitso contained the implicit promise of a more active and generous guardianship of the native interest. Yet in this unfledged status there were grave dangers, the more so because the older attitude that the natives were the "natural enemies" of the white man was still far from dead. It was so easy to allow a belief in the immaturity of the natives to become an administrative convenience, a device for exercising a control that was not altogether or honestly in the native interest.

From the magistrates in Basutoland came emphatic warnings and urgent prayers. Let the Government proceed more slowly. That the natives were politically voiceless did not condone a compulsion so curt and unbending. The prejudice that the guns in their hands predisposed them to sudden rebellion was dangerously wrong. Their proper management called for a sympathetic understanding. It would be better to take away their grievances and leave them their guns than to take away their guns and leave them their grievances. If only the law could be allowed to sleep, breathed one chief, until the hearts of the people were calmed. But the Government would not listen. Basutoland must be disarmed lest it become another Zululand.

The bewilderment of the Basuto, turning to anger, began to undermine a good will and an influence which had taken ten devoted years to build. Many who had learned to look to the European magistrates for counsel and guidance felt themselves thrust back into the arms of die-hard chiefs. A point was rapidly reached where the demoralization in Basutoland made force imperative. Colonel Griffith, the Governor's Agent, spoke bitterly. He did not deny the need of ultimate disarmament, but declared roundly that "the policy which has been forced upon me, by circumstances over which I have had no control, of carrying on the Government of a large tribe, like this, by what is known as 'moral force' or 'moral persuasion' has been played out".[1] Before the Basuto had risen in actual rebellion the Cape Government had made the use of force a necessity. As the Cape Mounted Rifles rode up to Basutoland Frere left South Africa. His going was a retreat from confederation and everything Carnarvon had hoped for.

In spite of warnings from every quarter the Cape Government committed the further blunder of esteeming too lightly the military strength of the natives. It sent up a handful of men instead of a force large enough to awe the headstrong, protect the loyal and mercifully proceed against insurrection before its infection could spread. When the Cape finally did call out the burghers it was found that there were too few efficient officers to organize the inexperienced forces quickly enough to make a vigorous show of force at the beginning of hostilities. Worse still, a force the purpose of which was to disarm the natives suffered itself for months from a poverty of arms and ammunition. Because the natives were given ample time to betake themselves with their cattle and their food into the mountainous country the campaign soon degenerated into desultory and forlorn attacks on hills and rocky fastnesses. In the days of assagais the military had chased the natives, captured their cattle and destroyed their grain. Now that they had guns the natives stayed and the Europeans unfortunately had to fight them. It was an unprofitable type of warfare that gave the burghers less opportunity to fill their waggons with grain and crack their stock whips over captured native cattle.

Up to Basutoland there marched not a single British soldier.

[1] C. 2755, 1881, p. 93, C. D. Griffith to H. E. Bright, 27 April 1880.

Sprigg declared that he did not want them; Hicks Beach and Kimberley retorted that he could not have them if he would. Not a soldier or a shilling. The Cape had refused to accept the British Government's policy of confederation. It could not well expect the help of British troops and money, although a few score experienced officers and Strickland's Commissariat would have been invaluable. The Colonial Office in its turn was convinced that the Cape Government had brought the war upon itself, and should therefore make what terms it could with the natives and its own conscience. "The decision of the Secretary of State", wrote Lord Cadogan, the Parliamentary Undersecretary, "that the Disarmament (whether right or wrong) is to be considered as the act of the Cape Government, the responsibility for which will rest on them, will not I hope be departed from."[1] The Cape, Kimberley averred, was a self-governing colony; in disarming the Basuto, or in making war upon them it was entirely within its constitutional rights. The Basuto War was the first war since the beginning of the century in which the British Government neither fought nor paid. For just such a lessening of its cares it had for a whole generation pursued and retreated and threatened and begged, making treaties and breaking them, annexing territories and abandoning them.

Yet Kimberley felt tugging at him an opposite impulse. Sprigg's heated protestations left him ill at ease. There was in some quarters of the Cape an immoderate language that foreboded a harsh ending to the war. In the Cape House of Assembly the Colonial Secretary himself explained that he saw no reason why Basutoland should continue to exist as a separate native territory, or why the Basuto should further exist as an independent nation. Kimberley remembered that they had been annexed to prevent their land being taken from them entirely. The Home Government could not stand passively by and see a vengeful Cape make another disastrous inroad upon that land. It would be the duty of the High Commissioner, he informed Frere's successor, Sir Hercules Robinson, to reserve any Act annexing Basuto territory for the Queen's pleasure. However much it was disposed to respect the rights of local self-govern-

[1] C.O. 291/5, D. 77, Wolseley to Hicks Beach, 10 March 1880, Minutes.

ment the Home Government did not thereby become an idle
and disinterested spectator. It could not be denied the right and
the duty to advise or caution, or even to act more drastically yet.
There were regions in which even self-government had to
respect the voice of the Home Government, and maybe yield
before it. Such a region was native policy.

Kimberley spoke decisively.[1] The Crown, he informed Robinson, would gladly lend its good offices to negotiate a peaceful
settlement. But if the Cape punished its enemies too cruelly or
if, as was not impossible, it failed to lay the storm it had raised,
the Home Government would be constrained to act in a positive
manner. In the event of a failure of Cape arms the British
Government would have to reconsider the conditions under
which the Cape controlled not merely Basutoland but the other
native territories as well.

Kimberley was teaching the British Government to walk again
on that tight rope on to which it had laboriously climbed after
the abandonment of the Sovereignty in 1854, and from which it
had decisively fallen with the annexations of Basutoland, the
diamond fields and the Transvaal. It was a difficult balance between a safeguarding of humanitarian interests on the one hand
and the limitation of military and financial responsibilities on the
other. A difficult balance it was indeed; for there was so much
to upset it. In the very midst of the Basuto War there came a
shock from the Transvaal that made equilibrium impossible.

The shot and shell that the little Cape seven pounders began
to rain upon the rocks of Basutoland in September had produced no apparent reverberation in the Transvaal, where all
seemed quiet as never before. Lanyon contemplated the result
of his labours and expressed satisfaction. People seemed pleased
with the new schoolmasters, the profitable quiet in the native
world, and the promise of a railway. An excess of revenue over
the estimates was assured. For 1880 the revenue would be
double that of the year before. Since the annexation Pretoria
had doubled in size. Prices were high. The Chief Justice was
paying £300 per year for rent. So many Government officials
were in debt that Lanyon had thought it wise not to publish the

[1] C. 2754, 1881, Kimberley to Robinson, 30 Dec. 1880.

Treasury regulations concerning officers in debt. Yet more spacious days had arrived. The time had come, Lanyon felt, for the Government and its officials to cut a better figure. The ladies of Government officers, he complained as if he were a South African born, had to stoop to the use of raw Kafirs for their servants, and even had to do much of their own housework. Such humiliation might have been acceptable under the Republic, but in one of Her Majesty's colonies, blessed with a surplus, it would not do. Just as little was it fitting that Government officials should leave their desks to work after hours for Pretoria merchants. All salaries, he told Downing Street, should be raised. For himself he contemplated leave. He was suffering from a sort of "scribbler's paralysis". The country was so quiet that there was every inducement to take a rest.[1]

The only disturbing note was the announcement by the Boer leaders of yet another mass meeting. The people would then decide what their answer to Gladstone's refusal to grant them their independence would be. It was evident that Kruger was determined that his sword should not smite in haste. Lanyon, like Wolseley and Shepstone, misunderstood such forbearance. Neither Wolseley nor he saw that the successive meetings had transformed the Transvaal. What had been divided was welded more closely together. Without arbitration or specific discussion men and districts were learning to submerge their differences and to acknowledge a common purpose. An idea had taken possession of them. It was their new Transvaal patriotism. It was their most binding cement.

Yet the historian, if he is to be impartial, must beware lest he accept too readily the belief that patriotism alone drove the Transvaal to arms. Sympathy is quickly aroused by the cry of oppression, and admiration is easily given to a call to freedom, else had Gladstone been less than Gladstone. It is an easy temptation, one that is pleasant to a heart stirred by generous and liberal feeling, to see in the uprising the desperate act of men to whom oppression and misunderstanding had become intolerable. That the cry for self-determination was genuine it would be absurd to doubt. It was an authentic note and it rang not less

[1] C.O. 291/6, Sep., Lanyon to Herbert, 3 Sept. 1880.

clearly because Bok translated it into the turgid jargon of the proclamations, with their wordy homilies, their appeals to the history of the Rights of Man, the American Constitution and many other things about which the Boers bothered not at all. The Dutch had, no less than the English, a natural instinct for liberty and a real love of free institutions. Such a people might tolerate the eclipse of its political liberty for a while. But it was a tolerance that could be withdrawn, for it is in the nature of severity and autocracy that they create dissidence amongst a freedom loving people, and of threats and neglect that they provoke disobedience and violence.

Yet it was also true that the political life of the Transvaal had been too brief and too troubled for its people to acquire in the true sense a capacity for orderly Government. There can be no doubt that in part at least the Boers of the Transvaal grew disaffected towards the British administration for much the same reasons as had helped to destroy the republican Government under Burgers. After the slipshod friendliness of Shepstone's rule they were subjected to a more rigorous Government which, although languid enough by ordinary standards of British Crown Colony Government, was efficient and domineering by the standards of the Transvaal. By the nature of the life he had lived for two generations and more the average Boer was bound to resist a form of Government which sought, even half-heartedly, to apply the rule of law, to withdraw the natives from the rough and one-sided jurisdiction of their white neighbours, and to refuse to allow the solvency of the state to remain at the mercy of whimsical taxpayers. The British administration was undone by an unwillingness on the part of the most vigorous section of the Boers to accept the end of its endeavours, which was the introduction of an average orderliness in law and finance, and by a complete refusal of the majority of the Boers to accept the instrument to that end, which was a narrow constitution that excluded from public affairs men in whom the habit and love of free political activity was too strong to be denied. That it was a harsh Government can scarcely be affirmed. If it could boast of few friends amongst the Boers it created fewer martyrs. Of material misery caused by war or taxation there could be no question. Even in the inflammable field of native policy it had thus far qualified its effort to improve the legal and territorial position of the natives by a willingness to accept most of Boer expansion and settlement as an accomplished fact.

The quietness of the country and the deferment of any decision led Lanyon to believe that agitation was lessening, and that only a handful of the irreconcilables prevented unrest from dying down altogether. A swift blow at the residue of malcontents, who were also mostly those whose taxes were in arrears, would permit the Government to begin the new year with the rule of law undisputed and the surplus assured. Lanyon was wrong. To try conclusions with the non-juring and tax-delinquent Boers was a hazardous undertaking enough. To quarrel with a man named Bezuidenhout was an egregious blunder. The British Government had quarrelled with that name in 1815 and South Africa had never forgiven it. Now once again in 1880 the British Government fell foul of the self-same name. Bezuidenhout had received a tax notice for £27. 10s. 1d. from the landdrost of Potchefstroom. He appeared at the office of the landdrost protesting that he owed only £14. He proved his contention but refused to pay a claim of £8 for costs which the landdrost assessed against him. His waggon was attached, a milling crowd of three hundred Boers led by Cronje dragged it off, and rebellion had at last raised head in the Transvaal.

Lanyon was unafraid. This overt rebelliousness was better than the skulking surliness of the last year. That it could be crushed he had no doubt. It could only have been with the deliberate intention of precipitating an outbreak that he now proceeded to arrest Celliers, editor of the *Volkstem*, for having printed a declaration that the Boers would not pay any more taxes, or if they paid them, would do so under protest. That the Boers could successfully resist the small and scattered troops he had at his disposal, did not at first enter Lanyon's mind. As the stirring and the muttering amongst the Boers grew he did somewhat more anxiously telegraph to Colley in Natal to send the 58th to the Transvaal, and ordered the companies of the 94th to march to Pretoria from their stations at Lydenburg and Marabastadt. But till the mine exploded beneath his feet he pooh-poohed the idea of any real danger, remaining to the end obstinately ignorant of the incendiary properties of personal resentment and popular patriotic emotion.

In Downing Street Lanyon's despatches were received with mounting uneasiness. They were too cocksure. Herbert was afraid that in deliberately provoking an outbreak so that he might crush it, Lanyon relied "too much on the notorious cowardice of the Boers, and had not allowed weight enough to the fact that cowardice prompts men to act in overwhelming numbers against small parties". That the Boers were not cowards only made his prophetic words more grim. Kimberley's sensitive and scrupulous mind received the smirking self-satisfaction of one of Lanyon's despatches with distaste. It was, he deplored, an "unfortunate despatch both on account of the mistaken estimate of the danger, and the general tone of the remarks on the state of feeling amongst the Boers". There was a certain rough and topical humour in comparing the Boers with the Irish; but even that was no reason for despising them or goading them into revolt. The Colonial Office, not for the first time, showed a better understanding of what was toward than the men on the spot. At the beginning of a conflict which had the Transvaal itself for a prize, Lanyon's administration had forfeited the sympathy of the Colonial Office. In Kimberley Lanyon had lost the only ally who could save him and his Government. Only a rabid prejudice could absolve the local British administration of an unusual responsibility for the disasters that overtook it. For once the fastidious pen of the historian may fairly choose a severer and harsher language. Lanyon was guilty of stupid ignorance of those whom he tried both to rowel and decoy into revolt. He deliberately wrested the control over events from the hands of Kruger and those who might still direct them along peaceable channels. "The Government has precipitated matters", Kruger complained with justice.[1] It had left the Boers no choice between being treated as rebels or exercising their eternal rights as a free people. If Lanyon acted stupidly as a politician his conduct as a soldier was conceited, fatuous and shortsighted. The cardinal sins of strategy were all his. He

---

[1] C. 2783, pp. 25–26.

despised his enemy, and overestimated his own strength. He provoked an outburst before he was prepared to meet the consequences. His forces were scattered, low in morale, weak in cavalry, and ignorant of South African warfare. Finally he allowed himself to be taken by surprise. Had he been either a good politician or a good soldier he might have prevented the outbreak or conquered it. Politically a more skilful man could at least have deferred revolt; militarily a better soldier could have avoided the extreme strategic and moral disadvantages of unpreparedness, surprise and early disorder.

The outbreak itself came with the suddenness of a flash. On 13 December 1880 the Triumvirate composed of Kruger, Pretorius and Joubert came into being; the Republic was declared and the Boers, convinced that law was on their side and God with them, rose. It was their land. They had inherited it violently and had no intention of any longer living in it meekly. At the moment, therefore, when the Government was sure that it had taken the measure of its enemies, the blow fell. The enemies were not a handful of malcontents, as Lanyon had expected and hoped. The entire Transvaal had risen. That was the surprise and the disaster. Boer patrols cooped Lanyon up in Pretoria. There he paged over the correspondence of the Government since the annexation and looked back upon his own administration, wondering where the movement had begun; for it seemed to have slunk upon him, gaining ground imperceptibly and overflowing suddenly to the surprise even of the Boer leaders themselves. He wrote a number of peevish despatches proving that the rebellion should never have happened, that it had been caused by "unscrupulous agitators, place hunters and foreign adventurers".

Lanyon soon regained his calm. If the outbreak had been sudden the collapse would be as sudden. Two-thirds of the Boers had been brought together against their will. They had no commissariat. They were incapable of any united or sustained action. They were mortal cowards, so that anything they did would be but a flash in the pan. All the British had to do was to wait calmly for reinforcements. It was rebellion, but it was not necessarily to be deplored. It had smouldered so long in dark places where probing had inflamed it without relieving it, that a free burning in the open was like a cleansing. The eruption was likely to gather together and thrust spontaneously to the surface the leading elements of unrest. Purged of them by a stern government, the country could be allowed at long last to subside into quietness and good order. A smart defeat, followed by a firm but gentle despatch in Sir Harry Smith's best manner, would work wonders. In Downing Street there was less confidence. "These do not now appear to us here like the clouds threatening an ordinary storm", said Herbert gravely when he received the first news of the outbreak. Kimberley read each despatch as it came grimly.[1] Lanyon's optimism impressed him hardly at all. "We must first 'catch our hare'; at present we appear to be caught ourselves", he warned his subordinates. And where Lanyon and Colley talked of defeating the Boers he himself grew more disposed to look attentively upon plans for withdrawal.

Not all of Lanyon's judgments of the Boers were wrong. Their weakness was actually great. A sustained rebellion calling for a long absence in the field was beyond them. They were poor in equipment, and it was one of their grievances that Lanyon had made the buying of ammunition difficult. Their commissariat was limited by what the individual burgher could carry with him, or forage in the country through which he passed. The internal economy of a commando was of the simplest, reinforcing a mobility already exceptionally great. Its *esprit de corps* was the sum of individual willingness; at its best it was excellent, at its worst it destroyed the commando. Being devoid of sanction it could disperse spontaneously when reward was lacking or conviction flagged. An acquisitive keenness for booty in cattle, or the need to protect property could keep it in the field against an enemy. Yet even then good rains and a promising spring could disorganize it. Its successes were the success of its mobility, although a commando was in no sense of the word cavalry. A Tartar charge of horsemen was utterly beyond Boer experience. Though there was initiative, endurance and courage in their warfare, they displayed little of the bravura of men born to the saddle. Horses were used to cover distance when out of the range

---

[1] C.O. 179/135, D. 247, Colley to Kimberley, 19 Dec. 1880, Minutes.

or the sight of the enemy. At close quarters they acted rather as individuals, dismounting to find each man his own vantage ground.

Their spontaneous military spirit found its proper strategy ready made in the hills and valleys of their country. Although it is called a plateau on the maps, the Transvaal high veld is of a deceptive levelness. Actually the country is over large areas broken up by local watersheds into a succession of valleys and steep hills. In 1880 it was a paradise for small bodies of snipers in the hills, and for quick moving horsemen in the flat country. In no particular place were they vulnerable. Infantry requires a simple battle front and clear cut objectives. The Boers provided none of these. The British infantry, on the other hand, could not scatter as they did, and by its very nature was forced to collect in relatively large bodies, which were therefore slow of movement and weighted down by their waggons and impedimenta. Against the Boer's pocket full of dried meat the commissariat waggon was at a disadvantage. For a force like the British infantry regiments dispersal was weakness and even invited disaster. Indeed the best use that could be made of infantry in the Transvaal was to let it sit down in a town where the Boers could besiege it until a mobile force could come to disperse them.

When the Boers rose against Lanyon the question was therefore which side would be betrayed first by its own weaknesses. The unpreparedness of the British forces, the incredible carelessness of certain officers and the light-hearted refusal to take the Dutch commandos seriously drew the initial reverses upon the heads of the British, destroying their confidence and building up the morale of their opponents. The Dutch success at Bronkhorstspruit over the 94th was of great strategic significance.

As early as 23 November the order had been given out for the 94th to return to Pretoria. Delayed by swollen streams it did not start till more than a week later, and was still on its way when the rebellion began. On 15 December Colonel Bellairs in Pretoria warned Colonel Anstruther to use his scouts and be careful of the hilly country about twenty miles from Pretoria. With a precise obedience to the letter of his orders Colonel Anstruther apparently concluded the Boers could not possibly attack him in any other place than that indicated by his superior officer. He felt that he could, on that fateful 20th of December, advance, with his train of waggons spread out half a mile, the ammunition boxes screwed down, his men eating peaches and the band playing a tune, to within seventeen miles of the locality of which Bellairs had warned him. It was no bravado but sheer folly. More incredible still was the circumstance that the officers actually knew at breakfast that there was a troop of Boers ahead of them. Although Anstruther only had four horses, there is no indication that he made full use of even these for advance scouting. He himself had actually ridden past the rocky koppie behind which the Boers had dismounted when the sudden silence of the startled band revealed the ambush to him. The Boers might have fired upon the 94th then and there. Instead they showed a certain chivalrous and scrupulous regard for the finer processes of warfare which has ever since provoked the respect of their enemies. Under a flag of truce they gave Anstruther two minutes to decide whether he would cross the little stream that was called Bronkhorstspruit or not. Meanwhile each Boer picked his position and marked his man. Anstruther replied that his orders were to go to Pretoria, and to Pretoria he would go. It is the decision of the soldier whether to accept the ignominy of surrender or to embrace the heroic pain of death and defeat, and the unmilitary critic can only withhold his comment in silence. In the first volley practically every officer fell; in ten minutes all the officers lay on the ground, and the dead and wounded numbered one hundred and twenty. The survivors threw up their helmets. The 94th had surrendered after all. Amongst the survivors it was ever afterwards a matter of debate whether the number of Boers killed had been two or only one.

Of glory it would be foolish to speak. The bleeding ranks and the broken flesh of the 94th had not yielded to a true victory. Its spirit was whole and its colours were saved, hidden first beneath a women's clothes and then smuggled away under a soldier's coat. Yet such an incident, trivial in the large scale of things, nevertheless shrivelled the blatant veil which Lanyon had pompously drawn before the British position in the Transvaal, betraying its weak and vulnerable anatomy.

Colley was the next to march to disaster and his own death.

He was in a quandary. If he waited for reinforcements from England and India, weeks would be consumed and the weak and poorly supplied garrison in Potchefstroom would almost certainly be lost. Concluding apparently that since Minorca British forces had always begun with an inspiring disaster, he decided to push into the Transvaal with what forces he had. He still insisted that the Boers would not be able to face trained forces. A firm front and a resolute advance could only hasten their inevitable dispersal. But Bronkhorstspruit had already set in motion events that were to make altogether futile Colley's efforts and doubly bitter his defeat and death at Majuba.

It was with a troubled mind that Downing Street now began to look upon the Transvaal. The commandos were rebels against Her Majesty, and militarily it was forbidden to yield before them. The War Office quite properly made preparations to throw an irresistible force against them, offering Colley two cavalry regiments and 1500 infantry. Yet the Colonial Office, and especially Kimberley, felt morally disarmed before the Boers. "I fear", he sighed, "that we have made many mistakes in dealing with these people."[1] Not the least mistake had been to attack them with a weak force. "Our belief that the Boers would not fight", Fairfield frankly avowed, "was not so much founded on reports from Colonel Lanyon that they were paying taxes, as from a disbelief in their possessing the necessary heroism, involved in risking death and defeat in the field; but I fancy it was always recognized that if they did brave death and destruction for the sake of independence, it would go far towards securing a *political* victory for the survivors." The Colonial Office called to mind that Sir Harry Smith had once declared that he would rather have a thousand "duffle jackets" than all the pipe clay on the frontier. "The whole history of the Boers is that of a very brave people skilful in war," went on Fairfield, "and we were misled in assuming that the present generation had degenerated in that respect." More grudgingly but just as ruefully Herbert admitted that "when a sufficiently strong cause stimulates them their 'Dutch courage' is apparently equal to great deeds".[2] And Bramston

[1] C.O. 291/14, A. Ikin to C.O., 1 Jan. 1881, Minutes.
[2] C.O. 48/499, D. 27, Strahan to Secretary of State, 11 Jan. 1881, Minutes.

even wondered whether the unclaimed balances of the compensation money due to Boer slave owners for the emancipation of their slaves in 1834 might not be paid to their descendants or given to some entirely Dutch institution. Strong indeed must have been the prickings of the British conscience if it was willing to confess and do penance for sins nearly fifty years old.

The lukewarmness which Lanyon's optimistic financial reports during 1880 had engendered went cold. As a colleague of Gladstone Lord Kimberley was himself somewhat of a connoisseur of surpluses. He seized upon Lanyon's vaunted figures and destroyed them. Did they take into account the imperial loans of £100,000? The reply came that they did not. Had Lanyon taken into account the money spent on British troops? Again the answer was no. Requested for a memorandum the War Office revealed that the annual cost of the garrison, now miserably cooped up in Pretoria and Potchefstroom, was £218,000. The net cost, which was the excess of expenditure caused by the force being in the Transvaal and not in barracks in England, was £136,000 a year. After the rebellion, if the Transvaal were retained, a larger garrison would be necessary, and for that the net cost could hardly be less than £200,000 a year. Thus contemptuously did Kimberley turn Lanyon's surplus into an "enormous and hopeless deficit".[1]

Financially Kimberley's criticism was not altogether sound or even fair. But he showed in the seclusion of the Colonial Office what Parliament would do more vigorously and unsparingly in public. It would be foolish to try to turn Parliament's attention away from the rebellion by pointing to Lanyon's empty figuring. Not even Gladstone could have made the ragged Transvaal finances look decently prosperous. If Kimberley ever rose to his feet in a debate on the Transvaal it could only be with apologies on his lips, and a prayer for more imperial money. Before a Parliament that already looked sourly on the previous Government and all its works, Transvaal policy had no adequate defence. The truth was, as Kimberley admitted, that "the policy in the Transvaal has been a failure.... It will require great tact and patience to restore a healthy feeling in South Africa."[2]

[1] C.O. 291/7, D. 199, Lanyon to Secretary of State, 8 Dec. 1880, Minutes.
[2] C.O. 291/14, *Daily News*, Minutes.

T

There was urgent need for a prompt settlement of the Transvaal crisis. Native insurrection was creeping from Basutoland into Pondoland and showed signs of jumping across Natal into Zululand where Wolseley's baker's dozen were faring but poorly. More alarming still was the fear that the Dutch and English might be at one another's throats outside the Transvaal as well. Eager to have a round in such a pretty quarrel, the town of Kimberley offered volunteers to deliver Potchefstroom. There were ugly rumours that the Boers of the Free State, not to be outdone, would rally to the support of their compatriots. The danger of such an embroiling of the races caused a shudder to run in South Africa and England alike. Messages from President Brand, Kruger himself and the never failing letter writers to the Colonial Office found the British Government prepared to come to terms with the Transvaal.

The political philosophy of those mid-Victorian Liberals to whom Kimberley and Gladstone belonged was one that counselled abstention rather than interference, and that saw self-help as a leading virtue of all self-government. In this view there were two proper states of colonial Government—Crown Colony Government for a colony that could not pay for itself or manage itself, and self-government for a colony that could. In the case of the Transvaal where the colony could not pay for itself and yet would not let Great Britain govern it the best solution seemed some form of independence.

In this second yielding to Dutch separatism British policy openly admitted defeat. In the minds of many the defeat was doubly bitter because the ignominy of Majuba imperatively called upon British arms to stay in the field till their honour had been vindicated. Then, if withdrawal had to come, it could come with flags flying and drums beating. Instead the British Government allowed its demoralized troops to shuffle out of the Transvaal in defeat. It was a sight that exaggerated the victory of the Boers and led many of them not unnaturally to misconstrue the causes that had restored them their independence; for it was not simply defeat nor even despair but also a sincerely generous spirit that animated British action. A love of peace and a respect for liberty enabled the British Government to put up again its sword into its place, and deny itself the glory of doing vengeance for its wrath. Between the one motive that was passive and neutral and the other which was active and aggressive British foreign policy had often been deeply embarrassed. But in the Transvaal there was a conjuncture of them both. The withdrawal of troops meant peace for England and liberty for the Transvaal. Otherwise it could never have been achieved with such relative ease. In this sense at least the restoration of Transvaal independence, even though qualified, was a genuine victory for the crusading spirit of liberal thought.

The Crown had taken; the Crown could restore. There was happily no need to ask Parliament to consent to the British withdrawal. There were too many militant members ready to say bitter and taunting things about Majuba, and philanthropic members eager to insist upon a native policy which could not be accepted without wrecking the negotiations with the Boers, or rejected without precipitating a difficult conflict in Parliament, and possibly a split in the Cabinet itself, where Bright and Chamberlain headed a powerful philanthropic group. In strict legality the Transvaal could have been relinquished completely, its independence unquestioned. It so happened that the South Africa Act which was introduced before the Transvaal was annexed, and passed while it was British territory, took no cognizance of the change in the Transvaal's status. Since the Act furthermore had remained inoperative it could be said that Parliament had not legislated for the Transvaal, and that consequently even the completest dereliction of British Sovereignty could be an act of the Crown. If this were not so the relinquishment of British Sovereignty at the Bloemfontein Convention would also be illegal. The grant of autonomy and independence to the Free State had been made by Order in Council and Proclamation without any Act of Parliament. Since it had been done with the knowledge of Parliament and had ever since been tacitly acquiesced in by Parliament, it had become a binding and valid agreement, and the most emphatic precedent for the Transvaal. *Fieri non debuit factum valet.*[1]

[1] It is impossible to do proper justice here to the many legal uncertainties involved in both the Bloemfontein Convention of 1854 and the Pretoria

The status of suzerainty for the Transvaal promised to avoid many pitfalls. Properly speaking suzerainty was not an English legal term, or at least it had a connotation so vague that as Lord Ellenborough observed it could, under British law, mean anything "from the palfrey of the King of Naples to full dominion". Precisely because it was an inexact concept did it become possible to represent the events after Majuba as a withdrawal, and as yet not a withdrawal, as giving to the Boers independence, and yet retaining their subjection, as giving to them complete self-government, and yet reserving in the hands of the suzerain control over native policy and foreign relations.

South Africa's haste was to forget. The confusion in the Transvaal was matched by confusion worse confounded in the Cape. For there the Basuto War was dragging to a wretched conclusion, most unfavourable to the Cape, and was in equal need of settlement. Sprigg had resigned, and his resignation removed the one man in the Cape Government who had been reasonably well disposed to confederation or closer union in South Africa. His misfortunes and resignation were so many reasons the more for not seeking to retain the Transvaal.

The Royal Commission appointed by Kimberley to come to terms with the Boers began its sittings on 13 June 1881. The commissioners, Sir Henry de Villiers, Sir Evelyn Wood, and the new High Commissioner, Sir Hercules Robinson, were confronted by suspicious and distrustful men. The Kruger of victory was not the milder Kruger of the years of annexation. Upon all the proceedings of the Royal Commission he looked with misgiving, as if its deliberations might end in deceit, and once more give the British Government an excuse for annexing the Transvaal. It was most noticeable during the weeks that followed how much

Convention of 1881. Actually the abandonment of the Orange River Sovereignty was not altogether legal. Cp. de Kiewiet, *op. cit.* pp. 70–71. It had only become legal because time and consent had made it an accomplished fact. The opinion given by Lord Chancellor Selborne in the matter of the Transvaal did not take into specific advisement whether the British Sovereignty over the Transvaal could be completely extinguished. The Lord Chancellor's opinion held that the relinquishment of sovereignty in 1854 was a precedent *a fortiori* for a step giving to the Transvaal the status of a Suzerain State involving not the total relinquishment and abdication of sovereignty, but only a partial restriction of it. The opinion however leaves little doubt that the Transvaal could have been abandoned entirely without reference to Parliament.

the Boers held the British Government in a distrust which not even the impartiality of de Villiers, the kindliness of Robinson or the tactfulness of Brand were able to dispel. Proposals were received gingerly. It was the outward and visible sign of a lack of confidence that had struck deep root in the Boer temperament. At times their minds almost seemed poisoned against the British Government. A scepticism of British faith was one of the most bitter fruits of Transvaal policy.

There were times when the Boer delegates stood back and let the Royal Commission settle its own differences first. Denied another battle with the Boers, Wood fought his battles in the Commission till the Boers grew to hate him. In the hope conceivably that Kimberley might still relent and at least not abandon the entire Transvaal, he kept up a constant stream of telegraphic complaints to Downing Street over the heads of his colleagues. The financial settlement of the Transvaal offered points for quarrel enough. At first it seemed that the new state would have to begin life staggering under a burden of debt of more than £1,000,000. Kimberley himself wondered for a moment whether it might not be possible to hold the Transvaal for the arrears of those taxes which had been so intimately concerned with the revolt. Gurdon did his duty gallantly as a representative of the Treasury. He haggled over detailed items, and was not without hope that the Boers in their new found patriotism might, like the French peasants ten years earlier, find it well to pay their arrears and lend their savings to the State at a low rate of interest.[1] In the end more moderate counsels prevailed. It was impossible to leave the Transvaal mired inextricably in debt, lacking credit with either local or European financial institutions, except at ruinous rates of interest. The more generous the settlement the better chance the British had of recovering any part of the debt. But even then Gurdon succeeded only too well. The agreement to accept but half a pound of flesh was still an ungenerous one. The British Government waived claims to a number of items of which the heaviest was £383,000 for the expedition against Sekukuni. The Transvaal was left with a total debt in excess of half a million pounds. The Colonial Office shook its head, feeling

---

[1] C.O. 291/12, Minutes under heading: Treasury.

that Gurdon had driven a lickpenny bargain.[1] "It seems almost a pity", said Hemming, "that whilst we were giving up so much politically we did not yield a little more financially and wipe out all claims for expenses incurred since the annexation...a couple of hundred thousand pounds more or less is nothing to Great Britain, but it will be a heavy if not impossible burthen on the Transvaal State....Generous and liberal treatment in the first place would probably have been more appreciated by the Boers than will any future revision." It was most truly spoken. The Colonial Office had no expectation and in a sense little desire that the Transvaal should live up to its bargain. "It is unfortunate", declared Herbert, "that we should commence our very difficult dealings with the new Transvaal Government by in-

---

[1] The total indebtedness as originally estimated was compounded as follows:

	£
Cape Commercial Bank	48,000
Railway Loan	85,667
Orphan Chamber	16,543
Deposits	13,965
Expenses of British administration (deficit)	279,550
Compensation	200,000
Abolition of Office	20,000
Sekukuni Expedition	382,522
	1,046,247

Gurdon originally claimed that the Boers were in debt to the British Government as follows:

	£
Imperial Grant	100,000
Overdraft Standard Bank	150,000
Crown Agents	15,000
Treasury Chest	50,000
Commissariat Stores	50,000
Compensation	200,000
Abolition of Office	20,000
	585,000

The final settlement read as follows:

	£
Compensation	136,900*
Debt to British Government	265,000
Other Debts	160,893
	562,793

* This sum was advanced by the British Government.

sisting...upon an obligation which is morally certain not to be fulfilled and which we do not believe the Transvaal capable of fulfilling without at least serious injury to the State."[1]

With concern did the Colonial Office follow the settlement of native questions. Its interest was genuine. Indeed, had the British Government decided not to leave the Transvaal, a most impelling reason would have been its concern for the Transvaal native population. Kimberley looked attentively upon every pro- posal that dealt with the natives. Even the suggestion that the European portion of the Transvaal should be attached to the Free State was not dismissed out of hand, for it had the virtue of leaving the British Government in control over the principal native areas. Or it might be possible to hold districts like Wak- kerstroom, Utrecht, New Scotland and Lydenburg as an insu- lation between the Boers and the Zulus, Swazis and Bapedi. But one by one these proposals and their variants were dropped. Sir Henry de Villiers insisted that the risks of retaining a part were greater by far than those involved in giving up the whole. Wood was firmly of the view that Great Britain should at least hold an insulating strip south of the Komati River and East of the water- shed of the Drakensberg. But he was opposed by the other soldiers, Colonel Bellairs and Lanyon. Bellairs was sure that any such restriction of Transvaal territory must lead to irritation and difficulties and vitiate all prospect of a good understanding with the British Government. Lanyon, caring now neither for Boers nor Bantu, muttered that "the sooner we get rid of contingent responsibilities the better for imperial interests. The recession of the Transvaal having been determined upon, the measure should be prompt and complete, without any fresh responsibilities being incurred to protect natives who are well able to protect them- selves."[2] Unless the British Government were prepared to main- tain peace and order by force it was inviting disaster to restore a mutilated Transvaal. Anyhow such a territory as Wood pro- posed would be worse than a second Griqualand West. Not even for the natives was Kimberley prepared to assume responsibility for such a "long, thin, poor, invertebrate, roadless, depopulated

[1] C.O. 291/12, Treasury.
[2] C.O. 291/18, Wood to Kimberley, 30 May 1881, Enclosures.

colony", inflammable every inch of it. In the mood of the British Government a difficult experiment in native policy was the least of its ambitions. In getting rid of the Transvaal it got rid both of the Boers and of the natives, escaping the danger and expense of native taxation, the settlement of land disputes, tribal jealousies, and of establishing the rule of law.

By waiving British claims to any part of the Transvaal the consent of the delegates was won to the exercise of the royal veto on native legislation and the appointment of a British Resident with a seat on the proposed Native Locations Commission, which was to create locations and protect native land rights, although it had no funds and had to reckon with the positive ill will of the Boers. It was a most insufficient provision for native interests. The device of a British Resident could not be satisfactory. The office was too weak and the will of the British Government too supine for any effective control of native policy to be effective. To believe that any Resident could supervise and direct Boer native policy was to misunderstand both Boer character and the nature of the native problem. Indeed the very first Volksraad, met together to ratify the Pretoria Convention, made it entirely clear that the thirty-three articles were hardly worth the paper they had been written upon. The Convention, it was complained in the Volksraad, was a glass of milk with thirty-three flies in it. The Volksraad quarrelled with the Transvaal's suzerainty, with the duties of the Resident, and only sulkily ratified the Convention because of the threat of renewed hostilities. At one moment ratification seemed so unlikely that Wood wondered whether he would be given another chance at Laing's Nek. The attacks upon the Pretoria Convention had begun before its ink was fairly dry.

It was undeniably a new South Africa. New notes more strongly discordant than ever before had been struck in popular feeling. At Majuba the Transvaal became the hub of Dutch political life, which was now acutely conscious of its distinct character and ambitions. At Majuba the Transvaal aroused in the breasts of Boers throughout the land a loyalty in which Dutch political and cultural movements could strike root. The feeling for political activity which the British administration had obstructed and denied was grown into a narrow if ardent nationalism, and its effects were not confined to the Transvaal. The Pretoria Convention spelled the triumph of localism. It elevated separatism at the expense of the ideal of political unity. In South Africa men henceforth drew breath in an unventilated political atmosphere stuffy with resentments and a mutual suspiciousness that was a standing menace to peace.

The agitation of the Boer leaders and the arms their followers had born undeniably contributed something of vital importance to South African life. It was the ardour of their political conviction. Had they accepted against their wishes a regime, however well meaning, that they did not desire, they would have shown that the prize of Carnarvon's efforts, namely confederation and self-government, had not been worth while. But that they resisted autocracy made it all the more imperative that such a conviction and such a spirit should be won for the self-government which was the soul of the new Empire. Their rebellion became a telling reason for keeping them within the Empire. The great blunder of British statesmanship, once the annexation was a fact, lay in not recognizing this need, or in recognizing it too late. The Transvaalers proved beyond a peradventure their attachment to the ideals of political liberty. Of their fitness to take part in the great experiment of self-government in the British Empire there could be no question. All the more pity then that the misunderstanding of men and the waywardness of events should have allowed their liberty to become clothed in a sullen racialism and a narrow separatism. These very qualities of their spirit that were invaluable to self-government became resentments that repelled co-operation, and deferred dangerously the day when the garment of South African life should again be seamless.

British policy failed also to recognize that the Transvaal of 1881 was no longer the Transvaal of even 1877. It was at the very time when the telegraph was an accomplished fact, and the railways were about to be rushed into a system of communications that the British Government withdrew. First diamonds, then gold and railways caused a new pulsing, which was the more rapid movement of men whose activities began to make political divisions dangerous and racial boundaries meaningless.

The truest of the prophecies in which Wolseley abounded was that the men who had come to Kimberley for diamonds and who were already coming to the Transvaal for gold, would ere long be numerous enough to challenge the Boers themselves.

The Transvaal could not be isolated from the rest of South Africa, nor South Africa from Europe. The merest glance at European politics showed convincingly the sheer impossibility of a British withdrawal from South Africa. Precisely because the country was not united a close dependence upon England was imperative if South Africa, its individual communities and its coastline were to be guaranteed against foreign interests. However much England ached to be relieved of its care, her withdrawal could only be incomplete. The dereliction of the Transvaal could not abate one jot her exercise of paramountcy. A fully independent Transvaal, sovereign in all its powers, was not feasible, for in 1881 the independence of the Transvaal had become in the full sense of the word, an international question.

CHAPTER XII

THE IMPERIAL FACTOR

LONG BEFORE the Convention had even been signed the
Zulu country smoked with the grass fires set by encroaching
Boers to hasten the growth of the young grass. On the
Transvaal south-western border Lieutenant-Colonel Moysey's
work of marking the new line was finally halted by the quarrels of
Boers and chiefs who agreed only in swearing to tear down his
beacons. It was clear that the Convention was attempting the
impossible. It exposed the Transvaal to temptation and deprived it of the means of resistance. It denied the Transvaal the
right to expand, yet insisted upon peaceful borders. Naturally
it was the merest folly to suppose that the pressure upon Zululand, Bechuanaland and ultimately Swaziland could be stayed
by a one-sided and unpopular instrument. The Pretoria Convention was part of an attempt to place the responsibility of acute
and unsolved native and territorial problems upon local communities, upon the Cape, exhausted and impoverished by the
Basuto War, upon the Transvaal, labouring under Gurdon's unworkable financial settlement. Since neither community could
bear such a charge, the withdrawal of British influence was
necessarily superficial and temporary.

In Zululand when the Black House went the White House did
not take its place. At first the Zulus had looked to Osborne, the
British Resident, to be the mouth that commanded them and the
ears that heard them. Their losses in cattle and grain during the
Zulu War had been enormous, so that their complaints and their
sorrows were many. Finding that the Resident did not propose
to exercise any real power the chiefs turned to renegade whites
whose "advice" bred mischief and degraded the reputation of
the British Government. The land returned to "eating up" and
confiscation. All of the year 1881 was loud with brawling and
contentiousness. At the end of August 1881 Sir Evelyn Wood
met the chiefs in an effort to patch up Wolseley's tattered settle-

ment. The chiefs agreed to the principle of a hut tax, and the appointment of official British Residents. Osborne begged Kimberley for authority for himself, urging that "the extension of Her Majesty's Sovereignty at once, over the whole of Zululand, will prove the only sure means of securing permanent peace and the welfare and civilization of its people ". Kimberley did not deny the failure of Wolseley's settlement. But the British Government had decided to "leave Zululand to take its chance"; and rather than try to keep the peace in Zululand itself, it would even allow Cetywayo to return from Cape Town, where the old paramount chief was gloomily spending his ten shillings of pocket money.

Whereas Zululand had at least been conquered before it was abandoned, the forces of the Cape had retreated from Basutoland in virtual defeat. Robinson's settlement was a failure from the start. The "rebels" had seized the land of the "loyals" during the war, and now refused to relinquish their booty. It was for land really that they had fought. It was for the fat acres that were still left in Basutoland that the burghers might fight again to revive the ebbing influence of the Cape. For land and Basuto labourers they might march once more. Such permission Kimberley strenuously refused. The Cape accordingly withdrew Robinson's award in April 1882, and, as a last resort, turned to Chinese Gordon. That famous man arrived in Cape Town in June, where quite incredibly Saul Solomon, the editor of the *Argus*, had never heard of him, his antecedents or his eccentricities. He arrived in Basutoland in September, just in time to check a quarrel between Lerothodi and Masupha which the harassed officials hoped might develop into an intertribal war and lead the Basuto to break their own strength. Gordon's conduct first bewildered the officials and then infuriated them. He talked as glibly and blithely as any frontiersman on native problems, though there fell from his lips one remark that proved that it was not always his ignorance of Basuto problems that was offensive. "I like the Boers", he confessed. "They are a fine people, but ask them outright which they like best—farms or Basutos." He reassured men that their troubles would be over in a fortnight, and horrified them by telling Masupha that in any case he would not fight against the Basuto. "His conduct has been that of a

man whose mind is unhinged", telegraphed the Secretary for
Native Affairs to the Premier, for Gordon had exhorted the
chiefs not to fight but to love one another. If they must crash
let them crash grandly together as an entire tribe. Such a man
and the frontiersmen could not work together, and he left com-
plaining of the ill feeling the officials had shown him. "The ill
feeling", growled one official, "should all I think come from my
side, but then I don't always talk about Jesus."[1]

The months that followed the departure of Gordon, soon to
die at the other end of the African continent, made more evident
the helplessness of the Cape in Basutoland. Finally East and
West, town and country were in agreement that the abandonment of Basutoland was inevitable. When the hope of carving
farms out of Basutoland died, the farmers saw little reason why the
Basuto should be retained. Indeed abandonment might succeed
where the commandos had failed—"clean the land" by plunging
the tribes into self-destructive conflict. Cape Town and the merchants welcomed abandonment, although for entirely opposite
reasons. The war had cost them their trade. If the British
Government would take over Basutoland—an essential condition
—they would lose the natives as their enemies but regain them
as customers. Thus the fate first of Zululand and now of Basutoland was placed squarely in the hands of the British Government.
To these territories circumstances now proceeded to add a third.

In the Pretoria Convention the weakest link was the settlement
of the Transvaal's south-western boundary. Quickly learning of
the repugnance in Downing Street to the Convention and all its
works the farmers began to cross the border in unprecedented
numbers into the Bechuana country beyond. Ostensibly they
came as volunteers to help their ally, His Honour David Massouw, against Mankoroane and Montsioa. It mattered little
whether a chief enjoyed the alliance or the enmity of these land-
hungry men. The reward they accepted and the punishment
they exacted were the same—land and yet more land. The areas
which in the latter part of 1882 became the separate Republics of
Stellaland and Goshen contained much, if not most, of the best
land which earlier encroachment had not absorbed. Stellaland

---

[1] C.O. 48/504, Conf., Robinson to Kimberley, 17 Oct. 1882, Enclosures.

contained some of the best native gardens near the Harts River. It was as good grazing land as could be found in that portion of the country. In the neighbourhood of Vryburg, which became the capital, there were invaluable permanent springs and streams. The Harts River itself, although not a running stream throughout the year, contained permanent water in its pools. Goshen was a smaller area, but more densely peopled by natives because of several "eyes" of rich land and water, greatly coveted by Moshette's Boer mercenaries. The number of these grew apace. Their "reward" soon threatened to cost Moshette the best of his patrimony.

The freebooters, as they were called in Robinson's alarmed despatches to England, were the sign of the Transvaal's unwillingness to adhere to the Pretoria Convention. Even more they were the sign of the Transvaal's inability to control them, and this weakness was not confined to the Republic alone. The depression which had threatened in 1876 now unloosed itself upon the entire country. In the Cape and Natal credit shrank, companies tottered and collapsed. Farmer and merchant were alike in their wretchedness. The disappointment over Basutoland revealed itself at the end of 1882 in a sudden effort of nearly two hundred frontier farmers to follow the example of the Stellalanders and "jump" land in Emigrant Tambookieland and Tembuland.[1] Not without the greatest difficulty did the Cape authorities control a movement so dangerous to the peace of the frontier. Depression and troubles of its own therefore caused the Cape to look askance at events beyond its borders. It was practising retrenchment within these borders, and would not expand outside them. The Imperial Government must take care of Bechuanaland.

In rapid succession these problems thrust themselves upon a Colonial Office less able than ever before of reaching an easy or swift decision. The minutes of the Colonial Office in the 'eighties bear witness to the amazing increase in the number and the complexity of colonial questions. The telegraph which promised to simplify and expedite the government of the Empire, actually increased its difficulties. It threw overwork upon the Executive

[1] C.O. 48/503, D. 219, Robinson to Kimberley, 12 June 1882.

and especially upon such offices as the Foreign Office and the Colonial Office. The calming effect upon the most excited despatch of lying unread for a month in the darkness of a mailbag was lost. Questions great and small, which formerly were decided on the spot, were now thrown upon the Home Government, not with the full information of a despatch, but with the elliptical curtness of cipher telegrams. Mr Mothercountry no longer lived in the Colonial Office. In the 'eighties colonial questions received the constant attention of Cabinet and Parliament as never before. The number of papers submitted to Queen and Cabinet increased greatly. In the filing system of the Colonial Office a new division was devoted to questions asked in Parliament. During all his period of office as Secretary of State for the Colonies Lord Derby wrote not a single minute on South African affairs that exceeded two or three lines. The reason, as he himself frequently explained, was that decisions lay outside the Colonial Office and in the Cabinet. Both the explanation and the direction of colonial policy lay more and more in the currents of national and imperial activity. A colonial question was also a parliamentary, a domestic, a financial and a foreign question. Conversely it is the simultaneous pressure of varied and contradictory interests upon colonial policy that helps to explain its irregular and hesitant course in these years. Not the least of a Colonial Secretary's worries was how to respond to the voices that rang in his ears, from colonists, merchants, missionaries, imperialists, Little Englanders, each capable of being very difficult and some capable of being very dangerous. In the frequent questions and discussions on South African affairs the Boers were either hailed as gallant and god-fearing Puritans or damned as slave drivers and the scum of South Africa. On the oft recurring question whether the British Government should aid the natives by throwing open to them the arms traffic the most irreconcilable views were stated. It should place an embargo on arms because otherwise the blacks would be armed against the whites. It should not place an embargo on arms because the British merchants would lose their trade to the Germans and Americans. It should control the arms traffic because the colonial laws forbade the sale of arms to the natives. It should not control the arms traffic because the "Aborigines People" would stigmatize it as an odious and inhuman act hindering the natives from protecting their land and their lives.

It was with a glum discomfort that the British Government watched the development of its relations with the Transvaal. A sense of guilt, especially at the financial settlement, burdened its conscience. When in August 1882 the Transvaal failed to pay the first settlement of £100,000 on the debt it had assumed at the Pretoria Convention, the Colonial Office was not surprised. "The Financial Clauses of the Convention", Fairfield admitted, "were hardly regarded as workable from the first",[1] and the Permanent Undersecretary, Herbert, advised a belated generosity since it was "not desirable to place the Trans Vaal Government in so impoverished a condition" that it could not govern the country properly "without imposing heavy taxation which will be resisted and heavy import duties restricting trade".[2] But gradually the Colonial Office, and indeed a large section of British public opinion, lost the respect and sympathy which the Boers had evoked by fighting for their independence. Though it would have preferred to leave the Transvaal alone, it felt that it could not. In overrunning the lands of the Bechuana and fighting them the Transvaal, even though it might disavow the freebooters, fell foul of the Convention, of British humanitarian sentiment, and not least of the memory and tradition of Livingstone and Moffat. The names of these men the British public had taken to its heart. Of all the South African tribes their protégés were the most likely to call forth active sympathy in England. While Herbert urged his colleagues to take every excuse for overlooking or minimizing the actions of the Transvaal Government, almost every mail brought fresh reasons for quarrelling with the Transvaal. Thus even though Ashley, the Parliamentary Undersecretary, confessed as early as November 1882 that he had long thought the Convention unworkable, and "rapidly becoming a dead letter",[3] he spoke strongly against any spontaneous or premature act of abandonment. Even the admission that the Trans-

---

[1] C.O. 291/16, D. 129, Robinson to Kimberley, 7 Aug. 1882.
[2] *Ibid.* D. 186, Robinson to Kimberley, 25 Sept. 1882.
[3] *Ibid.* D. 213, Robinson to Derby, 20 Nov. 1882.

vaal's debt had been ungenerously and unwisely imposed was made grudgingly. Thus was opportunity neglected for a frank and sympathetic gesture by wiping clean the slate. "I would *not* wipe out the debt", Ashley ejaculated most emphatically. "Such 'generosity' will not be appreciated by them any more than a reckless son appreciates his father paying his debts for him, and I should like to see the Boer Government having to proclaim itself and posted as a 'defaulter'. Then we may wipe off the account from our books but never from theirs."[1]

The relations between the Transvaal and the British Government were further embittered by a quarrel over the official name of the Transvaal. The name Transvaal State, used in the Convention, had originally been suggested by Kimberley purely as a convenience. There were two Republics in South Africa and the name South African Republic seemed ambiguous. The Boer protest to the name Transvaal State was eminently reasonable. Their sentimental attachment to the title of South African Republic had increased greatly, and its use was legally unobjectionable. But as Ashley said, the Boers were not liked and a "snub administered to them would be nowhere unpopular". Such a remark explains much of the failure of the Pretoria Convention. However bitterly Parliament and the Colonial Office inveighed against the Transvaal, the British Government regarded the Convention as a way of escape from South African responsibility. It endeavoured to maintain its position that it was not actively responsible for the execution of the treaty. Its opposition to Boer conduct was sentimental but it would not allow its heart to guide its hand. As Gladstone explained with unconscious humour to the House of Commons, the method of dealing with the Boers was by remonstrances. Not even to protect the natives of Kuruman itself would the British Government move in a positive manner to enforce the Convention. "A most miserable page in South African history", exclaimed Bramston, on reading Sir Hercules Robinson's account of filibustering in Bechuanaland, "but as we shall not attempt to coerce the Boers, Montsioa and Mankoroane must face starvation as best they can."[2]

---

[1] C.O. 291/16, D. 186, Robinson to Kimberley, 25 Sept. 1882, Minutes.
[2] *Ibid.* D. 221, Robinson to Derby, 7 Dec. 1882, Minutes.

U

The colonial policy of Lord Carnarvon had assumed that the Home Government, being paramount, could actively exercise its power in South Africa, even against the will of any single community. The Gladstone administration had inaugurated an almost opposite policy. Imperial interests in South Africa were not wide but narrow. The coastline, defence, relations with foreign powers, these clearly enough were the direct concern of the paramount power. But all else was colonial and the concern of the local communities. The Imperial Government was not unwilling to co-operate with them. It was prepared to be generous, and give them the benefit of its greater experience. But no longer would it willingly act as a principal, as it had done in annexing the diamond fields and the Transvaal. This policy was strengthened by the conviction that the colonies themselves maintained the same distinction, pursuing their own interests even when they collided with the Home Government. That was what Kimberley meant when he grumbled that the "Natalians may be very British, but they are not very loyal". And had not Sprigg been at great pains at the beginning of the Basuto War to forbid the Home Government to interfere in a purely colonial and local matter?

A new phenomenon dissuaded the British Government all the more from an active conduct in South African affairs. It was the growth of "Africander" sentiment throughout South Africa after the Transvaal War. Henceforth the common bond of feeling between the Dutch, regardless of domicile and allegiance, was a political factor of the first importance. What concerned the republics concerned the Cape "Dutch vote" also. To quarrel with the Transvaal and its Boers was to lose the co-operation of the Cape. In the Cape Colony no party or parliamentary group was strong enough to remain in power without the Dutch vote, although of seventy-two members in the House only twenty-four were actually Dutch. The influence of the Dutch leaders was mainly exercised by two organizations, the Africander Bond and the Farmers Protection Association, which, because they were extra parliamentary, forced the ministry to keep a wary eye, not upon the two dozen Dutch members, but upon the popular movement. That necessity was the special embarrassment of the successive ministries of Sprigg, Scanlen, and Upington. Each stepped gingerly on all questions affecting the Dutch vote, if only because the two groups had in themselves the makings of a political party based upon an exclusive Dutch feeling which might well sweep into Parliament on the votes of a Dutch majority.

The leaders of the two groups did not see eye to eye. The aims of the Association were more economic—the lowering of export duties and the excise, and legislation favouring the farmer. Those of the Bond were political. Its "Hollander" following was openly republican. Though it professed to welcome all South Africans who did not speak of England as "home" or Holland as the Fatherland, actually du Toit's vernacular newspaper *Di Patriot* was often abusively anti-English. It hated speculators and fortune hunters, was suspicious of Downing Street, and suspected that the admission of women to membership was "Socialistic and Nihilistic" and certainly "not quite Christian". Between the groups there was, however, mutual agreement on the burning question of native policy. In the meetings, speeches and writings of the two movements a very large amount of space and attention was given to questions of labour, native education, squatting, Masters and Servants Laws, and Basutoland. An active group within the Bond called upon the Government to restrict immigration because it took the responsibility of labour from the coloured people, many of whom were actually sending their children to school rather than to work. It was a popular comment at Bond meetings that to teach any person of colour to write was simply to enable him to commit a higher class of crime. Such sympathy as there was for the retrograde principle of voluntary education came from a belief that it would permit a withdrawal of funds from native education. The protest that the franchise was too low was nothing but an attack at a distance of half a century upon Ordinance 50 of 1828. From the Bond it was that came probably the strongest protest against the folly of governing Basutoland for the Basuto. If Basutoland could not be made to yield farms for European occupation, then Basutoland could go. There can be no question that the native policy of the Republics had returned to the Cape, and that the traditional liberal native policy of the Cape was on the defensive. In political life a humanitarian point of view was a handicap. The existence of these views had a direct effect upon Cape native policy and upon imperial relations, for however they were disguised all the important problems of the subcontinent were essentially native problems. It was, for example, with an eye on the Bond that the Cape Government forbore to publish the papers on the encroachment of farmers upon Tambookie territory. When in the Colonial Office Hemming called out that no South African Government "has any sympathy with natives, or will lift a finger to prevent them from being robbed and destroyed",[1] he at least recognized the now typically South African unwillingness to use influence, money, or men to protect native interests when these were opposed, as they were in Bechuanaland, to the interests of a vocal group of Europeans.

Never before had the necessity and justification of imperial intervention been more apparent. Yet never before had it been so clear that the British Government could not both espouse the native cause and enjoy the sympathy and co-operation of the European Governments. The more therefore the British Government insisted that it would only act in concert with the local Governments, the more surely it weakened its position as trustee and arbiter, abandoning native policies to the local communities without reserve or guarantee. It was in this spirit that Herbert spoke when he declared that if the Cape, the Orange Free State and the Transvaal were left to allot or apportion Bechuanaland, a solution would at least have been reached in which "it would not be very material whether they assigned the whole to the Transvaal or portions to more than one of the three Governments".

The British Government, it is important to recognize, was influenced by more than the narrow desire to save its shillings and spare its soldiers. Since Majuba had spelt the ruin of an active and independent imperial policy, it seemed to follow that the road to the confederation and common understanding which the Liberal administration desired not less ardently than its predecessors lay in withdrawal and non-interference. In the

[1] C.O. 291/16, D. 221, Robinson to Derby, 7 Dec. 1882, Minutes.

Transvaal War the British Government had glimpsed the twin spectres of an uprising of the Dutch throughout South Africa, and of a racial cleavage between English and Dutch. Thenceforth an unwillingness to fall foul of Dutch sentiment and above all a genuine respect for the right of local self-determination are important characteristics of South African policy. If left alone Dutch and English, republic and colony, even black and white might still compose their differences, settling in their own good time the terms of their closer association. If the French "Rip van Winkles" and the "pugnacious Presbyterians from Scotland" could agree to unite in Canada, there was hope for South Africa. In April 1881 Mr Grant Duff had told Parliament emphatically that the one consideration dominating "the whole policy which the present Government or any other Government must maintain in South Africa [was] the absolute necessity of preventing the development of race-hatred between men of British and Dutch descent". Two years later, in spite of the ill will that existed in the Colonial Office, Parliament and the Press towards the Transvaal, Gladstone insisted with equal emphasis that it behoved the British Government to weigh carefully its relations with the Dutch, for they were the dominant influence, one in sentiment in Republics and British colonies alike.[1]

It was but logical that the British Government should look with suspicion upon any attempt to commit it to action in Bechuanaland without the co-operation of at least the Cape. In July 1882 it consented to a proposal by Robinson that the Transvaal, the Orange Free State and the Cape should join with the Imperial Government to send a small force to the area of disturbance to round up the scallywags, deserters and violators of proclamations, and drag them back for trial within their proper jurisdictions. Both Republics refused. Another suggestion, the most acceptable of all to the British Government, was rejected out of hand by Scanlen. It was that the Cape extend the frontier of Griqualand West to protect the oppressed tribes. The protection of natives interested the Cape not at all. It had annexed the Basuto and then had fought them. If it annexed the Bechuana it would first have to fight the freebooters, and then,

[1] Hansard, series 3, vol. 277, col. 729.

as was the law of frontiers, the natives too. Mr Scanlen begged to be excused. In January 1883 Robinson expostulated against the violation of the Convention, demanding that it be denounced or enforced, one or the other. So strong were the words he used that the Colonial Office feared for their effect upon public sentiment and withheld them from the papers presented to Parliament. In February Derby offered to organize a police force against British subjects and deserters if the Cape Government would give "all facilities".[1] The answer from the Cape was vague, but the Colonial Office did learn that the force would require five hundred men, cost £100,000, and occupy the country for twelve months. Hurriedly Derby withdrew. It was not merely that five hundred police were too many police, and £100,000 too many pounds, but any British force that stayed in Bechuanaland for twelve months was certain to stay much longer. A policeman's lot was not a happy one. Yet another forlorn proposal that the Cape might take Montsioa, Mankoroane with their followers and locate them in the Cape was merely an admission that the natives had lost their land irretrievably. Robinson's telegraphic reply was curt and final. "Cape has already more native subjects and troubles on hand than it can cope with."[2] The Convention was doomed. The Cape, the Transvaal and the British Government had all helped to kill it.

The demise of that unfortunate document was hastened by happenings in Zululand. Where the Zulus had expected "one word" after the war they had been given thirteen. And the thirteen had built a tower of Babel. On 10 January Cetywayo set foot on Zulu soil, a king once again. But the British Government gave him back with one hand, not with two. Between the Umhlatusi and Tugela Rivers was created a separate reserve under the British Resident, while a large section of North-Eastern Zululand was given to Usibebu, who became immediately and necessarily a rival to Cetywayo. In the fighting that followed Bulwer begged for British action, for the sake of the Zulus, for the sake of Natal, for the sake of peace. His despatches for 1883 abounded in plans for British intervention to forestall the other-

---

[1] Telegram, Derby to Robinson, 23 Feb. 1883.
[2] C.O. 291/22, Telegram, Robinson to Derby, 17 March 1883.

wise inevitable encroachment and annexation by the Transvaal. Of all plans "the safest, the truest and the wisest solution" was the extension of British Sovereignty over all Zululand.[1] He pleaded in vain. Beyond the Reserve the British Government would not go. "I do not know of any reason", remarked Fairfield, "why, if the Zulu border can be made tolerably peaceful, the Boers and Zulus should not be allowed to intersperse their settlement." The Convention was truly dead.

Thrice during the first half of 1883 did Parliamentary opinion force debates on the Transvaal and the Convention. In each debate the Government speakers frankly admitted the failure of the Convention. Derby complained that the affairs of South Africa had been critical "not only ever since I had the honour to be appointed to my present office, but almost ever since I can remember".[2] What then was the British Government to do? he asked. Appeal to Pretoria? It had been done, and in vain. Send a force? Something of the sort had been done in Abyssinia and it had cost £9,000,000. Annex Bechuanaland? Bechuanaland was of no value for any English or for any imperial purpose. Politically it was of no consequence to England whether Boers or natives were in possession. Prevail upon the Cape Colony to annex it? The Cape Colony was thoroughly disgusted with the native responsibilities it already had. Annex the Transvaal? Surely the British people had learned their lesson and would not deliberately provoke the further resentment of the Dutch or create in South Africa another Ireland. Chamberlain came to Derby's aid and utterly disarmed so angry a critic of the Government as Forster by admitting that the British Government had, on the evidence before it, as good a *casus belli* as ever it had had for South African wars. Yet it declined to "send British residents here and British expeditions there".[3]

Faced with the alternative of maintaining British policy by force or establishing a *modus vivendi* with the people and government of the Transvaal, the administration had no hesitation in choosing the milder path of compromise. In the Colonial Office a memorandum on the Convention was drafted by Fairfield and

[1] C.O. 179/148, D. 211, Bulwer to Derby, 30 Nov. 1883.
[2] Hansard, vol. 280, col. 668.   [3] *Ibid.* vol. 278, col. 224.

sent to the Cabinet. A more impartial document Fairfield had never written. It confessed that the refusal to allow the Transvaal to style itself the South African Republic had been a petty and useless irritation. From the beginning the Convention had been a one-sided instrument disadvantageous to the Transvaal which could not effectively have controlled its errant subjects even had it shown more zeal. The Convention, said Herbert, had been of no value in securing any advantage to natives, British subjects, the colonies or the Transvaal. Hemming would fain have seen the British Government wash its hands of the Boers altogether, and Ashley, the Parliamentary Undersecretary, agreed that at least the suzerainty should be shaken off without delay.[1]

With the Convention disappeared also any hope of restoring the land to the natives. The effect of Derby's speeches against interference was a speculating and an auctioneering in Stellaland. The selling and the buying of land gave an air of legality to the presence of the whites, and set up claims that even Robinson agreed had to be recognized. Not how the interloping Europeans should be expelled, but how they should be governed was now the problem. Derby's refusal to rule the land and its natives provoked a cry that he rule the land and its Europeans. The hope that land prices would rise as the British flag unfurled turned speculators into loyalists. Most of them were unmindful that British annexation had not made prices to rise either in the Transvaal or in Famagusta where, as Fairfield wittily observed, the Sultan's banker had some fine blocks of bastions that he would be glad to sell for a song.

It was to be expected that the member of Parliament for Barkly West should be interested in Stellaland. That territory had been cut up into four hundred farms, all belonging to Europeans. Basutoland still belonged to its natives. For that reason Cecil John Rhodes was interested in Stellaland. By the middle of 1883 he was busy influencing opinion in the Cape and Stellaland in favour of his first imperial venture—the annexation of Bechuana territory to the Cape. On Saturday, 6 June, he had a long telegraphic conversation from Barkly West with Scanlen. They were urgent words which he sent over the wire. Scanlen's

[1] C.O. 291/24, Memorandum and Minutes.

replies were hesitant. In annexing Stellaland the Cape risked offending the Stellalanders, the Transvaal, and its own Dutch electorate. It had no stomach for fighting the first, or quarrelling with the second, or being unseated by the third. Yet to every objection Rhodes had the readiest reply. The Stellalanders desired annexation to the Cape. Every day the country contained less freebooters and more loyal Cape farmers. There was ample land for whites and blacks and to spare for Crown lands. On the other hand if the Transvaal got Stellaland and Goshen "you may as well stop your railways", for the Cape Colony would be entirely shut off from the interior trade. "Stop Lord Derby from giving the Transvaal the right to extend, and have the courage to give it to the Cape." Scanlen ventured the reply that the Cape might extend westwards only far enough to secure command of the interior trade, leaving the rest to the Transvaal. Back over the wire came the reply: "Don't part with one inch of territory to Transvaal; they are bouncing. The interior road runs at present moment on the edge of Transvaal boundary. You part with that and you are driven into the desert." When Scanlen spoke again of his fear of a quarrel with the Transvaal, Rhodes smoothly offered to "get a petition from Stellaland if that would help", and insisted that the Transvaal must be checked at all odds. "If you, gauging the feeling of the Colony, dare not propose annexation, do the next best thing to it. Stop Lord Derby from allowing the Transvaal to annex; they have the pluck of bankrupts, and given the right they would annex Egypt tomorrow, but are moving heaven and earth to annex Stellaland and Goshen." Scanlen continued to shake his head. It was useless to talk of annexing Stellaland unless the Cape's labouring shoulder was eased of Basutoland. How awkward it was that this question should arise just when the Cape had to meet a large deficiency in revenue. Still worse, Parliament was in its last session, and it was hopeless to expect it to assent to any measure that was considered adverse to the interests of the Transvaal. From such embarrassments the Cape could not escape without the aid of the Imperial Government.

Since 1881 the weight of Basutoland that galled the shoulder of the Cape had grown even heavier. Drink threatened to complete the havoc that war had begun and drought had continued. The liquor which was one of the most valuable of Natal's imports, reappeared again in the grogshops that thronged the Free State border. The prestige of Government had fallen so low that its principal function was little better than the conciliation of successful rebels. Not law and order but the avoidance of war was the real aim of administration. Even then the chiefs would have none of Cape rule. Let the Queen rule them, was their prayer. It pleased the Queen very little to listen to their prayer, yet it could not be denied. British policy could not permit a territory to drift rudderless in the midst of Natal, the Transkei, the Cape and the Orange Free State. It was a moral certainty that the anarchy would spread farther abroad, and provoke the aggression of the Free State, which had not forgotten nor forgiven the seizure of 1869.

The decision of the British Government to take over Basutoland from the Cape confirmed once again its territorial integrity. The subsequent economic and social development of South Africa has never ceased to testify to the wisdom of a policy that thus preserved a great tribe from the loss of its land. In both the practice and the theory of the modern Empire the idea of trusteeship is of paramount importance. Yet no measure so unquestionably beneficial and merciful was ever undertaken so glumly. The first of the great South African native protectorates was not the product of a willing conviction. It was a policy that the British Government initiated most grudgingly under the compulsion of circumstances. Her Majesty's Government, wrote Derby to Robinson, accepted "no permanent responsibility for the affairs of this part of South Africa. If the parties more immediately concerned should not, by assisting in every possible way, give proof that they appreciate the intervention now offered, Her Majesty's Government will not feel themselves bound to continue it."[1] So hesitant had been even this concession that four months later it was still a question whether Basutoland should not be completely abandoned after all. Not a single British soldier would march to Basutoland, for "Her Majesty's

[1] C. 3708, p. 39, Derby to Robinson, 14 June 1883. The Cape agreed to pay a sum not exceeding £20,000 a year to support Basutoland.

Government has only undertaken to try the experiment of ruling the Basutos, and should preserve its right to retire and leave it to anarchy without fighting the Basutos if they after all prove rebellious".[1]

With Basutoland off their minds and shoulders Scanlen and Robinson both proceeded to England to help Derby in coming to an understanding with the Boer delegates. These came to the Colonial Office declaring that the Transvaal objected to the entire Pretoria Convention, the manner of its making, its working, its every word. It was an alien instrument forced upon them, and they would accept nothing less than the full independence they had once enjoyed under the Sand River Convention. Although the Colonial Office knew itself to be guilty of many faults, publicly it repented of no sin. It received the Boer delegates upbraiding them for the Transvaal's financial default, its failure to establish an effective Government, its inability to respect its legal boundaries or the rights of the natives beyond its boundaries. Not the Transvaal but the British Government really denounced the Convention. It was a tactical advantage a little unfairly obtained, but useful in the negotiations that followed. Out of the wreckage of the Convention Derby had decided after all to salvage some guarantees for the natives. The Transvaal could have the same internal sovereignty as the Orange Free State; the British Government was prepared to make a more generous financial settlement. But the Cabinet still shrank from scuttling the native interest. It would not protect them, yet could not openly abandon them. In the Colonial Office Robinson pleaded for the protection of the Trade Route, and insisted that without the presence of British influence no convention devised would ever bring the Transvaal to respect its borders. Outside the Colonial Office Mankoroane's missionary, the Reverend John Mackenzie, rallied the men of Exeter Hall by preaching against Boer encroachment on the tribes, and inspired the imperialists by supporting Robinson's plea for some extension of British influence. The Transvaal was less popular in Parliament and the Press than in the Cabinet. "The public", commented Ashley, "are beginning to be very tired of Transvaal

[1] C.O. 48/508, G. Williams to C.O., 24 Nov. 1883, Minutes.

Boerdom and would like a rap on their knuckles."[1] In his uncertainty Derby turned to Scanlen, and asked what the British Government could expect from the Cape if the Road were kept open. In reply Scanlen made it clear that he could not commit the Cape Parliament. But for himself and fellow-ministers he gave a promise to support the British Government in protecting the natives outside the new Transvaal western boundary which the Convention would establish. He promised also to make a financial contribution to the Government of Bechuanaland in lieu of customs dues. Thus fortified Derby turned to the delegates. The new line which he forced them to accept gave the Transvaal the territory of its vassals Massouw and Moshette.[2] It was good land, but only a fraction of Stellaland and Goshen. To the remaining territory Mackenzie returned as Deputy Commissioner, the agent, be it noted, not of the Cape Government but of the Imperial Government. Great Britain's unwilling feet were seized again in the slough of dominion.

The Convention, in the words of Derby, had arranged matters to the best of English ability, and left the rest to Providence. Providence was not kind. Forbidden an outlet into Bechuanaland the Transvaal's land-hungry farmers immediately turned to Zululand. Cetywayo had finally died in February of a fatty heart. By April four hundred Boer volunteers were in Zululand to fight for the rights of Dinizulu. Their success was such that there were soon a thousand men in Zululand, and each man claimed a farm. Telegram after telegram Bulwer sent home pleading for British action, but at each Derby shook his head more emphatically. The Cabinet was "not much disposed to annexation".[3] That it had agreed to a protectorate over Bechuanaland was no reason why the British Government should object to the presence of the Boers in Zululand. The men of the Republic of Goshen had been filibusters *pur sang*, whereas the men of the New Republic had taken most of their land from their friends, only rounding off their farms with territory taken from their enemies. Moreover the British Government would never

---

[1] C.O. 291/24, Transvaal Delegates to C.O., 26 Nov. 1883, Minutes.
[2] See R. I. Lovell, *The Struggle for South Africa*, p. 57.
[3] C.O. 179/152, Bulwer to Derby, 5 May 1884.

have insisted on keeping open the Road and establishing British rule in Bechuanaland if Scanlen had not very distinctly promised his co-operation.[1] Such assurances Natal was altogether too weak and too poor to give. Yet without them the risk of becoming saddled with expensive and dangerous responsibility was too great.

Like the rest of South Africa Natal had ridden high on the tide of British expenditures. 1876 was the last year in which the budget had been in equilibrium. Railways and public works had caused the public debt to soar from £331,000 in 1875 to £3,000,000 in 1884. A year later it was £3,865,445. In 1885 the charge for the service of the debt was £191,271, or nearly £7 per head of the white population.[2] The boom started by the annexation of the Transvaal collapsed in 1881. The sudden drop in the purchasing power of the Transvaal punished Natal severely for its overtrading and speculation. The years that followed drove it ever deeper into depression. Bad seasons and a decline in the world prices of sugar and wool curtailed its imports and its exports. The effect of the incorporation by the Cape of Griqualand West was spectacularly seen in a complete drop of Natal's rum exports to the diamond fields from 68,920 gallons to nothing at all. Traders importing through Delagoa Bay were selling their fiery Hamburg rum in the Free State at half the price quoted by Natal merchants. The rebates granted by the Cape on goods destined for the interior brought Cape merchants unto the very borders of Natal itself. Imports slumped from £2,213,538 in 1882 to £1,751,107 in 1883. Annual deficits destroyed Natal's credit balance entirely, to the exceeding damage of its standing on the London money market. South African securities already stood lower than those of the other colonies. Cape debentures quoted at £95. 10s. 4d. in July 1882, fell to £91. 19s. 1d. in July 1883. Those of Natal were still lower. In 1883 the Crown Agents invited tenders for £700,000 Natal debentures at 4 per cent. They managed to dispose of only £469,800 at a discount, and of this amount £200,000 remained on the hands of the bankers.

The Colonial Office itched to disallow estimates that each year showed rising expenditures. It did not do so because by

---

[1] C.O. 417/2, D. 202, Robinson to Derby, 17 Sept. 1884, Minutes.
[2] C.O. 179/159, D. 156, Bulwer to Stanley, 17 Oct. 1885.

disciplining Natal's finances it increased its own responsibility. By 1883 the idea of responsible Government for Natal was popular in the Colonial Office. It was after looking at the estimates for 1884 that Meade declared that "responsibility should follow the power" already exercised by the Natal Assembly.[1] Deficits and debts were moreover not the only ills from which Natal suffered. Much as it had grown to distrust every mention of the native interest, the Colonial Office shrank from leaving Natal undefended by British troops. Natal could not agree to self-government without a British garrison, and the Home Government could not agree to it with one. Natal could have self-government, suggested Fairfield, on certain conditions. It must permanently secure a vote of some £60,000 for Mounted Police, to be placed under the immediate control of the Governor; it must hand over the proceeds of the native hut tax, vest in the Governor the native locations and as much of the Crown Lands as were inhabited by natives, allow the Crown the right of disallowing all legislation affecting native interests; the Governor must have control over the Department of Indian Immigrants, control external and supervise internal native affairs. It was, of course, an involved way of refusing self-government to Natal. But it was also a revealing explanation of British Zulu policy. Great Britain would not, and Natal could not rule Zululand. Natal's relations with the native subjects it already had grew more difficult under the stress of bad times. The throwing of the Crown Lands on the market and the passage at the end of 1883 of a Bill to provide for the collection of rent from native squatters on Crown Lands were clearly depression measures, and calculated to make still more precarious the attachment of the natives to the land. Numerous were the complaints of natives about land before the Native Commission of 1881–2. In its report the Commission was all but silent upon these grievances. Native rents continued to rise. In 1884 H. C. Shepstone, Secretary for Native Affairs, reported that rents on private farms ranged from £3 to £30 per hut per annum.[2] Relations between natives and

[1] C.O. 179/151, D. 4, Bulwer to Derby, 7 Jan. 1884, Minutes.
[2] C.O. 179/154, D. 215, Bulwer to Derby, 25 Nov. 1884. A more reliable account derived by Bulwer from actual returns submitted by local magistrates showed much less exorbitant rents, ranging between 10s. to £12 a year. D. 149, Bulwer to Stanley, 10 Oct. 1885.

European landlords were increasingly marked by evictions and sales of personal property. Sir Theophilus Shepstone himself confessed that although the natives paid their taxes well, native grievance was acute. "The truth is", he wrote in a confidential memorandum, "that the colony contains a larger native population than, with its white inhabitants it can conveniently or safely, under present conditions of native life, accommodate; for a long time this had been year by year growing apparent; attention has been frequently called to the increasing pressure and the proportionately increasing danger."[1] The less such a country had to do with Zululand the better, was in effect the decision of the British Government.

In Zululand the British Government again insisted on the difference between imperial and colonial interests. The annexation of Zululand was not an imperial interest. Since the Zulu and Transvaal Wars the opinion had gained strength in the Colonial Office that the soundest humanitarian doctrine was to leave the natives alone as far as possible. A protective annexation, such as Bulwer asked for Zululand, was likely to end in a punitive expedition. It was almost true to say that for once the Government was "agin" its subjects. Bantu, Boers and British, Downing Street looked upon all of them with a distrustful eye. Whether British regiments fought for them or against them, the British Treasury got its pockets picked, and neither the War Office nor the Colonial Office got any thanks. For years the story was told in the Colonial Office of the Boer who satisfied his patriotism by fighting against Colley at Majuba, and his pocket by hiring his waggons to the British Commissariat. To it were added the tales of renegade Englishmen with service medals on their coats busy stirring up trouble in Zululand or jumping land in Bechuanaland. Upon efforts to save natives or punish them the Colonial Office looked with especial distrust. Wheresoever they marched, in Basutoland, Zululand, or Bechuanaland, the Queen's horses and the Queen's men were like unto a "Salvation Army" ministering to the welfare of the colonists. The sufferers were too often the natives and the Chancellor of the Exchequer. The constant complaints from the Cape and the Free State of Basuto restlessness finally goaded Herbert to the declaration that "the

[1] C.O. 179/140, Conf., Mitchell to Kimberley, 2 Jan. 1882, Enclosure.

next attempt to get 2 or 3 millions of money expended for the benefit of the whites in South Africa will probably be by pressing Her Majesty's Government to undertake what seems to me a wholly unnecessary Basuto war ".[1] A letter that arrived at the Colonial Office in December 1884 brought a delighted chuckle from Fairfield. "This is the most clear headed correspondent we have ever been fortunate enough to have. He says that all South African wars are swindles got up to encourage expenditure from army funds."[2]

A distinction between imperial and local interests could be maintained only on the assumption that the British Government and the colonists were alone in the subcontinent, associated in an essentially domestic relationship, unheeding of the outside world in the discussion and settlement of their problems. Before 1883 the colonial newspapers had spoken occasionally of a Russian menace, and since 1871 a little more frequently of a German menace, but generally in the vague manner in which distant and unlikely events are discussed. In England as late as the end of 1882 it was much more of Russia and France than of Germany that imperial sentiment was afraid. It was, for example, of Russia's colossal expansion in Asia and of friction with France in Madagascar, on the Niger, the Congo, and in the Pacific Ocean, that Sir Charles Dilke complained to Herbert Bismarck in November 1882.[3] Even then it was assumed that the real danger to which South Africa was open was that of a maritime attack upon Cape Town and Simon's Bay. Of foreign settlement there was remarkably little mention. It was taken for granted in an entirely uncritical fashion, unsupported by official maps or definite treaties, that on the east and west coasts there were Portuguese interests and British interests. Where the first left off the second began. With this assumption the German "Kolonial-menschen" disagreed.

The story of Germany's invasion of South Africa's separateness and the annexation of Angra Pequena has often been told,[4] and need not be told again. The Duke of Buckingham had

---

[1] C.O. 417/7, D. 397, Robinson to Stanley, 14 Oct. 1885, Minutes.
[2] C.O. 179/155, G. E. Fawcus to C.O., 3 Dec. 1884, Minutes.
[3] *Die Grosse Politik*, vol. I, pp. 40 ff.
[4] R. I. Lovell, *op. cit.* pp. 81 ff.

seriously considered some British settlement north of the Orange River as early as 1868. Sir Bartle Frere, had he been given his way, would have annexed the entire coastline as far as Portuguese limits. The British Government would only permit him to annex Walfisch Bay, and his only real encouragement came from a lunatic youth in Brighton with an unexpected fondness for empire building, who forged a letter purporting to come from the private secretary of Hicks Beach. The letter requested Frere to annex all the country north of the Orange River, and excused its private character on the grounds that the British Government did not wish to appear in the matter. Frere did not fall into the trap.

Bismarck's shadow fell across South Africa at the very moment when British policy was disillusioned and dreaded action. The movement of British policy, where it was not passive, was rather the movement of retreat than advance. Its flaccid and disenchanted temper was manifested by short views, and a positive shunning of enterprises that were not justifiable by immediate and practical benefits. It had certainly no desire to make itself directly responsible for an area like Namaqua-Damaraland which was, if anything, the concern of the Cape. " I believe ", said Fairfield in February 1883 with relief, " that the agitation for the annexation of Damaraland, if it ever was genuine, is now quite dead, as the Colonists now see no hope of throwing on us the expense and trouble. The Cape Ministry has just declined to entertain a proposal for the extension of the limits of the Territory."[1] So far neither the Cape nor the Colonial Office had taken very seriously Herbert Bismarck's enquiry earlier in the month about what protection the British Government would give to a German factory on the south-west coast. More than seven months later the Colonial Office was still unperturbed by the complaints and reports it had heard of the doings of the German merchant Lüderitz, and still insistent that any annexation would have to be the work of the Cape and not the British Government. In the Colonial Office it was taken for granted that it was only the irresolution of the Cape that prevented a definite answer being given to Germany. " They cried out like children for it," joked Fairfield, "and now that it is offered to them, they hesitate to

[1] C.O. 48/506, D. 51, Robinson to Derby, 26 Feb. 1883.

W

take it." Neither he nor his colleague Bramston felt that any
pressure should be put upon the Cape. "Walfisch Bay", commented the latter, "is hardly required for any purpose of Imperial
Gov[ernmen]t, and if the Cape will not take it over, we had
rather abandon it." With even greater frankness did Fairfield
proceed to question the value either to the Cape or the British
Government of any annexation beyond the Orange River.
Annexation or the extension of a protectorate "would mean
perpetual hostilities, in which the Cape would after a time try to
make us the catspaw, as they have done in Basutoland successfully, through the backing of the Aborigines people". Even a
simple annexation of part or all of the coastline was undesirable,
should there ever be a maritime war in which England was
neutral. "It would make the whole of these waters British and
throw on us the responsibilities of neutrals in regard to them.
For these reasons the Duke of Buckingham in 1868, and Sir
M. E. H. Beach in 1878 declined to take the step. The Alabama
and other troubles with the Americans were then fresh in
memory."[1]

Almost to the middle of November the Colonial Office gave no
indication that it had taken seriously the prospect of a German
settlement in South-West Africa. On 2 October the Foreign
Office was informed that the islands adjacent to Angra Pequena
had been annexed to the Cape Colony, but that Her Majesty's
Government had no claims or jurisdiction over the mainland.[2]
Had this unequivocal statement been conveyed to the Germans,
it would have destroyed utterly the British case. In the Foreign
Office Sir Julian Pauncefote hesitated to relay to the German
ambassador such a complete surrender of Angra Pequena. After
a delay of six weeks he called upon Herbert. The result of their
conversation was that Bismarck never came to know how nearly
Angra Pequena had dropped into his lap. Together the two
officials elaborated the policy which was officially adopted by
their Government. They agreed that the German Government
should be informed that it had been always understood that no
foreign sovereignty or jurisdiction was admissible between the

---

[1] C.O. 48/507, D. 292, Smyth to Derby, 8 Oct. 1883, Minutes.
[2] C.O. 48/508, F.O. to C.O., 17 Nov. 1883, Minutes.

southern point of Portuguese jurisdiction at latitude 18° and the frontier of the Cape Colony, although Her Majesty's Government had not proclaimed the Queen's sovereignty along the whole coast, but only at certain points such as Walfisch Bay and the Angra Pequena Islands. Although there were British traders with long-established interests on the coast the British Government trusted that it might be found practicable to make such arrangements as might enable the German traders to share in the occupation of Angra Pequena.[1] It is clear that the very private minutes of the Colonial Office give some colour to the German accusation of bad faith against the British Government. "We cannot allow German adventurers", declared Herbert to his colleagues, "to seize country already granted to British subjects, nor under the circumstances, can German sovereignty be established at Angra Pequena, but we shall probably do well to arrange for the occupation of some part at least of the coast by these German traders and promise that they shall have equal treatment with British subjects."[2] Yet the ill faith of the British Government was more apparent than real.

The minutes and correspondence of the Colonial Office are quite clear that there was till the eve of the German annexation much uncertainty in London concerning German intentions. As late as the end of May 1884 Ampthill could still write from Berlin that Bismarck had hitherto shown no inclination to satisfy the German craving for colonies beyond sending Dr Nachtigal to report generally on the west coast of Africa. The declaration by Herbert Bismarck to Granville in the middle of June that it was not the intention of the German Government to establish "State Colonies" was ambiguous enough to cause the Colonial Office to enquire, after the German flag had been raised at Angra Pequena, whether the protectorate was personal, to be exercised over German traders, or territorial. While the British Government was almost naively ignorant of the trend of German policy, Bismarck, in his turn, was guilty of a misapprehension of many details of British colonial law, history and practice. He was ignorant of the reliance of the Foreign Office on the Colonial Office in colonial matters, and more ignorant still of the relationship between the

[1] *Ibid.*   [2] *Ibid.*

Colonial Office and a self-governing colony like the Cape. It was
with real justification that one official complained that "a great
deal of Bismarck's feeling against us evidently comes from his
inexperience in the rule of possessions in wild countries. He
evidently has not the slightest idea of how difficult the management of a distant possession may become." Least of all did
Bismarck understand, or care to understand, the distinction which
the British Government was trying to draw between imperial and
colonial interests. Against England he quoted from Parliamentary
Papers the *ipsissima verba* of her Secretaries of State to colonial
Governors. Kimberley's despatch of 30 December 1880 to the
Governor of the Cape, for example, had stated explicitly that the
Orange River was the northern boundary of the Cape, and that
the acquisition of the coast beyond was undesirable on imperial
grounds. But these words had been used, so the Colonial Office
felt, by a Secretary of State to a British colony. Though published they were declarations of a domestic policy, not to be
listened to by the world outside the Empire. For fifty years, ever
since the Great Trek, the Home Government had solemnly and
habitually declared that it would not budge another step toward
the uncomfortably magnetic Zambesi, refusing dominion over
Natal, the Orange River Territory, Basutoland, the diamond
fields, the Transvaal. Yet it proceeded to annex them each in its
turn. Thus when Kimberley and his successor disclaimed dominion over the south-west coast, they did not mean that Great
Britain had no more right or interest than France, Russia, or Germany. Nor did they deny the possibility of annexation sooner or
later by the Cape. Indeed such a possibility was strengthened, for
the denial of imperial interest was a negative mode of stating that
the British Government would under certain circumstances recognize and further colonial interests. "If there had been any apprehension", declared Fairfield, "of an annexation of this coast by a
power not concerned in the promotion of South African policy,
Great Britain as the paramount South African power, would have
taken possession of it long ago."[1] But Bismarck refused to recognize that Kimberley's outright denial of any British interest beyond the Orange was, in its full context, merely a phase of a long

[1] C.O. 417/1, Telegram, Robinson to Derby, 18 Aug. 1884, Minutes.

drawn out negotiation between Mother Country and Colony about responsibility. He could not see that the British Government had been forced by the exigencies of its South African policy to say and unsay, do and undo for fifty years.

The Colonial Office would fain have kept Germany at a distance from both colonies and Republics. To this reluctance the presence of the Boer delegates in London gave special point, for, as Herbert remarked, "their notion of marching to the Atlantic may be healthily cooled by the knowledge that we have not given up Angra Pequena".[1] It was, in his view, most desirable that some British authority should undertake control of the coast. It was not "a matter of little importance to South Africa that a new Foreign authority should be introduced and further complicate the already confused political questions with which we and the colonies have to deal".[2] In the whole broad Empire there was not another region that was so vexed with problems, so ill-contrived in its organization, so ready to war, so inopportune with its disasters. Nothing could be more natural than that the British Government should see with a sinking heart the attempted entry of a foreign influence into such a very troubled land. The attitude of the British Government could only unfairly be described as that of the dog in the manger. Yet it is altogether a mistake to suppose, as Bismarck himself did, that the British Government was stubbornly and wilfully opposed to any consideration of the German claim. Contemporary and subsequent criticism has done too little justice to the judicious temper of the officials of the Colonial Office. From the beginning there had been every disposition to give Lüderitz equal rights to trade with British subjects. Ashley was prepared to go even further, objecting that "I myself do not see why we should object to Germany, if she chooses, occupying other parts of this coastline, where we may not previously have gone. It is a long way from everywhere."[1]

The Colonial Office also recognized that it was one thing to lay claim to a coastline and yet another to substantiate that claim. An examination of the specific acts establishing British priority

[1] C.O. 48/507, D. 322, Smyth to Derby, 6 Nov. 1883, Minutes.
[2] C.O. 48/509, Admiralty to C.O., 23 Jan. 1884, Minutes.

revealed no great strength. Governor Wodehouse's proclamation of 1866 annexing the Guano Islands, and the Letters Patent annexing the islands to the Cape, were both silent as to the harbour of Angra Pequena or any other part of the mainland. On being consulted the Admiralty dug up from its files the fact that Captain Alexander of H.M.S. *Star* had taken possession of the Bay in 1796. Bramston readily admitted that "this taking possession without subsequent occupation will hardly do to fight the Germans with".[1] Taken in connection with Wodehouse's proclamation it might be maintained that the British Government had taken possession only of the islands in 1866 because Captain Alexander's annexation of 1796 had made unnecessary any specific declaration of British rights on the mainland. Such reasoning was manifestly specious, and the Colonial Office was aware that on strictly legal grounds, on such grounds as might be submitted to a court of arbitration, its case was weak. An even greater weakness was its own uncertainty whether it was prepared to annex the coastline in order to exclude Germany. The British Government at least, considered Herbert, possessed a good "holding title". But was it "prepared to occupy the property and discharge the duties of owner"? Was it prepared to give a satisfactory answer to Münster's questions as to what institutions the British Government possessed at Angra Pequena which would secure protection for German subjects and relieve the German Empire of the duty of providing for their protection itself? The answer was perfectly plain. If there was to be annexation the Cape must undertake it. If there were to be institutions the Cape must maintain them. To imperial annexation Derby was quite opposed.

Rightly or wrongly the Colonial Office was convinced that the Cape would not undertake the responsibility for the coast itself. "Unfortunately at this moment", commented Herbert, "the Cape Government (forming a strong contrast to the Australasian Governments) is shrinking from all obligations beyond the present boundaries of the Colony, and will, I conclude, allow Angra Pequena to pass into foreign hands, whither Walfisch Bay will probably soon follow it." With Herbert's contention that it

[1] C.O. 48/510, Admiralty to C.O., 23 Jan. 1884, Minutes.

was in consequence difficult to resist the representations of the German Government, Derby was quite agreed. "It is awkward", he wrote in a minute that was lengthy for a man so sparing of words, "to contend that though we exercise no *de facto* authority there, we must forbid all other Powers doing so."[1] The disposition to yield to Germany grew stronger as the early months of 1884 passed with no sign from the Cape. A telegram dispatched on 3 February received the reply that Scanlen's absence deferred any decision. When at the end of April still no reply had been received from Cape Town it was taken in the Colonial Office as proof sufficient that the Cape would not assume responsibility for the south-west coast. And since there was no prospect of the Imperial Government doing so, surrender to German insistence seemed inevitable. The best the British Government could do, opined Herbert, was to make an effort to guard the interests of British merchants on the coast by pressing for the appointment of a joint Anglo-German commission to regulate the rivalry of British and German merchants. The Parliamentary Under-secretary Ashley was even more emphatic. "We have no choice", he insisted. "We cannot show any title to this large territory (apart from Angra Pequena and Walwich Bay) even if we were disposed to assert it and to take steps to provide sufficient protection to traders. There may probably be compensatory advantages in the presence of the German flag to counterbalance the evils."[2]

The Cape broke the silence of months at last on 29 May. Not eagerly but reluctantly did the new Upington ministry declare its policy on the south-west coast. It would rather not act at all, but if needs must it would consent to annex the coastline to a depth of five or ten miles. "Ministers do not desire to extend the responsibilities of the Colony into the interior." With such a belated and grudging document the Colonial Office could not be entirely pleased. Bismarck was out of patience and British Egyptian policy was beginning to suffer the discomfort of a hostile German diplomacy. Bramston's grumbling minute expressed the feeling of the Colonial Office. "If Mr Scanlen had

[1] *Ibid.*
[2] C.O. 48/510, F.O. to C.O., 25 April 1884, Minutes.

been willing to do this, the Angra Pequena question would have solved itself long ago."[1] Now of necessity the issue, which was so close to settlement by default of the British Government, was opened again. To the German note of 30 December the Cape had at long last provided a formal answer, and the Foreign Office was asked to inform the German Government that arrangements would be made for providing protection under the British flag to German and British traders duly established on the coast. The communication was diplomatically correct. There is no evidence that Derby was trying to bluff the Germans, nor is there the least reason for discussing the accusations of wilful deception held against Derby. Few documents have been as uniformly ambiguous and so calculated to cause misunderstanding as these produced by the wrangle between Great Britain and Germany over Angra Pequena. Even the reasons for Great Britain's withdrawal in favour of Germany have been partly misunderstood. It was true that Herbert Bismarck in his three interviews with Granville in June impressed upon that apologetic minister the serious effects upon British interest in Egypt and elsewhere of a quarrel with Germany. One hand, Bismarck had said, must wash the other. But the British Government did much to contribute to its own defeat; for from the beginning its position had been greatly weakened both by its own unwillingness to proceed to direct imperial action and by the laggard disinclination of the Cape Colony.

The unique isolation of the Empire was shattered. Step by step the wide vague rights which it had taken for granted were challenged and reduced. Even in dealing with her own colonies Great Britain had the eyes of the world upon her. The former distinction between papers foreign and papers colonial was gone. A colonial problem was like many problems of foreign policy, fully as difficult and often as dangerous. In South Africa the German intrusion made the British position doubly difficult. Just when the British Government was resolutely trying to carry out and defend a policy of non-expansion and non-intervention, German sovereignty took its place beside Cape self-government and republican independence. And the German flag was manifestly

[1] C.O. 417/1, D. 57, Robinson to Derby, 6 June 1884, Minutes.

disposed to wander still farther afield in search of more con-
quests. It would respect a *fait accompli*, or claims too explicit to
be challenged, but it would pounce upon indecision. How was
the British Government to protect the unannexed coastlines and
their hinterland and yet assume no responsibility for them itself?
It was a difficult predicament. Not to annex them was to forfeit
at least part of them to the "hot fit" of colonization in Germany.
To annex them was to be a catspaw for the colonies. There was
really only one answer. The British Government was forced
back into South Africa. The attempt to juggle unannexed territories in mid air between itself and Germany gave way first of all
to an effort to steer between annexing too little and annexing too
much and finally to an unequivocal return to South Africa as a
principal if not as a partner. The new imperialism moved with
leaden feet. *Eppur si muove.*

In the month that saw the German flag hoisted at Angra
Pequena, another Dutch republic was born in Zululand. Its
five million acres were the price the Zulus had paid for an
"alliance" with the Boers which had made still more desperate the
already cruel effects of war and famine. Into the Reserve poured
a dispersed and starving mass to stress Bulwer's plea that Zululand be annexed ere it be destroyed. Yet the British Government
looked with equanimity upon a scene which ten years before
would have provoked it to indignation and alarm. Indeed it
almost welcomed the New Republic. In such minutes as Meade
and Bramston wrote there was not a breath of concern for the
natives. The British Government, averred Meade, no longer
held "to that portion of the recent Convention with the Boers
by which they were to observe the borders of the South African
Republic".[1] Openly scornful of any benevolent inclination
Bramston suggested that "if we do not stand too much on our
dignity and virtue [the Boers] may according to all appearances
serve as assistants, in maintaining peace and order in Zululand.
There is no question now of driving the Boers out of Zululand
and we ought not to turn would-be friends, however little their
friendship may be worth, into dangerous enemies, by refusing to
recognize them as soon as they have established some form of

[1] C.O. 179/155, Reuters, 21 Aug. 1884, Minutes.

settled Government."[1] Unfortunately for such a policy of dereliction Zululand had a coastline, unannexed and therefore attractive to Germans. In the last months of 1884 there appeared in the Zulu country a most frank German traveller named Schiel who insisted on writing to Bulwer accounts of the chaos in Zululand. He visited Dinizulu with the German flag flying on his waggon, wearing the uniform of a member of the "General Staff of Baden". After teasing Bulwer with hints of an intimate understanding with Bismarck he left that now thoroughly nervous Governor, promising to return in a German man-of-war.

The British reply to German "intrigues" in Zululand was to send H.M.S. *Goshawk* in December 1884 to raise the British flag at St Lucia Bay. This act made clear how jaded was Great Britain's imperial appetite. Not merely because an annexation of the entire coast would have been grossly tactless during the sessions of the Congo Conference in Berlin, but because the British Government still hoped that by this single gesture it could wave Germany away without going to the extreme of extending British sovereignty from the Natal border to Delagoa Bay, did it raise its flag at a single point. Only under pressure would it advance farther. In Zululand as in the rest of South Africa its deliberate effort was to avoid all action until events had accumulated to a point where action was inescapable. The annexation of Zululand was being slowly forced upon a Government which took every step with distaste, deferring it as long as it might. It might have been indefinitely content to see Zululand in a state of anarchy, admitted Ashley, "so long as it was only the Zulus". But advance it must now that the Germans were straining at the leash. The only object of annexing at all, said Fairfield, was to prevent the Germans "shaking hands" with the Boers of the South African Republic or the New Republic. "This cannot be prevented as long as any hole is left in the cordon." Thoroughly aroused by Germany's emphatic championship of colonization in Africa and the Pacific, parliamentary and public opinion would not forgive a second and greatly more serious surrender of South Africa's coastline. Willy nilly British policy did not dare find itself again "in the ridiculous position

[1] C.O. 179/154, Bulwer to Derby, 11 Nov. 1884, Minutes.

we were at Walfisch Bay—hung up *en l'air*—and looking foolish ".
The total exclusion of Germany from the entire south eastern
coast was forced upon England as a principle which British
policy could not desert. For this reason the annexation of Zululand and by the same token Pondoland was bound to come, and
Germany's promise not to interfere on the coast could only
postpone it.[1]

In Bechuanaland Rhodes' Traders Road was like the Zululand coastline; once it had become a British interest the territory
about it was bound to become a British interest too. The first
step was the appointment of the missionary John Mackenzie as
Deputy Commissioner of Bechuanaland. He was already known
to the Colonial Office for his unique offer to solve the problem of
the Transvaal, which was to place Dutch-speaking Scotch
Presbyterian ministers and dominies in every Transvaal village.
Ireland was Ireland because it lacked them, Scotland was for
ever Scotland because the wayward spirit of Jacobite High-
landers had been tamed and won by them. On his return to
England in 1883 the Colonial Office received him coolly because,
like Mr Forster, he declared that it was England's "business" to
protect the natives. His appointment, although urged by Robinson, was a little doubtfully agreed to in the Colonial Office, and
was immediately unpopular in both the Cape and the Transvaal. As a missionary and a "Kafir friend" his every move was
suspect to the Boers, and his every step an offending. Mackenzie
tried to be a realist, agreeing with Robinson that the land titles of
the Stellalanders must be recognized. But his past and Rhodes
were both against him, and his inexperience betrayed him. His
following was a little gang of shopkeepers and speculators, greedy
of imperial funds, villains some of them and few any better than
Bethell, who had left England for cheating at cards in a London
Club. In August Robinson replaced him by Rhodes, whose
quality it was that he was interested in land and not in natives.

The Colonial Office saw Mackenzie's departure from Bechuanaland with relief. It was not its intention that the creation of a

---

[1] Zululand outside the New Republic was annexed in 1887. Pondoland
remained independent till 1894, when it was annexed to the Cape. In
January 1885 a British protectorate was declared over its coastline.

Bechuanaland protectorate should be a humanitarian measure, for essentially the protectorate was not over the natives. A protectorate was simply a device which proclaimed British interest but not British sovereignty. If it protected anything at all it protected British interests, which were to close Bechuanaland to Germany and the Transvaal and yet to avoid expense and responsibility.

"What information have we respecting Mr Rhodes?" asked Herbert on hearing of his appointment. He was a "sensible" man, replied Fairfield, but inexperienced like Mackenzie and untrained in administrative work. However he "would do very well as a stop gap".[1] The success which Rhodes achieved was pleasing in the eyes of the Colonial Office. He promised the Stellalanders that their land was safe, and they in return promised to accept Cape rule when it came. Land not natives, Rhodes had said, and he was true to his word. The only part in the Bechuana country that was choicer was the area at Rooigrond in the Land of Goshen. There Montsioa threw the land into unrest by fighting to retain the only spot where irrigation was possible. Above the din the voices of Rhodes and Joubert remained unheard, till at last Kruger himself deliberately upset the apple cart by annexing Goshen. Now let the British Government declare what was the meaning, and what were the responsibilities of a protectorate.

The decision of the British Government to send five thousand men under General Warren to Bechuanaland was of capital importance. Not a soldier or a shilling, British policy had declared in effect in the Pretoria Convention, and again in the London Convention. Yet once more troops of the line marched a thousand miles from Cape Town and South Africa had returned to its accustomed place in the British estimates. It was vain to insist that Warren marched solely to keep the peace, and that he served not the interests of the United Kingdom but those of the Cape colonists. He had Union Jacks in his baggage and it would be strange indeed if he did not leave them behind flying over another addition to the Empire.

The truth was that British policy was variously moved to action. An instinctive dislike for disorder was reinforced by the

[1] C.O. 471/1, Telegram, Robinson to Derby, 30 Aug. 1884.

fear of outside interference. The annexation of Angra Pequena, the quarrel over the Zulu coast, and Kruger's annexation of Goshen were but local manifestations of a world-wide pressure upon real and fancied imperial interests. A lash of the lion's tail would have salutary effects both near and far. Warren's force was thus much more than an expedition against the "gang of pirates" in Goshen. It announced that circumstances were once again forcing the British Government to admit that if South Africa did not have unity it must have supervision—actively exercised by the paramount power. Over the Republics, and especially over the Transvaal, British suzerainty was virtually re-established. No clauses in conventions were needed to make that clear. Not simply the external activity of the Transvaal but also its internal condition and policies became progressively and more directly the concern of the British Government. "I am told", remarked Bramston significantly, "that British and foreign gold diggers are becoming unmanageable by the weak Government of the Transvaal." The logic of Warren's expedition was, of course, not immediately nor fully evident. In January Bramston could still regard with apparent equanimity the prospect of a German seizure of the Transvaal, believing that the Germans would be "better neighbours than the Portuguese or the Boers—and if they are going to absorb the Transvaal and to enforce law within it we shall not be injured unless they take a strip right across the continent".[1] Actually it was more likely that not Germany but Warren's troops would find the road into the Transvaal. Still many a year was destined to elapse before such a possibility became a vivid and desperate reality. Yet in 1885 the return of the Transvaal under the British flag was something that British policy felt in its bones. Said Hemming, the imperialist of the Office: "That the Transvaal would be able to maintain itself as an independent state I have never thought probable. That we should resume the Government of it is, I fear, a hope not likely to be realized. That Germany will take it under her protection, i.e. annex it, seems if we hold back, an almost certain contingency."[2]

[1] C.O. 179/156, Telegram, Bulwer to Derby, 11 Jan. 1885, Minutes.
[2] *Ibid.* Conf., Bulwer to Derby, 19 Jan. 1885, Minutes.

Rarely had the British Government watched a force proceed into a distant interior with more misgiving. Till Warren had reached Bechuanaland and found no fighting to do, it wondered nervously whether Warren would fall foul of the Transvaal or a hostile Cape Boer population. It was the latter fear that caused Fairfield to make the startling suggestion that it might be necessary "to coerce the Cape Ministry into behaving properly, by means of a fleet at Cape Town, where they are vulnerable to our power". As Warren began work Khartoum fell and the South African cable broke. In order that the Boers might not take their cue from the Mahdi and trap Warren a thousand miles from help, the Colonial Office speculated seriously, and in the event foolishly, whether it might not be wise to seize the cable and let no news of Gordon's fate pass over it until Warren had effected his settlement.[1]

Much deeper was the fear that the expedition would end in saddling Great Britain with another Crown Colony. A protectorate, it is important to observe again, did not have the modern connotation in 1885. It was deliberately intended to be a device and not an admission of trusteeship or responsibility. It established title without admitting sovereignty or the obligations of sovereignty. In the period during which two such highly important native protectorates as Basutoland and Bechuanaland came to be established in South Africa, the idea of a protective imperial trusteeship was definitely unpopular in the Colonial Office and the Cabinet. The view was held that the mass of the natives were already irrevocably under the control of the colonies and republics. The creation of protectorates with the specific intention of withdrawing the natives from colonial control was not a popular policy. "The Native question", declared Fairfield in response to a suggestion that the High Commissionership be separated from the Governorship, "cannot be solved except in friendly co-operation with the local communities, and a policy which would amount to a declaration that all confidence is withdrawn in them would be disastrous both to us and our protégés. All the mischief and misery nearly that has ever been inflicted on the Natives in South Africa has been inflicted by Imperial

[1] C.O. 417/4, Conf., Robinson to Derby, 14 Jan. 1885, Minutes.

Officers.... Once we get Natives under the management of the much abused Cape Colonists, and leave the Cape Colonists alone, everything goes right. They understand Native management much better than we do."[1] Constant was the grumbling during 1885 about Basutoland and Zululand, that *damnosa haereditas* that could not long remain unannexed.

Warren had marched northwards firm in his resolve to be a good soldier and a good statesman. He would confront the filibusters "with their own style of fighting, confuse them with cavalry and confound them with artillery". Yet his battle cry was: "There is room for all." The British Government, he announced, was prepared to expand European settlement rather than restrict it. "It is impossible to ignore the fact", he told Derby, "that in process of time the white colonists will extend through the country, no matter what impediments are put in their way." It was a policy after Rhodes' own heart. Yet by April Robinson was ready to resign in protest against Warren's doings, and drag Bechuanaland into a public and parliamentary debate. In succession Warren quarrelled with Rhodes, the Governor, the local Boers and the Transvaal. The despatches to England were loud with their quarrel, and often unpublishable because of their animus. Warren discovered that under Rhodes' hands the boundary of Stellaland had wandered farther afield, and that the map of Stellaland used for the London Convention had been "superseded" by another map of a bigger and better Stellaland. Thereafter he ignored Rhodes and turned to Mackenzie. Rhodes struck back at Warren with weapons that were not always scrupulous, and sometimes disgracefully dishonest.[2]

Warren had gone to Bechuanaland to prepare for the coming of the Cape. That consummation, so devoutly desired by Downing Street, was now indefinitely deferred. And every act that Warren undertook was calculated to estrange both the Cape and all Boerdom. He suddenly announced that there could be no further encroachment by Boers upon native land, and that the government of Bechuanaland by the Cape would be inconsistent with the native interest. Under the Cape Bechuanaland would become

[1] C.O. 417/6, Telegram, Warren to Stanley, 27 July 1885.
[2] *Ibid.* Warren to Stanley, 6 Aug. 1885.

the prey of land speculators and an area for fighting the battles of Cape politicians who would attempt to catch the Dutch vote by bringing more and more Boers into the native territories. Had Warren taken his stand on the single principle that it was the responsibility of the Imperial Government to protect the natives against further loss of land, he would at least have deserved well of the natives. But he degraded his principle by sheer and indefensible racial prejudice, by a virulent anti-Dutch sentiment that necessarily alienated every element in the Cape and England that aimed to conciliate Dutch opinion.

Standing on the Traders Road Warren had decided to do a little Empire building on his own account, thereby forcing from Fairfield the groan that the plan of "entrusting able and experienced officers on the spot with a wide discretion does not work". The Colonial Office groaned again when there came in succession threats of "disturbances" in Khama's country, a "magnificent offer" from Khama to the Empire, and finally Warren's grandiose scheme: a British Crown Colony. Struggling to be free the British Government grew more engaged. In the Colonial Office there was indignation that Warren should have become a filibuster on a larger scale than any Goshenite and have fallen victim to the "Mackenzie fallacy of a great inland Crown Colony" which was, by all accounts, so inhospitable and so dry that the only settlers it could maintain were Scotch crofters and broken down drunkards.[1]

Every step Warren had taken proved to be as unpalatable to the Colonial Office as to the Cape. It did not want a native protectorate, and still less a Crown Colony. It wanted to see Bechuanaland annexed to the Cape. Any settlement that was unacceptable to the Cape, or tended to embroil the Home Government with the local communities was for these very reasons unpopular. Any attempt, said Herbert with feeling, "made by persons of limited political information to set up an antagonism between Dutch and English in Africa, and to saddle this country with an impracticable pro-English policy are fatal and mischievous". It was an Empire without fustian and that moved with a schoolboy's unwilling mood. The Home Govern-

---

[1] C.O. 417, Telegram, Robinson to Derby, 28 May 1885.

ment felt no compulsion to interpose itself either between Boer and Britain or between white and black. There was no real divergence of interest or feeling between Dutch and English in South Africa, was the belief of the Colonial Office. The real divergence was between colonists, whether Dutch or English, and the "Imperial Factor". Far better it were to let the whites quarrel and fight with their natives. Boer encroachments were admittedly serious, yet they were insignificant by the side of the "intense antagonism between the white races" and the "terrible difficulty" that would be caused by an unwelcome imperial interference in South African native affairs. It was actually true that in 1885 the British Government had its heart set upon retreating as far from South Africa as it could. Yet Warren stayed, though his superiors itched to withdraw him. They dared not because they feared the "swarm of parliamentary and other hornets" that Warren's recall would unloose. When finally he was recalled the honours were his. In March 1885 Bechuanaland had become an Imperial protectorate. In September the land south of the Molopo River became the Crown Colony of British Bechuanaland. Fairfield sighed for the more spacious days when the interior was no concern of the British Government. "The policy embodied in the Sand River Convention", he said, "gave us 25 years of peace and freedom from anxiety. We abandoned it, and we have been ever since in a horrid mess. We shall no doubt revert to it again some day, and be once more at rest. We are very far from being at rest now."

Not now nor for many bitter years to come would Great Britain be at rest in South Africa. Fairfield, the most charming, witty and honest of men, was destined to die of a broken heart and of the grief caused by the Jameson Raid, and a bitterly tragic war would have to be fought, before that rest would be achieved. Deeply and more deeply yet was the British Government drawn into the slough of dominion. This most convulsed of centuries was fated to end in a last agony more costly and bloody than all the previous wars put together. Yet British policy had by 1886 already suffered an irretrievable defeat. The first discoveries of gold on the Witwatersrand in 1886 announced a great new age of growth and achievement. To that age British

X

policy had failed to contribute what had been the ideal of its most enlightened minds—whether nurtured in England or South Africa, whether of Dutch or British stock—a social and economic order in South Africa in which a greater tolerance of race, a more ardent trusteeship, a more inspired social wisdom should be the mark of the peace and unity and liberty for which the century had suffered so grievously.

BIBLIOGRAPHY

A. OFFICIAL MANUSCRIPT SOURCES

These are all in the Public Record Office, and constitute the most important sources for this period. A large proportion of the incoming and outgoing despatches were destroyed. The instructions for finding printed copies are, however, included in the bound books.

1. Cape Colony. C.O. 48, vols. 464–511 (1872–1885).
2. C.O. 336. Register of Correspondence, vols. 7–11.
3. Natal. C.O. 179, vols. 111–162 (1872–1885).
4. C.O. 357, Register of Correspondence, vols. 5–9.
5. Griqualand West. C.O. 107, vols. 1–9 (1875–1880).
6. Transvaal. C.O. 291, vols. 1–26 (1877–1884).
7. C.O. 510, Register of Correspondence, vols. 1–3.
8. South Africa. C.O. 417, vols. 1–9 (1884–1885).
9. F.O. 64, vols. 1101–1106 (1883–1885).

B. OTHER MANUSCRIPT SOURCES

1. Carnarvon Papers. (Deposited in the Public Record Office.) G.D. 6. The volumes that bear on South Africa are 23, 32–34, 36, 38, 49, 80–84, 116, 131.
2. Granville Papers. (Deposited in the Public Record Office.) G.D. 29.

C. OFFICIAL PUBLICATIONS

1. Parliamentary Papers, 1872–1885. An excellent list will be found in the bibliography in volume VIII of the *Cambridge History of the British Empire*, pp. 889 ff.
2. Hansard Parliamentary Debates, 3rd series, 1872–1885.

D. BRIEF LIST OF SECONDARY WORKS

AYLWARD, A. *The Transvaal of Today.* 1878.
BUTLER (Sir) W. F. *The Life of Sir George Pomeroy Colley.* 1899.
Cambridge History of the British Empire, vol. VIII, South Africa. 1936.
COLENSO, F. E. and DURNFORD, E. *The History of the Zulu War.* 1881.
CUNYNGHAME, A. T. *My Command in South Africa.* 1879.
ENGELBRECHT, S. P. *Thomas François Burgers.* 1933.

GARVIN, J. L. *Chamberlain*. 3 vols. 1932–1934.

HARDINGE, Sir A. *The Life of Henry Howard Molyneux Herbert, Fourth Earl of Carnarvon*. 1925.

HICKS BEACH, Lady VICTORIA. *The Life of Sir Michael Hicks Beach*. 1932.

JORISSEN, E. J. P. *Transvaalsche Herinneringen*. 1897.

KIEWIET, C. W. DE. *British Colonial Policy and the South African Republics*. 1929.

KOTZE, Sir J. *Biographical Memoirs and Reminiscences*. 1934.

LAURENCE, Sir P. *The Life of John Xavier Merriman*. 1930.

LEYDS, W. T. *The First Annexation of the Transvaal*. 1906.

LOVELL, R. I. *The Struggle for South Africa*. 1934.

MACKENZIE, J. *Austral Africa*. 1887.

MARTINEAU, J. *Life and Times of Sir Bartle Frere*. 1895.

MAURICE, Sir J. F. and ARTHUR, Sir G. C. A. *The Life of Lord Wolseley*. 1924.

MOLTENO, P. A. *The Life and Times of Sir John Charles Molteno*. 2 vols. 1900.

UYS, C. J. *In the Era of Shepstone*. 1933.

WALKER, E. A. *Lord de Villiers and his Times*. 1925.

WILMOT, Count A. *The Life and Times of Sir Robert Southey*. 1904.

WORSFOLD, W. B. *Sir Bartle Frere*. 1913.

INDEX

Aborigines Protection Society, 178
Adelaide, 170
Afghanistan, 83
Africa, South, effect of European colonization, 2, 3; British policy in, 5, 20, 57, 91, 136, 299; imperial interests in, 7; need of credit in, 10, 256; industrial revolution in, 15; problem of capital and labour, 52; native problems of, 55, 157, 201, 202, 263; Cobden recommends self-government in, 67; an international problem, 83, 84; British sovereignty on east and west coasts, 83–4, 220, 221; importance of gold discoveries in, 96; Sir Bartle Frere and, 126–47; financial condition (1878), 181; effect of Isandhlwana on British policy in, 234–5; poverty in, 254; General Gordon in, 290–1; Lord Derby and, 293, 301, 302, 304, 305–6, 317; effect of German intrusion in, 318–20; Fairfield and native policy in, 324–5
Africander Bond, 296; policy of, 297–8
Agriculture, native, wasteful methods of, 150–1, 152, 163
Alexander, Captain, and Angra Pequena, 316
Alexis, Grand Duke, visit to Cape Town, 128
Amahlubi tribe, dispersion of, 37
American Civil War, 6
Angra Pequena, 310, 316, 318; German traders and, 313; Herbert and, 315–16; German annexation of, 319, 323
Anstruther, Colonel, defeat at Bronkhorstspruit, 276–7
Arms, traffic in, 18–19, 65, 90, 293–4; London Conference (1876) and traffic in, 155; as incentive to war, 263
Ashanti War, cause of, 37
Australia, 5, 27, 65
Austrian Bourse, effect of collapse of, 17, 138
Aylward, Alfred, filibuster, 49, 54, 55

Bank, Insinger of Amsterdam, 97; Cape Commercial, 104–5, 142–4
Bapedi, raids of, 179
Baralong territory annexed by Transvaal, 22
Barkly, Sir Henry, High Commissioner and Governor of Cape Colony, and Cape self-government, 12; his dislike of the Republics, 19–20, 29, 71, 102; opposes Republican independence, 24–5; views on Transvaal, 26; an obstacle to confederation, 73–5; and Froude, 77–9; reply to Carnarvon on co-operation, 79; and British intervention in Transvaal, 112–13
Bashee, River, 150, 169, 170
Basuto, social problem, 2; disarmament of, 262–3, 265–8; unrest among (1876), 263
Basuto War, cause of, 263; no imperial help for Cape in, 267–8
Basutoland, native reserve, 11; annexed by Cape, 12; liquor traffic in, 17–18; and native labour, 155; drought in, 161, 265; native overcrowding in, 264; economic conditions in, 265; Sprigg visits, 265–6; Robinson's settlement of, 290; taken over by British Government from Cape, 304
Batlapin, in revolt, 179
Bechuana, social problem, 2
Bechuanaland, as native reserve, 11; Rhodes' Traders Road in, 321, 326; British policy in, 322; Warren's expedition to, 322–7; an imperial protectorate, 327
Bedford, land tenure in, 160
Berlin Congress (1878), 139
Bezuidenhout, Johannes, Boer farmer, 272
Bismarck, Herbert, German ambassador, 310, 312, 318; and German colonization in south-west Africa, 311, 313–15, 317
Bloemfontein, as federal capital, 87; English churches active in, 93
Bloemfontein Convention, 15, 281
Bloemhof, 21